A
COMPANION
TO
MURDER

A COMPANION
TO MURDER

A DICTIONARY OF

Death by Poison / Death by Shooting
Death by Suffocation and Drowning
Death by the Strangler's Hand

1900 — 1950

BY

E. SPENCER SHEW

WITH A NOTE ON THE BRITISH JUDICIAL SYSTEM

19   61

Alfred·A·Knopf • New York

L. C. catalog card number: 61-14626

THIS IS A BORZOI BOOK,

PUBLISHED BY ALFRED A. KNOPF, INC.

FIRST AMERICAN EDITION

for
MY WIFE

FOREWORD

OF the cases presented here, some have been chosen because the people involved in them are strange and remarkable people, passionate, revengeful, avaricious, stupid, ambitious, resourceful, pitiable, tragic, even comic, beyond the ordinary. Others have been chosen because the interplay of motive behind the crime has some special interest; others for the sake of some brilliant stroke of detection. Other cases are to be valued for their particular atmosphere or mood; others because they illustrate some tenet of the law as it applies to the crime of murder; others, again, because they display the forensic skill of a great advocate, the *élan* of a Marshall Hall, the precise and persuasive logic of a Norman Birkett.

In these pages will be found choice murders by poison, by the pistol, the rifle and the revolver, by suffocation, by strangulation and by drowning—a collection of cases recorded in Great Britain during the first half of the century, each of which has some claim to be distinguished from the unrewarding mass. Also included are biographies of judges and counsel associated with those cases, together with some discussion of various principles bearing upon the law of murder, as amended by the Homicide Act of 1957.

I wish to express my grateful thanks to my wife and to my friend Philip Evans, F.R.I.C.S., for their assistance in handling a mass of intractable material.

E. SPENCER SHEW

A NOTE UPON
THE BRITISH JUDICIAL SYSTEM
AND UPON
THE STYLES AND DIGNITIES OF
HER MAJESTY'S JUDGES AND COUNSEL

In England the High Court of Justice is one of the two branches of the Supreme Court of Judicature, the other being the Court of Appeal.

The High Court has three divisions: Queen's Bench Division, Chancery Division, and Probate, Divorce and Admiralty Division. Judges of the High Court, who must be barristers of at least ten years' standing, are appointed for life and may be removed from office only by resolution of both Houses of Parliament. Appointment rests with the Crown upon the nomination of the Lord Chancellor, who, besides being the head of the justiciary, is Keeper of the Great Seal of the Realm, Keeper of the Queen's Conscience, Speaker of the House of Lords and a high-ranking member of the Cabinet. The ordinary channel of promotion is (1) Lord Justice of Appeal and (2) Lord of Appeal in Ordinary, who sits in the House of Lords, the supreme judicial authority for Great Britain and Northern Ireland and the ultimate Court of Appeal.

The office of Lord Chief Justice (formerly Chief Justice of the King's Bench, first appointed in 1268), who is President of the Queen's Bench Division and, as such, senior Common Law judge, carries with it immense prestige and authority. The Lord Chief Justice ranks next to the Lord Chancellor in the legal hierarchy, and upon appointment is usually created a peer of the realm. Another prize is the post of Master of the Rolls, who heads the appeal judges, and another the Presidency of the Probate, Divorce and Admiralty Division.

By custom, a judge of the High Court receives a knighthood upon being raised to the Bench, but he is styled 'Mr. Justice', and in court is addressed as 'My Lord' or 'Your Lordship'. (Thus, the most famous criminal judge of his time was known in private life as Sir Horace Avory, but in court he was Mr. Justice Avory, or, in the formal language of the Law Reports, Avory, J.)

In practice, an indictment for murder, or such other serious crime as lies outside the jurisdiction of the inferior courts, is tried by a judge of the Queen's Bench Division (sitting with a jury), although, in theory, any judge of the High Court of Justice has power to try any cause, civil or criminal. Murder trials take place: in the capital, at the Central Criminal Court, better known under its ancient name of the Old Bailey, the seat of the Assize for the City and County of London and certain parts of the home counties; in the provinces, at Assize courts in the Assize towns, which are grouped together in one or other of seven 'circuits'.

Three times a year the judges of the Queen's Bench Division, travelling in quasi-royal state as the representatives of the Sovereign, visit the various Circuit towns to try all indictable offences, and also such civil causes as are down for hearing, and which would otherwise be brought in the Queen's Bench Division (or in the divorce courts) in London. Judges so engaged are said to be 'going circuit'; they have been doing so now for nearly eight hundred years, ever since the system of travelling justices, originated by Henry I (1100-1135), was developed and made permanent by Henry II at the Assize in Nottingham in 1176.

At their meeting at the Law Courts in London on the first day of Michaelmas Term (1st October-21st December) the Queen's Bench judges allocate the various circuits amongst themselves, the first choice resting with the most senior of them, and so on through the list in order of seniority. Originally, two judges visited each Assize town. Nowadays the number varies between one and four; normally there are two courts sitting at the same time, one to try criminal cases (known as the Crown Court), the other to try civil actions. Where there are two judges, the one who tries the criminal cases is known as the judge 'in commission' (sometimes called the 'red judge'), and takes precedence of his colleague at the various ceremonies which have for centuries attended the holding of an Assize.

A prisoner convicted on indictment of a criminal offence may appeal to the Court of Criminal Appeal (established 1907) which has power to quash a conviction on the ground that the jury's verdict was unreasonable or against the weight of the evidence, or that the judgment of the trial court was wrong in law, or that there was a miscarriage of justice. It may also reduce (or increase) the sentence passed upon the prisoner, unless fixed by law, as in the case of murder. It has no power, however, to order a new trial. Normally the Court consists of the Lord Chief Justice and two Queen's Bench judges.

The robes of the judges vary with the seasons of the ecclesiastical year. During Michaelmas and Hilary terms (the winter season) a Queen's Bench judge trying criminal cases wears a scarlet robe trimmed with ermine; a 'scarf', so-called, although it is, perhaps, better described as a broad stole of black silk; a sash of scarlet cloth known as a 'casting hood', which is worn diagonally from the right shoulder to the waist at the left side; a girdle, collar bands of plain lawn; and a bob wig without curls, called a tye wig. He carries white gloves and Black Cap, a square of limp black silk dating from the early 16th century which was formerly laid corner-wise on the judge's wig when he passed sentence of death. In trying civil cases a black robe with a scarlet sash is worn. For the ceremonies at the opening of an Assize, including the reading of the Queen's Commission, and at church for the Assize service, a Queen's Bench judge is attired in full dress, consisting of a Court suit of black velvet with knee-breeches, black silk hose and buckled shoes; a scarlet robe trimmed with ermine; an ermine-lined scarlet mantle; a scarlet hood trimmed with ermine; a 'scarf', a girdle, plain bands, full-bottomed wig, three-cornered hat, white gloves and Black Cap. The so-called 'summer robe' of scarlet, worn during Easter and Trinity terms, is trimmed with slate-coloured silk, instead of ermine. The Lord Chief Justice wears lace cuffs and a lace stock (instead of bands), but the most distinctive badge of his high office, worn upon all occasions of state, is a gold chain of medieval design which once formed part of the livery of the royal house of Lancaster. All his robes have trains, which are borne by his clerk. Between 1st May and 30th September judges trying cases at the Old Bailey carry posies of garden flowers, a practice which survives as a curious reminder of the days when prisoners put up for trial brought with them into court the 'prison smell' of old Newgate, the ill-famed gaol which stood close by. (The scent of flowers was thought to ward off gaol fever. As an additional precaution the courts were strewn with rue, as they still are to this day, in the summer months, although it is getting on for a hundred and fifty years since there was any danger of infection. Tradition at the Old Bailey is too tough to die so soon.)

Counsel appearing before a judge of the High Court wear bob wigs (with tight curls), lawn bands and black gowns—stuff gowns for junior barristers, silk gowns for Queen's Counsel. Thus, a junior barrister who becomes a Queen's Counsel is said to 'take silk'. Similarly, Q.Cs are often referred to as 'silks'.

A Queen's Counsel is appointed by letters patent to be 'one of Her Majesty's counsel learned in the law'. Application for a silk gown is made to the Lord Chancellor, it being a matter of general acceptance that such an application—for 'a seat within the Bar,' as it is called— shall be submitted only by barristers of at least ten years' standing. In civil actions, and, in general, at criminal trials also, a Queen's Counsel may not appear in court without the assistance and support of a junior barrister; he is thus said to 'lead', and his junior customarily alludes to him as 'my learned leader'.

A barrister with a large junior practice often hesitates to 'take silk', since he cannot be sure that as a Queen's Counsel (who is expensive to employ) his services will be in anything like the same demand; the gain in status is sometimes painfully offset by a loss of income. Some busy juniors never take the risk at all. But it is one which must be accepted by the ambitious man who aims to get to the top, for in the profession of the law the silk gown is the way to preferment. (A High Court judgeship, for instance, rarely comes the way of a junior barrister—but see Mr. Justice McCARDIE for an example of leap-frog promotion from the junior Bar to the judicial Bench.)

Barristers who become Members of Parliament—as so many of them do—are entitled by custom and courtesy to a silk gown, if they choose to apply for it. M.Ps who do apply have to put up with hearing themselves described as 'artificial silks'; legal jokes are not always very subtle.

The leader of the Bar is the Attorney-General, the senior Law Officer of the Crown and chief legal adviser to the Government, of which he is a member; he sits in the House of Commons. His deputy, the Solicitor-General, junior Law Officer of the Crown, is also a member of the Government, although there have been instances of a Solicitor-General receiving his appointment whilst still without a seat in the House of Commons; in such cases it has been usual for the Government of the day to use its influence and powers of patronage to find a 'safe' seat for him as soon as that may conveniently be done. The Law Officers of the Crown are always Queen's Counsel 'learned in the law'.

Only very rarely do the Law Officers appear in the criminal courts. But an indictment for murder *by poisoning* is, by long custom, usually handled in person either by the Attorney-General or Solicitor-General. (See Herbert Rowse ARMSTRONG, Beatrice PACE, the SEDDONS, VACQUIER, and others.)

Treasury Counsel, so called, are barristers nominated by the Attorney-General to appear for the Crown in criminal prosecutions initiated by the Director of Public Prosecutions at the Old Bailey and at the Middlesex and London Sessions, which are inferior courts of limited jurisdiction. Six of them are permanently engaged at the Old Bailey. A Treasury Counsel is a junior barrister; he may not 'apply for silk' whilst he still continues to hold the appointment.

Every barrister practising at the English Bar must be a member of one or other of the Inns of Court, viz., Lincoln's Inn, the Inner Temple, the Middle Temple and Gray's Inn, all of them being of ancient foundation. Upon attaining his professional qualifications by examination, the fledgling barrister is 'called to the Bar' by the 'Benchers' (governing body) of the Inn to which he belongs; he needs no further licence or permission to begin practice.

Barristers may act only upon the 'instructions' of solicitors, who belong to the so-called 'lower branch' of the profession and rank as the 'professional clients' of counsel they employ. Thus, for example, whilst a barrister briefed to defend a prisoner on a charge of murder is responsible for the conduct of the case in court, he relies upon the solicitor who 'instructs' him to prepare the case and to collect the necessary material. (Needless to say, the solicitor does this in close consultation with counsel.)

Scotland has its own High Court and its own criminal code, which differs markedly in many respects from the practice in England. For example, it is open to a Scottish jury to arrive at a verdict by a majority. Again, it may if it chooses return a verdict of 'Not Proven', which is something separate and distinct from an acquittal. (See John Donald MERRETT.)

The administration of justice in Scotland rests primarily upon the Court of Session (established 1532), which consists of the Outer House or Courts of First Instance (seven judges) and the First and Second Divisions of the Inner House, or Courts of Appeal. At the head of the First Division is the Lord President; at the head of the Second Division the Lord Justice Clerk.

The seat of the courts is the old Parliament House at Edinburgh.

Trials for murder and other serious crimes take place within the High Court of Justiciary, which is presided over by the Lord President in his capacity of Lord Justice General. The other members of the High Court of Justiciary—which sits at Edinburgh and the circuit towns, including Glasgow—are the Lord Justice Clerk and, beneath him, all the other judges of the Court of Session, who, for this purpose, have the style of Lords Commissioners of Justiciary.

A Scottish judge bears the formal title of Senator of the College of Justice in Scotland and has the rank of a life peer. (Thus, Lord Russell, not Mr. Justice Russell.)

The Law Officers of the Crown in Scotland are the Lord Advocate and the Solicitor-General for Scotland (assisted by 'advocates depute'). Both are members of the Government and ordinarily sit in the House of Commons.

Counsel setting up in practice in Scotland are said to be 'admitted to the Faculty of Advocates', which is the collective term used to designate the members of the Scottish Bar.

E. SPENCER SHEW

NOTE

The figures which appear in italics at the foot of many of the entries refer to books listed under the corresponding numerals in the Bibliography.

They aim to be of use to the reader who wishes to be informed where he may find treated in greater detail than is possible here those cases which have attracted his especial interest.

Cases included in the *Notable British Trials* series are indicated by the figure *1*, and in the *Old Bailey Trials* series by the figure *2*. Since the volumes in these well-known series provide verbatim records of the trials with which they deal it has not, as a rule, been thought necessary to refer the reader to other sources, which, however interesting, are bound to be less complete.

For purposes of cross-reference, the first appearance in any entry of a subject having an entry of its own in another part of the book, is printed in CAPITAL LETTERS.

TABLE OF MURDER

TABLE OF MURDER

xvi

TABLE OF MURDER

TABLE OF MURDER

Some poison'd by their wives, some sleeping kill'd;
All murder'd

Shakespeare : *King Richard II*

A
COMPANION
TO
MURDER

A

An ounce of poison in one pocket.
Lord Macaulay: *Frederic the Great*

'**Acid Bath' Murders.** *See* John George HAIGH.

Alverstone, Viscount (1842-1915). Lord Chief Justice of England
(1900-13). Born Richard Everard Webster, son of Thomas Webster
Q.C., he was called to the Bar by Lincoln's Inn in 1868, at the age of
twenty-six. By the time he took silk ten years later he possessed one of
the largest practices at the Bar, being principally engaged in patent
cases, assessment appeals, arbitrations, and shipping disputes. In 1885
he became Attorney-General in Lord Salisbury's administration, and in
the same year he entered the House of Commons as Conservative
Member for Launceston. Three times he held the office of Attorney-
General (June 1885 to January 1886; August 1886 to August 1892;
July 1895 to May 1900). In May 1900 he accepted the office of Master
of the Rolls, and a month later was raised to the peerage as Baron
Alverstone of Alverstone in the Isle of Wight. The death of Lord
Russell of Killowen in the following August left vacant the office he
most coveted—that of Lord Chief Justice. He was appointed on 22nd
October 1900, and held the post until October 1913, when ill-health
compelled him to retire. Upon his resignation he was created a Viscount.
He died two years later, on 15th December 1915. At his death the title
became extinct, his son having pre-deceased him. Although he lacked
the polish of a Coleridge or the dignity of a Cockburn, and was not
distinguished for any great wealth of erudition, Lord Alverstone matched
his great predecessors in the office of Lord Chief Justice as much by his
uncanny gift for reducing the most complicated set of facts to a coherent
and deceptively simple narrative, as by the dominating force of his
personality. A kindly man, who was always particularly helpful to young
and inexperienced barristers, he could, when occasion demanded it,
be as stern and inflexible as any martinet who ever sat on the Bench;
it was fatal, as many counsel found to their cost, to attempt any liberties
with him. His impressive appearance—he was a big man with an

enormous head and heavy features—contributed notably to the ease with which at all times he maintained the great traditions, and indeed the majesty, of his office. Lord Alverstone presided over some of the most sensational murder trials of his time, notably those of Herbert John BENNETT; Horace RAYNER; Madar Lal DHINGRA; and—most notorious of all—Hawley Harvey CRIPPEN.

Anderson, Thomas Weldon, a middle-aged actor, was found dying outside the back door of an empty ground-floor flat at 17 Clifton Gardens, Prince of Wales Road, Battersea Park, on the evening of 16th June 1910. He had been shot twice at close quarters, in the face, and in the left temple. After a protracted but fruitless inquiry, a coroner's jury returned an open verdict of 'wilful murder against some man unknown'. There the matter rested, and there it still rests, for nobody has ever been able to suggest the identity of the murderer, or even a likely motive. The facts are these: Thomas Weldon Anderson, whose stage name was Atherstone, was a married man living apart from his wife; there were two sons of the marriage, both of them dear to their father. For some ten years past he had been living with a lady, formerly an actress, but more lately engaged as a 'teacher of expression' at the Academy of Dramatic Art in Gower Street, Bloomsbury. It was a liaison punctuated by violent quarrels and doubtful reconciliations, of which the main cause was undoubtedly Anderson's almost insane jealousy. Until some eight weeks before his death he had, when not on tour, been sharing a flat with this lady at 17 Clifton Gardens; at first it was the ground-floor flat, and then the flat above on the first floor. After a particularly violent quarrel during which he had, quite falsely, accused his mistress of having entertained another man in the flat, Anderson stamped furiously out, shouting that it was 'all over'. He had found a room for himself in Great Percy Street, King's Cross, and had sent for his things; this time the separation had all the air of being final and complete. On the evening of 16th June, Anderson's elder son, a boy of seventeen, went to dine at the flat at 17 Clifton Gardens, and it may, or it may not, be relevant to add that he had, a few days before, told his father of this engagement. Scarcely had they sat down at the table, the boy and the woman whom he had looked upon for so long almost as a mother, than they were startled to hear two shots in the yard below. They ran to the back door, which gave access to the yard by an iron staircase, just in time to see a man climbing over the wall into the yard of the adjoining house. A quarter of an hour later, a police officer having been summoned, Thomas Weldon Anderson was found unconscious, huddled under the staircase immediately outside the back door of the ground-floor flat, which was untenanted. It was obvious that before he had been shot he had had a violent struggle with his assailant. Anderson was wearing carpet slippers, and had in his hip pocket a strip of insulated cable eighteen inches long, wrapped in brown paper and tied with string, so that it had all the appearance of an innocent parcel rather than of the lethal weapon it undoubtedly was. On the mantelpiece of a room in the empty flat were Anderson's boots, wrapped in brown paper. The man whose hurried escape was watched from the first-floor flat was also marked by five other witnesses; some saw him drop from the wall, others met him running as hard as he could in the direction of the river. As so often happens, these witnesses supplied the police with widely differing descriptions of the man; the only thing on which they were all agreed was that he was young and active and very short. (One of them estimated his height at only 5 *ft.* 3 *in.*) It is a fascinating puzzle. Presumably we are to take it that Anderson went there that night intending either to do his mistress some mischief, or to settle his account with his imaginary rival, and that he changed into carpet slippers in the empty flat below so that he would not be heard as he crept up the outside staircase. Jealous as he was, he had always encouraged his mistress in her friendship for his two sons, and freely acknowledged what he and they owed to her for her motherly care of them. Why, then, should he have chosen the very night that he knew his elder son would be there? And what about the little man who came so mysteriously out of the night? Was he some Sir Galahad who appeared in the nick of time to protect the lady upstairs? How did he know that Anderson would be there that evening? Or was it that by some peculiar coincidence *two* persons, each of them unknown to the other, chose the same evening and the same hour to enter the ground-floor flat? Did one surprise the other? One of them we know, but who was the second man? A burglar, perhaps? But why should a burglar break into an empty flat? Or did the two of them come together? Or meet by appointment at the flat? If so, what was the rôle of the second man to be? And why did they quarrel? Why did this furtive meeting end in murder? The questions come flocking, but at the distance of fifty years there are still no answers.

[*120, 130, 210.*

Antiquis, Alec de. *See* Charles Henry JENKINS.

Armstrong, Herbert Rowse, was a Master of Arts of Cambridge University and a solicitor practising at Hay, on the Brecon border, where he was clerk to the Justices of the Peace. Much liked and respected in the district, this pernickety, rather self-important little man— he weighed only seven stone—was also a murderer, who, having safely poisoned his wife with arsenic, engaged himself disastrously in an attempt by the same means to dispose of a fellow solicitor whose competition for the legal business of the town he found inconvenient. Had Major Armstrong—he set great store by his wartime substantive rank—been content with one murder only he might have counted upon dying in his bed, a blameless ornament to the community; it was by his ill-judged attempt at a second murder, handled so much more clumsily than the first, that he was undone. In August 1920, Major Armstrong and his wife, Katherine Mary, had been married for thirteen years. They lived with their three children in a house called Mayfield at Cusop Dingle, just outside the town of Hay. Mrs. Armstrong was a cultured and intelligent woman, but severe to the point of fanaticism, and she ruled the little major with unbending severity, sparing him none of the day-to-day humiliations of the 'henpecked' husband. She thought nothing, for example, of interrupting a set of lawn tennis at a neighbour's house by a sharp-voiced reminder to her husband that it was time for him to be going as it was his 'bath night'. He suffered it all in silence and without complaint, giving no sign even of a wish to revolt. It was in the summer of 1920 that Mrs. Armstrong's peculiarities were recognized as the symptoms of some form of mental derangement, and on 22nd August she was certified as of unsound mind and removed to Barnwood Private Asylum. Shortly before her departure Mrs. Armstrong was taken so gravely ill that she could scarcely make the journey. She herself put it down to 'one of my bilious attacks', but in the light of after events there seems to be no doubt that in fact she had been given a severe dose of arsenic by her husband, who had already embarked upon a premeditated course of murder by instalments. Mrs. Armstrong was in the asylum for five months. On 22nd January 1921 she was permitted to return home 'on leave'. She fell ill almost at once and by the middle of February the local practitioner, Dr. 'Tom' Hincks, was making daily calls at Mayfield, where a mental nurse had been installed. On 18th February Mrs. Armstrong lost complete use of her limbs, and on 22nd February she died. The doctor's certificate gave the cause of death as heart disease. That might have been the end of the Armstrong story; instead, it was the prelude to one of the most macabre episodes in the murder records of this country. On 22nd October, eight months to the day after Mrs. Armstrong's death, Mr. Oswald Norman Martin, a rival solicitor whose office was just across the street, received from the little major a pressing invitation to tea at Mayfield. A few days later he went. During tea his host handed to Mr. Martin a buttered scone with the apology, 'Excuse my fingers'. Mr. Martin ate the scone. Hardly had he got home before he was seized with the most violent pains, which by the next day had reduced him to a condition of extreme weakness. Dr. Hincks was called in. He prescribed as for a severe bilious attack, but all the same he was not entirely satisfied—he could not account for the extremely rapid pulse. The doctor decided to submit a specimen liquid discharge to analysis. It was found to contain one thirty-third of a grain of arsenic. This startling fact set Dr. Hincks thinking again about the circumstances of Mrs. Armstrong's last illness. What if the neuritis which had been regarded as a functional disorder was, in fact, peripheral neuritis—a well-known symptom of arsenical poisoning? And what of the other symptoms? The vomiting, the peculiar 'high-stepping' gait, the discolouration of the skin? The more Dr. Hincks pondered the matter, the plainer he saw his duty to put the facts before the Home Office. Police inquiries were begun, so discreetly, so cautiously, that right up to the last Major Armstrong suspected nothing. For poor Mr. Martin the weeks that followed were a continuous nightmare; few men have ever been tried so hardly as slowly, very slowly, the processes of the criminal law came into action. He now began to receive a regular fusillade of invitations to tea at Mayfield. The major was perpetually on the telephone: 'Will you look in for tea this afternoon?'—'Come to tea tomorrow'—'Why haven't you come? Tea has been waiting for you for half an hour.' Mr. Martin was at his wits' end to find fresh excuses not to go. It will be appreciated that by this time he was acting under the instructions of the police, who had enjoined upon him that he was on no account to accept any of Major Armstrong's invitations—he scarcely needed that injunction—but, far more difficult, not to let anything appear in his manner which might serve to put the would-be murderer on his guard, or allow him to suspect that he was under police surveillance. Ever more insistently the tea-cups rattled. Major Armstrong took to having tea served in his office; day after day Mr. Martin was invited to 'step across the road' for a refreshing cup— and a buttered scone. In sheer self-defence Mr. Martin began taking tea in his own office, so as to have a colourable excuse for not accepting this new battery of invitations. At length the baffled major resorted to an invitation to Mr. and Mrs. Martin to dine with him at Mayfield. Desperately, Mr. Martin temporized, but was driven at last to accept. Fortunately for his peace of mind, by the time the day came round the police had completed their clandestine inquiries, and Major Armstrong was already in custody. It was on 31st December 1921 that he was arrested, on a charge of attempted murder. Two days later the body of Mrs. Armstrong was exhumed in Cusop churchyard, where it had lain at rest for just over ten months. Three and a half grains of arsenic were found in those parts of the body which were examined. (Two grains may be a fatal dose.) In April 1922, Herbert Rowse Armstrong was put on trial at Hereford Assizes for the wilful murder of his wife, the presiding judge being Mr. Justice DARLING, hen on his last circuit before his retirement. It is difficult to read the transcript of the trial without being struck by the generous supplies of arsenic that were available at Mayfield. Major Armstrong, a diligent gardener, was perpetually at war with dandelions and plantains, was never without stocks of weed killer, and, in addition, bought arsenic himself to make up a weed killer of his own. He was also shown to have purchased a quarter of a pound of white arsenic on 11th January 1921, shortly before Mrs. Armstrong returned from the asylum. Nothing was more damaging to Major Armstrong than a lengthy exchange between himself and Mr. Justice Darling upon the use he had made of this. In the witness-box the major described how he had taken one ounce of the white arsenic and, with a penknife, had divided it into twenty roughly equal parts. He had put each part into a separate packet. Nineteen of these packets he had used to attack the roots of nineteen separate dandelions—it was the twentieth, the only one left, which had been found in his pocket on his arrest. Here is a sample question, and a sample answer:

> *Mr. Justice Darling:* Did you realize it was just a fatal dose of arsenic, not for dandelions only, but for human beings?
> *Armstrong:* No, I did not realize that at all. I only studied chemistry at school.

The gravamen of the defence, brilliantly conducted by Sir Henry CURTIS BENNETT K.C., was that Mrs. Armstrong, being of unsound mind, had poisoned herself. It was rejected by the jury, which, after a ten-day trial, found Armstrong guilty. He was hanged at Gloucester Prison on 31st May 1922.

[*1.*

Atherstone, Thomas Weldon. *See* Thomas Weldon ANDERSON.

Atkin, Lord (1867-1944). Born Richard Atkin, he was called to the Bar by Gray's Inn in 1891, and quickly established himself as a leading commercial counsel. He took silk in 1906, and in 1913 was appointed to the Bench as a judge of the King's Bench Division. His experience as a judge developed and matured the remarkable clarity of thought and exposition for which he had been conspicuous at the Bar, and earned for him an outstanding reputation amongst lawyers. In legal memoirs which look back affectionately to the first quarter of the twentieth century there are frequent references to Mr. Justice Atkin as a 'humane' judge, a 'courageous judge remarkable for the tenacity of his opinions', and as the possessor of the 'perfect judicial temperament'. Promotion was inevitable. First he became a Lord Justice of Appeal, and afterwards a Lord of Appeal in Ordinary, when a life peerage was conferred upon him. He died in office on 25th June 1944, at the age of seventy-seven. Murder trials over which he presided included those of John STARCH-FIELD; and David GREENWOOD.

Atkinson, Sir Cyril (*b.* **1874**). Called to the Bar by Lincoln's Inn in 1897, he practised on the Northern Circuit, became a King's Counsel in 1913, and was raised to the Bench in 1933, when he received a knighthood. During his fifteen years as a High Court judge—he retired in 1948 at the age of seventy-four—he presided over some most notable murder trials, including those of Thomas Joseph DAVIDSON; and Udham SINGH.

Autrefois Acquit: Autrefois Convict is the expression of the Common Law principle that a man must not twice be put in peril for the same offence. This is to say that he may not be tried a second time for the offence of which he has already been either acquitted or convicted, even if the former trial took place in a foreign country. It must, however, be shown that the trial ended in a final verdict. If, for any reason—as, for example, failure to agree—the jury were discharged without returning a verdict, there would be no bar to a second trial.

Avory, Sir Horace Edmund (1851-1935). Judge of the King's Bench Division of the High Court (1910-35). Mr. Justice Avory was a severe man, severe in his judgments, severe in the sentences he meted out, severe—icily severe—in his manner and in the conduct of his court. Although to the 'old lag' he was known, disrespectfully, as 'Horace', or even 'Old Horace', and barristers would sometimes in their more unbuttoned moments refer to him as 'The Acid Drop', in Court there were few indeed who did not stand in awe of him. From his seat on the Bench Mr. Justice Avory maintained an iron discipline, demanding from counsel who appeared before him the loftiest standards of professional practice. If an indignant barrister, sternly checked for some departure from the strict legal code, thought fit to protest that he had often taken a similar line in another court without complaint, he would be certain to draw from Mr. Justice Avory the icy retort, 'I do not doubt that you have, but you will not do it in this court.' He distrusted rhetoric and was utterly unresponsive to any appeal directed to the emotions rather than to the reasoning intelligence. If it seemed to him that counsel had fallen back upon a few fashionable tricks of oratory to confuse the jury and to conceal from them some circumstance unfavourable to his case, he would, when the time came for him to sum up, hammer away at the carefully built up façade of argument and inference until at last only the hard, naked facts remained. He was, indeed, a Man of Law; he swore by the Law and the Tablets of the Law, and there were moments when, as one sat in his court and glanced up at the erect, motionless figure of this most 'upright judge', one had the odd fancy that the wrinkled parchment face beneath the bob wig was the face of The Law itself. Stern and unyielding though he was, Mr. Justice Avory was not without a dry, wintry humour of his own, and it is surprising how often the aphorisms which circulate among barristers like small change may be traced back to Avory, J., rather than to some recognized judicial wit like Lord DARLING or Mr. Justice Rigby SWIFT. 'To find a packet of three and a half grains of white arsenic in a solicitor's pocket is surely rare', is a remark which has the sharp, authentic bite of Mr. Justice Avory. Horace Edmund Avory, the second son of Henry Avory, Clerk of the Court at the Old Bailey, was called to the Bar by the Inner Temple in 1875, took silk in 1901, and became one of His Majesty's judges in 1910, when he received the customary knighthood. He continued to sit on the Bench until the end of the Easter sittings of 1935, when he retired, being then in his eighty-fourth year. He died suddenly on 18th June of the same year. According to Mr. F. W. Ashley, the clerk who served him at the Bar and on the Bench for fifty-four years, Mr. Justice Avory presided over 163 murder trials. They included those of Edith BINGHAM; Edward HOPWOOD; Jean Pierre VAQUIER; Alfonso SMITH; BROWNE and Kennedy; and Frederick STEWART.

B

But the father answered never a word
A frozen corpse was he.

Henry Wadsworth Longfellow:
The Wreck of the Hesperus

Baguley, Ada. *See* Dorothea Nancy WADDINGHAM.

Bailey, George Arthur, was, in January 1921, tried at Aylesbury
Assizes before Mr. Justice McCARDIE for the murder of his wife,
Kate, by poisoning her with prussic acid. It was the first murder trial
at which women—there were three of them—were summoned to
serve on a jury. The Court handled them gingerly. Typical of the
solicitude with which these pioneering (and somewhat self-conscious)
ladies were treated was the judge's decision to have a brief adjournment
each afternoon so that they could be sustained with tea. In spite of this,
it was remarked by the Press that they had 'obviously felt the strain', and
for its report of the fourth and final day of the trial *The Times* put up the
headline: JURYWOMEN'S ORDEAL. It seems to have been an ordeal for
counsel, too. Being required to put various delicate matters to witnesses,
they were at such pains to avoid using words no lady ought to hear that
the judge had to tell them there was no need to be mealy-mouthed
simply because of the unaccustomed presence of women in the jury-box.
But even Mr. Justice McCardie felt it necessary to impress upon this
particular jury the need to be firm, as if he feared the male members of
it were likely to succumb altogether to feminine softness, sentimen-
tality, and lack of logic. 'I ask you', he said, on a note pitched a little too
high, 'to arrive at your verdict without flinching and to deliver it with
unswerving firmness.' They did. Setting aside Bailey's defence that his
wife, being determined to commit suicide, had swallowed the prussic
acid herself—out of an egg-cup—they brought in a verdict of 'Guilty'.
Bailey was sentenced to death, and executed on 2nd March 1921.

Baker, Alice. ⎤
Baker, Percy. ⎦ *See* John Edward GARTSIDE.

Barney, Elvira Dolores, was in 1932 the central figure in a *cause célèbre* for which the newspaper headlines almost wrote themselves: MAYFAIR BEAUTY IN SHOOTING DRAMA, BANKER'S SON DEAD AFTER COCKTAIL PARTY, KNIGHT'S DAUGHTER ON MURDER CHARGE—every one a winner. It was the period in which the Bright Young People of the 1920s had already gone into a decline. They were still, in spite of the Great Depression, aggressively 'bright', but some of them were no longer particularly young, and the merriment had gone a trifle sour. The brittle, self-indulgent existence of Elvira Barney precisely reflected the tone of that sadly diminished 'set', whose 'amusing' parties were somehow ceasing to amuse; behind them were too many stale dawns. But although the fun had wilted it was still doggedly pursued, and right up with the pack was Mrs. Barney, the good-time girl. She was the daughter of wealthy parents—town house in Belgrave Square, a 'place' in the country—and had all the money she required for a kind of life that obviously needed plenty. In 1932 she was twenty-six, a blonde with a pretty face and figure, both showing signs of going to seed. She had sloughed off a husband, an American cabaret artiste, who had gone back to the States after a spell of marriage which Mrs. Barney described, succinctly, as 'Hell'; she now had a house in Williams Mews, Knightsbridge, London, and a lover of whom she was fiercely possessive. This was William Thomas Scott Stephen—everyone called him Michael— a young man of her own age who had no income of his own and no occupation, although he vaguely called himself a dress designer. On 30th May 1932, Mrs. Barney gave a cocktail party, a characteristically noisy affair, glumly regarded by her long-suffering neighbours. When, at about 9.30 p.m., the last of the guests had gone, Elvira and Michael set out on their usual round. They supped at the Café de Paris, went on to a night club in Soho, and got back to Williams Mews shortly after midnight. At 3 a.m., the peace of the Mews was shattered by a row of titanic proportions between Mrs. Barney and her lover. It rose to an uproarious climax and ended in the sharp staccato of a revolver shot. A little while later the telephone rang at a doctor's house near by. Mrs. Barney's agitated voice was on the line: 'There has been a terrible accident; for God's sake come at once!' When the doctor arrived, it was to find Michael Stephen lying dead at the top of the stairs with a bullet through his lung, and close beside him a revolver containing five cartridges, two of which were spent. Mrs. Barney was on the edge of hysteria. She was darting about aimlessly, repeating over and over again, 'He cannot be dead, he cannot be dead,' and then, 'I will die, too. I want to die. I loved him so.' The subsequent arrival of the police destroyed the last shred of what remained to her of her self-control. She shrieked at the officers to leave, called them 'vile swine', snatched the telephone from one of them when he tried to use it, slapped another in the face; she screamed, laughed, and wept alternately. Mrs. Barney recovered her calm at the local police station, where later that morning she signed a statement containing an entirely coherent account of how Michael Stephen had met his death; she never afterwards departed from it. She had, she said, quarrelled with Michael over a woman he was fond of. He had picked up a revolver which she kept in the house, saying that he was going to take it away for fear that she might kill herself. She had struggled with him for the possession of the weapon— and it had gone off. Mrs. Barney was allowed to go, but three days later the police, having made an investigation and being no longer satisfied of the truth of her story, arrested her at her parents' house in Belgrave Square, and charged her with murder. In the following July she stood her trial at the Old Bailey before Mr. Justice HUMPHREYS, when the Court was treated to an exhibition of skilled advocacy by her counsel, culminating in a speech to the jury which the veteran judge described as one of the finest he had ever heard delivered at the Bar. The King's Counsel who earned that tribute from a judge notoriously sparing with his compliments was Sir Patrick HASTINGS, a man who practised little in the criminal courts, and who confessed that he hated trials for murder. He had, on the face of it, a formidable case to answer. One of Mrs. Barney's neighbours was prepared to say that just before the fatal shot was fired she heard Mrs. Barney cry, 'I'll shoot you!' Another swore that two shots were fired, not one, an assertion which appeared to be supported by the fact that the mark of a bullet was found on the bedroom wall. Both these statements were clearly damaging to a defence which rested upon the accidental discharge of a revolver during a struggle. Another neighbour—a woman—had a story to tell of a violent quarrel between Mrs. Barney and her lover a few days earlier. This had ended in Michael Stephen walking out of the house. Where-upon, Mrs. Barney had screamed out of the window, 'Laugh, baby, laugh for the last time', and had fired a revolver at him. Mrs. Barney's version of this earlier quarrel was that when Michael had left the house she had fired at the bedroom wall to frighten him into thinking that she had carried out her threat to commit suicide. But the woman neighbour insisted that the shot had been fired out of the window—she had even seen a 'puff of smoke':

Sir Patrick Hastings: I suppose you didn't know Mrs. Barney's revolver contained cordite cartridges?

Witness: No.

Sir Patrick Hastings: And I suppose you don't know that cordite cartridges don't make any smoke?

Nothing more was heard of the 'puff of smoke'. The prosecution lost one deadly point when the neighbour who in the court below had sworn she had heard Mrs. Barney scream, 'I'll shoot you', now went into the witness-box and amended this simply to 'I'll shoot', words which Sir Patrick was able to represent as a threat by a half-demented woman to shoot *herself*. As for the neighbour who said she had heard *two* shots fired, Sir Patrick made no attempt to suggest directly that she was wrong, but, instead, led her dextrously into the position of seeming to say that there had been not two, but *five* shots. 'Quite a fusillade,' he observed sardonically. In the witness-box, Mrs. Barney, although obviously suffering from intense strain, told her story clearly and well. There was one immensely dramatic moment during Sir Patrick's examination. 'I want the revolver put on the ledge of the box exactly in front of the witness,' he said. This was done. Sir Patrick turned as if to address the judge, but suddenly whipped round and, in a harsh, even violent tone, rapped out, 'Pick up that revolver, Mrs. Barney!' Mrs. Barney gave a start, and picked up the revolver—with her right hand. The Court gasped, for the witness who had described Mrs. Barney shooting at Michael from the window had sworn that she had fired the revolver with her *left* hand. Sir Patrick Hastings' closing speech to the jury made no concession to sentiment, sternly avoided rhetoric, or what he himself contemptuously described as 'flatulent oratory'. As a classic example of the appeal which is aimed at the head and not at the heart it could hardly have been better judged. After a retirement of one hour and fifty-five minutes the jury came back into a tense, expectant court with the verdict of 'Not Guilty' that set Elvira Dolores Barney free.

[*89, 126.*

Barrow, Eliza Mary. *See* Frederick Henry SEDDON.

Baumberg, Anton. *See* Lieutenant Douglas MALCOLM.

Baxter, Jeannie, fair, frail and twenty-four, sat in the dock at the Old Bailey one June day in 1913, and heard an eminent King's Counsel describe the story that had brought her there as one which would need the 'pen of a Zola and the brush of a Hogarth' to do it justice. Those words were used by Edward Marshall HALL, who, in protecting the interests of his clients, seldom erred on the side of understatement. Yet perhaps there is something here which suggests a new *Rake's Progress* or an additional chapter to a novel by the author of *Nana* and *L'Assommoir*. For some years Jeannie Baxter had lived under the 'protection' of a wealthy North Country man. But the *ménage* had not survived the entry into her life of Julian Bernard Hall, young, dashing, and rich, a patron of the prize ring and a pioneer airman; he lived at a flat in Denman Street, just behind Piccadilly Circus, and had a notorious fondness for the bottle. Hall made Jeannie his mistress and set her up in a flat at Carlton Mansions, Maida Vale. Jeannie hoped to marry him, but at the same time she did not allow her North Country lover to disappear entirely from her life. Indeed, this man had bought a house for her in the country, and in December 1912 was pressing her to go back to him. He came up to London to see her, and that evening at the Carlton Mansions flat there occurred an extraordinary scene of jealousy and violence. Before the arrival of the man from the North, Hall turned up at Jeannie's flat, and at once made plain that this was to be an unusual evening by taking out a revolver and firing it at random in the sitting-room. He had brought with him two magnums of champagne; one of these he opened and drank, so that by the time Jeannie's former protector—we will call him Mr. X—reached the flat Hall was very drunk and in a fighting mood. To Mr. X he threw out a challenge. He produced two revolvers and proposed that each should take one, that each should light a cigarette, and then, all the lights having been turned out, each should fire at the other in the darkness. The challenge being refused, Hall took aim and fired at a photograph of Mr. X on the wall. 'Do you love this girl?' he demanded. Courageously—for Hall had drunk himself into a condition in which he was clearly capable of anything— Mr. X replied that he did. Hall thereupon turned out the lights and fired several shots—one of them hit Jeannie's photograph. As a parting gesture, he fired his revolver over his shoulder through the sitting-room door. Jeannie was now to see some chance of her hopes coming true, for Hall promised her that if she would send Mr. X away, he would marry her. Plans were made for the wedding to take place on 15th April 1913. But when Jeannie went to the Denman Street flat on the morning of 14th April she found to her dismay that Hall, who was sitting up in bed drinking brandy, had made no arrangements at all for the following day. 'Drink', he told her, 'is killing me. I can't stand it.' At about noon shots were heard in Hall's bedroom, and then a woman's screams. A friend of Hall who was staying at the flat swore that a distraught Jeannie had come running out of the room crying, 'Come and see Jack. I have shot him. He dared me to do it!' Hall was found lying on the bed; he had been shot in the chest and arm, and a few moments later he died. At her trial before Mr. Justice ROWLATT Jeannie Baxter told what happened in Hall's bedroom to lead to the fatal shots. When Hall admitted to her that he had done nothing about the wedding arrangements, she told him: 'Jack, I think you are a coward to treat me so.' Hall then struck her in the face, took a revolver out of a drawer, and helped himself to a brandy and soda. 'Bill,' he said (he always called her Bill), 'you and I will never get on if we are married. I cannot keep my promise. It is better to finish it.' He then began to 'whistle' down the barrel of the revolver. 'I told him to put the revolver down,' said Jeannie. 'He said, "Do you think you could take it from me?" He was holding it with the muzzle towards himself, and he asked me to pull the trigger. I said, "I am not such a coward." At the same time I tried to take the revolver away from him, but before I knew what had happened I saw him bend down to pick up the revolver. I snatched it up and fired four times at the ceiling as rapidly as I could. I then rushed to the door and shouted, "Jack has been shot".' Her counsel exerted his tremendous powers to secure Jeannie's out-and-out acquittal, but the jury, although they acquitted her of murder, found her guilty of manslaughter. Jeannie Baxter was sent to prison for three years.

[*30, 131.*

Beard, Arthur, a night watchman, was sentenced to death at Chester Assizes in October 1919 for the murder of a thirteen-years-old girl named Ivy Lydia Wood, whom he suffocated while committing rape upon her. It was a featureless and utterly sordid crime, yet it is famous in English criminal law as *Rex v Beard*, the source of one of Lord Birkenhead's most notable judgments from the Woolsack. Beard was drunk when he committed the crime; it was this circumstance which led the Court of Criminal Appeal to reduce the finding of murder to one of manslaughter. The ground for this reversal was that Beard, being in a state of intoxication, was incapable of forming an *intention* to murder the girl, and therefore could not have acted with that 'malice aforethought' which the law of murder requires. The Crown took the case of Arthur Beard to the House of Lords, and there, on 5th March 1920, the judgment of the Court of Criminal Appeal was reversed. The Lord Chancellor, Lord Birkenhead, ruled that while Beard might have been too drunk to form an intention to kill, he had not been too drunk to form an intention to commit the felony of rape. Since the girl's death was caused by an act of violence done in furtherance of a felony, it followed that, in law, Beard was guilty of murder. Seated between two warders, Beard made a dejected and incongruous figure in the soberly dignified setting of the House of Lords, whilst the implications of his repellant crime were argued back and forth by the most learned lawyers in the land; it was, indeed, a feast of reason from which his sluggish understanding could snatch no crumb. But at least he knew that he was not going to hang, for the Home Secretary had already intimated that, whatever the outcome of the legal argument, he would advise a reprieve. In the event, he was sentenced to a long term of imprisonment. An odd feature of

Rex v Beard was that Lord Reading sat both in the Court of Criminal Appeal and in the House of Lords. At the end of Lord Birkenhead's reserved judgment he said only that he agreed with his 'learned friend on the Woolsack' and had nothing to add, thus acquiescing in the reversal of his own judgment in the court below.

[*149.*

Beck, Elizabeth Ann. } *See* Richard BRINKLEY.
Beck, Richard.

Bennett, Herbert John, had by the time he was fifteen already begun to display some of the more unpleasing characteristics of the petty cheat and sneak thief. At seventeen he met a girl named Mary Jane Clark, a music teacher, three years older than himself, and on 22nd July 1897 he married her at West Ham register office. Mrs. Bennett does not appear to have been over-burdened with moral scruples herself, and for some time she and her husband obtained a dubious living by selling faked violins. (Sometimes Mrs. Bennett posed as a young widow forced by straitened circumstances to part with her late husband's cherished violin.) Mr. Bennett combined this profitable venture with a variety of petty swindles and, it is surmised, blackmailing transactions also. By 1900, when he purchased a grocer's shop at Westgate-on-Sea—which, having been suitably insured, conveniently burned down—Bennett had long since tired of his wife. Their landlady at Plumstead, to which they moved after the fire, later recalled a fierce passage of arms between them. 'Herbert,' Mrs. Bennett had stormed, 'I will follow you for the sake of the baby, and if you are not careful, I can get you fifteen years.' To which Bennett had retorted, 'I wish you were dead, and if *you* are not careful you soon will be.' Bennett now obtained a job at Woolwich Arsenal. His wage was only thirty shillings a week, but this meagre return did not prevent him from cutting a dash with a new acquaintance, Miss Alice Meadows, an attractive parlourmaid to whom he posed as a single man; soon they were 'walking out' together. On 28th August 1900 Bennett presented her with an engagement ring, and it was settled that they should marry in the following June. Mrs. Bennett was now in deadly peril. On 14th September Bennett visited her at Bexley Heath, where she was living at this time; it appears that he proposed that she should take a little holiday. The next day, which was a Saturday, Mrs. Bennett set off for Yarmouth, where, in the name of 'Mrs. Hood', she engaged a room in the house of a Mrs. Rudrum. To her new landlady, 'Mrs. Hood' confided that she was a widow living at York, and had been escorted to Yarmouth by her brother-in-law, who was in love with her and was madly jealous. (Mrs. Bennett was never at a loss for a romantic story.) On the following Thursday Bennett lamented to the unsuspecting Alice Meadows that he would not be able to see her at the week-end, as he had to go to Gravesend, where his grandfather was dangerously ill. On the Saturday—22nd September—Bennett set out from his lodgings in Woolwich—but he did not go to Gravesend. That same night, at about 11 o'clock, a young man and his girl were sitting together in a lonely hollow on the South Beach at Yarmouth when they noticed another couple on the sloping sand some thirty yards away. Presently, out of the darkness, they heard a woman's voice calling 'Mercy, mercy,' followed by a moaning cry. They got up and passed within a few yards of the other couple. The man was crouching over the woman, and as they walked unconcernedly by—they had no idea they were witnessing anything more terrible than a bit of skylarking—he turned his head to look at them; it was too dark for them to see his face. At 11.45 a man later identified as Herbert John Bennett walked into the Crown and Anchor Hotel, Yarmouth; he was out of breath, as though he had been running. He explained to the Boots that he had lost the last tram to Gorleston and wanted a bed for the night. Early next morning he was up and away. At about that same hour a bathing-machine boy came upon the body of a woman lying on her back on the beach. A mohair bootlace, fastened with a reef knot, followed by a granny knot, was drawn so tightly about her neck that it was embedded in her flesh. It was not until some six weeks later that—through the tracing of a laundry mark—the body was identified as that of Mary Jane Bennett. Two days later—on 4th November—Bennett was arrested in the street. The police searched his lodgings, and in a portmanteau was found a gold chain and, among other miscellanea, a woman's wig, a man's wig, and a false moustache. At Bennett's trial for the murder of his wife, which was transferred to the Old Bailey because of the intense local animus against him, the gold chain turned out to be the pivotal point of the case. Witnesses swore that it was the identical chain which Mrs. Bennett was wearing at Yarmouth shortly before her death; if this were so, it was obvious that this was a chain whose slender links would hang the prisoner. It happened that at Yarmouth Mrs. Bennett had had her photograph taken by a beach photographer. It showed her wearing a gold chain. The question was: Was it *the* chain? Mr. Edward Marshall HALL K.C., appearing for the defence, concentrated all his energy and skill into an attempt to discredit this damaging evidence. The photograph, he contended, showed a 'rope chain of the Prince of Wales pattern', whereas the chain found at Bennett's lodgings was of the link variety; maddeningly, the chain Mrs. Bennett was wearing in the photograph was so blurred that it could well be either. The trial was not without its sensations. On the fifth day Marshall Hall produced, without warning, a 'secret' witness, who, he told the jury, would say that it was 'impossible for this man to have murdered his wife on September 22nd'. This 'secret' witness proved to be a Mr. Douglas Sholto Douglas, a fancy goods manufacturer, who described how, whilst he was out walking near Eltham on the evening of 22nd September, an affable stranger had forced his company upon him. As they walked along the man had pointed to a signboard over a barber's shop and had remarked, 'By the way, a namesake of mine lives there.' The name on the board was 'F. K. Bennett'. He had no doubt that the stranger was the prisoner in the dock. This alibi, had it been established to the jury's satisfaction, must have secured Bennett's acquittal, since by the time Mr. Douglas had fallen in with his talkative companion the last train for Yarmouth had already gone. But there was a disastrous weakness. For fear of exposing Bennett to the relentless cross-examination of prosecuting counsel, Mr. C. F. GILL K.C., Marshall Hall did not dare put his client in the box to explain what he was doing at Eltham on the day his wife was killed. After a summing-up markedly in Bennett's disfavour, the jury took only thirty-five minutes to arrive at a verdict of 'Guilty'. The presiding judge, Lord ALVERSTONE, only lately appointed Lord Chief Justice of England, was a great deal more distressed by the terrible words of the death sentence than was the prisoner, whose absolute composure, maintained throughout the trial, did not desert him now. It was still unshaken in the condemned cell at Norwich Prison, and indeed on the scaffold itself, where Herbert John Bennett perished on the morning of 21st March 1901.

[*I*.

Bentley, Police-Sergeant Robert. *See* SIEGE OF SIDNEY STREET.

Benton, Wallace, seventy, short-sighted, cantankerous, and almost totally deaf, being charged at Norwich Assizes in June 1929 with the murder of a smallholder named Thomas Henry Williamson, reduced the immensely experienced judge who tried him, Mr. Justice HUMPHREYS, to the helpless admission that he had 'never felt so completely unable to control a Court'. The 'atmosphere of pantomime', upon which the judge comments in his reminiscences, was created not only by the old man's physical infirmities—his counsel actually had to go into the witness-box with his client and bellow questions into his ear through a speaking-tube—but also by his insistence upon giving a dramatic demonstration to the learned Clerk of Assize in open court to show how the gun had accidentally gone off and killed the unfortunate Mr. Williamson. The old man, ragged and unkempt, oblivious to every direction of the judge, forced the embarrassed Clerk to play the part of the victim while he waved the gun about in front of him, his finger playing with the trigger; for most of the time the muzzle was within a few inches of the Clerk's head. In vain, judge, counsel, ushers tried to stop him; once he was wound up the whole majesty of the Court was powerless to check the words that poured out of him in an uncontrollable flood. The macabre 'pantomime atmosphere' prevailed right up to the last, for after he had been found guilty of murder, the death sentence had to be shouted into Benton's ear one word at a time. When Mr. Justice Humphreys had spoken the final sentence, 'May the Lord have mercy upon your soul', and this had been stentoriously repeated, the old man in the dock looked around him and murmured, 'I am not at all sure of that; I don't see why He should.' Still muttering, he was led to the cells below. The old man did not hang. The jury had added a strong recommendation to mercy, and almost at once he was reprieved. Benton had been living on a small farm at Tilney St. Lawrence, near King's Lynn, Norfolk, for some twenty-five years. With advancing age, he got into financial difficulties, and in 1925 he was forced to mortgage the property. As he had failed to pay the interest for three years running, an ejectment order was made against him in January 1929, and in the following March the mortgagees moved to compel him to leave by means of a warrant. At this time, the man who was to have the reversion of the tenancy of Benton's farm, Thomas Henry Williamson, was already working the land. On 21st March, the day before he was to be ejected, if necessary by force, Benton came upon Williamson in the stable near the house. There was the sound of a shot, and fifteen minutes later Benton walked into the house of the local policeman and said, 'There's been an accident, a bad gun accident. That man that comes on the place is shot.' Later he added, 'It was his own fault. What he got he deserved.' Williamson was found lying dead on the floor of the stable. The Crown case was that Benton had peered round the open stable door with his gun 'at the ready', and that when Williamson, who was pitching hay with a fork, turned round, the old man had fired at him at a range of six feet, letting him have the full charge on the left side of the head. [95, 97.

Bertron, Suzanne (otherwise Naylor). *See* Max KASSEL.

Bingham, Edith Agnes, had the unique experience of being charged with a triple murder committed in the very building in which she was tried—and acquitted. The explanation of this extraordinary circumstance is that each of the three victims was done to death in historic Lancaster Castle, which besides being a museum and art gallery also houses the Assize Court. This led to a curious result. Witnesses, on being asked to describe an incident or conversation bearing upon the crime, were quite likely simply to point across the courtroom and say, 'He was lying there, my Lord', or 'She was sitting on that chair in the corner.' The Bingham family had a long association with Lancaster Castle. Mr. William Hodgson Bingham was resident caretaker there for thirty years, and when he died in January 1911 his son, James Henry, was appointed in his place. The new caretaker invited his sister, Margaret, to act as his housekeeper at the Castle, but she had scarcely taken up her duties before she died—quite suddenly. She was succeeded as housekeeper by her half-sister, Edith Agnes Bingham. This arrangement worked anything but smoothly, and by August 1911 Miss Bingham's conduct had become so displeasing to her brother that he engaged a new housekeeper. She was to move in on 14th August, but on 12th August, after eating a steak cooked by his sister, Edith, Mr. Bingham was taken ill whilst showing some visitors over the Castle; he died three days later. A post-mortem examination revealed traces of arsenic. The inquest was adjourned while the bodies of William Hodgson Bingham, the father, and his daughter, Margaret, were exhumed on a Home Office order. When it was resumed the county analyst stated that the bodies of all three, father, son, and daughter, contained enough arsenic to presuppose that each had been given a fatal dose. Edith Agnes Bingham was arrested on the coroner's warrant, and later committed to Lancaster Assizes to stand her trial before Mr. Justice AVORY for the murder of her brother, James Henry Bingham. There it was shown that there had been quarrels between brother and sister. It was also proved that the prisoner at least had access to weed killer which was used for the paths of the Castle grounds; this contained 97 grains of white arsenic to the fluid ounce, or two grains, a fatal dose, in ten drops. Much more than a fatal dose could be administered in a beef steak without being detected by the palate. But the case against the prisoner could not be pressed home with sufficient force to convince the jury that it rested upon anything more solid than mere suspicion, and it took them only twenty minutes in deliberation to return a verdict of 'Not Guilty'. No evidence was offered on either of the two other indictments charging Miss Bingham with the murder of her father and half-sister, and the jury was therefore directed to find a formal verdict of 'Not Guilty' in each case. Miss Bingham was discharged, and retreated into obscurity.

[206.

Birkett, Lord (b. 1883). Norman Birkett belonged to the last decades of what is now looked back upon as a Golden Age of advocacy. An erudite lawyer, formed by nature to argue intricate points of law in the passionless atmosphere of the Court of Appeal or the House of Lords, he also had that within him which made him one of the greatest pleaders at the Criminal Bar, where skill in the interpretation of a statute counts for less than a knowledge of life and of the good and evil in men's hearts. He had at his fingertips the subtle arts by which the great criminal advocate can always be recognized; he was a master of timing and tactics and of the mechanics of 'handling' a jury, so unjustly despised by counsel who fancy themselves a cut above the Old Bailey. He had something else besides. He had a *passion* for justice and fair play, which led him time and again to lay aside his fashionable and immensely lucrative civil practice, to do battle in the criminal courts for some friendless prisoner whose life or liberty he believed to be unjustly threatened. His methods were based upon argument, analysis, reason, persuasion. He never hectored a witness, seldom even raised his voice. Usually when he addressed a jury, it was to discuss the case with them in conversational tones, as if he were admitting them to his confidence. At the same time, when his liberal sympathies were engaged he could be splendidly eloquent. Not least among his assets was a beautiful voice, perfectly modulated and controlled, which he used with great skill. There is no doubt that it had something of a mesmeric effect upon juries who, as his long record of forensic successes might suggest, were for the most part content to lie within the hollow of his hand. Norman Birkett was born in September 1883, at Ulverston, in Lancashire, the son of a local draper. He had a grammar school education, then went on to Emmanuel College, Cambridge, from which he graduated with the degrees of M.A. and LL.B. In 1913 he passed his Law tripos and was called to the Bar by the Inner Temple, receiving his early training in the chambers of Sir Edward Marshall HALL K.C. He became a King's Counsel in 1924. His Liberal convictions took him into politics, and he twice represented East Nottingham in Parliament, first in 1923-4, and again in 1929-31. But like many other lawyers of the first distinction, he was not a conspicuous success in the House of Commons. He was knighted in 1941, upon becoming a judge of the King's Bench Division of the High Court. In 1950 he was appointed to be a Lord Justice of Appeal, but perhaps the true climax to his remarkable legal career had come five years earlier, when, as one of the two British judges, he was invited to be a member of the Nürnberg tribunal, which called the leading Nazi war criminals to account. He retired at the end of 1956 and was made a baron in the New Year's Honours of 1958. During his twenty-eight years in practice at the Bar, he appeared for the defence in a long series of famous murder trials, including those of Mrs. Beatrice PACE; Mrs. Sarah HEARN; Mrs. Ethel MAJOR; Dr. Buck RUXTON;

and Edward Royal CHAPLIN. He led for the Crown against Alfred
Arthur ROUSE; Nurse WADDINGHAM; and Frederick NODDER.
As junior counsel, he took part in the prosecution of Ronald LIGHT.

Black, Edward Ernest, an insurance agent, living with his wife and
stepdaughter at Tregonissey Lane End, Cornwall, bought two ounces of
white arsenic in the nearby town of St. Austell on 29th October 1921.
He said he wanted it to kill rats. Two days later Mrs. Black, a woman
eighteen years older than her husband, was taken ill, apparently with
gastritis, an hour after eating a breakfast of cake, bread and butter,
and tea, which he had prepared. For the next week Black looked after
her assiduously. Then, on 8th November, he left the house, never to
return. He was in serious financial difficulties and was, in fact, running
away from a charge of fraud which was being brought against him in
connection with his insurance business. Two days later Mrs. Black's
condition took a turn for the worse, and on 11th November she died.
A minute quantity of arsenic—only 3.73 milligrams, or one-seventeenth
of a grain—was found in the organs of the body submitted for analysis;
it was calculated that in the body as a whole there would be about one-
sixth of a grain, considerably less than a fatal dose. Nevertheless, expert
medical opinion at the Home Office was satisfied that Mrs. Black had
met her death through arsenical poisoning. This view was based on a
theory which was, at least, consistent with the small quantity of arsenic
found in the body. It was said to be the residium of a dose administered
more than five days before Mrs. Black's death, which the patient had
been unable to eliminate because of a diseased kidney condition; it was
this failure which was the immediate cause of death. Black was later
arrested in Liverpool and was put on trial before Mr. Justice
ROWLATT at Bodmin Assizes, in February 1922. Neighbours gave
evidence of Black's attentions to his wife during her last illness. One
said that Mrs. Black was sick after taking the medicine her husband
gave her; another, that she had complained that it 'burned her mouth
like pepper', and that she would not take another drop, 'even if she were
to die that minute'. No one was able to suggest an adequate reason why
Black should have wished to kill his wife. But, as was afterwards pointed
out in the Court of Criminal Appeal, it was not incumbent upon the
prosecution to establish motive; it certainly did not do so. In the witness-
box, Black swore that he had never had poison of any kind in his
possession. What had he to say, then, of his purchase of white arsenic
at St. Austell two days before his wife took to her bed? Simply that
there was no such purchase. But was not that his signature in the
poison book recording the transaction? It was, he agreed, 'somewhat
similar', but it was not, in fact, his signature. The evidence of the two

assistants in the shop, both of whom knew him, was brushed aside as mistaken. These were fatal denials, and probably contributed more than anything else to the jury's finding of 'Guilty'. Black was sentenced to death and was executed at Exeter Prison on 24th March 1922.

Bodkin, Sir Archibald (1862-1957), knighted in 1917, succeeded Sir Charles MATHEWS as Director of Public Prosecutions in 1920, after twenty-eight years as Treasury Counsel at the Old Bailey, during which time he helped to send many notorious murderers to the gallows, including George Joseph SMITH, the 'Brides in the Bath' killer. As prosecutor, he conceived it to be his primary duty to place *all* the relevant facts before the Court, whether they told against the prisoner or not. This has since become the established tradition of prosecuting counsel, a fact which undoubtedly owes something to the example of Sir Archibald Bodkin, whose term of office saw the end of what still remained of the brutal and even vindictive methods of securing a conviction which had once disfigured Old Bailey practice. He held the post of Director of Public Prosecutions for ten years, retiring in 1930. He died on 31st December 1957 at the age of ninety-five. Archibald Bodkin was called to the Bar by the Inner Temple in 1885, and appointed Junior Treasury Counsel at the Old Bailey in 1892. In that capacity he assisted in the prosecution of George CHAPMAN; the Baby Farmers, Annie Walters and Amelia SACH; and Arthur DEVEREUX. In 1908 he became Senior Treasury Counsel. Murder trials in which he led for the Crown during the next twelve years included those of John STARCHFIELD; and George Joseph SMITH. He also assisted the Attorney-General of the day in the prosecution of Madar Lal DHINGRA; and Lieutenant-Colonel RUTHERFORD.

Bonati, Minnie. *See* John ROBINSON.

Boyce, Arthur Robert. *See* Elizabeth McLINDON.

Breaks, Harriet Elsie (Kitty). *See* Frederick Rothwell HOLT.

'Brides in the Bath' Murders. *See* George Joseph SMITH.

Brinkley, Richard, provides a perfect example of the well-known legal doctrine that a person who, in attempting to murder A, unintentionally kills B, is nevertheless guilty of the crime of murder. Brinkley was a jobbing carpenter who cherished the idea of acquiring money without working for it. To this end, he assiduously cultivated the friendship of a German widow of seventy-seven named Johanna Maria

Blume, who lived with her granddaughter in her own house at Fulham, and possessed, in addition, a modest fortune of £800. To secure both the house and the £800, the jobbing carpenter hit upon the deceptively simple device of making out a will which left all the old lady's property to himself. All that was then required was Mrs. Blume's signature, and the signatures of two other persons as witnesses. This presented little difficulty to a man of Brinkley's ingenuity. What, he asked the old lady, could be nicer than a little outing in the country or to the seaside when the weather improved? He had in his pocket, he said, a list of persons who were willing to take part in this pleasing little jollification. Why should not Mrs. Blume add her own name to it? Brinkley then produced a sheet of foolscap which was folded in such a manner that the old lady could not see what was written on it. Would Mrs. Blume be so good as to sign just there? Mrs. Blume obediently did as she was asked, imagining that she was adding her signature to a list of other names. Above the fold of the paper was the form of the will which Brinkley had concocted. He now proceeded by exactly the same stratagem to secure the signatures of two other people—one of them a man named Parker—and thus put himself in possession of a document which, on the face of it, appeared to be Mrs. Blume's last will and testament, duly signed and witnessed, in accordance with the require-ments of the law. Two days later Mrs. Blume died. An inquest was held at which a verdict of natural death from cerebral hæmorrhage was recorded. All was now ready for Brinkley to enter into his inheritance. He called at the house, announced that he was 'master here', and in proof of that claim, produced the supposed will, inviting Mrs. Blume's granddaughter to inspect the signature. The granddaughter had to confess that it appeared to be genuine enough. Wisely, however, she consulted a solicitor, who in due course entered a caveat against the will. Brinkley was now faced with the necessity of proving the validity of the will. To murder the witnesses seemed to him to be the easiest way out of that particular difficulty. Brinkley decided to make a start with Mr. Parker. Accordingly, on 20th April 1907 he called at this man's lodgings at Croydon on the pretext that he had come to buy a bulldog that was for sale. He brought with him a bottle of oatmeal stout, which he genially recommended for its restorative qualities. Brinkley and Parker then went out to inspect the bulldog. Whilst they were away, Parker's landlord, a man named Richard Beck, and his wife, Elizabeth Ann Beck, came into the room with their young daughter, saw the bottle of stout on the table, and in a disastrous moment decided to sample it. The daughter merely sipped hers; Mrs. Beck took one mouth-ful and promptly spat it into the fire, declaring that it tasted like bitter almonds; Mr. Beck drank heartily. All three collapsed, and in a few moments both Mr. and Mrs. Beck died in convulsions from the effects of poisoning by prussic acid. The daughter was taken to hospital unconscious, but fortunately recovered after a few days. 'Well, I'm sugared!' exclaimed Brinkley when he was arrested. 'That's very awkward, isn't it?' On 5th May—five months after her death—the body of Mrs. Blume was exhumed, but examination and analysis proved completely negative. Brinkley was put on trial at Lewes Assizes for the murder of Mr. and Mrs. Beck, the unintended victims of his desperate plot to get rid of an inconvenient witness. He was convicted, sentenced to death by Mr. Justice Bigham (later Lord MERSEY), and hanged at Wandsworth Prison on 13th August 1907.

[*134, 145.*

Brown, Ernest, groom to a rich Yorkshire cattle factor named Frederick Ellison Morton, forced his attentions upon his employer's wife, Dorothy Louise, and presently made her his mistress. The clandestine affair continued for several years, although it appears that whatever feelings Mrs. Morton may once have had for Brown had long since withered; on her side, at least, it had become a relationship of hate and fear, fear of what Brown might do if she denied him, for he was a man of ugly temper and aggressively jealous. At the beginning of 1933, Mr. and Mrs. Morton went to live at Saxton Grange, an isolated farmhouse at Towton, near Huddersfield. In the following June, Brown threw up his job in a fit of pique because he was ordered to mow the lawn, a chore he could reconcile neither with his duty, which was to look after his master's hunters, nor with his pleasure, which was to look after his master's wife. Mrs. Morton may have thought that she was to be free at last of her uncomfortable lover, but within a few days Brown was badgering her to get her husband to give him his job back. Under threat of violence, she agreed to do as he asked, and so far prevailed upon Mr. Morton that he agreed to take Brown back—as an odd-job man. Brown took what was offered, but he considered himself to be greatly ill-used, and repeatedly during the months that followed the banked fires of his anger and resentment would burst into flame, at which times he would curse his employer—though never to his face—and threaten to 'clout him under the clock' and even to 'wreck the place'. In this simmering atmosphere of hate and fear and frustration the seeds of murder slowly ripened. They came to a terrible flowering in the autumn of the year. On 5th September 1933, Mr. Morton went out in one of the two cars that were kept at Saxton Grange, telling his wife that he would not be back until supper time. Brown was also away for part of the day. When he returned in the evening there was a violent scene between himself and Mrs. Morton, following upon her admission that she had been out swimming with a man of whom Brown chose to be jealous. It ended with Brown knocking Mrs. Morton down. At about 9.30 p.m. Mrs. Morton was in the kitchen with her companion-help, a young woman named Ann Houseman, when from somewhere close to the house there was the sound of a shotgun being discharged, and the rattle of pellets against the window. The two women ran out of the kitchen and into one of the front rooms. They were both terribly frightened, so much so that Mrs. Morton, unnerved by the scene with Brown earlier in the evening, threw herself on the floor and hid under the table. Brown came in shortly afterwards and said that he had been shooting at a rat near the cowshed. At 9.40, the tension-charged silence of the house was broken by the shrilling of the telephone. The two women ran to answer it. It was a call for Mr. Morton. The caller was invited to ring again. He did, eight minutes later, but found that the line was 'dead'; in the interval, the telephone wire outside the house had been cut. For the two women there now began a night of terror. For hours they waited, hoping in vain for the reassuring sound of Mr. Morton's car returning. At midnight they went upstairs, but they were too frightened to go to bed. Mrs. Morton locked herself in the bath-room; Ann Houseman kept watch from the window of her bedroom, from which she saw Brown crossing the yard towards the back door. She slipped away and joined Mrs. Morton in the bathroom; from behind the locked door the two women heard Brown moving about the house. They stayed in the bathroom for an hour, fearful of every creak on the stairs. Then they stole out and went together to Ann Houseman's room, where they resumed their vigil. Again they heard Brown wander-ing about. At about 2 a.m. the house fell silent, and there was no further alarm until, at about half-past three, the two women were startled by a loud explosion outside. Mrs. Morton pulled aside the blind, to see the garage on the other side of the yard ablaze. They ran to the telephone, but, finding that the instrument was 'dead', they fled back upstairs again. Mrs. Morton picked up her baby, and then the two women ran out of the house and into the protection of the open fields, where they lay down under a hedge, leaving behind them the furnace-roar of the flames, which were reddening the night sky. Later they stumbled on across the fields until they reached the village, and there they gave the alarm. Meanwhile Brown was racing about the yard rescuing the horses and cattle from the outbuildings adjoining the garage. Then he got out the horse-box and drove into Towton to rouse the farm bailiff, who went back with him to Saxton Grange. By that time the fire had spread to the adjacent outbuildings. It blazed so fiercely that it was not until 9 a.m. that it was possible to get near enough to the burned-out garage to examine the debris. In it was found all that remained of Mr. Morton's two cars, and in the one in which he had been out driving the day before was the charred trunk of a man. The head and arms had been burned away, but there could be no doubt that these were the remains of Frederick Ellison Morton. A post-mortem examination later in the day established that he had been dead before his body was burned, a hole at the bottom of the ribs being consistent with the wound a gunshot would inflict if fired at close quarters. Brown made a statement to the police in which he said that Mr. Morton, who 'appeared to have had something to drink', had returned home at 11.30 that night. He had put the car away, but had told Brown that he would be going out again. Brown had then gone quietly off to bed. Mr. Morton, he said, had sometimes slept in the car in the garage; he was a heavy smoker. Brown was charged with murder and put on trial at Leeds Assizes before Mr. Justice HUMPHREYS. The Crown case was that Mr. Morton had returned to Saxton Grange, not at 11.30, but at about 9.30; that Brown had shot him as he sat in the car after he had garaged it; and that immediately afterwards he had fired a second shot closer to the house, so that if anyone had heard the first—nobody had—the explanation that he was firing at a rat would serve convincingly for both. After cutting the telephone wire to isolate the house and make it as difficult as possible for the outbreak to be brought under control before the car had been destroyed, and with it the body of Mr. Morton, he had set fire to the garage, feeding the flames with petrol. (It was this which had caused the loud explosion the two women had heard as they kept their vigil upstairs.) Brown, in the witness-box, adhered to the story he had told the police. He denied the suggestion that he had terrified Mrs. Morton and her companion so that they would be afraid to go outside and 'see something he did not intend them to see'. The jury returned a verdict of 'Guilty'; Brown was sentenced to death, and in due time was hanged at Armley Road Prison, Leeds.

[97, 219.

Brown, Thomas Mathieson, a retired colliery manager, in the winter of 1906 sent an iced shortcake through the post as a present to his wife's uncle, Mr. William Lennox, who lived at Old Cumnock, Ayrshire. With it he enclosed a card: 'Hearty greetings to an old friend'. Mr. Lennox ate a small piece of the cake; so did his housekeeper, Grace McKerrow. Both of them were taken ill; Mr. Lennox recovered, but Miss McKerrow died. The shortcake was submitted for analysis, and the icing was found to contain a considerable quantity of strychnine. Brown, who had been assiduous in calling at the house to express his condolences, was arrested, and put on trial within the High Court of Justiciary at Edinburgh. The mental condition of the accused man was the only serious issue; medical evidence was given to show that this could be described as one of chronic epileptic insanity. Brown, who had been an epileptic for the past forty years, was found 'Guilty but Insane', and was ordered to be detained during His Majesty's pleasure. [72.

Browne, Frederick Guy, shared the guilt of the brutal murder of P.C. Gutteridge of the Essex Constabulary with a shiftless, weak-willed degenerate named **William Henry Kennedy,** called by his cronies 'The Fair-haired Sniper' or 'Two Gun Pat', because he boasted of having been a Sinn Feiner. The two men shared one shining talent, a facility for stealing other people's property, and one grave weakness, a facility for getting caught; all their lives they had been in and out of prison; indeed, it was at Dartmoor that they are said to have had their first meeting. Both had seen Army service in the 1914-18 war; both had been discharged under the stigma of dishonesty, Browne with an 'indifferent character' (a curiously mild phrase), Kennedy with 'ignominy'. Such were the two men who, on the evening of 26th September 1927, set out together from the garage at Clapham where Browne carried on an occasionally honest business. That night the business was strictly dishonest—they were going to Billericay in Essex to steal a car. At 6 o'clock the next morning Police-Constable George William Gutteridge of the Essex Constabulary, stationed at Stapleford Abbotts, was found lying dead beside the little-used Romford-Ongar road, about a mile from his home. A trail of blood led from the other side of the road to the bank against which he had fallen. His helmet lay on the ground beside him, and near it his notebook; his right hand gripped a pencil. The constable had been shot four times. Two of the bullets had entered the cheek and—a stroke of brutality from which the mind revolts—a bullet had been fired into each eye. Some three and a half hours before the discovery of the body, a Morris-Cowley car had been stolen from the garage of a Dr. Lovell at Billericay, about thirteen miles away; one hour after the discovery the car was found abandoned at Brixton. In it was a spent cartridge and on the running-board there were marks of blood. It was not until January 1928 that Chief-Inspector James Berrett of the C.I.D. was ready to make a charge. On 20th January Browne was arrested at his garage for stealing a car the previous November. A search of the garage brought to light various medical instruments and appliances which Dr. Lovell had had in his car on the night it had been stolen, the night of the murder. In the pocket by the driver's seat in Browne's own car was a loaded Webley revolver; it was proved that at least one of the shots which had killed P.C. Gutteridge had been fired from it. On 25th January, Kennedy was

27

arrested at Liverpool. He made a long, intensely graphic statement in which he described how he and Browne had stolen the doctor's car at Billericay by forcing open the door of the garage. He went on to tell how, with Browne at the wheel, they were driving along the Ongar road in the early hours of the morning when someone standing on the bank flashed a lamp at them as a signal to stop. The statement continued: 'We drove on, and then I heard a police whistle and told Browne to stop. He did so quite willingly and when the person came up we saw it was a policeman. . . . The policeman came up close to the car and stood near Browne and asked him where he was going and where he came from. Browne told him we had come from Lea Bridge Road garage and had been out to do some repairs. The policeman then asked him if he had a card. Browne said, "No." He then asked Browne, "Have you a driving licence?" Browne again said, "No." The policeman then again asked him where he came from, and Browne stammered in his answer, and the policeman then said, "Is the car yours?" I then said, "No, the car is mine." The policeman flashed his light in both our faces and was at this time standing close to the running-board on the off-side. He then asked me if I knew the number of the car, and Browne said, "You'll see it on the front of the car." The policeman said, "I know the number, but do you?" I said, "Yes, I can give you the number," and said, "TW 6120." He said, "Very well, I'll take particulars," put his torch back in his pocket, and pulled out his notebook and was in the act of writing when I heard a report, quickly followed by another one. I saw the policeman stagger back and fall over by the bank at the hedge. I said to Browne, "What have you done?" and then saw he had a large Webley revolver in his hand. He said, "Get out quick." I immediately got out and went round to the policeman, who was lying on his back, and Browne came over and said, "I'll finish the bugger," and I said, "For God's sake don't shoot any more, the man's dying," as he was groaning. The policeman's eyes were open, and Browne, addressing him, said, "What are you looking at me like that for?" and, stooping down, shot him at close range through both eyes.' In law, this statement was evidence only against Kennedy, not against Browne; no doubt, in making it, Kennedy was seeking to exculpate himself, but in this he was bound to fail, since whoever was responsible for the actual shooting, both men were equally guilty of murder, for both were jointly engaged upon a felony, and both were united in a common resolution to resist by violence anyone who should oppose them. Their trial for the murder of P.C. Gutteridge took place at the Old Bailey in April 1928, and lasted for five days. Browne gave evidence in his own behalf; he made a violent, excitable, almost uncontrollable witness. He was asked: 'Is there any truth in all that statement that you went to Billericay?' He replied, 'It is a horribly concocted statement that has taken hours to consider. That is my opinion.' For his part, Kennedy did not go into the witness-box, but he made a statement from the dock, in which he said that Browne killed P.C. Gutteridge in an 'absolute mad frenzy'. He added a footnote which, in the circumstances, can only be called nauseating: 'I can only now express my deep regret to Mrs. Gutteridge that I should have been in the car on the night of the crime.' The jury returned a verdict of 'Guilty' against both men. As Mr. Justice AVORY prepared to pass sentence of death, first Browne, then Kennedy, made a short speech from the dock, in which each admitted that he had had a fair trial. 'I would not wish to be tried by a better judge,' said Browne. 'I am quite content to leave it, but I am not guilty according to the One above who knows. I am not guilty, but the Court says I am. I am quite content; my conscience is clear.' As for Kennedy, he declared himself to be the victim of a 'preordained fate' to which the judge and jury were 'mere accessories'. On 31st May, Browne was hanged at Pentonville, Kennedy at Wandsworth.

[I.

Bryant, Charlotte, born Charlotte McHugh, was a violent, bad-tempered slut. Frederick John Bryant had the ill-luck to meet her in the course of his Army service at Londonderry in 1920-2; he had the even greater misfortune to marry her and to bring her back with him to England, where he found work as an agricultural labourer. In 1925 the couple moved to Over Compton in Dorset, and there they occupied a tied cottage belonging to the farmer by whom Bryant was employed. Bryant seems to have been an amiable, trusting character; either he did not see, or, more likely, he chose to ignore, the lewd behaviour of his wife, who was widely known in the neighbourhood as 'Black Bess', 'Killarney Kate', or 'Compton Liz'. At Christmas 1933 a horse dealer named Leonard Parsons, a man of gipsy blood, entered the disordered life of the Bryants. He came to lodge at the cottage, and promptly became Charlotte Bryant's lover. This led to so much scandal in the village that within a few months Bryant lost his job. He found another, this time with a farmer at Coombe, near Sherborne, and in March 1934 the Bryants moved into the cottage that went with it. The ubiquitous Parsons, part lover, part lodger, followed them; there can be no doubt that Mrs. Bryant, whose numerous other affairs were casual to the point of forgetfulness, was extremely fond of him. On Monday, 13th May 1935, Bryant was taken violently ill, but quickly recovered. On 6th August he fell ill again, but within a few days he was back at work; a countryman born and bred, he was not at all an easy man to kill, which no doubt contributed to Mrs. Bryant's vexation. His third illness began on 11th December and was of a much more serious character. Ten days later he took a sharp turn for the worse, and on the afternoon of 22nd December he died. The doctor refused to issue a death certificate and informed the police of his suspicions. Dr. Roche LYNCH, the Home Office analyst, subsequently reported that he had found four grains of arsenic in the body. The Bryants' cottage, which was in an indescribably filthy condition, was subjected to a minute search. Furniture was removed, floors swept, floorboards lifted, soot taken from the chimneys. Altogether more than 150 samples of dust and scrapings were submitted for analysis. Parsons was able to satisfy the police that although he might have been the cause of the murder he had had no hand in it. He reported that Mrs. Bryant had more than once told him that she was 'going to be a widow', and that then they could marry, to which he had retorted, 'I wouldn't marry any woman.' Mrs. Ostler, a widow who helped with the housework, described how one day Mrs. Bryant had picked up a tin of weed killer and had said, 'I must get rid of this.' Some ten minutes later she had come back into the room without the tin. 'If nothing is found,' she had remarked, 'they can't put a rope round your neck.' A renewed search of the cottage and its surroundings yielded an old, battered, scarcely recognizable tin, which had been thrown away. Scrapings from it were found to contain 58,000 parts per million of arsenic. The manufacturers identified it as a tin similar to those they used for their product, a weed killer which turned out to be tasteless in milk or tea, and scarcely noticeable even in water. Mrs. Bryant was tried and convicted at Dorchester Assizes, where, on 30th May 1936, Mr. Justice Macnaghten sentenced her to death for the murder of her husband. She was hanged at Exeter Prison on 15th July.

[92, 103, 151.

Buchowski, Jan. *See* Ludomir CIENSKI.

Buckingham, John William. *See* Thomas John LEY.

Bucknill, Sir Thomas Townsend (1845-1915). Judge of the King's Bench Division of the High Court (1899-1914). Known affectionately as 'Sentimental Tommy', this genial man never lost the ingenuous, even boyish charm which was so great an asset to him during early days at the Bar when he was building up a prosperous junior practice on circuit. Most of the stories of 'Sentimental Tommy', of which there are many in the legal memoirs of the period, highlight his tender-heartedness. Capital cases must have been an agony to him, and it is on record that when he had to pass sentence of death he would do it with the tears running down his cheeks. The son of a well-known specialist in mental diseases, he was called to the Bar by the Inner Temple in 1868. He sat in the House of Commons as Conservative Member for Mid-Surrey from 1892 until 1899, when he was elevated to the Bench as successor to Mr. Justice Hawkins (Lord Brampton). He made an excellent judge, not by virtue of any great legal erudition, but because of his indestructible common sense, and his ability to sift the truth from a mass of contradictory evidence; incidentally, there never was a judge more completely free from arrogance or conceit. Off the Bench he was known as a keen horseman and rider to hounds. He retired in 1914 and died in October of the following year, aged seventy. To students of murder he will always be remembered as the judge who presided over the trial of the SEDDONS.

Burnham, Alice. *See* George Joseph SMITH.

Burton, Walter William, was employed by the squire of Gussage St. Michael, Dorset, to keep the rabbits down at the Manor Farm, and to do odd jobs about the house. Gussage St. Michael was, in 1912, when this peculiar story begins, an isolated village of 160 souls, seven miles from the nearest railway station, its only regular link with the outside world a twice-weekly bus service to Dorchester and Blandford. In such a place everybody knows everybody else's business, and that makes it all the more difficult to understand how the brutal murder of a young woman could go undetected for more than a month, in spite of the clues, each more sinister than the last, which were scattered with almost insolent casualness beneath the very noses of the unsuspecting villagers. Winifred Mary Mitchell came from the neighbouring village of Manswood. In October 1912, when she was twenty-four, she took a situation as cook at the Manor Farm, and at once attracted the roving eye of the twenty-nine-years-old odd-job man, who had a great relish for his own reputation as a seducer of women, and an unpleasant habit of boasting about his conquests. But the new girl 'up at the farm' was inconveniently virtuous, and it took him until the following January before he could bring her to the frame of mind in which she was willing to become his mistress. By this time he was already talking about leaving his wife and child—he was married to the village post-mistress, a woman twelve years older than himself—and of making a fresh start in Canada with Winifred Mary Mitchell at his side; he even went so far as to make an abortive attempt to raise the money for the fares. He was, however, unable to scrape together more than £5. By March he had tired of the girl and was seeking a way to be rid of her; he believed her to be pregnant and, in one way or another, likely to become a very great nuisance. The much-discussed elopement was now presented as something which was likely to happen within a few days; all unsuspecting, Winifred Mary was made to assist in the preparation of her own violent end. She was to tell her mother that she had taken a new situation in London. She was to send home such of her belongings as she did not wish to take with her. She was, in short—although this was not how the matter was put to her—to do all that could be done in advance to provide a convincing explanation against the time when she was no longer to be seen about the village. All this she dutifully did; her thoughts were all on Canada, Burton's thoughts much nearer home. On 29th March Burton proposed that the girl should meet him near Sovel Plantation, a small wood on the hillside near the Manor Farm, to discuss plans for the elopement with 'a man with a motor car'. At the last moment Winifred Mary was unable to keep this appointment; Burton did not allow this to hinder his preparations. The next day, which was a Sunday, some children picking primroses in the little wood on the hill came upon a hole which someone had dug in the moist earth. It was long and wide and deep and had all the appearance of an open grave, which was exactly what it was. The children were full of this odd discovery when they got home, but nobody troubled to listen. On the following afternoon, shortly before 4 o'clock, Winifred Mary Mitchell, wearing her best clothes, left the Manor Farm on her bicycle, telling the housemaid that she had to be 'up on the hill'; she was keeping the appointment she had not been able to keep two days before. Perhaps it was some sudden premonition that she might not return which compelled her to add, 'If I am not back at a quarter-past four you will know something has happened to me.' She rode away on her bicycle and she did *not* come back. But nobody imagined that anything had 'happened' to her. The talk in the village was that Winifred Mary had gone up to London to take a new and superior situation in domestic service, so well had the ground been prepared. No one remembered the open grave; no one even appeared to think it remarkable when, later on, it was discovered that the grave had been filled in with freshly turned earth; no one thought to make anything of the fact that on the day Winifred Mary Mitchell had disappeared the odd-job man at the Manor Farm had borrowed a gun and three cartridges to 'kill a cat', and had presently returned it, with one of the cartridges missing. On 6th April a dairyman walking in the Sovel Plantation picked up three false teeth, probably on the very spot where the girl had been murdered, but all he did with them was to take them home and set them up on his mantelshelf. There they remained until 29th April, when the rector's wife, hearing of this odd discovery, prevailed upon her husband to report it to the police. At last things began to move.

On 2nd May the body of Winifred Mary Mitchell was recovered from the grave so carefully prepared. It was found that she had been shot from behind at a distance of a few feet. Burton was arrested, and, being put on trial at Dorchester Assizes, before Mr. Justice RIDLEY, was convicted and condemned to death. He had the doubtful distinction of being the last man to be hanged at Dorchester Prison.

'Button and Badge' Murder. *See* David GREENWOOD.

C

Confusion now hath made his masterpiece !
Most sacrilegious murder hath broke ope
The Lord's anointed temple, and stole thence
The life o' the building.

Shakespeare: *Macbeth*

Calvert, Louie, a crafty liar with an evil temper and a rich fund of pious talk—she often appeared in a stolen Salvation Army bonnet—kept body and soul together by prostitution and petty pilfering. Early in 1925 this little scrap of a woman went as housekeeper to a night watchman named Arthur ('Arty') Calvert, who lived in Railway Place in the Hunslet district of Leeds. After she had been with Calvert for some six months she told him, falsely, that she was pregnant, and by this means induced him to marry her. As the months went by, and there was still no sign of the approaching birth, Calvert was naturally suspicious, and by March 1926 he was constantly pressing his wife to say precisely when the baby was expected to arrive. The method she chose to relieve herself of the embarrassment of her husband's persistent inquiries was characteristic of the tortuous, even fantastic, nature of this woman's mind, which always preferred the involved to the simple solution. Instead of telling Calvert that she had been mistaken and that she was not going to have a baby after all, or even pretending that she had had a miscarriage, she decided to procure a new-born baby and pass it off as her own. As a first step, she showed her husband what purported to be a letter from her sister in Dewsbury, inviting her to go there for her confinement. The next day she left home, saying that she was going to her sister, and indeed she did actually go to Dewsbury, where she stayed long enough to send a telegram to her husband advertising her safe arrival, then returned to Leeds. There she took lodgings with a Mrs. Lily Waterhouse, an eccentric widow who dabbled in spiritualism, and who occupied a three-roomed house in Amberley Road, only about two miles away from Railway Place. There she set about the task of finding a suitable baby. An advertisement in a Leeds evening paper offering adoption quickly provided her with what she

34

wanted. A seventeen-years-old unmarried girl had given birth to a daughter in a Leeds nursing home a few days before. The girl's mother saw the advertisement, answered it, and after an interview with Louie Calvert agreed to allow her to adopt the unwanted child. She arranged to hand the baby over on 31st March, which was in about three weeks' time. At the end of the three weeks, Louie Calvert returned home—with the baby. 'Arty' Calvert, firmly imagining himself to be a father, was overjoyed. The next morning—it was Maundy Thursday—he was mildly puzzled to find a suitcase in the sitting-room, a suitcase which he had not seen before. Louie explained that her sister in Dewsbury had given it to her, and that it contained baby clothes. That evening the police called upon Louie Calvert, and presently charged her with the murder of Mrs. Lily Waterhouse, who had been found strangled at her home in Amberley Road, her hair matted with blood from savage blows on the head by a poker or hammer. The mysterious suitcase, then being opened, was found to contain bits and pieces of cutlery, cracked cups and saucers, and some oddments of household linen—a pitiful haul, but Mrs. Waterhouse's poverty-stricken home had offered nothing better. At Mrs. Calvert's trial at Leeds Assizes, before Mr. Justice Wright, the Court listened to the chequered story of Mrs. Waterhouse and her strange lodger; of how pieces of crockery and articles of clothing had begun to disappear; how Mrs. Waterhouse suspected who the thief was, but was so frightened of Louie's savage temper that she had not dared at first to accuse her openly; how in the end she had gone to the police, who had arranged for her to take out a summons and had instructed her to appear at the Magistrate's Court on Maundy Thursday. Before that day came she was already dead. It now transpired that in the early hours of the day following her return to Railway Place, Mrs. Calvert had gone back to the house in Amberley Road, where Mrs. Waterhouse was lying dead. Letting herself in with a key, she had filled up a suitcase with the odds and ends of crockery and linen. The Assize jury convicted Louie Calvert of the murder, and she was sentenced to death. In the condemned cell, she is said to have confessed to another murder, committed in Leeds four years earlier, when a man named John William Frobisher, who had employed Louie as his housekeeper, was found drowned in a canal. Mrs. Calvert was executed at Strangeways Prison on 26th June 1926.

[94.

Camb, James, steward in the Union Castle liner *Durban Castle*, was convicted of the murder of twenty-six-years-old Eileen (Gay) Gibson, whose body he pushed through the porthole of Cabin 126, so that it was lost for ever in the trackless ocean. At the time of her death Miss

Gibson, having already had some stage and radio experience, was hopefully looking forward to fresh engagements on the strength of the success she had had in repertory in South Africa. She was now on her way home to England as a first-class passenger in the *Durban Castle*, which had sailed from Cape Town on 10th October 1947. At 12.40 a.m. on 18th October, Miss Gibson retired to her cabin, having spent the evening dining and dancing with some shipboard acquaintances. At two minutes to three, the bell rang in the first-class pantry on A deck; the indicator showed that someone was ringing in Miss Gibson's cabin on B deck. Frederick Steer, night watchman, went to the cabin. Two lights were showing outside the door, indicating that both the steward and the stewardess had been rung for. Steer knocked and made to enter the cabin. The light was on. He opened the door a few inches. It was then shut in his face. As it closed, Steer had a quick glimpse of a man wearing a sleeveless singlet and a pair of blue trousers, a man he recognized as one of his shipmates. He returned to the pantry and reported to James Murray, the head night watchman, that James Camb, a steward on the promenade deck, was in Miss Gibson's cabin. Together, they went along to the cabin, but although they waited outside the door for four or five minutes, they heard no sound. It was time now for Murray to make his routine report to the bridge. To the Second Officer of the Watch he described what Steer had seen, but being reluctant to make trouble for one of the stewards, he allowed the officer to infer that the man in Cabin 126 was a passenger. The officer dismissed him, remarking that the morals of the passengers were their own affair. Miss Gibson was missed at breakfast-time and, after fruitless attempts to find her, Captain Patey, master of the *Durban Castle*, gave the order to reverse course. It was a hopeless search, and after an hour the captain set the liner on her course again. Steer now informed the captain that it was Camb he had seen in Miss Gibson's cabin. Camb promptly denied that he had stirred from his own quarters after he had gone to bed at 12.45. Later in the day he was examined by the ship's surgeon, who found that on the steward's right wrist were marks which appeared to be consistent with scratches made by fingernails. An examination of the bed in Cabin 126 revealed bloodstained saliva stains on the sheets. When the *Durban Castle* arrived at Cowes Roads on the night of 24th–25th October, Camb was taken to police headquarters in Southampton, where it was pointed out to him that to persist in his denial that he had been in Cabin 126 when Steer had knocked at the door would only make it the more difficult to accept any reasonable explanation of Miss Gibson's disappearance that he might later have to offer. Said Camb: 'You mean that Miss Gibson might have died from a cause other than being murdered? She might have had a heart attack or something?' The Crown suggested that this was the genesis of the defence Camb was afterwards to develop at his trial, which took place at Winchester Assizes before Mr. Justice HILBERY the following March. In the witness-box, Camb told how he had gone to Miss Gibson's cabin at about 11 p.m. on 17th October to ask her if she required a supper tray. There, half jokingly, he said, 'I have a good mind to bring a drink down and join you.' To which Miss Gibson replied, 'Please yourself; it's up to you.' At about 2 a.m., he went along to Cabin 126, where he found Miss Gibson lying on the bed wearing a yellow quilted dressing-gown. He sat on the edge of the bed talking to her for ten or fifteen minutes. Then he climbed on to the bed and lay down beside the girl, who undid her dressing gown; he saw that she had nothing on underneath it. Whilst he was making love to her she suddenly heaved, as if she were gasping for breath. Her body stiffened for a fraction of a second and then went completely limp. 'I was rather stunned for a moment,' said Camb. 'First of all I listened and felt for heart-beats. I could not find any, and I attempted, by massaging the stomach towards the heart, to bring back circulation. . . . I should say I was twenty or twenty-five minutes trying to revive her.' He was standing by the bed applying what he knew of artificial respiration when Steer tried to enter the cabin; he closed the door upon him. He did not think he had been recognized, yet a feeling of 'complete panic' overcame him. For about fifteen minutes longer he continued in his fruitless attempts to revive Miss Gibson; at length he was forced to conclude that the girl was dead. He went on: 'I confess now it sounds very foolish, but I hoped to give the impression that she had fallen overboard, and deny all knowledge of having been to that cabin, in the hope that the Captain's further inquiries would not be too severe. I lifted her up and pushed her through the porthole.' In cross-examination by Mr. G. D. Roberts K.C., who led for the Crown, Camb was asked:

Q: What would you expect a passenger to do who, in the night, objected to the advances of a member of the crew?
A: Shout.
Q: Not much good shouting. Is not ringing the bells a much better thing for a passenger to do?
A: They both amount to the same thing.
Q: That is what she did, is it not?
A: She didn't touch the bell.
Q: Who did then?
A: I don't know.
Q: Are you suggesting the bells went off on their own accord?
A: I cannot suggest how the bells were rung.

Q: Did you have to work quickly to silence her before the bell was answered?
A: I didn't have to silence her at all.
Q: I suggest that is what you did, and got those scratches on your right wrist?
A: No.

The medical evidence was clearly of vital importance. Some of the best-known pathologists in the country were called. All agreed that the usual features of strangulation were present—the bloodstained saliva marks on the sheet, the scratches on Camb's wrist, suggesting that the girl had tried to tear the murderer's hands from her throat. Two eminent medical men who were called for the defence considered, however, that the signs were equally consistent with death from natural causes. Camb was found guilty and was sentenced to death—but he did not hang. He was condemned whilst Parliament was preoccupied with the 'no hanging' clause which the House of Commons added to the Criminal Justice Bill and which the House of Lords took out. The Home Secretary had publicly stated that there would be no executions whilst the matter was still at issue between the two Houses. Thus was James Camb's life preserved. He was released from prison in September 1959.
[*I.*

Casserley, Georgina May.⎱ *See* Edward Royal CHAPLIN.
Casserley, Percy Arthur. ⎰

Casswell, Joshua David, Q.C. Official Referee of the Supreme Court of Judicature since 1951. He was 'called' in 1910, but his career was interrupted by distinguished service in the 1914-18 war, and it was not until the late 1920s that he built up his great reputation as a pleader at the Criminal Bar. Special mention may be made of his conduct of the defence at the two trials of Reginald WOOLMINGTON (1934 and 1935), whose conviction for murder was quashed by the House of Lords; and of his brilliant, but unavailing, fight to save Charlotte BRYANT from the gallows. He took silk in 1938, and during the next thirteen years he appeared for the defence in a long series of murder trials, of which perhaps the most remarkable was the trial of Neville HEATH. Others he defended include Elizabeth JONES (Jones and Hulten); and James CAMB.

Catterall, John Bernard. *See* George KELLY.

Chaplin, Edward Royal, was a solace to Mrs. Georgina May Casserley in her loveless marriage to a man more than twenty years older than herself. Percy Arthur Casserley, fifty-eight, ex-director of a brewery, drank heavily, was apt to be quarrelsome, and had the habit—a fatal one, as it turned out—of keeping a loaded revolver at hand. From time to time he went as a patient into what was tactfully described as a 'nursing home for nervous complaints', and during these absences Edward Royal Chaplin, a builder's foreman, quite often lodged at the Casserleys' affluent home at Wimbledon; alternatively, Mrs. Casserley stayed with him at his flat. In March 1938 she was about to become the mother of his child. Mr. Casserley returned from the last of his visits to the 'nursing home' on 22nd March. On the following evening, Mrs. Casserley ran to a neighbour's house, crying out that whilst she had been away from home an intruder had broken in and had injured her husband. Casserley was found lying on the floor of the lounge, having been shot through the head. There were lacerated wounds on the back of his head, abrasions and bruises on his face and back and forearms. He died soon after the police arrived. Table silver and cups and goblets from the sideboard were laid out on the floor of the dining-room, together with a heavy torch, which was dented and stained with blood. Casserley's revolver was missing. Superficially, all this suggested that Casserley had surprised an intruder in the dining-room as he was about to make away with the family silver, had gone into the lounge for his revolver, and had been hit on the head with the torch during a struggle. The would-be thief had then, it would appear, wrested the revolver from him and had shot him in the head. The police were suspicious of this explanation from the start. Inquiries into the Casserleys' family circumstances led them irresistibly to Edward Royal Chaplin, who not only made a statement admitting that it was he who had struggled with Casserley for the possession of the revolver, but also led the police to the spot where he had hidden it. His account of the events of 23rd March was that he had gone to Casserley to have a talk with him about a situation which urgently required a solution, now that Mrs. Casserley was going to have a baby. When Chaplin had admitted that he was the father, the outraged husband had flown at him. There had been a fierce struggle, in the course of which Chaplin had hit out at Casserley in self-defence, using the torch he had brought with him as a weapon. Casserley had further injured himself by blundering into the furniture and falling down in his blind rage. Then Casserley had snatched his revolver from a drawer in the bureau. To save himself, Chaplin had thrown himself upon him, and as he was trying to take the revolver away from him it had gone off. Mrs. Casserley had then come into the room, and between them they had faked the evidence to suggest that a burglar had broken in and had been surprised in his thieving. Chaplin was charged with murder, Mrs. Casserley with being an accessory after the fact. (Because she was too ill to be taken into custody, she was allowed to go to friends, and afterwards into a nursing home.) Tried at the Old Bailey before Mr. Justice HUMPHREYS, Chaplin was found guilty only of manslaughter, and for this he was sentenced to twelve years penal servitude. Mrs. Casserley was tried separately—before the same judge—as an accessory, and received a sentence of eleven days imprisonment, which meant, in effect, that she was immediately released.

[34, 47.

Chapman, George, devoted many of his most active hours to the pursuit, possession, and poisoning of women. His real name was Severin Klosowski, but, perhaps because 'Chapman' is more easily pronounced, he is best remembered in the halls of infamy under that casual alias, which he picked up at some stage in his squalid career. The son of the village carpenter, he was born at Nagornak in Poland on 14th December 1865, and died on the scaffold in Wandsworth Prison on 7th April 1903. During his short life-span, he was known to have poisoned three women—apparently for the pleasure of watching them slowly die—and it is possible that he murdered many more. For George Chapman rests under the suspicion that he may have been 'Jack the Ripper', of abominable memory. In his youth, Chapman was apprenticed to a surgeon, and at one time seems to have held some sort of hospital appointment at Praga in Poland. He arrived in England some time in 1888 and obtained a situation as an assistant at a barber's shop in Whitechapel. He did not stay there long. Indeed, he was constantly on the move, working at various barbers' shops in Tottenham, Shoreditch, and Leytonstone. In August 1889 he acquired a wife, who presented him with two children, and eventually, after a brief sojourn with him in America, parted from him, being no longer willing to tolerate his persistent infidelities. In 1895, some two years after the break-up of the marriage, he met, whilst working at Leytonstone, a certain Mary Isabella Spink, the wife of a railway porter. It was not long before they were living together. With Mrs. Spink's money, he leased a hairdressing business in Hastings. Later, he and Mrs. Spink returned to London, where Chapman became the licensee of the Prince of Wales Tavern in Bartholomew Square, off the City Road. They had been there only a few months when Mrs. Spink began to suffer from severe vomiting attacks and abdominal pains. A doctor was called in. He prescribed various relieving medicines, but Mrs. Spink continued to grow steadily weaker, and on the morning of Christmas Day, 1897, she died. Chapman was prostrated with grief. The doctor was sympathetic, made no difficulty about granting a certificate, in which phthisis was named as the cause of death. A few months later, Chapman advertised for a barmaid. Among the applicants for the job was a young woman named Elizabeth (Bessie) Taylor. She was engaged, and almost at once succumbed to her employer's apparently irresistible charm. Very soon, her health began to fail, and as she grew thinner and weaker, Chapman treated her with increasing brutality. The Prince of Wales was given up for a public house in Bishop's Stortford. Later still, Chapman became the landlord of the Monument Tavern in the Borough. By this time Bessie Taylor had become a semi-permanent invalid. Several doctors attended her; none of them seemed to understand her case. Yet another doctor, Dr. Stoker, was called in. The treatment he prescribed seemed to be having some beneficial result, when there was a sudden deterioration in the patient's condition, and in the early hours of 13th February 1901, Bessie Taylor died. Dr. Stoker obliged with a certificate, in which death was attributed to 'exhaustion from vomiting and diarrhoea'. Chapman composed a touching verse for Bessie's gravestone:

> Farewell, my friends, fond and dear,
> Weep not for me one single tear;
> For all that was and could be done
> You plainly see my time was come.

In the following August, a Miss Maud Eliza Marsh of Croydon advertised for a situation as a barmaid. It was answered by the landlord of the Monument Tavern, and Miss Marsh was duly engaged. She quickly became Chapman's mistress. Almost immediately, the same pattern of illness began. Maud Marsh began to suffer excessively from vomiting, diarrhoea, stomach pains, and eventually became so ill that she was admitted to Guy's Hospital. Meanwhile, Chapman removed to the Crown, a public house further along the street. In hospital, Miss Marsh gradually recovered, but as soon as she was able to return home the same symptoms began to recur. Dr. Stoker appeared on the scene again; he was as much perplexed by the condition of the patient as he had been in the equally puzzling case of Bessie Taylor. No inkling of the truth dawned upon him. It was left to Maud Marsh's mother to mention the word 'poison'. She confided her suspicion to her husband who, in turn, passed it on to his own doctor, Dr. Francis Grapel. As a result, Dr. Grapel called at the Crown on the afternoon of 21st October 1902, and had a consultation with Dr. Stoker; he also examined the patient. Thoroughly alarmed, Chapman acted quickly. On the day after Dr. Grapel's visit Miss Marsh died. As soon as Dr. Grapel heard of this he telegraphed a warning to Dr. Stoker; thinking over the case, he had come to the conclusion that the patient might be suffering from arsenical poisoning. (He was wrong about the poison—it was antimony.) Dr. Stoker, to Chapman's evident surprise and annoyance, refused to grant a death certificate. On 25th October, the day of the Coronation of King Edward VII, Chapman was arrested. The bodies of Mrs. Spink and Bessie Taylor were exhumed; analysis disclosed in each case the presence of tartarated antimony. Chapman was indicted for the murder of Maud Marsh before Mr. Justice GRANTHAM at the Old Bailey in March 1903, the Crown case being presented by the Solicitor-General, Sir Edward Carson K.C. The prisoner's plight was hopeless from the start. His counsel, Mr. George ELLIOTT, did his best for him, but it took the jury only eleven minutes to find Chapman 'Guilty'. Sentence of death left him paralysed with terror, and he had to be assisted from the dock. Chief-Inspector Abberline, who had charge of the investigation of the gruesome murders which spread terror through the mean streets of Whitechapel in the 1880s, firmly believed at one time that Chapman, the sadist, and 'Jack the Ripper' were the same person; later, it is true, he changed his mind. The evidence was summarized by Mr. Hargrave L. Adam in his introduction to *The Trial of George Chapman* in the *Notable British Trials* series:

JACK THE RIPPER	CHAPMAN
First murder of the series committed in August 1888.	Chapman arrived in London some time in 1888: worked and lived in Whitechapel.
Other murders committed during 1888.	During this time, Chapman was within easy reach of the scenes of these murders.
It was thought that Jack the Ripper had medical knowledge.	Chapman had been a medical student.
Description given of the man seen with the woman Kelly: 'Height. 5 ft. 6 in.; age, 34 or 35; dark complexion, with moustache curled at the ends.'	This is a most faithful description of Chapman.
The Americanisms in the letter and card written to the police.	Chapman passed himself off as an American and used Americanisms in conversation.
The grim and callous joking tone of the messages.	Chapman was very callous, and was in the habit of indulging in pleasantries of this sort.

Last murder in London, July 1889.	Chapman still in the vicinity.
No Ripper murders in England, but similar murders in America, in the locality of Jersey City.	Chapman and his wife left in May 1890 for America, where Chapman opened a barber's shop at Jersey City.
At the beginning of 1892 Ripper murders cease in America.	Chapman left America and returned to London in May 1892.

It has been surmised that Chapman gave up the 'Ripper' murders as being too dangerous, and took to the safer method of poison for his sadistic enjoyment. This, of course, is only one of many theories that are, or have been, held as to the identity of 'Jack the Ripper'. It cannot be said that it is much in favour with later commentators, for whom it leaves too much unexplained.

[*I*.

Charles, Sir Ernest Bruce (1871-1950). Judge of the King's Bench Division (1928-47). Mr. Justice Charles was not a judge of any great profundity, but he possessed an inexhaustible fund of hard sense, which, combined with a wide knowledge of the world and its wickedness, served him just as well. During his career at the Bar, he had had the reputation of being 'good with a jury', and this quality did not desert him on the Bench, where he continued to make use of his special talent for expounding complicated issues in the plain, honest terms most readily understood by the plain, honest man in the jury-box. Rubicund and benign, yet resolutely unsentimental, he dispensed justice in a down-to-earth manner, which, if it lacked subtlety, was yet astonishingly effective—seldom were his judgments disturbed on appeal. He held strong opinions on a variety of subjects, and since he was exceedingly forthright in his expression of them, it was not surprising that the name of Mr. Justice Charles should be constantly appearing in the newspapers, often under some such convenient headline as BACHELOR JUDGE HITS OUT. (Incidentally, he had been a good amateur boxer in his youth, and all his life retained an interest in the prize ring.) Himself the son of a High Court judge, Ernest Bruce Charles was called to the Bar in 1896—when he was twenty-five—and took silk in 1913. He was one of two new judges appointed in February 1928—the late Sir Travers HUMPHREYS was the other. Retiring in 1947, he died in May 1950, being then in his eightieth year. Murder trials over which he presided during his nineteen years on the Bench included those of Mrs. Ethel MAJOR; Frederick FIELD (second trial); JONES and HULTEN; and Leonard HOLMES.

Chesney, Ronald John. } *See* John Donald MERRETT.
Chesney, Vera.

Chevis, Lieutenant Hubert George, a regular officer in the Royal Artillery, who occupied a bungalow at Blackdown Camp, near Aldershot, sat down on the evening of 21st June 1931 to a dish of roast partridge. A brace of birds, supplied by a poulterer in Aldershot, cooked together and basted in the same fat, were served to the young officer and his wife. Lieutenant Chevis took one mouthful, found that the meat 'tasted horrible', and refused to eat any more. He asked his wife to taste the partridge on her plate. She merely touched it with her tongue; it had, she agreed, a 'fusty' taste. Lieutenant Chevis told his batman, who was serving the dinner, to take the birds away and have them destroyed, as he did not want his dog to get hold of them. Fifteen minutes later he was taken violently ill. He lost the use of his legs, was shaken by terrible convulsions, and, being removed to hospital, died the next day in great agony. Mrs. Chevis was also seized with severe pains shortly after the meal, but after being treated by a doctor she presently recovered. In the case of Lieutenant Chevis, the stomach content, as examined by Dr. J. H. Ryffel, Home Office analyst, yielded a large amount of strychnine. He also found strychnine in the dripping and more in the gravy. Dr. Ryffel concluded that the total quantity of strychnine associated with the partridges amounted to at least two grains. (The minimum fatal dose of this poison is half a grain.) After twice adjourning the inquest to allow the police to complete their inquiries, which produced no result, the Deputy Coroner for West Surrey had no option but to instruct the jury that the only proper verdict was: Asphyxia following strychnine poisoning caused by eating partridge, with insufficient evidence to show how the poison came to be in the bird. The jury duly returned an open verdict. There is, however, no doubt at all that Lieutenant Chevis was murdered. No difficulty arises over opportunity. After delivery by the poulterer in the morning, the cook placed the partridges in an open meat safe which was kept outside the bungalow, and there they remained until they were required for the oven. It need only have been a matter of moments for anyone who was so disposed to inject the birds with a solution of strychnine by means of a hypodermic syringe. But who could have wished to murder this young officer, popular in the regiment, happily married, a young man who did not appear to have an enemy in the world? A strange, and hateful, feature of the case was that on the morning of the funeral a telegram, handed in at Dublin, was received by Sir William Chevis, the young man's father. All it said was: 'Hooray Hooray Hooray.' It had been sent by a man who wrote the name 'J. Hartigan' on the back of the form, together with the address of a well-known Dublin hotel. Immediate inquiries were made at the hotel, but no one of that name was, or had been, registered there; nor was there any 'Hartigan' on the staff. A week or two later, Sir William Chevis received a postcard which had been posted in Belfast. It read: 'It is a mystery they will never solve. J. Hartigan. Hooray.' The card was prophetic. After a quarter of a century, the Mystery of the Poisoned Partridges is still without a solution.

[*72, 206.*

Choat, Police-Constable Walter Charles. *See* SIEGE OF SIDNEY STREET.

Christie, Ethel.
Christie, John Reginald. } *See* Timothy John EVANS.

Cienski, Lieutenant Ludomir, a distinguished officer attached to Polish naval headquarters in London during the second World War, was displaced in the affections of his wife by a brother officer, Lieutenant Jan Buchowski. On 12th April 1943, Lieutenant Buchowski called by invitation at Cienski's flat in Victoria. The two men went into the sitting-room together, closing the door behind them. A few minutes later three shots rang out. Cienski's landlord rushed into the room. Buchowski was half-sitting, half-lying in an armchair by the fireplace. Lieutenant Cienski was standing with a revolver in his hand. To the police he said: 'I tried to get him to promise not to see my wife again. He refused. I handed him my revolver and asked him to shoot me. If he shot me it didn't matter. He fired at me. When he did so I jumped at him and caught the hand holding the revolver. There was a struggle. I heard shots. He fell back in his chair. I didn't shoot him.' Mr. Justice HUMPHREYS presided over Cienski's trial at the Old Bailey. There, the landlord spoke of the three shots having been fired one after another in quick succession, or, as he put it—pouf, pouf, pouf. This was awkward for the defence, since if Cienski's story were true there ought to have been an interval after the firing of the first shot. Also, Sir Bernard SPILSBURY, the Home Office pathologist, insisted that the third shot must have been fired after Buchowski was dead, which was scarcely consistent with Cienski's story that the revolver had gone off by accident in the course of a struggle. On the other hand, the case for the defence was strongly supported by the fact that a bullet mark had been found near the window facing the chair in which the dead man was lying; this showed that one of the shots, presumably the first, had been fired in the opposite direction from the other two. But it was an extra-ordinary omission on the part of the police that made a likely acquittal a certainty. *The revolver had not been tested for fingerprints.* Sir Patrick HASTINGS K.C., who defended Cienski, made effective use of this point in his cross-examination of the police officer in charge of the case:

Q: If the prisoner's story is true, the dead man must at some time have held the revolver in his hand?
A: Yes.
Q: In that case you would have expected to find the dead man's fingerprints upon the revolver?
A: Possibly.
Q: Were the dead man's fingerprints on that revolver?
A: I don't know.
Q: Why not? Is it not the duty of the police to search for finger-prints? Were they ever taken in this case?
A: No.

'Why not? Why not?' snapped Sir Patrick. 'Has somebody made a grave mistake?' There was no answer. After that exchange no jury would have taken the risk of convicting the prisoner. If the gun had been tested for fingerprints, it might have proved Cienski's story to be false; it might equally have shown it to be true. Inevitably, the jury's verdict was one which set this gallant officer at liberty.

[*89.*

Clapperton, Alexander. *See* John James HUTCHISON.

'Cleft Chin' Murder. *See* Elizabeth Maud JONES.

Clements, Dr. Robert George, debonair, dapper, very much the ladies' man, committed suicide at Southport, Lancs, where he practised, upon learning that the police had stopped the funeral of his fourth wife, Amy Victoria. There had seemed no reason to doubt that Mrs. Clements' death—in the summer of 1947—was due to natural causes. But if, in any quarter, suspicion should still have lingered, then surely it must have been dispelled by Dr. Clements' own suggestion that there should be a post-mortem examination. This was carried out by a young and highly gifted doctor, and appeared to confirm that there was nothing in the circumstances of this woman's death to warrant further inquiry. The vital organs submitted for examination were thereupon destroyed. Arrangements were made for the funeral, but at the last moment the

police authorities received a letter from a woman doctor who, on the strength of what she knew of the dubious activities of Dr. Clements when he was resident medical officer at a hydropathic establishment in Lancashire, earnestly suggested that it would be unsafe, without further investigation, to allow the body to be interred. Acting upon this disturbing letter, the police suddenly stepped in—and, as suddenly, Dr. Clements took his own life. Subsequent inquiry was made infinitely more difficult than is usual in a case of this kind, first, by the fact that the young doctor who had conducted the post-mortem had since killed himself, and secondly that the organs of the body normally used to establish cause of death had been destroyed. Such other parts of the body as were capable of yielding any positive reaction were submitted to a meticulous examination, conducted with exemplary patience by Dr. J. B. Firth, Director of the Home Office Forensic Laboratory at Preston, Lancs. The most promising specimen was a piece of the spinal cord weighing only one ounce. Day after day for over a fortnight this was subjected to every known test for arsenic, strychnine, and other poisons. All failed. Eventually, under the microscope, a pin-head fragment of the spinal cord, measuring no more than one sixteen-thousandth part of an inch, was observed to change colour when treated with a chemical reagent. This clue was the starting point for days and nights of minute calculation, as the result of which Dr. Firth was at last able to show that Mrs. Clements had died from morphine poisoning extending over a period of months, and that the last and fatal dose had been injected by a hypodermic needle somewhere in the region of the spine, possibly whilst she was unconscious. There have been few feats of pure scientific detection more impressive than this; it was sufficient to establish to the satisfaction of the coroner's jury in Southport that Dr. Clements had murdered his wife. The suspicion that at least one of Dr. Clements' earlier wives may also have been murdered by him is difficult to resist, especially since, in one case, it was the doctor himself who had signed the cremation certificate.
[65, 68.

Coleridge, Lord (1851-1927). Judge of the King's Bench Division of the High Court (1907-23). Bernard John Seymour Coleridge, eldest son of the first Baron Coleridge, sometime Lord Chief Justice of England, inherited his father's famous charm and the cultivated tastes of his distinguished family. His 'advanced' political opinions—and for his time they were considered to be very advanced indeed—were all his own. He belonged to the extreme left wing of the Liberal Party, and during the nine years (1885-94) he sat in the House of Commons as M.P. for the Attercliffe division of Sheffield he supported a variety of progressive causes, particularly Irish Home Rule, to which he was a convinced adherent. He was deprived of his seat in 1894, not because of electoral defeat but through his father's death, by which he was translated to the House of Lords as the second Baron Coleridge. He had successfully combined his active Parliamentary career with practice at the Bar, to which he had been called by the Middle Temple in 1877; he was now to be the first peer to practise as a barrister. In 1907, on the nomination of Lord Chancellor Loreburn, he was raised to the Bench, which he continued to grace for the next sixteen years. Retiring in 1923, he died on 4th September 1927, in his seventy-seventh year. Lord Coleridge sentenced to death John Alexander DICKMAN, the railway murderer.

Collins, James Thomas, a twenty-six-years-old private of the 2nd Battalion, East Kent Regiment (the Buffs), was on a musketry course at Hythe, Kent, in the summer of 1926. He broke camp in the early hours of 13th June, taking his rifle with him, and later that same morning he came upon two women and a thirteen-years-old girl, all of them complete strangers to him, picnicking in King's Wood at Challock, near Ashford. He shot the three of them dead—the elder woman died with the sandwich she was eating still in her hand—put the three bodies in the car which had brought the picnic party to that treacherously peaceful spot, and drove off in it. After going some little distance, he jettisoned the bodies not far from the road and drove on to London, where he garaged the car. Then he telephoned New Scotland Yard and said that there were 'three women badly injured on the road between Ashford and Chatham'. Asked for his name, Collins said, 'Don't ignore it', and hung up. On the following day he was stopped by a policeman at East Barnet. He aimed his rifle at the officer—Police Constable Chapman—and said, 'I shall have a hangman's rope round my neck in three days time. I have shot Lance-Corporal Collins of the 2nd Battalion, the Buffs.' P.C. Chapman, who behaved throughout with considerable courage, replied coolly, 'Surely you are not going to shoot me.' Said Collins, 'I shall not shoot you, providing you do not touch me.' The police constable tried every ruse to get possession of the rifle, but with the wary cunning of the insane, Collins held on to it. P.C. Chapman pretended to ride away on his bicycle, then, leaving the machine at the side of the road, doubled back and followed Collins along the road, using the protection of the hedge. Collins was not deceived. 'Don't be foolish, following me,' he called out. The officer blew his whistle to summon aid. Collins scrambled over the fence on to the railway line and ran along the track towards the nearby golf course. For the moment he eluded his pursuers, but shortly afterwards he was seen crossing a field. A strong force of police closed in upon him. He fired at one of the officers at a range of thirty yards, then discharged his rifle five or six times into the air. A policeman knocked the rifle out of his hand from behind, whereupon Collins remarked in the level tones of the fatalist, 'All right, I think that's the lot.' In a statement to the police, he said, 'I don't remember shooting the three women. I lose my temper sometimes.' On being charged a little later, he added, 'I am terribly sorry. It's a diabolical thing. No regrets of mine can be accepted.' The three victims of Collins's maniacal attack were Mrs. Janie Tremayne Swift, aged sixty-nine, manager of Ye Olde Sportsman's Inn at Seasalter, near Whitstable; her daughter, aged thirty-five, with the same Christian names as herself, who was married to Mr. Thomas Stemp, landlord of the White Hart Inn, Wadhurst; and the Stemps's thirteen-years-old daughter, Peggy. Collins was put on trial at Maidstone Assizes before Mr. Justice (John Anthony) HAWKE in the following November. He was found 'Guilty but Insane' and was sent to Broadmoor during His Majesty's Pleasure. As a melancholy instance of how some families seem to be dogged by malignant fortune, it may be mentioned that on a January afternoon in 1956, more than twenty-nine years after Mr. Stemp lost his wife and daughter, a jet aircraft crashed in the High Street at Wadhurst and destroyed the bungalow in which he had been living since his retirement as landlord of The White Hart. The next day, Mr. Stemp died in hospital from his injuries, having been cut down by a stroke as cruel—and as casual—as that which had dispatched his wife and daughter and mother-in-law as they picnicked under the trees and enjoyed the drowsy stillness of that far-off summer morning. [34, 166.

Connolly, Charles. *See* George KELLY.

Constructive Malice. The doctrine of Constructive Malice, first expounded by Chief Justice Coke in the first half of the seventeenth century, but modified by later practice, was abolished by the HOMI-CIDE ACT, 1957. In its extreme form, the doctrine held that death brought about *by any unlawful act* is murder. (Coke gave the example of a man who shoots an arrow at another's cock or hen and by chance kills a man.) The doctrine was modified a century later by Chief Justice Holt, who restricted it to cases where the unlawful act was a *felony*. In the early years of this century—as the Royal Commission on Capital Punishment, 1949-53, pointed out—the development of the common law was tending to limit the doctrine to cases where the felonious act was *likely to cause death*, which would be murder in any event. But this development was checked by a series of decisions of the House of Lords and of the Court of Criminal Appeal in cases where death was caused in the commission or attempted commission of rape or robbery. The report of the Royal Commission adds (*page* 30): 'Although the exact effect of these decisions may be uncertain, they seem to justify the conclusion that, where death is caused in the commission of a felony involving violence, a lesser degree of violence may justify a verdict of murder than would be necessary in other circumstances.' (The Commission quotes with approval the interpretation of the Editor of the latest edition of Stephen's *Digest*: 'The fact the prisoner was engaged on a felony increases the risk for him that upon death accidentally resulting from his felonious enterprise, he will be held guilty of murder.') The Commission concluded: 'So far as we are aware, the doctrine that any killing in the course of the commission of any felony is murder has never been expressly overruled by the courts; and judicial witnesses gave it as their opinion that in strict theory this was probably still the law. They hastened to add, however, that in practice it has been dead for many years, and that if the killing was unintentional a modern judge would direct the jury to bring in a verdict of manslaughter unless the felony was one involving violence. But although it may be accepted that the old rule in its full vigour is no longer in practice applied by the courts, it is not easy to formulate accurately the scope of the rule as it is now applied.' The law was put beyond doubt by the Homicide Act, 1957, which lays it down (Clause 1; Sub-section 1):

Where a person kills another in the course or furtherance of some other offence, the killing shall not amount to murder unless done with the same malice aforethought (express or implied) as is required for a killing to amount to murder when not done in the course or furtherance of another offence.

For these purposes, 'a killing done in the course or for the purpose of resisting an officer of justice, or of resisting or avoiding or preventing a lawful arrest, or of effecting or assisting an escape or rescue from legal custody, shall be treated as a killing in the course or furtherance of an offence.'

Crippen, Hawley Harvey, with his bulbous eyes, straggling moustache, choker collar, mild manners, indestructible air of respectability, florid wife, and mouse-like mistress, is the central figure of the one indisputable murder 'classic' of the twentieth century. Born in Coldwater, Michigan, in 1862, he took his diploma as an eye and ear specialist at the Opthalmic Hospital in New York, and set up in practice as a doctor at Detroit, at Santiago (where he married his first wife, Charlotte

Bell), Salt Lake City, Philadelphia, and other American cities. After only a few years of marriage, the first Mrs. Crippen died, and in 1892 the doctor took to himself a second wife, a seventeen-years-old girl he had met in New York, and whom he knew as Cora Turner. (He later discovered that her real name was Kunigunde Mackamotzi, her father being a Russian Pole, her mother a German.) The second Mrs. Crippen possessed a small but pleasing voice and a disproportionate ambition to sing in grand opera. Dr. Crippen indulged his wife's fancy sufficiently to pay for singing lessons for her in New York. In 1900 he came to London as manager for a patent medicine business, Munyon's Remedies. He was followed a few months later by his wife, who had given up her singing lessons, and with them the prospect of an operatic career. She now saw herself as a 'Queen' of the music hall, then in its heyday, and equipped with the promising stage name of Belle Elmore and a dazzling wardrobe, provided by her acquiescent husband, she set out to capture the town. The town refused to be captured, and after a few highly unsuccessful appearances at minor music halls the stage career of Belle Elmore, who was conspicuously without talent, languished and presently expired. In 1905 the Crippens moved from Bloomsbury to 39 Hilldrop Crescent, a small semi-detached house off the Camden Road, in North London. At about this time, also, a certain Miss Ethel Le Neve applied for and obtained a situation as book-keeper and typist at the offices of the patent medicine business which Dr. Crippen managed. The cast is now assembled. First, Dr. Crippen, small, slight, insignificant, peering mildly at the world through gold-rimmed spectacles, always courteous and soft-spoken, shouldering without complaint an immense variety of household chores, tolerant of his wife's infidelities, patient with her in her many extravagances, although these were putting an ever-increasing strain upon his finances. Secondly, Mrs. Crippen, vain, vivacious, dominating, boldly handsome, with raven-black hair and fine dark eyes, always elaborately dressed in bright, emphatic colours, much addicted to jewellery (probably not all of it given to her by her husband) and to regulating every detail of the little doctor's day-to-day existence, even to the extent of arranging with the tailor the cut and pattern of his next new suit. Thirdly, the typist, to the grateful Dr. Crippen the embodiment of everything his wife was not—quiet, neat, reserved, unassuming, obedient, methodical, above all *lady-like*, the element of repose in the hectic, restless life imposed upon him by his wife's flamboyant temperament. The interaction of these people upon each other led to results of which some could have been foreseen by any moderately percipient person and some could not, for murder when it comes is almost always a surprise and a shock. Who could reasonably have foretold that for the sake of the typist the little doctor, so mild and complaisant, would poison his wife, cut her up, dispose of the bones, limbs, and head (on a trip to Dieppe, it was said), and bury what remained of the body beneath the brick floor of his coal cellar? Something must have happened in the first days of January 1910 to plant a murderous seed in the heart of this long-enduring man. It may have been some word or action by his wife which he saw as a threat to his relationship with Ethel Le Neve, a relationship he was determined to preserve with all the obstinacy of a man who, after many years in subjection to a superior will, has at last gone out and done something on his own. Mrs. Crippen was perfectly well aware of her husband's liaison with his typist; she may have signed her death warrant by threatening to interfere with it. Or was the thing that happened independent of any pressure from outside? Was it not, perhaps, the result of some disturbance of the moral nature, which seemed sudden only because the slowly working changes which made this harmless little man into a murderer left no ripple on the placid surface? These questions can never be finally answered. The only certain thing is that on 17th January 1910, Dr. Crippen ordered five grains of hyoscin from Messrs. Lewis and Burrows and that, either on 1st February or 2nd February, he poisoned his wife with it. Although Cora Crippen had by this time given up her tenuous stage career—it might be truer to say that her career had given her up—she still liked to think of herself as a member of the theatrical profession, even if temporarily out of an engagement. She subscribed to theatrical magazines and kept in touch with the 'profession' in various ways, but particularly through her work for the Music Hall Ladies Guild, of which she was honorary treasurer. One of the members of the Guild was a Mrs. Clara Martinetti. On the evening of 31st January, she and her husband, Paul Martinetti, a retired music hall artiste, dined at Hilldrop Crescent with Dr. and Mrs. Crippen. After the meal the four of them played whist. The game went on so long that it was 1.30 the next morning before the Martinettis were ready to leave. Mrs. Crippen, who was obviously in the best of health and spirits, stood at the top of the steps to see them off. 'Don't come down, Belle,' said Mrs. Martinetti. 'You will catch a cold.' Mrs. Crippen went back into the house, closed the door upon the departing visitors, and that was the last that anyone ever saw of Cora Crippen until pieces of her skin were passed around the court at the Old Bailey on a soup plate, watched with grave and courteous attention by the little man in the dock. A week after the dinner party at Hilldrop Crescent, Mrs. Martinetti was startled to hear that Belle had gone to California. It was now that Dr. Crippen had need of the utmost caution and patience, for his wife had a host of friends who were sincerely attached to her, and they were naturally mystified by, and inclined to be suspicious of, her unexplained departure. He did not display even the rudiments of either. On 20th February Ethel Le Neve accompanied him to a dinner-dance in aid of the Music Hall Benevolent Fund. She was wearing a brooch which had belonged to Mrs. Crippen. Many of Belle's friends saw and recognized it. The effect of this indiscretion can easily be imagined. On 12th March Dr. Crippen took Miss Le Neve to live with him, more or less openly, at the house in Hilldrop Crescent. It was not long before Belle's friends, already sufficiently outraged, suffered an even worse shock. In the early hours of 24th March, Mrs. Martinetti received a telegram from Dr. Crippen informing her that Belle had died in Los Angeles at six o'clock the previous evening. Later, in reply to messages of condolence and inquiry, he supplied the information that Belle had been cremated, and that her ashes were being sent home. A memorial notice, inserted by Dr. Crippen, appeared in the theatrical paper, *The Era*. Letters streamed out of Hilldrop Crescent on black-edged paper: 'I hardly know how to write to you of my dreadful loss. . . . My poor Cora is gone and, to make the shock to me more dreadful, I did not even see her at the last. . . . She is being sent back to me, and I shall soon have what is left of her here.' (In fact, Dr. Crippen already had 'what was left of her' under the cellar floor.) Mrs. Crippen's friends were not reassured. At the end of June, one of Belle's friends, a Mr. Nash, went to Scotland Yard, where he set in train the inquiries which were to uncover the most famous murder case of the century. Chief-Inspector Walter Dew, accompanied by Sergeant Arthur Mitchell, called upon Dr. Crippen at his office on 8th July. The doctor made no bones about admitting that the story he had told about his wife's death was untrue. In fact, everything he had said to account for his wife's disappearance was an invention, fabricated by himself to conceal the unpalatable fact that Belle had left him for a man 'who was better able to support her'; he did not know who the man was. (It was his belief that his wife had gone to Chicago.) Dr. Crippen showed every desire to help the officers in their inquiries. He accompanied them to 39 Hilldrop Crescent and showed them over every room in the house, from attic to cellar. They found nothing to arouse their suspicions, and they went away. If there were ever a moment in a man's life when his future was in the balance, to be tilted one way or the other by the wisdom or folly of a single action, that moment had come for Dr. Crippen. At that stage the police investigation was virtually over. It had exposed Dr. Crippen as a liar who was prepared, perhaps understandably, to go to extreme lengths to try to conceal the fact that his wife had left him for another man. That was all. There was no reason for Inspector Dew to suspect that, besides being a liar, Dr. Crippen was also a murderer, and in fact he did not suspect him. But Dr. Crippen lost his nerve. The day after the officers' call he left England with Ethel Le Neve. From Rotterdam they went to Antwerp, where they booked passages for Quebec in the s.s. *Montrose*. They sailed on 20th July, Crippen under the name of John Philo Robinson, Miss Le Neve, somewhat sketchily disguised, as his son John. They left behind them in London a situation dramatically transformed. On 11th July, Inspector Dew paid a routine call at Dr. Crippen's office to check one or two unimportant details in his statement. The doctor was not there, and no one seemed to know where he had gone. His suspicions immediately aroused, the inspector hurried to 39 Hilldrop Crescent, found the house void, and submitted it to a thorough search, giving particular attention to the coal cellar. He discovered nothing. The following day, the inspector went back to the house once more and conducted another inch-by-inch search—still without any result. With a dogged pertinacity which made his reputation, Inspector Dew returned again the next day—13th July—and made a minute examination of the brick floor of the coal cellar. He discovered that it was possible without any great difficulty to prise out some of the bricks. He got a spade from the garden and began to dig the clay uncovered by the removal of the bricks, and at a depth of a few inches he came upon animal remains, which were shown by expert examination to be a human body, from which the head, limbs, bones, and sex attributes had been removed. On 16th July a warrant was issued for the arrest of Dr. Crippen and Miss Le Neve, and there was a nation-wide hue and cry. On the second day out from Antwerp, the captain of the *Montrose*, Captain Kendall, thought he recognized in 'Mr. Robinson' and his 'son' the two fugitives whose descriptions had been circulated by the police. He communicated his suspicions to London in a radio message which turned out to be historic, for this was the first time that wireless telegraphy, then in its commercial infancy, had ever been used to prevent the escape of a criminal. On 23rd July, Inspector Dew sailed from Liverpool in the s.s. *Laurentic*, a faster ship than the *Montrose*, which he boarded at Father Point, disguised as a pilot. He confronted Dr. Crippen—who had shaved off his moustache—in the captain's cabin, and arrested him for the murder and mutilation of his wife. Dr. Crippen said nothing then, but a little later he turned to the inspector and remarked, 'I am not sorry; the anxiety has been too much.' Following extradition proceedings at Quebec, Dr. Crippen and Miss Le Neve were brought back to England in custody. The trial of Dr. Crippen opened at the Old Bailey before the Lord Chief Justice, Lord ALVERSTONE, on 18th October, and was notable for the relentless cross-examination of the accused by the formidable Richard MUIR, one of the most damaging ever witnessed, even in that famous court. The trial ended three days later in a verdict of 'Guilty'. In sentencing Dr. Crippen to death, Lord Alverstone implored him to 'make his peace with Almighty God'. 'I still protest my innocence,' said the doctor. His farewell letter to Ethel Le Neve, written in Pentonville Prison on 22nd November, the eve of his execution, was deeply moving; there can be no doubt of his true and selfless love for her. From the moment of his arrest, it must be said, his first care was for her. He insisted that because of the absolute trust she placed in him, Miss Le Neve had been content to follow his lead without question, and without seeking to know the reason for any decision he thought fit to make. Ethel Le Neve was tried at the Old Bailey on 25th October as an accessory after the fact. She was found 'Not Guilty' and discharged. [I.

Crocker, Eileen Alice.
Crocker, Phyllis Elizabeth. } *See* Lionel Rupert Nathan WATSON.

Culpable Homicide is the equivalent in Scottish law of manslaughter in England.

Cummins, Gordon Frederick, has earned an evil notoriety as a modern 'Jack the Ripper'. Like the Whitechapel killer of dreadful memory, he picked up women in the streets, murdered them, and inflicted upon their bodies sadistic mutilations of the most revolting description. This twenty-eight-years-old R.A.F. cadet found his first victim in Miss Evelyn Margaret Hamilton, a chemist's assistant, whose body was found in an air-raid shelter in Montagu Place, Marylebone, in the early hours of 9th February 1942, not very far from where she lived. She had been strangled, and the murderer had tightly wound the woman's own silk scarf around her nose and throat. Marks on the throat suggested to Chief-Superintendent Cherrill of the Fingerprint Bureau, New Scotland Yard, that the murderer was left-handed. It was only when the killer struck again that the full value of this piece of deduction was appreciated. This happened on the very next night, the second victim being a Mrs. Evelyn Oatley (also known as Nita Ward), formerly a showgirl at the Windmill Theatre, who was strangled in her flat in Wardour Street, Soho. Her nearly naked body was found lying across the bed. It had been savagely mutilated with a tin-opener. There were fingerprints on the handle—the impressions of a left hand. The Fingerprint Bureau had no record of these prints in its files, and they were thus of no immediate value to the police, other than to establish that whoever the murderer was, he was not a man with a criminal record. The knowledge that a new and no less terrible 'Jack the Ripper' was at large in London's pitch-black streets spread fear, then panic, especially among the prostitutes who plied for hire on the dingy edges of the

West End. Two days passed without news of further attack. Then on 13th February the almost naked body of Mrs. Margaret Florence Lowe, known in the neighbourhood as 'Pearl', was discovered lying on the bed in the flat she occupied, and used for her trade, in Gosfield Street, off Tottenham Court Road. A silk stocking was tightly knotted around her neck. Even more shocking mutilations had been inflicted upon her than upon the body of Evelyn Oatley. Fingerprints were detected on a glass candlestick and on a partly emptied bottle of stout. These again seemed to point to a left-handed man as the killer. Within a few hours of this gruesome discovery the police were called to a flat in Sussex Gardens, Paddington. There, clad only in a dressing-gown, a scarf knotted tightly about the neck, was the fourth victim of the 'Blackout Ripper'—Doris Jouannet, wife of a London hotel manager. The body had been savagely slashed. A wave of terror rippled across the square mile within which the four murders had been committed. None knew where the killer would find his next victim, but that he would strike again was tolerably certain, for clearly this was a man in the grip of an insatiable lust for blood. And Cummins *did* strike again. Within a few hours of the murders of Margaret Lowe and Mrs. Jouannet, he accosted a young woman in a public house off Piccadilly. When she left he followed her into the street, and in the Haymarket he pushed her into a doorway. 'You must let me kiss you good-night,' he said, and immediately seized her by the throat and held on until she lost consciousness. Fortunately, he was frustrated in his murderous intention by the approach of a passer-by, who was just in time to see a shadowy figure melt into the blackness of the night. In the vacant doorway the police found an Air Force respirator which the woman's assailant had left behind. Meanwhile, Cummins had picked up another woman and had gone with her in a taxi-cab to a flat in Southwick Street, Paddington. There he seized the woman by the throat and tried to strangle her. She managed to free herself from his choking hands and roused the whole house with her screams. Cummins got away, but in his desperate haste he left behind the belt of his R.A.F. cadet's uniform. It was a simple matter of routine to trace the owner of the respirator left in the doorway. It bore the number 525987, and led the police to a billet in north London, where they arrested Gordon Frederick Cummins, later to be charged with the murders of Mrs. Oatley, Mrs. Lowe, and Mrs. Jouannet. (There was not at that time sufficient evidence to connect him with the murder of Miss Hamilton.) At Bow Street, where he was formally charged, his fingerprints were taken. Asked to sign the fingerprint form, Cummins did so—with his left hand. He was tried at the Old Bailey before Mr. Justice Asquith in April 1942, but following the usual practice in such cases, he was indicted for only one of the four murders, that of Mrs. Oatley. He was found guilty, sentenced to death, and on 25th June he was duly hanged. [34, 35, 42.

Curtis Bennett, Sir Henry Honywood, K.C. (1879-1936). No advocate who ever practised at the Criminal Bar knew and understood more accurately the habits of thought and behaviour of the man in the jury-box than did Henry Curtis Bennett. It was this flair for 'handling' a jury which was at the root of his prodigious success, and which won him his indisputable place amongst the great criminal pleaders of the first half of the twentieth century. Again, no advocate ever exploited his personality more adroitly for the purposes of his profession. It was a warm, rich, singularly engaging personality, which, like the physical presentment of the man, seemed somewhat larger than life. Curtis Bennett even made his girth—they called him the 'Falstaff of the Bar'— part of his stock in trade, just as he did his fine 'actor's voice'. The word 'actor' would not have displeased him. He possessed a very keen 'sense of the theatre', and he rightly regarded it as a valuable part of his professional equipment. Indeed, he once remarked that it might be a good thing if he had an orchestra to play 'soft music' while he made the speech for the defence. This theatrical sense of his came out very strongly in his well-known 'entrances' into Court, which were as carefully prepared as those of Sir Edward Marshall HALL himself. First would come Sir Henry's clerk carrying The Brief. Under the fascinated eyes of the jury, a battery of coloured pencils would be set out on the desk before the empty place soon to be so amply filled, and beside them a box of Sir Henry's favourite throat lozenges. It was astonishing how that little box of cough sweets seemed to dominate the Court during those last pregnant moments before the opening of a great murder trial. At the last possible moment Sir Henry himself would appear, and there would be the inevitable stir and flutter in the Court, the flattering whisper, 'Here he is.' He was, in short, an exponent of the Grand Manner, which is but sketchily represented at the Bar in our own declining day. He was not only a great advocate—he looked like one. Nature seemed to have shaped him for the part; he had the weight, the size, the stature, the bold commanding presence, the necessary virtuosity of voice and manner, above all the supreme self-confidence that is possible only to a barrister who has a perfect mastery of his brief and a familiarity with every detail not only of his own case, but of his opponent's case as well. In private life he was a delightful and amusing companion, a wit and, like the Falstaff he resembled, a cause of wit in others; a *bon vivant* who loved Society (with a capital S) and went about a great deal in it; a diligent first-nighter; a top-flight after-dinner speaker in constant demand. He ended his full and successful life in the flush of his vitality, and in a manner which he might well have selected for himself, had the choice been left to him. In October 1936, being then in his fifty-eighth year, he succeeded Sir Percival Clarke as Chairman of the County of London Sessions. A week or two later—on 2nd November—he attended the annual dinner of the National Greyhound Racing Society at the Dorchester Hotel in London. At twenty minutes to eleven that night he rose to reply to the toast of 'Our Guests'. He made a characteristic speech, witty, perfectly timed. As he was fond of doing, he told a joke against himself on a pet subject, his own vast size. And while the company was still laughing, Sir Henry Honywood Curtis Bennett K.C. dropped dead at the table from a coronary thrombosis. His father, Chief Metropolitan Magistrate, had died in similar circumstances twenty-three years before—on 2nd June 1913, after speaking at a meeting at the Mansion House. Sir Henry left behind him what he liked to call his 'greatest memorial'— a collection of between four and five hundred letters from men and women he had defended in the courts, expressing their appreciation of his services. The leading events in the professional life of this great criminal advocate can be briefly stated: Called to the Bar by the Middle Temple, 1902; King's Counsel, 1919; Conservative M.P. for Colchester, 1924-6; knighted, 1922. His name will forever be associated with some of the most memorable murder trials of the 1920s and 1930s, including those of Herbert Rowse ARMSTRONG; Madame FAHMY (with Sir Edward Marshall HALL); Jean Pierre VAQUIER; Wallace BENTON; and Sidney FOX.

D

Delightful task! to rear the tender thought
To teach the young idea how to shoot.

James Thomson: *The Seasons*

Darling, Charles John, first Baron Darling of Langham (1849-1936), a judge of high distinction and much wit, was called to the Bar in 1874 and became a bencher of the Inner Temple in 1892. His practice being almost entirely confined to the Oxford Circuit, as a lawyer he made little impression outside it, and his appointment as a judge of the High Court in October 1897 led to an outcry in the Press, and especially in the Radical newspapers, which did not hesitate to describe it as a piece of political jobbery. As Conservative Member for Deptford, he had sat for nearly ten years in the House of Commons, and there he had acquired the reputation of a vigorous, combative 'party man'. Since he was thought little of as a lawyer, it was perhaps hardly surprising that an uncharitable construction should have been placed upon the action of the Conservative Lord Chancellor, Lord Halsbury, in offering him a judgeship. The *Daily Chronicle* considered that the whole transaction was 'grossly scandalous', whilst the *Westminster Gazette* declared with much bitterness that Lord Halsbury, having apparently exhausted the list of his relatives, was now 'ready and willing to be a party as well as a family man'. Lord Darling's biographer, Mr. Derek Walker-Smith, admits that it was a 'bold' appointment. But then, Lord Halsbury was a bold Lord Chancellor, and having discerned certain rare judicial qualities in the man the Temple regarded merely as 'a political silk who did a little work on circuit', he was ready to back his judgment and to abide by the result. He knew that only time could justify the wisdom of his choice, and this is what time most handsomely did. Lord Darling made no claim to possess all the qualities of a great judge; he was never to become a profound or erudite lawyer; he had, says Mr. Walker-Smith, a 'certain natural and instinctive impatience in his approach to cases of which the subject matter did not command his interest'. But he was, in the words of a just appraisal of him by Lord HEWART, 'a wise, experienced, and humane judge, with a consummate knowledge of human nature and the world', and with that epitaph he would certainly have been content. Mr. Justice Darling remained a judge for twenty-six years, and even after his retirement in November 1923 he more than once returned to the Bench to deal with arrears that were hindering the work of the Courts. In January 1924 he was raised to the peerage under the style of Baron Darling of Langham. He died in May 1936, being then in his eighty-seventh year. Long before his retirement from the Bench the name of Mr. Justice Darling had become a household word, the wit with which he delighted and sometimes exasperated his Court being zealously collected and retailed by the newspapers, for which he was, and remained to the end, 'front page news'. In appearance Lord Darling was immensely distinguished. He had a trimly elegant figure—they called him 'Little Darling'—and there was that in his face, the high cheek-bones, the deep-set eyes, the sensitive modelling of the lips, which proclaimed his fine breeding and the humane, eminently civilized quality of his thought and speech. The trial of Herbert Rowse ARMSTRONG was perhaps the most famous of the many murder trials over which he presided.

Davidson, Thomas Joseph, poultry farmer, aged thirty-four, was charged at the Old Bailey in September 1934 with the murder of his eight-years-old son, John Desmond, of whom nothing had been heard since his disappearance in the previous December. The jury returned a verdict of 'Guilty', thus disproving a legal fallacy which for some minds appears to have a remarkably durable attraction—the fallacy that without a body there can be no conviction for murder. (*See* James CAMB; John George HAIGH.) The body of Davidson's little boy was never found, nor was any part of it. The father three times confessed—first in a letter to a police inspector, then in a signed statement, and finally in a letter to his wife—that he had drowned the child in a canal and destroyed the body on a burning refuse dump at Yiewsley in Middlesex. It was, however, impossible to confirm his statement by independent evidence, since the spot at which Davidson said he had burned the body had long since been covered over with thousands of tons of rubbish; even if this mass of waste material could have been cleared away there would still have been little chance of recovering anything that could be identified. All trace of the crime having been destroyed by time and mischance, Davidson chose at his trial, before Mr. Justice ATKINSON, to retract his confession; he now swore that he had *found* the child's body in the canal. After Davidson's conviction —to which the jury added a recommendation to mercy—it was argued in the Court of Criminal Appeal that in murder cases in which the body had not been discovered, independent evidence, other than that given by the prisoner himself, must be produced to show that a crime had been committed. But in giving the judgment of the Court, the Lord Chief Justice, Lord HEWART, held that it had been open to the jury to conclude that the child was dead, and, after hearing Davidson's evidence, to disbelieve the retraction of his confession and accept the statement he had previously made, namely that he had been the cause of the child's death. The appeal was dismissed, but Davidson did not hang. The death sentence was commuted.

De Antiquis, Alec. *See* Charles Henry JENKINS.

Derham, John Adam Tytler. *See* Alfonso Francis Austin SMITH.

Devereux, Arthur, a chemist's assistant, sealed the bodies of his wife, Beatrice Maud Devereux, and his twin sons, Lawrence Rowland and Evelyn Lancelot, aged two years, in an air-tight trunk, which he deposited in a warehouse at Kensal Rise, London. There, on 13th April 1905, nearly three months later, it was discovered and opened by the police. The cause of death in each case was poisoning by salts of morphine, but Devereux protested to the last that he had had nothing to do with it. His story was that he had returned to his lodging in Milton Avenue, Harlesden, to find his wife and twin sons lying dead in their beds. A poison—a compound of chloroform and morphine—which he always kept by him lest he should be forced to commit suicide 'rather than face starvation', was missing from his writing-desk, and he concluded that his wife had made away with the two children and had then destroyed herself. Because of his many quarrels with his wife and the ill-feeling which existed between himself and his mother-in-law, Mrs. Gregory—it was Mrs. Gregory who eventually called in the police —he was afraid to face an inquest. So he packed the bodies into a trunk, contriving, out of pieces of wood screwed together and coated with glue mixed with boric acid, an air-tight cover, which he fitted inside the lid to prevent the smell of decay escaping. At his trial at the Old Bailey before Mr. Justice RIDLEY in July 1905, he was unable to persuade the jury that he had not poisoned his wife and infant sons. Nor do they seem to have been much impressed by the evidence of a well-meaning clergyman that Devereux had always been regarded as 'a little bit off the top' and had 'done some extraordinary things', such as posing as an American millionaire in Malvern. Medical evidence was offered by the defence to show that Devereux was a man of weak intellect and even a mental degenerate, but there was no attempt to prove an infirmity of mind sufficient to relieve him of responsibility for his actions. A verdict of 'Guilty' was returned; Devereux was sentenced to death and hanged at Pentonville Prison on 15th August 1905.

[34, 79.

Dhingra, Madar Lal, twenty-five-years-old Indian student, completing an engineering course at University College, London, applied for and obtained a licence to carry firearms, and having purchased a Colt automatic revolver, thereafter attended a shooting gallery in Tottenham Court Road, where, by dint of practice three days a week, he presently acquired considerable skill as a marksman. Upon a final visit to the gallery on 1st July 1909, eleven of his twelve shots took effect on the target—which was about the size of a man's head. That evening, Madar Lal Dhingra went to a concert at the Imperial Institute, to which he had been invited by the honorary secretary of the National Indian Association, a benevolent organization which existed to help and advise Indian students working in England. He took with him his Colt revolver, a Belgian pistol (both fully loaded), and a dagger. Also attending the concert with his wife was Sir William Hutt Curzon Wyllie K.C.I.E., for many years a distinguished servant of the Crown in India, and at this time political *aide-de-camp* to the Secretary of State; he was also honorary treasurer of the National Indian Association, being keenly interested in the welfare of Indian students. The concert ended at about 11 p.m., and as the audience was dispersing Dhingra approached Sir Curzon Wyllie in the vestibule and engaged him in what was to all appearances a friendly conversation. Suddenly, without warning, the student drew the Colt automatic from his pocket and fired five shots at Sir Curzon. Since they were fired at point-blank range they made no call upon the marksmanship he had so diligently acquired, but no doubt the opportunity for assassination had turned out to be more favourable than he had anticipated. Sir Curzon was killed instantly, four of the bullets entering his head, the fifth merely grazing his chest. For one horror-struck moment those in the vestibule stood paralysed with shock. First to recover his wits was an Indian doctor from Hong Kong named Cowas Lalcaca, who was on a visit to London. He sprang forward to seize the assailant, but before he could close with him, Dhingra fired at him twice, wounding him fatally; he died a few minutes later. The student now had only one shot left in the automatic. He turned it on himself, but it misfired, and before he could make a second attempt upon his life, Dhingra was overpowered and disarmed. At his trial before the Lord Chief Justice, Lord ALVERSTONE, at the Old Bailey, Dhingra declared himself to have been inspired by motives of the loftiest patriotism. In a statement which was read to the

Court, Dhingra declared: 'English people have no right to occupy India and it is perfectly justifiable on our part to kill the Englishman who is polluting our sacred soil.' When the jury returned the verdict which convicted him of the double murder, Dhingra refused to acknowledge the authority of the Court. 'You can pass sentence of death on me,' he said. 'I don't care, but remember that one day we shall be all-powerful, and then we can do what we like.' Sentence of death having been passed upon him, the young student, with a deep salaam to the judge, protested the pride he felt in being given the honour of laying down his life for his country's cause. He was hanged at Pentonville Prison on 17th August. (*See* Udham SINGH.)
[*113.*

Dickey, Jacob. *See* Alexander Campbell MASON.

Dickman, John Alexander, being in desperate straits for money, killed a colliery clerk and book-keeper named John Innes Nisbet in a third-class compartment of a train between Stannington and Morpeth on the North Eastern Railway, and decamped with a small leather bag containing £370. 9s. 6d., mostly in gold and silver, which the murdered man was taking to pay the wages at the Stobswood Colliery, near Widdrington. It was a regular journey of the sort which Mr. Nisbet made every other Friday, when he invariably had with him the cash for the colliery wages, a fact which was well known to Dickman, himself a former colliery secretary, but now existing precariously on commission from various bookmakers. On this particular Friday—18th March 1910 —he joined the train at Newcastle-upon-Tyne with the unfortunate man he was plotting to kill, sharing a compartment with him in the carriage immediately behind the engine. The train, which was due to stop at every station between Newcastle and Alnmouth, left at 10.27 a.m. Somewhere between Stannington and Morpeth, a six-minutes run, Dickman shot Nisbet dead, pumping five revolver bullets into him, and pushed the body under the seat. At Morpeth he alighted from the train, surrendering to the ticket collector the outward half of a return ticket to Stannington and 2½d., being the correct excess fare. From there, or so it was conjectured at his trial, he made his way to the Isabella pit, less than two miles away, and disposed of Nisbet's black leather bag, first slitting it open and taking the money; it was found eleven weeks later at the bottom of an air shaft, empty save for nineteen shillings in coppers. The gruesome discovery of the body under the seat was made when the train reached Alnmouth. Dickman was arrested three days later, and in the first week of July he was tried for murder before Lord COLERIDGE at Newcastle Summer Assizes. He was found guilty and sentenced to death. Scarcely had the chaplain said 'Amen' before Dickman cried out from the dock, 'I declare to all men that I am innocent.' The Court of Criminal Appeal declined to quash the conviction, in spite of counsel's strictures upon the police in regard to the conditions in which at least one of the witnesses was invited to identify the prisoner. Dickman was hanged at the prison in Newcastle on 10th August 1910. [*1.*

Diminished Responsibility. Formerly admissible only in Scottish law, the plea of Diminished Responsibility may now be entered in the English Courts. The authority rests upon Section 2(1) of the HOMICIDE ACT, 1957, which says that:

> Where a person kills or is a party to the killing of another, he shall not be convicted of murder if he was suffering from such abnormality of mind (whether arising from a condition of arrested or retarded development of mind or any inherent causes or induced by disease or injury) as substantially impaired his mental responsibility for his acts and omissions in doing or being a party to the killing.

The late Lord Alness, Lord Justice Clerk, established an alternative definition which governed Scottish practice long before the Homicide Act incorporated the principle into English law. He said that to sustain the plea:

> There must be a weakness of mind; there must be some form of mental unsoundness; there must be a state of mind which is bordering on, although not amounting to, insanity; there must be a mind so affected that responsibility is diminished from full responsibility to partial responsibility.

If the plea be sustained the effect is to reduce the crime of murder to one of manslaughter (in Scotland, culpable homicide).

Dobkin, Harry, Russian-born, aged forty-nine, bald, squat, bull-necked, added his own private, unambitious murder, the slaying of his wife, to the mass killings of the German air raids on London in 1941. For over a year—from April 1941 to May 1942—he was employed as a fire-watcher at a paper store-room behind a blitzed Baptist chapel in St. Oswald's Place, Kennington. During this period, although many bombs dropped on East London, none of them fell close enough to give Dobkin any trouble. But in the early hours of 15th April 1941, a fire did break out in the area of his watch, that is to say, in the cellar under

64

the vestry of the partly destroyed chapel. Although it was not caused by an incendiary bomb, or any other form of enemy action, it was certainly a fire which involved the fire-watcher. In fact, it was he who started it, using straw torn from an old mattress to set the place alight. He was trying to destroy the mutilated body of his wife, Rachel, who had been making a nuisance of herself by pestering him to come back to her. Neither the origin nor the purpose of the fire came to light at the time—after all, in London at the height of the Blitz there was little time or opportunity to bother much about an outbreak which had done no more than char an already uninhabitable building—but both became sufficiently clear fifteen months later. On 17th July 1942, a workman engaged in tidying up the damaged site prised up a large paving stone at the far end of the chapel cellar and discovered under it a scorched skeleton. The remains being removed to the Southwark mortuary, they were examined by Dr. Keith Simpson, Home Office pathologist, who reported that the head and arms had been clumsily severed from the trunk, clearly by somebody who had no knowledge of anatomy, and that the tissues had been stripped from the head, as if to make identification more difficult. He gave it as his opinion that the bones, which had been exposed to flame, were the remains of a woman of between forty and fifty, about 5 ft. 0½ in. in height, who had died twelve or eighteen months previously; from the fracture of a certain small bone in the throat he deduced that the cause of death was manual strangulation. The pathologist's findings directed the attention of the police to an entry in the record of missing persons which showed that on Saturday, 12th April 1941, a few days before the unexplained fire in the chapel cellar, a woman had reported the disappearance of her sister, a Mrs. Rachel Dobkin, aged forty-nine, of Cookham Buildings, Bethnal Green, who was living apart from her husband. Dobkin was put on trial at the Old Bailey before Mr. Justice Wrottesley in November 1942. In spite of the pains that had been taken to conceal it, the identity of the corpse was convincingly established, especially through the testimony of Mrs. Dobkin's dentist, who was able to recognize the curious shape of the top jaw, as well as certain features of the teeth and gums. Dobkin was found guilty. Three weeks later he was hanged at Wandsworth Prison.

[2.

Donald, Jeannie, aged thirty-eight, wife of an Aberdeen hairdresser, was convicted in July 1934 within the High Court of Justiciary, Edinburgh, of the murder of an eight-years-old child named Helen Wilson Robertson Priestly. This little girl lived with her parents on the first floor of a tenement building in Urquhart Road, Aberdeen, immediately above the Donalds. There was no love lost between the two families; in fact, Mrs. Donald and Mrs. Priestly had not been on speaking terms for some years. On 20th April 1934, the child having returned from school for her dinner, she was sent to buy a loaf of bread at the Co-operative store a hundred yards away. She was seen on her way back with the loaf in a shopping-bag, but she never reached her home, and, indeed, nobody ever saw her alive again. At 5 o'clock the next morning, after a day and night search in many different parts of the city and the neighbouring district, the mutilated body of Helen Priestly was discovered in a sack under the stairs leading to her own front door, although there had been no sign of it there only half an hour before. There were superficial signs that the child had been interfered with, but it appeared from a subsequent medical examination that, in fact, she had not been raped, and from this it was conjectured that the killer was a woman who, by simulating the sort of injury that would be looked for in the case of a violation, had hoped to make it self-evident that the murder had been committed by a man. The cause of death was asphyxiation, but although there were marks on the neck, suggesting manual pressure, the balance of medical opinion was that the later injuries, inflicted while the child was still alive, had made her sick, and that this had choked her. The police carried out exhaustive inquiries in the neighbourhood during the next few days. On 25th April they were at the Donalds' home for something like thirteen hours, and round about midnight both husband and wife were charged with murder, and driven to the police station through a bitterly hostile crowd, who hurled imprecations and shook their fists at the retreating police van. The husband, Alexander Donald, was released some weeks later, the police being by that time satisfied that he had had nothing to do with the murder, which had been committed shortly before 2 p.m.—about half an hour after the purchase of the loaf—and at a time when he was at work at his hairdressing saloon. Because of the intense local animus against Mrs. Donald, her trial was transferred to Edinburgh, where it took place before Lord Justice Clerk Aitchison. It was chiefly remarkable for the medical and scientific evidence offered by the Crown, the case against Mrs. Donald being built upon the careful correlation of minute physiological, chemical and other details, observed and recorded in laboratories in many different parts of the country. The defence, which was in the able hands of Mr. D. P. Blades K.C. (afterwards Lord Blades), fought hard to show that the injuries to the child were consistent with sexual violation by a man, for, obviously, if this could have been established—which it was not—there would have been an end to the case against the accused. Mrs. Donald seems to have been of little help to those whose task it was to defend her. She took the line that as she knew nothing at all about the child's death there was no useful information she could impart. She committed herself to silence, and her course was unalterable; she did not go into the witness-box. The trial lasted for six days, and it was only at the very end that the impassive calm of this strange woman deserted her. When the foreman of the jury spoke the word 'Guilty' she collapsed, and after sentence of death had been passed upon her, was carried moaning from the dock. On 6th August, a week before the date fixed for the execution, Mrs. Donald was reprieved and her sentence commuted to one of life imprisonment. Ten years later—on 26th June 1944—she was released on special licence.

[*1.*

Dougal, Samuel Herbert, a coarse-grained vulgarian of goatish tastes and habits, belonged to a type which, on the surface, a well-bred maiden lady of impeccable refinement might be supposed to find repellent. However, he possessed a certain crude virility. Since none of the conventional safeguards appear to afford much protection to the inhibited female when really put to the test, this no doubt sufficiently explains how it was that Miss Camille Holland, a devout spinster in comfortable circumstances, and with more than her share of the polite Victorian accomplishments—she painted in water-colours and wrote sentimental verses, which she set to tinkling little tunes of her own—should have been willing to set aside the restraints and prejudices of a lifetime to go away with a man who made no pretence of offering her marriage, and who, at a period when such distinctions were thought to be important, was so much her social inferior. It is not known precisely how these two became acquainted, but probably it was the result of a chance meeting at the Earl's Court Exhibition. Whatever the circumstances, it was providential for Dougal, who was at the time at his lowest financial ebb. He had lost his job, had lost his third wife—who had left him because of his persistent cruelties and infidelity—and had lost his Army pension, which he had forfeited upon his conviction at the Old Bailey on a charge of forging a cheque. He was fifty-five years of age, still a fine figure of a man, with bright grey eyes, a neatly trimmed beard, and a bluff, hearty manner. All his life, twenty-one years of which had been spent in the Royal Engineers, he had been a skilful exploiter of women, and under his expert attentions Miss Holland was completely infatuated with him within a few weeks of their first meeting, which took place towards the end of 1898. In December of that year she left the boarding house in Elgin Crescent, Ladbroke Grove, where she lived, and went to share a furnished house with Dougal at Hassocks, near Brighton. But Dougal had a fancy to set himself up as a country gentleman in a small way; it need hardly be said that he planned to do this at the expense of Miss Holland, who possessed invested capital amounting to between six and seven thousand pounds. With her money he bought a property at Quendon, near Clavering, Essex, known as Coldham's Farm—which he re-christened the Moat Farm—although at the last moment Miss Holland insisted upon herself being named in the contract as purchaser. On 27th April 1899, Dougal and Miss Holland took up residence at the Moat Farm, a small, isolated, dreary house, set among dark fir trees, and surrounded by a moat. Three weeks later— on Friday 19th May—she went out with Dougal in his pony trap. Florrie, the servant girl, stood at the door and watched her mistress drive away in a white sailor hat and dark dress; against the clip-clop of the hooves echoing across the flat Essex fields Miss Camille Holland was ushered out of life. When she came back from the ride there was a bullet through her brain. Four years later—on 27th April 1903—after an inch-by-inch search of the house and grounds, the police found all that remained of Miss Holland in the spot where Samuel Herbert Dougal had buried her, the deep end of a drainage ditch in the farmyard, which had later been filled in and planted with trees. In the four years that had elapsed between burial and discovery Dougal had lived on at the Moat Farm with a succession of mistresses, his tastes running to buxom, apple-cheeked country wenches, who presented him with a numerous progeny. During those years, too, he applied himself by various forgeries to getting Miss Holland's little fortune into his hands. By September 1901 he had sold out part of her capital, and had transferred nearly three thousand pounds from her banking account into his own. He had also, by means of a letter bearing Miss Holland's forged signature, had the ownership of the Moat Farm conveyed to himself. It was his many scandalous amours, which in this small country place had everybody gossiping, that eventually directed attention to matters that Samuel Herbert Dougal would have preferred to have kept decently covered. People began to ask what had happened to the lady who used to call herself Mrs. Dougal, and who had, within a few weeks, so mysteriously 'gone to London'? In the end the police acted. A nephew was able to state definitely that the signature on one of her purported cheques was not that of his aunt. It was decided to proceed against Dougal on a charge of forgery, and on 18th March 1903 he was arrested in London. At once an intensive search of the Moat Farm was begun, the police sleeping in the house and carrying on with the search day after day for five fruitless weeks. It was then that the police got to know about the drainage ditch which Dougal had caused to be filled in. After some hours' digging the body of a woman in an advanced stage of decomposition was uncovered, together with a tortoiseshell

comb, some hairpins, a wire hair-pad, and an out-of-date bustle. The police had found what they were looking for, and retribution for the untimely death of Miss Camille Holland, with her water-colours, her verses, and her music, was drawing near for Samuel Herbert Dougal. He was found guilty of murder on 23rd June 1903, after a two days' trial at the Old Bailey, and was sentenced to death by Mr. Justice WRIGHT. On 8th July he was hanged at Chelmsford Prison.
[ʐ.

Duboff, Yourka. *See* SIEGE OF SIDNEY STREET.

Dudley, Florence. *See* Edward HOPWOOD.

Duff, Edmund Creighton, lived in a pleasant house in South Hill Park Road, Croydon, Surrey, with his wife, Grace, and their two children. His mother-in-law, Mrs. Violet Sidney, a barrister's widow, lived near by, sharing a house in Birdhurst Rise with her unmarried daughter, Vera, sister of Mrs. Duff. An even closer neighbour was Mr. Thomas Sidney, brother of Grace and Vera, who lived with his wife and children further along South Hill Park Road. The members of this prosperous middle-class family moved easily and elegantly through their well-ordered world. But sinister forces were at work behind the cool façade. On the evening of 26th April 1928, Edmund Creighton Duff returned from a fishing holiday in Hampshire to a light supper of cold chicken, served with potatoes, and washed down by a bottle of beer. Shortly afterwards he complained of cramp in the calves of his legs. Dr. Binning, the family physician, was summoned the next morning and diagnosed a mild attack of colic. By the evening Mr. Duff was dead. Certain organs were removed for analysis, but no trace of poison could be found, and at the inquest a verdict of death from natural causes was returned. Nearly a year went by, and then, on 14th February 1929, after lunching at home with her mother, Miss Vera Sidney was taken violently ill. By the next day, Miss Sidney, a strong, athletic woman of forty, unaccustomed to illness, was apparently sufficiently recovered to get up and go out in her car. Later, however, she fell desperately sick, and all that night and all the next day was in extreme pain. A specialist was called in and agreed with Dr. Binning that the patient was suffering from severe gastric influenza. That night Miss Sidney died. A third death was soon to follow. On 5th March, Mrs. Sidney, who had been distraught by the tragic loss of her daughter, took a dose of the well-known proprietary tonic which Dr. Binning had prescribed for her, and at once complained to her maid that it 'tasted nasty'. After lunch she was taken ill, the symptoms of her condition—vomiting, cramp

—being precisely the same as in the case of her daughter and son-in-law. In a few hours she was dead. Now the Home Office acted. On 22nd March the bodies of Mrs. Sidney and her daughter were exhumed in Croydon Cemetery. An examination by the eminent pathologist, Sir Bernard SPILSBURY, established that in both cases death was due to arsenical poisoning. It was then decided to exhume the body of Edmund Creighton Duff, in spite of the fact that the earlier post-mortem had failed to discover any traces of poison. The exhumation was carried out on 18th May, and this time the examination was entrusted to Sir Bernard Spilsbury, who found that on the previous occasion a great part of the intestines had in some way been overlooked. Renewed analytical tests revealed the presence of arsenic and established that a fatal dose had been taken within twenty-four hours of death. Whatever else may have been left in doubt by this extraordinary case it was clearly established that Mr. Duff had been poisoned by the beer he had drunk with his supper, Vera Sidney by the soup she had taken at lunch, Mrs. Sidney by her tonic. The question was: Who had put arsenic into the beer, into the soup, into the tonic? This seemed to be a united family, living in amity; no member of it was in any financial need; no other motive was ever openly suggested. The possibility was considered that, perhaps, the murder had been committed by some outside person who had managed to gain admittance by the methods of the sneak-thief, and had then found the opportunity to tamper, first, with the beer, afterwards with the soup, and finally with the bottle of tonic, but this theory plainly involved some formidable difficulties; they proved insuperable. The inquests, which were taken separately, dragged on for months, but they dragged on in vain. When, for want of further material, they at last came to an end in August 1929, the best that the coroner's jury could do, both in the case of Vera Sidney and Edmund Creighton Duff, was to record a verdict of wilful murder against some person or persons unknown. In the case of Mrs. Sidney the jury's verdict was even more inconclusive; they found there was insufficient evidence to show whether she had killed herself or had been murdered. Nothing has since emerged which could serve to take the inquiry a single step further, and the case remains today in the same state of frustration in which it was left in August 1929.

[8, 34, 138, 168, 186.

Dunn, Reginald, twenty-five-years-old ex-corporal in the Irish Guards, and his fellow Irishman, **Joseph O'Sullivan,** twenty-four, also an ex-soldier of the 1914-18 war, were hanged at Wandsworth Prison on 10th August 1922 for the murder of Field-Marshal Sir Henry Wilson, former Chief of the Imperial General Staff, who was shot on the doorstep of his home at 36 Eaton Place, London. As the hour struck for their execution mourners carrying the Sinn Fein colours knelt in prayer outside the prison and sang the Irish funeral hymn, *Wrap the Old Green Flag Around Me.* For the assassination of this famous soldier was a political murder, nurtured and encouraged by the many acts of lawless violence which troubled the early days of the Irish Free State, after Michael Collins and the other negotiators of the 1921 Treaty had been denounced by the Republicans as traitors to the cause of Irish independence. Dunn and O'Sullivan, two young Irishmen living in London, looked upon themselves as patriots and martyrs, and indeed at their trial at the Old Bailey Dunn had spoken openly of their 'rights and wrongs in ridding the world of a scourge'. Sir Henry Wilson, after retiring from the post of Chief of the Imperial General Staff in February 1922, had immediately accepted an invitation to stand as a candidate at a by-election for one of the Ulster seats (North Down), and had been returned to the House of Commons unopposed. He had lately been in Belfast as adviser to the Northern Ireland Government on ways and means of dealing with bomb outrages and other forms of Southern Republican terrorism. On 22nd June 1922 he was at Liverpool Street station—in uniform, and wearing his sword—to unveil a memorial to railway workers killed in the late war. He returned home by taxi-cab just after 2.30 p.m., and was about to let himself in at the front door of his house—on the corner of Eaton Place and Belgrave Place—when there was a sharp report and a revolver bullet, fired from close range, pierced the left upper panel of the door. It was followed immediately by another shot. The Field-Marshal turned towards his assailants and made to draw his sword, but at least six more shots were fired at him; as the two assassins made off, he collapsed on the doorstep. Lady Wilson came running to the door and, although in great distress, helped to carry her husband into the house, where he died a few moments later. Dunn and O'Sullivan were chased along Eaton Place and eventually into Chester Terrace, firing their revolvers upon their pursuers as they ran. Two policemen, P.C. March and P.C. Sayer, and a civilian named Alexander Clarke, were severely wounded before the two armed men were captured in Ebury Street, where only the strenuous efforts of the police prevented them from being lynched by a hostile crowd. When the news of the Field-Marshal's assassination reached Westminster later that afternoon, the House of Commons at once adjourned as an unprecedented mark of respect. (Mr. Lloyd George's Government was later to be severely criticized for having withdrawn police protection from everyone menaced by Irish disaffection save only the former Chief Secretary for Ireland, Sir Hamar Greenwood.) At the trial on 18th July, Mr. Justice Shearman refused to allow Dunn to read to the jury a statement he had prepared, since he held it to be an irrelevant 'political manifesto' and a 'justification of the right to kill'. After a verdict of 'Guilty' had been returned against both the men, Dunn attempted another political oration, but again the judge declined to hear him. Dunn had the last word, however, for the death sentence having been pronounced, and the judge having added the customary phrase, 'And may the Lord have mercy on your soul,' he exclaimed in a loud voice: 'He will, my Lord.'

[*43, 145.*

Durand-Deacon, Olive Henrietta Olivia Robarts. *See* John George HAIGH.

E

Even butchers weep!
John Gay: *The Beggar's Opera*

Edgar, Police-Constable Nathaniel. *See* Donald George THOMAS.

Edmunds, Mabel Jennings. *See* Frederick William Maximilian JESSE.

Elliott, George, K.C. (1860-1916). This genial man, short, stubby, with rosy cheeks and a homely sense of humour, was for many years a familiar figure at the Old Bailey, where he was engaged for the defence in many of the most famous murder trials of his time, notably those of George CHAPMAN; Samuel Herbert DOUGAL; Arthur DEVE-REUX; and Horace George RAYNER. He was called to the Bar by the Inner Temple in 1882 and entered the chambers of the famous leader, Sir Edward Clarke Q.C. He built up a prosperous practice on the South-Eastern Circuit, specializing in Criminal Law cases, and took silk in 1909.

Elmore, Belle. *See* Hawley Harvey CRIPPEN.

Evans, Timothy John, twenty-four, a van driver, tubercular, entirely illiterate, brought his eighteen-years-old wife, Beryl, and their infant daughter, Geraldine, to live in two rooms on the top floor of 10 Rillington Place, a depressing cul-de-sac (since renamed) in the Notting Hill Gate district of London. Occupying the ground floor at the same grimy address were John Reginald Halliday Christie, a forty-nine-years-old ex-War Reserve policeman, and his wife, Ethel. Some eighteen months later, on or about 14th November 1949, Evans went to stay with his aunt at Merthyr Tydfil, South Wales. On 30th November he walked into the local police station, where he made a statement, the burden of which was that, upon returning to his home on the evening of 8th November, he had found his wife lying dead and that he had 'put her body down a drain'. On 2nd December the bodies of Beryl Evans and the baby, Geraldine, were discovered in the washhouse in the back yard of 10 Rillington Place; they had been strangled. Whereupon Evans made a second statement in which he accused Christie of having caused Beryl's death by an abortion. He was brought to London, where at Notting Hill Police Station he made a third statement. In this he confessed to killing his wife on 8th November and the baby two days later, and to concealing their bodies in the washhouse after Mr. and Mrs. Christie had gone to bed. At his trial at the Old Bailey before Mr. Justice Lewis, on 11th January 1950, Evans, who was indicted only for the murder of the baby, retracted his confession and held Christie responsible for both murders. 'That is a lie,' said Christie, in the witness-box. Evans was found guilty, and was sentenced to death. (Christie improved the solemn occasion by bursting into tears.) An appeal to the Court of Criminal Appeal was dismissed on 20th February, and on 5th March Evans was hanged. Rather more than three years later, on 22nd June 1953, John Reginald Halliday Christie stood in the dock at the Old Bailey on a charge of having murdered his wife, Ethel, whose body had been discovered under the floorboards of the ground-floor front room at 10 Rillington Place in the previous March. The bodies, or the bones, of five other women were discovered in that appalling death house, three of them—Rita Nelson, Kathleen Mahony, and Hectorina MacClennan—in a recess cupboard in the kitchen. A few days later, digging by the police in the back yard uncovered human bones making up the almost complete skeletons of the other two—Margarete Fuerst and Muriel Eady—who had been buried there since 1943 and 1944 respectively. At his trial, not only was Christie's responsibility for the deaths of all five women not denied, but he also gave detailed evidence which purported to show that he had killed Mrs. Beryl Evans as well, by strangling her with a stocking. He denied, however, that he had killed the baby; he 'took it' that this had been done by Evans. The revelations at Christie's trial caused a great deal of public disquiet. The matter was raised in the House of Commons, and, on 6th July 1953, the Home Secretary, Sir David Maxwell Fyfe Q.C. (afterwards Viscount KILMUIR), announced that he had appointed Mr. John Scott Henderson Q.C. to inquire into the evidence and report whether, in his opinion, there was any ground for thinking that there might have been a miscarriage of justice in Evans's conviction. Mr. Scott Henderson heard evidence from twenty-three persons on 8th, 9th, and 10th July. One of these persons was Christie himself, who, his insanity plea having failed, was then under sentence of death and awaiting execution at Pentonville Prison. (The sentence was carried out a few days later.) Christie was asked by Mr. Scott Henderson if he could remember whether or not he had had anything to do with Mrs. Evans's death. He replied: 'Well,

I am not sure. If somebody came up to me . . . and told me that there was definite proof that I had something to do with one of them, or both of them, I should accept it as being right, that I must have done it, but I want to know the truth about it as much as you do.'

> *Q:* So that if there is no proof that you had anything to do with Mrs. Evans's death are you prepared to say you were responsible?
> *A:* Well, I cannot say that I was or was not.

In his report, Mr. Scott Henderson called particular attention to the evidence given by the Rev. W. G. Morgan, Chaplain at Pentonville Prison, who had had two conversations with Christie. Christie had told him that he had 'gained the impression that it was necessary for him to confess to murders'. Said the Chaplain: 'The actual phrase he used stuck in my mind because of its incongruity. It was "The more the merrier".' Mr. Scott Henderson reported: 'I am satisfied that Christie gradually came to the conclusion that it would be helpful in his defence if he confessed to the murder of Mrs. Evans.' He summarized his findings as follows:

(1) The case for the prosecution against Evans, as presented to the jury, was an overwhelming one.
(2) Having considered all the material available relating to the deaths of Mrs. Evans and Geraldine Evans, I am satisfied that there can be no doubt that Evans was responsible for both.
(3) Christie's statements that he was responsible for the death of Mrs. Evans were not only unreliable but were untrue.

Mr. Scott Henderson's report was sharply criticized in Parliament, and to meet various objections to his conclusions he afterwards submitted a Supplementary Report. In his book, *The Man on Your Conscience*, which purports to show that Evans was made the victim of an appalling miscarriage of justice, Mr. Michael Eddowes writes: 'One becomes convinced that there could not possibly have been two incredible monsters living in the same house perpetrating murders and disposing of the victims' bodies in the same ghastly way.' It is this element of 'coincidence' in the Evans-Christie case which undoubtedly still troubles many minds.

[*1, 56, 154.*

Everard, Lydia Mary. *See* Sarah Ann HEARN.

Everitt, Frank. *See* Marian GRONDKOWSKI.

Excusable Homicide is of two sorts: (1) by misadventure, and (2) in self-defence. The first kind occurs in cases where a person going about a lawful act performed with due caution kills another accidentally, and without any prior intention to do bodily harm. An obvious example is the air gunner who overshoots at a ground practice target and kills some of his comrades (*Justice at Work*, James Avery Joyce). The second kind is homicide committed out of *unavoidable necessity* by a person protecting himself against attack in the course of a sudden brawl or quarrel. To establish this as Excusable Homicide it must be shown that the person committing the act had, out of a genuine desire to avoid bloodshed, retreated as far as he possibly could before turning upon his assailant to kill him. A man may not seek to avoid the guilt of deliberate murder *under colour of self-defence*; if two persons agree deliberately to fight, and if one makes an onset upon the other, who retreats as far as he safely can before delivering the fatal blow, then that is murder, *because of the previous malice and concerted design.* (Jervis, *On The Office and Duties of Coroner*). *See* JUSTIFIABLE HOMICIDE.

Exhumation. A body may *at any time* be exhumed, provided it can be shown that there is a good and sufficient reason for doing so. It may not be done because of some technical irregularity at the time of burial, or in cases of accidental death in which a medical certificate may have been granted through a genuine inadvertence, and no civil or criminal action is in question. Jervis, *On The Office and Duties of Coroner* points out: 'Many murderers have been convicted in modern times through the exhumation of the bodies of their victims months and years after burial.' Numerous cases (for example, Herbert Rowse ARMSTRONG) are recorded in this book.

F

For murder, though it have no tongue, will speak
With most miraculous organ.

Shakespeare: *Hamlet*

Fahmy, Marguerite, formerly **Laurient,** an elegant, sophisticated
Parisienne, had had the misfortune to attract a young, fabulously rich
Egyptian, and to be attracted to him in return. He had wooed her
ardently, bombarded her with extravagant letters, until in December
1922 she had agreed to marry him. Six months later she was repenting
in bitterness and tears. Ali Kamel Fahmy Bey was a sadist of vicious
sexual habits, who treated his wife with calculated brutality. To terrify
her, he would aim a revolver at her and fire over her head. Because she
was frightened of his coloured servants he set an enormous Negro to
watch over her. To his sister-in-law he wrote: 'Just now I am engaged
in training her. . . . With women one must act with energy and be
severe.' Madame Fahmy went in fear of her life. Only a few weeks
after the marriage her husband had solemnly sworn on the Koran
that he would kill her. As the months passed she was driven inexorably
to the edge of what is endurable. In July 1923, Ali Kamel Fahmy Bey,
his unhappy wife and his secretary-companion, Said Enani, arrived in
London and engaged a suite at the Savoy Hotel. On 9th July, after
they had been staying at the hotel for two or three days, the three of
them were lunching in the restaurant when the leader of the orchestra
went up to Madame Fahmy and asked her if she would like any particular piece of music to be played. Madame Fahmy made a most curious
reply. 'Thank you very much,' she said, 'my husband is going to kill me
in twenty-four hours, and I am not very anxious for music.' The
startled band leader backed away. 'I hope you will be here tomorrow,'
he stammered. That night London was shaken by the most violent
thunderstorm experienced there for many years. It broke in fury
round about midnight, and for more than two hours the thunder was
incessant and the sky was illuminated by brilliant flashes of lightning.
At some time after 2 a.m., the storm then reaching its climax, a porter
wheeling luggage along one of the corridors of the Savoy Hotel heard,

77

piercing through the sound of the thunder, three pistol shots fired in quick succession. He burst into Madame Fahmy's bedroom, to find her kneeling beside the dead body of her husband, who was lying on the floor in his pyjamas, with the blood trickling out of his mouth. The night manager was summoned. To him, Madame Fahmy cried out, in French: 'What have I done? What will they do to me? Oh, sir, I have been married six months, and I have suffered terribly!' To the doctor who was called she said, also in French, 'I have pulled the trigger three times.' The trial of Madame Fahmy for the murder of her husband attracted the most intense public interest, and for the six days it lasted the Old Bailey was under siege by large, noisy, excited crowds. Two of the most brilliant criminal lawyers of the day, Sir Edward Marshall HALL K.C. and Sir Henry CURTIS BENNETT K.C., had been briefed for the defence; their junior was Mr. Roland Oliver, afterwards a High Court judge. Marshall Hall's conduct of the case was a classic piece of advocacy, which showed him at the peak of his extraordinary powers. There was no denying that Madame Fahmy had killed her husband. Many thought that her counsel would seek a verdict of manslaughter. Instead, he went all-out for an absolute acquittal. His case was that when Madame Fahmy had pressed the trigger she had not known that the pistol was in a condition to be fired. Earlier she had tried to unload it by opening the breach, but had not been able to pull back the breach cover. Whilst she had been struggling with it the gun had gone off, the bullet spending itself harmlessly. In her complete ignorance of firearms, Madame Fahmy had thought that the gun was now unloaded, whereas, in fact, with the discharge of the first cartridge the second had automatically come into the firing position. On 9th July she had had a painful scene with her husband. It had been necessary that she should undergo a serious operation, and she had wished it to be performed in Paris. But Fahmy had refused to let her go; she had been without money, and he had refused to give her any. In the early hours of the next morning he had come into her room at the height of the storm, had flourished banknotes in her face, and had told her that she could have them to pay for her journey to Paris if she would submit to his perverted sexual demands. She had refused. In the witness-box, Madame Fahmy, weeping bitterly, struggled, through an interpreter, to describe the terrible scene that had followed:

> He crouched to spring on me and said, 'I will kill you. . . .' I now lifted my arm in front of me, and, without looking, pulled the trigger. The next moment I saw him on the ground, without realizing what had happened. . . . I do not know what had happened, and I asked the people what was all the trouble. I saw

Fahmy on the floor and I fell on my knees alongside of him. When I saw him lying on the floor, I caught hold of his hand, and said to him, 'Sweetheart, it is nothing. Speak, oh, please speak to me.' While I was on my knees the porter came up, but I was so touched that I understood nothing.

> *Sir Edward Marshall Hall:* When you threw your arm out as the pistol was fired, what were you afraid of?
> *Madame Fahmy:* That he was going to jump on me. It was terrible. I had escaped once. He said, 'I will kill you, I will kill you!' It was so terrible.

Marshall Hall's speech to the jury has long since passed into forensic history. It was indeed a masterly performance. When he came to describe the actual shooting, he assumed, there in the crowded court-room under the spellbound eyes of the jury, the stealthy crouch of the Egyptian as slowly he advanced upon the terrified woman. 'In sheer desperation,' said Sir Edward, 'in sheer desperation—as he crouched for the last time, crouched like an animal, like an Oriental, retired for the last time to get a bound forward—she turned the pistol and put it to his face, and to her horror the thing went off.' Marshall Hall pointed the pistol straight at the jury, and then let it drop, so that it clattered on to the floor—just as Madame Fahmy must have dropped it when she saw her husband stagger and fall. Marshall Hall always said afterwards that he had dropped the pistol by accident. Accident or not, there can be no doubt of its galvanic effect. The macabre scene in the hotel room had been re-created with so much vividness that there were many in court who cried out sharply when the pistol fell clattering to the floor; it was an attack upon the nerves as violent as a physical blow. After a summing-up by Mr. Justice SWIFT, markedly in favour of the prisoner, the jury were out for just over an hour. They returned with a verdict of 'Not Guilty' of murder, at which there was an outburst of cheering, clapping, and stamping which so angered the judge that he at once ordered the court to be cleared. Not until the public gallery had been emptied did he allow the clerk to ask the jury if they found the prisoner guilty of manslaughter. 'Not Guilty,' said the foreman. Madame Fahmy was discharged.

[*15, 61, 131.*

Fairfield, Lord (1863–1945). Born Frederick Arthur Greer, the son of a Liverpool merchant, he was called to the Bar by Gray's Inn in 1886 and acquired a large commercial and shipping practice on the Northern Circuit. He continued to practise as a Liverpool local until

1907, when he transferred to London; three years later he took silk. When Lord Birkenhead became Lord Chancellor in 1919, one of his first legal appointments was to make his former colleague at Liverpool a judge of the King's Bench Division. Mr. Justice Greer promptly established his reputation as a judge of quite exceptional capacity. He was a mild-mannered, even-tempered man, invariably courteous and considerate to counsel who practised in his Court. But he also possessed a vigorous, independent mind, a fact which became even more strikingly apparent when in 1927 he was appointed a Lord Justice of Appeal. He retired in 1938, and in the following year was raised to the peerage as Baron Fairfield of Caldy in the County Palatine of Chester. He died in 1945, being then in his eighty-second year; the barony then became extinct. As Mr. Justice Greer, he presided over the trial, *inter alia*, of Frederick Rothwell HOLT.

Federoff, Osip. *See* SIEGE OF SIDNEY STREET.

Field, Frederick Herbert Charles, went into the witness-box at Westminster Coroner's Court, in October 1931, to tell what he knew about the death of a prostitute named Annie Louisa (called Norah) Upchurch, whose body had been found lying in the passageway of an empty shop in Shaftesbury Avenue a few days previously. Field worked for a firm of signboard fixers, and had been at the shop the day before that grim discovery was made. He told the Coroner, Mr. Ingleby Oddie, that he had gone there to take away a 'To Let' board. A man wearing plus-fours had come up to him as he was removing it, told him that he had an 'order to view', and had asked for the keys. He had handed them over, being under the impression that this was the man who was about to rent the empty shop. When, some years later, Mr. Ingleby Oddie came to write his autobiography, *Inquest*, he vividly recalled the scene:

> I had many questions to put to Field to test the truth of his story. He was an impudent and self-confident fellow, but as I asked him those awkward questions I could see as he faced me that he knew that I *knew* who had committed this murder! Indeed, at one point I felt certain he was going to confess. But at that psychological moment a woman fainted in court, and had to be carried out. By the time this disturbance was over, Field had recovered his complacency, and he made no confession—then.

But twenty-one months later, he did. On 25th July 1933 he walked into the office of the *Daily Sketch* and told the news-editor that he wished to confess to the murder of Norah Upchurch. In a long, detailed statement, he described how he had lured the girl into the empty shop, had strangled her and had made off with her handbag; this he had afterwards thrown into a ditch at Rose Hill, Sutton. Field later repeated his confession to the police. It was put in in evidence at his trial, which took place at the Old Bailey before Mr. Justice SWIFT in the following September. Here is an extract from it:

> I lost my temper and gripped her round the throat. . . . She seemed to faint away and fell back out of my hands on to the floor. She did not scream or speak. I knew that something was seriously wrong when she fell back, and lost control of myself, and cannot remember exactly what happened.

But when this cunning man went into the witness-box he took back every word of his confession. He said that ever since his encounter with Mr. Ingleby Oddie at the inquest 'the finger of suspicion' had been pointing at him, and he had 'wanted the whole thing cleared up properly'. He went on: 'I wanted to be arrested, because by doing that I could have my innocence proved properly.'

> *Mr. Justice Swift:* It is a peculiar way of proving your innocence to say you are guilty of murder.
> *Field:* It was the only way.

There was no independent evidence against Field. The whole case against him rested upon his own confession. Since this had now been repudiated, the judge had no option but to direct the jury to return a verdict of 'Not Guilty'. Field left the Old Bailey in the comfortable knowledge that he had been too smart for the law. Since no man may be tried twice for the same offence unless the jury shall have disagreed, it did not matter to him now what evidence might thereafter come to light to connect him with the murder of Norah Upchurch; he had made himself perpetually free from the danger of arrest. Shortly afterwards, this 'impudent and self-confident fellow' joined the R.A.F. as an aircraftsman. Nothing more was heard of him for nearly three years. Then, on 4th April 1936, the naked body of a middle-aged widow named Beatrice Vilna Sutton was found lying on a bed in her flat at Elmhurst Mansions, Clapham; she had been suffocated with two pillows. Employing the same technique which had served him so well three years before, Field confessed to the murder of Mrs. Sutton, and so made a second appearance in the dock at the Old Bailey, this time before Mr. Justice CHARLES. Once again the confession was put in in evidence. 'I went to her place and done her in, and, as you might say, put myself on the spot. . . . I just murdered her because I wanted to murder someone. I had not the guts to take my own life, and I knew that by doing it I should lose my own life.' Once again, when Field, a man of limited imagination, went into the witness-box, he repudiated the confession. He said that whilst on the run as a deserter from the R.A.F. he had slept for two or three nights in a cupboard under the stairs at the block of flats where Mrs. Sutton lived. On the night of the murder he had been about to crawl into the cupboard once more, when he heard the sound of a quarrel going on. Then a man had come out of Mrs. Sutton's flat, leaving the front door open. Field went on:

> I thought I would go in and see what was wrong. I saw the woman on the bed. She had a pillow over her face. For a moment I did not know what to do. I knew if I called the police they would only say what was I doing there. Then it occurred to me that if I were to take the blame for anything wrong in there I could accomplish what I had not the courage to do—commit suicide.

But this time Field had said too much. His confession was far too detailed; it included references to matters which only the killer could have known. Neither did the Crown need to rely upon Field's confession alone—this time there was plenty of independent evidence. The jury required only twenty minutes to make up their minds. Field was sentenced to death, and on 30th June 1936—almost five years after Norah Upchurch's body had been found in the empty shop—he was hanged.

[*145, 148, 219.*

Fox, Charles William. *See* Stanley Eric HOBDAY.

Fox, Sidney Harry, was the type of man who, being cursed with expensive tastes and having neither the talent nor the inclination to gratify them by honest means, exists precariously between one prison sentence and another, by bilking tradespeople, cheating hotel keepers, committing petty forgeries and thefts, passing 'dud' cheques, trading upon the infatuated tenderness of elderly ladies, and indulging in sundry acts of blackmail. To the criminal courts the type is wearisomely familiar. It is usually to be recognized by its engaging manners, frank, boyish charm, cultured accent (genuine or synthetic), and extreme plausibility. Sidney Fox possessed most of the identifying characteristics and, given time, might well have become a perfect specimen of the type. But within him, side by side with the perverted talents of the swindler, the sneak thief, and the 'con man', there slumbered a ruthless egotism, which, when the time came, did not shrink from one of the most repulsive and unnatural crimes in the calendar. With one stride he left his petty crimes behind and stepped straight into the Chamber of Horrors. For a mess of insurance money he killed his mother. At the time of her death, Mrs. Rosaline Fox was sixty-three, a heavily built woman with snow-white hair, a benevolent expression, a distinctive shuffling gait—she suffered from *paralysis agitans*, which made her seem older than her years—and notions of financial morality little, if at all, superior to those of her son. She was the wife of a railway signalman, from whom she had parted; afterwards she had set up house with a man who also worked on the railway—as a porter—and it was he who was the reputed father of Sidney Harry, the fourth and youngest of her children, and the apple of her eye. Unfortunately for himself, Sidney chose to believe that his father was someone far grander than a railway porter, or even a railway signalman. He liked to think that he had noble blood in his veins, and this undoubtedly encouraged his distaste for settling down in some humdrum, if honest, occupation. Thus, he took quite early to a life of crime, specializing in forgery, but not despising the dishonest penny wherever it was to be found. Fox served his first prison sentence—three months hard labour for defrauding a Brighton tradesman—as early as 1918; he was then a youth of nineteen. During the next ten years he was in and out of gaol with fair regularity, on convictions for forgery, larceny, and fraud. In March 1929, after serving a fifteen months sentence for a jewellery theft, he took his mother away from St. Mary's Hospital, Portsmouth, to which she had been admitted as an indigent person twelve months before. A few months later, mother and son set out upon a dreary and, it might have been thought, perilous round of hotels in the South of England, decamping when they could no longer avoid paying the bill. This was made all the easier by the fact that they had no luggage, and indeed only the most sketchy toilet necessities. Mrs. Fox had two dresses, which she wore one on top of the other, one undergarment, a top coat, a 'fur piece', two pairs of stockings, and a pair of shoes; she had no nightdress or washing materials. Sidney just had the clothes he stood up in. They were thus in a good position to make a quick get-away. On Wednesday, 19th October 1929, the wanderings of this curious pair brought them to the Hotel Metropole at Margate. On the Sunday following their arrival at the hotel, Sidney told the manager that his mother had had a fainting fit. A doctor was called in, found little wrong with the old lady, and prescribed a simple tonic. The manager suggested that Fox and his mother should move into rooms having a communicating door. Thereupon, Mrs. Fox was moved into room No.

66, on the second floor, her son into the adjoining room, No. 67. Fox was hurrying on with the necessary preliminaries to his terrible act. Two days earlier he had gone to Ramsgate and had taken out an insurance policy with Messrs. Pickfords, agents for the Ocean Accident and Guarantee Corporation Ltd. The policy was for £1,000, payable in the event of Mrs. Fox's death from 'external accidental means'. (The premium was 2s., quite a large sum for Fox to have to find, since he was practically penniless.) The next thing he had to do was to scrape together his railway fare to London, where he had further insurance business to transact. This he did by the familiar method of persuading a local shopkeeper to cash one of his worthless cheques. Thus equipped, on Tuesday, 22nd October, he went up to London, where he obtained from the Cornhill Insurance Company an extension of a £2,000 policy, so that it would become payable to him if his mother were to die from an accident before midnight on 23rd October. He also secured from the head office of Messrs. Pickfords an extension of the Ramsgate policy, to expire at the same hour of the same day. These various insurance transactions required Mrs. Fox's signature; everything we know of her suggests that she was willing to sign anything her son chose to put in front of her, without knowing, or seeking to know, its purport. On the fateful Wednesday evening—23rd October—the insurance policies having only a few more hours to run, Sidney Fox escorted his mother into the hotel dining-room with his customary solicitude. After dinner, he assisted her back to her room, bringing with him, as a special treat for the old lady, a half-bottle of port, for which he had actually paid cash—three shillings. Nothing more was seen of Mrs. Fox. Later in the evening, however, her son made an appearance in the hotel bar. It will never be known whether by that time he had already strangled his mother in her bedroom, or whether he was having a drink to nerve himself for the deed. In either case, he must have been thinking about the narrow margin of time which was left to him. To enable him to collect the insurance money it would be necessary to establish that his mother had died before midnight, and even if he had already killed her, a substantial part of his plan still remained to be carried out. He had no watch of his own, and it is said that he timed the operation by keeping an eye on the illuminated clock tower opposite the hotel. Whatever may be the truth of that, at twenty minutes before midnight Mr. Samuel Hopkins, a commercial traveller staying in the hotel, was startled to see Fox— naked except for his shirt—come running down the stairs in a state of great agitation, calling out, 'Where is the "boots"? I believe there's a fire!' Mr. Hopkins shouted an alarm and followed Fox upstairs. Pointing to the door of No. 66, that distraught young man cried out, 'My mother is in there!' Mr. Hopkins tried to get into the room, which was dense with thick black smoke, but was beaten back. He made a second attempt, this time crawling on his hands and knees, and succeeded in groping his way to the bed. His hands came in contact with the bare legs of Mrs. Fox, which were dangling over the edge. Somehow, he managed to drag the old lady off the bed and into the corridor. She had nothing on save a small vest. Mr. Hopkins, who was in the last extreme of exhaustion, wrapped her in his raincoat; then he collapsed. Meanwhile, two other commercial travellers staying in the hotel had managed to get into No. 66, by way of Fox's room. One of them, by crawling on his knees, fought his way through the blinding smoke to where an armchair was burning in front of the gas fire, which was lighted. The carpet immediately under the chair was in flames. The chair was dragged into the corridor, where the flames were put out. Downstairs in the entrance hall unavailing efforts were being made to revive Mrs. Fox by artificial respiration; she was already dead. The doctor who had been sent for broke the news to Fox. He asked if he could see his mother for the last time, and the doctor took him upstairs to the room where the body had been placed. Fox walked up to his mother, looked at her, touched her; when he came out, his eyes were full of tears. To assume that these were necessarily crocodile tears is to take too simple a view of human nature. For a few days Fox's luck held. An inquest was held and a verdict of 'Accidental death' returned. A Margate solicitor, to whom Fox had committed the charge of his affairs, advanced him £40 on the strength of the insurance policies. On 25th October Fox left the Hotel Metropole with the sympathy and good wishes of the residents and staff, but without, as usual, paying his bill. On 29th October he attended his mother's funeral, at Great Fransham in Norfolk. He probably thought by this time that he had 'got away with it'. But he had not. There are few people in the world who have a wider experience of chicanery than claims assessors for the great insurance companies; to one such the papers relating to the various policies of Mrs. Rosaline Fox suggested only one thing—murder. The companies communicated with Scotland Yard. On 3rd November Fox was arrested in Norwich on six separate charges relating to frauds upon hotels, including the Hotel Metropole, Margate, and the Royal Pavilion Hotel, Folkestone. But before he could be brought to trial, Fox faced another and graver charge—the charge of murdering his mother. He was put on trial before Mr. Justice ROWLATT at Lewes Assizes in March 1930. The prosecution was in the hands of the Attorney-General, Sir William Jowitt K.C. and Sir Henry CURTIS BENNETT K.C. Mr. J. D. Cassels K.C. led for the defence. The prosecution presented a formidable and, as it turned out, unanswerable case. The facts that told most strongly against Fox were: (1) the unburned strip of carpet between the gas fire and the spot where the blazing armchair had been standing; this disposed of what might otherwise have been a colourable explanation of the blaze; (2) the mass of charred newspapers which were found in a position suggesting that they had been immediately underneath the armchair, and bearing the plain inference that it was in this way that the fire had been started; (3) the discovery of a small cane chair, which, although it was standing by the window, far away from the area of the fire, had been partly burned, thus clearly indicating that some person had been in the room after the fire had started and had moved it out of the way of further damage. Nothing did greater harm to Sidney Fox than his own showing in the witness-box. He described how he had awakened during the night and had smelt smoke. 'Then', he said, 'I suddenly remembered that I had left my mother sitting by the fire and wondered whether she had turned the fire out, or whether something was scorching. I opened the communicating door and a volume of smoke met me and I could not get into the room.' This led to a celebrated exchange of question and answer between Fox and the Attorney-General.

> Q: Did you realize when you opened the communicating door that the atmosphere in the room was such as would probably suffocate anybody inside?
> A: If I had stayed in there three or four moments I should have been suffocated.
> Q: So you must have been greatly apprehensive for your mother?
> A: I was.
> Q: Fox, you closed the door?
> A: It is quite possible I did.
> Q: Can you explain to me why it was that you closed the door instead of flinging it wide open?
> A: My explanation for that now is that the smoke should not spread into the hotel.

The crowded courtroom greeted this last fatal reply with an audible gasp of horrified incredulity. The jury returned a verdict of 'Guilty', and Fox was sentenced to death. He was hanged at Maidstone Prison on 8th April 1930.

[*I.*

Fox-Davies, Arthur Charles, K.C. (1871-1928). Called to the Bar by Lincoln's Inn, he enjoyed a high reputation as a barrister, achieving the almost unprecedented feat of doubling a practice in the Chancery and criminal courts, but was, perhaps, even better known as a genealogist and authority on heraldry, on which he published a number of standard works. (As light relief from his more serious literary activity, he wrote a series of agreeable 'thrillers'.) He appeared for the defence in some of the most notorious murder trials of the 1920s, including that of Alexander Campbell MASON.

Frampton, Walter (1871-1939). In his day, one of the best-known juniors practising at the Bar, he was associated with Sir Patrick HASTINGS K.C. in the defence of Mrs. Elvira BARNEY. With Mr. E. F. Lever he also defended Frederick Guy BROWNE (Browne and Kennedy). A rubicund figure of genial proportions, he was, in build, not unlike his friend Curtis Bennett; like him, too, he was a brilliant criminal lawyer, who found in the tense atmosphere of a trial for murder at the Old Bailey the best and most natural outlet for his talents, although he had a large divorce and licensing practice as well. Called to the Bar by the Middle Temple in 1901, he died some weeks before the outbreak of the second World War in 1939.

Frobisher, John William. *See* Louie CALVERT.

Fulton, Sir Eustace Cecil (1880-1954), was one of the three sons of Sir Forrest Fulton, for twenty-two years—1900 to 1922—Recorder of the City of London. Called to the Bar by the Middle Temple in 1904, he practised successfully in London, on the South-Eastern Circuit, and at sessions in the Home Counties. He was appointed one of the junior prosecuting counsel at the Old Bailey during the 1914-18 war, in which he served with some distinction; in 1932 he became senior prosecuting counsel. Four years later he accepted the post of Chairman of the County of London Sessions. He retired in 1949 and died in October 1954. Murder trials in which he prosecuted included those of Madame FAHMY; Alfred Arthur KOPSCH; Frederick FIELD (both trials); Theodosis PETROU; and Thomas Joseph DAVIDSON.

Furnace, Samuel James, a jobbing builder who had formerly been a ship's steward, and had served in the Black and Tans during the Irish 'troubles', pencilled a crisp note for the Coroner on the evening of 3rd January 1933. It read: 'Good-bye all. No work. No money. Sam J. Furnace.' Later that same evening, fire broke out in a shed at the back of 30 Hawley Crescent, Kentish Town, London, which Furnace rented for the purposes of his business. After the blaze had been brought under control, firemen dragged from the damaged shed the charred body of a man; they also recovered Furnace's note, with its plain implication of an intention to commit suicide. But the Coroner who conducted the inquest, Mr. (afterwards Sir) Bentley Purchase, was not satisfied that (*a*) this was a case of suicide, (*b*) the dead man was Sam J. Furnace, in spite of a confident identification which appeared to put the matter beyond doubt. His personal examination of the corpse confirmed his suspicions on both scores. First, there was a bullet wound in the back which could not possibly have been self-inflicted; secondly, the teeth were those of a much younger man than Furnace. But if the body were not that of Samuel James Furnace, whose body was it? A Post Office savings book in a pocket of what remained of the man's charred jacket provided an answer. It had been soaked with water used to put out the fire, but the name on it was still decipherable—Walter Spatchett. This clue led to the body being positively identified as that of a rent collector for a firm of estate agents in Camden Town. Walter Spatchett had last been seen when he left his employers' office at 5 p.m. on Monday, 2nd January, the day before the fire, at which time it was thought that he must have had on him some thirty-five or forty pounds in rent money. It was established that Furnace had been a friend of Spatchett; indeed, he had known him well enough to borrow £60 from him, although the prospect of his being able to repay the loan had grown steadily more remote as his financial difficulties had mounted. The full resources of the Metropolitan Police were mobilized to find Samuel James Furnace. At one time it was said that half the entire police forces of the United Kingdom were engaged in the hunt, one of the most elaborate that had ever been staged. In the end, Furnace was run to earth through his own incaution. On 14th January—eleven days after the fire—he wrote a letter to his brother-in-law, a Mr. Charles Tuck-field. In it, he said:

Just a line to you in hope that I shall be able to see a friend before I end it all. . . . I am at Southend, quite near the station, making out I have been ill with the 'flue. So have been able to stay in all the week. I am far from well through want of sleep. I don't think I have slept one hour since the accident happened. Now what I want you to do is not for me, but for May and the kiddies. My days are numbered. I want you to come down Sunday, on your own, please. Catch the 10.35 from Harringay Park, that gets you down in Southend at 12.8. Come out of the station, walk straight across the road and down the opposite road. Walk down on the left side. I will see you. I am not giving my address in case you are followed. Just walk slowly down. If you come will you bring me 15½ shirt and two collars, any colour will do. Also one pair of socks, dark ones and one comb. I think that is all now. Best of luck. Mine is gone.

Mr. Tuckfield handed this letter to the police. Acting upon their instructions, he went to Southend on the Sunday, and carried out in every detail the directions given in the letter. He walked along Whitegate Road—the street which faced the station—keeping to the left side, as instructed. Presently, he saw Furnace draw back the curtains of a ground-floor room at No. 11, and beckon to him. He went into the house. It need scarcely be said that, although nobody seemed to be about, certainly no one who appeared to be interested in Mr. Tuckfield's little stroll, all this had taken place under the scrutiny of the police, who were operating under the direction of Superintendent G. W. Cornish and Chief-Inspector G. Yandell, the Scotland Yard officers in charge of the case. Entering the house through the scullery at the back, the officers took Furnace by surprise. Furnace was taken back to London, and at Kentish Town police station he made a statement in which he said that Spatchett had been with him in the shed at Hawley Crescent during the early evening of 2nd January. Furnace had shown him his revolver. Furnace went on: 'I was showing him through the door, with the gun in my left hand, and as he was going through the door the gun went off and shot him. He fell to the ground groaning. I realized my position and lost my head. I went out. When I got back there I found he was dead.' Furnace left him in the shed and went home. 'The idea struck me to destroy the body by burning it, making out that the body was mine. [See Alfred Arthur ROUSE.] The idea at first seemed too terrible, but no other way seemed possible.' The next afternoon, therefore, he put the body on a chair and poured oil and spirits over it. 'I screwed up a lot of paper on the floor and set a candle, which I lit, in the middle of it. . . . I came outside and pulled the outer door to, locking it.' Had Furnace ever come to trial, the issue would have depended upon how far he could have made good his story of the accidental discharge of the gun. But he never was brought to trial. After making his statement, Furnace was shut in a cell at the police station. He spent most of the night pacing restlessly up and down. At 7 o'clock the next morning, a police constable looked into the cell, in time to see Furnace put a small bottle to his lips. He rushed into the cell, but Furnace had already swallowed some of the contents—hydrochloric acid. He was taken to St. Pancras Hospital, where he died twenty-four hours later. A Coroner's jury found Furnace guilty of Spatchett's murder. One of the wreaths at his funeral bore the inscription: 'To err is human, to forgive divine.'

[78, 92, 102, 219.

Fyfe, Sir David Maxwell. *See* Viscount KILMUIR.

G

Guilt was my grim chamberlain
That lighted me to bed
And drew my midnight curtains round
With fingers bloody red.

Thomas Hood: *The Dream of Eugene Aram*

Gall, Christina. *See* Peter QUEEN.

Gardner, Margery. *See* Neville George Clevely HEATH.

Gardstein, George. *See* SIEGE OF SIDNEY STREET.

Gartside, John Edward, aged twenty-four, called upon a furniture dealer in the West Riding of Yorkshire on 22nd May 1947. He said that he was parting from his wife, was rejoining the Royal Air Force, and had a houseful of furniture to sell. The dealer agreed to purchase the furniture for £300, and the vendor signed a receipt for the money—in the name of 'P. Baker'. Sent to collect the furniture from the house, which was at Standedge Tunnel, on the slopes of the Pennines, the removal men were loading it into a van when a Mrs. Doughty called. She had come to visit her friends, Mr. and Mrs. Percy Baker, and was surprised and distressed to hear that they had given up the house and had sold their furniture. The whole proceeding seemed to Mrs. Doughty so peculiar that she telephoned her husband, who told her to make a note of the name and address of the dealer. The following day Mr. Doughty, together with another friend of Mr. and Mrs. Baker, went to see the dealer, and asked him for a description of the man who had signed himself 'P. Baker'—in a hand which neither of them was able to recognize. From what the dealer said, it was obvious to them that whoever had sold the furniture, it was not their friend Percy Baker. The dealer called in the police. He told them that, besides taking away the furniture, he had, on 'Mr. Baker's' instructions, also removed eight suitcases from the house, and had delivered them to a shop in Saddleworth. Inquiries showed that this shop was rented by John Edward

Gartside, general dealer. There was no one at the shop when the police visited it. A constable was detailed to keep watch. Presently, a man drove up in a motor car. Questioned by the constable, he persisted in calling himself Percy Baker, but later admitted that his name was Gartside. At the police station, he said that he had bought the furniture from Baker for £250 a few days before, and had given him another £200 for his car. Asked why he had used the name 'Baker', he returned the perplexing reply: 'That was his idea. He's parted from his wife, and he didn't want the neighbours to know.' He had no idea where the Bakers were now. The suitcases delivered to the shop were found to contain a large quantity of clothing, household linen, and personal effects, which were identified, at least in part, as the property of Mr. and Mrs. Baker. The Bakers' house was searched from cellar to attic. There were bloodstains in the dining-room, and on the floor the mark of a bullet. The Chief-Inspector in charge of the case told Gartside that he had reason to believe that some person might have been killed in the house. 'Who has been killed?' Gartside asked. 'It may be Mr. or Mrs. Baker,' replied the officer. Whereupon, Gartside came out with the fearful question, 'What if it is both of them?' He went on to make a written statement, in which he admitted that he had buried the dead bodies of Percy and Alice Baker on the moor, some three-quarters of a mile from the house. Next morning, as soon as it was light, Gartside conducted the police to the spot, and there, after a few minutes' digging, the two naked bodies were uncovered. Baker had two bullet wounds in his head; his wife, one. 'What am I supposed to say now?' Gartside asked, upon being charged with murder. He then made a new and much amplified statement, in which he described how he had gone to the house to buy furniture, Percy Baker being a friend of his. He went on:

> Baker suggested I bought a bedroom suite and Mrs. Baker objected.... There was quite an argument about it between the two of them.... He made some remark about this gentleman friend of hers, and she asked him what he was meaning. There was a suggestion from him that she had seen him regular. He had brought a rifle and revolver in and placed them on the settee. They were both loaded, as we intended to try them out. When he suggested she had been seeing this gentleman friend regularly, she stooped and got hold of the poker, and he grabbed hold of the rifle and fired whilst she was holding the poker in the air. She dropped instantly. I went over to try to take the revolver off him, and there was a struggle, during which the gun went off. He was making a great deal of noise and was squirming in agony, and after a bit I

grabbed my rifle and fired two more shots to put him out of the agony.... I know there was two rifle shots, anyway ... I went into a panic. I decided that, as they were both dead, I had got to dispose of them some way or other, and make it look as though they'd disappeared.... As soon as it was dark I dragged them up the bank and over the moor one at a time, and buried them on the moor, all of which took several hours, and it was daylight before I'd finished.

Gartside, it will be seen, decked out his story with a good deal of detail. This, from his point of view, was a mistake, for it gave the police repeated opportunities to test the truth of it; it did not survive that test. Gartside was tried at Leeds Assizes in July, where he was found guilty and sentenced to death; he was duly hanged.
[85.

Geraghty, Christopher James. *See* Charles Henry JENKINS.

Gibson, Eileen (Gay). *See* James CAMB.

Gill, Sir Charles Frederick, K.C. (1851-1923). This tall, strikingly handsome Irishman possessed few of the qualities thought to be characteristic of his race. He was an Irishman without eloquence or wit. He was slow, even halting, in speech, ponderous in manner, in argument logical and restrained. The total impression was one of stolidity and dourness. Yet he enjoyed a very large and fashionable practice, and, in his heyday, no *cause célèbre* was complete without him. Primarily, he owed his success to a quite extraordinary capacity for mastering the smallest detail not only of his own but also of his opponent's case; he was thus usually forearmed against any eventuality and was rarely surprised. Charles Gill was born in Dublin on 10th June 1851. He was called to the Bar by the Middle Temple in 1874; was junior counsel to the Treasury (1889-92); senior counsel (1892-9). He was knighted in 1921, and died on 22nd February 1923. Famous murder trials in which he appeared for the Crown included those of Herbert John BENNETT; and Samuel Herbert DOUGAL.

Goddard of Albourne, Baron (b. 1877). Lord Chief Justice of England (1946-58). It was unfortunate that in the public mind Lord Goddard should have been so prominently identified with the last-ditch defence of capital punishment and that at every attempt at reform he should have appeared as a Cassandra-like figure prophesying woe.

Depending upon the individual viewpoint, Lord Goddard tended to be regarded either as a sadist with an unlovely relish for the gallows, or else as a people's champion doing battle with 'abolitionist cranks and sentimentalists', who would have us all murdered in our beds. Either presentment is an absurd caricature of Lord Goddard, whose true reputation rests, or ought to rest, upon his brilliant qualities as a judge learned in the law and wise in the affairs of men. On the Bench, as in private life, he was an odd mixture of sternness and geniality. He publicly attacked approved schools, probation, and modern penology in general, and lamented the abolition of flogging as a punishment for crimes of violence; on the other hand, he was vigilant in the protection of persons whom he believed to have been treated roughly, either by unjust decisions of inferior courts, or by great corporations, or municipalities, or even by Whitehall itself. Off the Bench, his abrupt manner had a way of melting under the influence of good talk and good food, of both of which he is a connoisseur. (He is also a great expert on port.) Rayner Goddard was born in 1877, the son of a solicitor. He was called to the Bar (Inner Temple and Gray's Inn) in 1899; thereafter his career advanced by orderly stages to the topmost reaches of his profession—King's Counsel, 1923; Judge of the King's Bench Division of the High Court, 1932; Lord Justice of Appeal, 1938; Lord of Appeal in Ordinary (with life peerage) in 1944. In 1946 he succeeded the late Lord Caldecote as Lord Chief Justice of England. He retired in September 1958 at the age of eighty-one, and was replaced by Lord Justice Parker, an appointment which, like his own, was 'non-political'. Murder trials over which he presided included those of Nurse WADDINGHAM; William TEASDALE; and LEY and SMITH.

Grantham, Sir William (1835-1911). Judge of the King's Bench Division of the High Court (1886-1911). Mr. Justice Grantham was perhaps better suited to his rôle of benevolent country squire than he was to the Bench, where his pronouncements often reflected political opinions and prejudices which he seemed quite unable to conceal, and which made nonsense of the principle of judicial impartiality. He was, however, a tremendous 'character', and, as such, a popular figure with the public, though hardly with the members of the Bar, who suffered much from his notorious intolerance and occasional eccentricities. By birth, tradition, instinct, and preference he was a country gentleman, and it is at first glance a little odd to find him engaged in a learned profession which has nothing of the flavour of the countryside about it. In term-time, he rode on horseback every day from his home in London's Eaton Square to the Law Courts, and the spectacle of the bluff, ruddy-faced judge mounted on his iron-grey cob was for many years one of the sights of the town. On circuit, Mr. Justice Grantham offered princely hospitality to the Bar and to the county notabilities, his dinner parties at the judge's lodgings being distinguished by the fine wines which graced his table, and by an almost legendary punch whose preparation was the special secret of a butler, who was said to owe his place in the entourage entirely to this one shining talent. It was a paradox of the judge's character that, off the Bench, he should have shown himself to be a genial companion, a delightful host, a kind, generous, warm-hearted man—and, in Court, only too often a rude, brusque, cantankerous person, much given to hasty, dogmatic judgments that had to be corrected on appeal. In dealing with any case having the faintest political flavour, his partisanship—he was a rabid Tory of the old school—was so blatantly evident that his fitness to hold judicial office was repeatedly questioned in Parliament. Strong efforts were made to persuade him to resign, but he resisted all efforts to dislodge him, and continued to sit on the Bench until, after twenty-five years as a High Court judge, he died on 30th November 1911. He was then in his seventy-seventh year. A barrister of the Inner Temple, William Grantham sat in the House of Commons as Conservative M.P. for East Surrey (1874-85) and for Croydon (1885-6). He was promoted to the Bench in 1886, being one of Lord Halsbury's famous 'political selections', which were so fiercely criticized at the time. (In this connection, see Lord DARLING.) Murderers sentenced to death by Mr. Justice Grantham included George CHAPMAN.

'Green Bicycle' Case. *See* Ronald Vivian LIGHT.

Greenwood, David, is still remembered, at a distance of more than forty years, as the 'Badge and Button' murderer. He was traced by a badge; he was convicted by a button. Few cases exhibit more strikingly how a man may be trapped by a trifle and caught by a coincidence. It was on the evening of Saturday, 9th April 1918, that Nellie Grace True, a sixteen-years-old junior clerk employed at Woolwich Arsenal, left her parents' home in Juno Terrace, Welhall, to change her library book. By midnight she had not returned home, and her father went to the police. At 8.20 the following morning, the body of Nellie True was found on Eltham Common, barely a quarter of a mile from her home; she had been raped and strangled. By her side was her handbag and her library book, *The Adventures of Herr Baby,* and near by, half-trodden into the mud, a cheap replica of the famous 'tiger' badge of the Leicestershire Regiment. The trampled grass also yielded a plain button, which looked as if it had come off an overcoat. A piece of metal wire was threaded through two of the four holes; one end of it had been sharpened, the other broken off. Photographs and a description of button and badge were circulated to the Press, and were published in almost every newspaper in the land. They were seen by a man named Edward Farrell, who was one of the fifty employees of the Hewson Manufacturing Company of Newman Street, Oxford Street, which, at this critical stage of the 1914-18 war, was engaged in the production of aeroplane parts. Farrell thought he recognized the badge. He had seen one of his workmates, twenty-one-years-old David Greenwood, a turner, wearing it—or one very like it—in the lapel of his overcoat. Farrell was certain that when he and his mates knocked off work at Saturday lunchtime, Greenwood had been wearing the badge. Now—on Monday morning—it was missing. He asked Greenwood what had happened to his badge, and the young man replied that on the Saturday afternoon he had sold the badge for two shillings to a man he had met on a tram between Welhall and Eltham. Greenwood's workmates told him that to 'clear' himself he ought to go to the police. He did. At Tottenham Court Road police station he gave a detailed description of the man in the tram to whom he had sold the badge. ('His accent appeared to me as though he came from Belfast. . . . I should say he was a man that had had an outdoor life', and so on.) Later, at an interview with a Scotland Yard officer at the Hewson works, Greenwood was shown the badge found at the scene of the murder, and admitted, unhesitatingly, that it was his. The officer asked Greenwood to accompany him to Scotland Yard. On the way, sitting beside him in the car, he suddenly asked Greenwood, 'What buttons have you on your coat?' and added, 'Why, I see they are all off.' It was true. Greenwood's overcoat was entirely without buttons. He explained that they had been 'off for a long time'. The inspector then drew Greenwood's attention to the fact that the bottom button but one appeared to have been torn away, leaving behind a small ragged hole. 'That is where it was pulled out, I suppose,' said Greenwood. The police now turned their attention to the piece of wire which had apparently been used to fasten the button on. This was found to be spring steel of a peculiar make in use at Hewson's, which the manager positively identified. Greenwood was tried at the Old Bailey before Mr. Justice Atkin (afterwards Lord ATKIN) in the following April. In his evidence he said that he had never liked his overcoat, which had been issued to him upon his discharge from the R.A.M.C. in 1917; he was not wearing it on the day of the murder. As to the buttons, they had been only lightly sewn on, and had quickly begun to come off. The jury were not impressed. They found Greenwood guilty, and he was sentenced to death—only to be reprieved. The late Mr. Justice HUMPHREYS wrote in his *A Book of Trials*:

When at the Bar, it was my practice, in my later years, to talk with the junior members of my Chambers on such topics as circumstantial evidence. Greenwood's case was a favourite one on these occasions, when we found it interesting to discuss the problem: 'If Greenwood had used thread instead of wire to fasten the lowest but one of his overcoat buttons would there have been enough evidence to justify a conviction?' I leave the answer to others. Meanwhile, one impudent pupil, as I remember, observed: 'It only shows how careful one ought to be in these small matters of dress.'

[97, 99.

Greenwood, Harold, was in the summer of 1919 living with his wife Mabel, their daughter Irene, aged twenty-one, and their ten-years-old son Kenneth in the village of Kidwelly, near Llanelly, where he was in practice as a solicitor. It was a comfortable *ménage*. Rumsey House, the Greenwoods' home, was a substantial three-storeyed mansion standing in its own grounds at the edge of the village; three indoor servants were kept—cook, parlourmaid, between-maid—and also a gardener. Mr. Greenwood's practice would hardly have sufficed to enable him to live in such a style, but his wife, a younger sister of Sir Vansittart Bowater, Bart., had ample means of her own. Mabel Greenwood had been in poor health for some years, but, in spite of a weak heart and other disabilities, she played a leading part in the affairs of the village and the social activities in and around it. She was much liked in the neighbourhood. The same could not be said of her husband. He seems to have had few friends, although there were many women who found him attractive. He was what used to be called a 'ladies' man', which, in his case, probably meant no more than that he took pleasure in the company of a pretty woman. The neighbours looked on in sour disfavour. To understand the tragedy of Rumsey House correctly, it is essential to see it against this perpetual background of scandal-mongering and gossip, some of it merely thoughtless, some of it malicious and vindictive. To their friends and acquaintances and, perhaps more significantly, to the servants who lived under the same roof with them, the Greenwoods seemed a happy and harmonious couple. On the morning of Sunday, 15th June 1919, the family breakfasted late. Thereafter, Mrs. Greenwood occupied herself with writing letters and reading on the lawn, whilst her husband overhauled his motor car. Irene Greenwood was emphatic that her father did not go into the house at any time during the forenoon. Hannah Williams, the parlourmaid, on the other hand, was to swear at the trial that her master had come in at 12.30 p.m., had gone into the china pantry, and had stayed there for a quarter of an hour. She said that she had never seen him do this before, and declined the suggestion that it was her master's regular habit when he came in from the garden to wash his hands at the pantry sink, so as to save himself the trouble of going upstairs to the bathroom. The quarter of an hour which Greenwood was supposed to have spent in the pantry that Sunday morning was vital, for it was then that he was alleged to have added a fatal dose of arsenic—in the form of diluted weed killer—to the bottle of Burgundy which was destined for his wife's lunch. Luncheon consisted of a joint, vegetables, gooseberry tart and custard. More important was who drank what. Hannah Williams swore that Greenwood drank whisky, Irene Greenwood and the boy, Kenneth, water; only Mrs. Greenwood drank the wine. During the meal, Miss Florence Phillips, a friend and neighbour of the Greenwoods, called at Rumsey House. Mrs. Greenwood came out of the dining-room and asked Miss Phillips to supper that evening; she 'looked very ill, and could hardly speak'. After lunch, Mrs. Greenwood retired to her bedroom to rest, and a little later on went into the garden and sat in a deckchair on the lawn. Tea was served in the drawing-room at 4.30 p.m. —nothing, at that time, seemed to be amiss. Certainly Mrs. Greenwood was sufficiently well to go out into the garden again between 5 p.m. and 6 p.m. But at about 6.30 she complained to her husband of pains in the region of her heart. Greenwood gave her brandy; she was very sick. With some difficulty her husband, assisted by Irene, got her upstairs to her bedroom. Greenwood sent for Dr. Thomas Griffiths, who lived opposite, and who had been the Greenwoods' family doctor for the past sixteen years. To Dr. Griffiths, Mrs. Greenwood said that the gooseberry tart had disagreed with her. The doctor directed that she should be put to bed and given sips of brandy and soda-water. Later he sent over a bottle of medicine containing a bismuth mixture. At 7.30 p.m., Miss Phillips arrived for supper. Greenwood told her that his wife was 'very ill'; Miss Phillips at once went for the district nurse, Elizabeth Jones, who lived a short distance away. Nurse Jones arrived at about 8 p.m. She found the patient in a 'serious state of collapse'. Believing that the medicine Dr. Griffiths had sent over was a heart stimulant, she gave Mrs. Greenwood another dose of it—one dose had already been taken. Mrs. Greenwood complained that it 'caught her at the back of the throat'. Dr. Griffiths paid repeated visits during the evening, but throughout the course of Mrs. Greenwood's illness saw nothing inconsistent with a gastric disturbance. Miss Phillips had supper in the dining-room with Greenwood and his daughter Irene. Again it became of importance to know what was drunk with the meal. At Greenwood's trial, Miss Phillips was asked: 'Was there any wine on the table?' To which she replied: 'I know there was no wine on the table. If there had

been, I should have had some.' But Irene Greenwood was also questioned about this when she was giving evidence for her father.

Q: What did you drink for supper yourself?
A: I drank Burgundy.
Q: Was that from the same bottle you got the Burgundy from for
the lunch?
A: Yes.

Irene said that she had offered Miss Phillips the Burgundy, but she had
refused it. Miss Phillips left the house soon after 11 p.m. By 1 o'clock
the next morning, Mrs. Greenwood must have realized that she was
mortally ill, even if the doctor did not. She asked Nurse Jones if she
were going to die, and afterwards the nurse heard her praying. By this
time, the bismuth mixture had been supplemented by some pills which
Dr. Griffiths had prescribed. At the trial a great deal of attention was
paid to these pills and what they had contained. The only thing certain
about them was that after taking them Mrs. Greenwood went into a
coma and never woke again; she died shortly after 3 a.m. Dr. Griffiths
certified that death was due to valvular disease of the heart. Almost at
once the whispers began. Up and down the village street the gossip
eddied and flowed. Suspicion hardened to certainty in many minds
when, within four months of his wife's death, Greenwood married
again. His new bride was Miss Gladys Jones, a woman of over thirty,
belonging to a family well known and respected in Llanelly. Greenwood
had been a friend of the family ever since he had first come to practise
in the town twenty years before. No suggestion that there had been
any guilty or improper association between himself and Miss Jones
during the lifetime of the first Mrs. Greenwood was ever established.
But gossip does not wait for facts—it supplies its own. The village of
Kidwelly had no doubt at all that it knew the truth. The second marriage
took place on 1st October 1919. The newly married couple had scarcely
returned from their honeymoon before Police-Superintendent Samuel
Jones and Inspector Nicholas of Llanelly were calling upon Greenwood
at his office asking him for a statement about the death of his former
wife. On 30th October the police informed him that, having regard to
current rumours, they would have to apply for an order to exhume the
body. 'Just the very thing,' said Greenwood. 'I am quite agreeable.'
It was not until the following April, however, that the remains of Mrs.
Greenwood were exhumed from the grave in Kidwelly churchyard,
where they had lain for more than nine months. The body was found
to contain rather more than a quarter of a grain of arsenic. From this it
was calculated—by Dr. William Willcox, consulting medical adviser

to the Home Office—that a dose of at least two grains had been swallowed by Mrs. Greenwood at least nine hours before she died. In Dr. Willcox's opinion, the arsenic was taken in soluble form, probably between 1.30 p.m. and 6 p.m. on the fatal Sunday. An inquest was held. At the end of it, the jury returned the following verdict: 'We are unanimously of the opinion that the death of the deceased, Mabel Greenwood, was caused by acute arsenical poisoning, as certified by Dr. Willcox, and that the poison was administered by Harold Greenwood.' Greenwood was arrested the same day, and in the following November he appeared in the dock at Carmarthen Assizes, before Mr. Justice Shearman, to answer an indictment charging him with the wilful murder of his first wife. Sir Edward Marlay Sampson K.C. led for the Crown, and Greenwood was defended by Sir Edward Marshall HALL K.C., whose conduct of the case was marked by some highly characteristic 'scenes' between himself, the judge, and opposing counsel. The prosecution emphasized Greenwood's purchases of Eureka weed killer in February and April 1919—purchases which he had made no attempt to conceal or deny. This was shown to contain sixty per cent. arsenic, to be easily soluble, and, *if dissolved in red wine*, not detectable either by taste or colour. Marshall Hall based the defence upon the argument that Mrs. Greenwood died, not from arsenical poisoning, but from the effects of the pills prescribed by Dr. Griffiths. During the police-court hearing, Dr. Griffiths had said that each of the two pills he had given to Mrs. Greenwood had contained half a grain of morphia. Marshall Hall intended to call expert evidence to show that this was a dangerous dose. But at the trial the doctor said that the pills were opium pills, and each had contained only one-fortieth of a grain of morphia. This correction was a sharp blow to the defence, and led to some rough handling of the doctor by Marshall Hall, who did not hesitate to suggest that the so-called bismuth mixture supplied to Mrs. Greenwood had been, in reality, Fowler's solution of arsenic; by 'an unfortunate mistake, colossal in its results', he said, one had been substituted for the other. (The judge, in his summing-up, pointed out that if this were true, Dr. Griffiths would be liable to criminal prosecution, and it would be open to a jury to find him guilty of manslaughter.) However, it was not the attack upon Dr. Griffiths and his supposed negligence which destroyed the case against Harold Greenwood. What did that was Irene Greenwood's calm insistence that she and her mother both drank Burgundy *from the same bottle* at lunch on the Sunday, and that she herself had had another glass of the wine at supper that evening. Mr. Justice Shearman recognized that this was so when, in his summing-up, he said: 'If the daughter partook of the wine, then there is an end to the case.' The jury recognized it, also. They returned a verdict of 'Not

Guilty', and Harold Greenwood went free. He made an abortive attempt to take up his old life again, but his social and professional ruin was complete. Eight years later—on 17th January 1929—he died at Walford, Ross-on-Wye, where, dogged by poverty and ill-health, he had been living under the name of Pilkington.

Greer, Frederick Arthur. *See* Lord FAIRFIELD.

Grondkowski, Marian (thirty-three), and his friend, **Henryk Malinowski** (twenty-five), Polish Army deserters operating in London during the immediate aftermath of the second World War, were profitably engaged in a variety of black market speculations and foreign currency deals. Their partner in these various transactions was an international crook named Reuben Martirosoff, known as 'Russian Robert', a Caucasian by birth, with a prison record in Paris, Berlin, Vienna, Istanbul, and London. On 1st November 1945, between 5 a.m. and 6 a.m., Martirosoff was found lying dead on the back seat of a small saloon car parked near a bombed site in Chepstow Place, Notting Hill, London. He had been shot with a small-calibre revolver at very close range. Police inquiries among Martirosoff's known associates led to the arrest of Grondkowski—whose fingerprints were on the steering-wheel of the car—and later of Malinowski as well. In custody, the two men turned upon each other. Grondkowski described how on the evening of 31st October he and his friend Malinowski had met 'Russian Robert' at Edgware Road underground station, and had gone with him in his car to a public house, where they had discussed projected black market deals. After they had come away from the pub, the car had refused to start. With Martirosoff at the wheel, the two of them had pushed the car for a little way, and it was then, said Grondkowski, that his friend had whispered to him that he was going to 'finish Russian Robert off'. As soon as he had got the car to start, Grondkowski had seated himself next to the driver, whilst Malinowski had clambered into the back. They had driven for only a short distance when Malinowski had whipped out a revolver and had shot 'Russian Robert' through the back of the head. Coerced by threats that if he resisted he would share the same fate, Grondkowski had helped to lift the body into the back of the car. Malinowski had rifled the dead man's pockets, and the pair of them had shared his money between them. Malinowski's account of what had happened did not differ substantially. But there *was* this one important difference—it was Malinowski who had sat in the front seat, and it was Grondkowski who had done the shooting. Grondkowski had asked him to help to lift the body into the back of the car, but he had refused. Thereupon, Grondkowski had done it single-handed. In point of fact, it did not matter which of the two men had fired the shot; in law, they were equally guilty of murder. On New Year's Day 1946, the two men were tried at the Old Bailey. They were found guilty, sentenced to death by Mr. Justice Croom-Johnson, and, in due time, hanged. Rather less than a fortnight before the murder of 'Russian Robert', the body of a man named Frank Everitt had been discovered jammed into a narrow aperture in the wall of a disused National Fire Service pump-house on Lambeth Bridge. He had been shot with a small-calibre revolver at very close range. Everitt, aged fifty-six, a Brixton taxi-driver, had, because of his style of living, been known admiringly as 'The Duke', ironically as 'Honest Fred'. Besides a country house in Gloucestershire, he had a flat in Streatham, another flat in Battersea, and a substantial balance at the bank. Clearly, 'The Duke' had not relied entirely upon his earnings as a taxi-driver. The inference was that he had been an operator in some profitable sector of the black market, which by the end of the war had become an intricate and elaborately organized network of dishonesty. Presently a witness came forward to say that he had seen Everitt pick up two well-dressed men close by the Richard Cœur de Lion statue outside the Houses of Parliament some time after midnight on 18th October. The police were following up this fruitful line of inquiry when the murder of 'Russian Robert' came to light, after which, significantly, the investigation was dropped. Although the connection between the two murders was never formally established, the police were confident that the same two men were responsible for both.

[66, 122.

Gutteridge, Police-Constable George William. *See* Frederick Guy BROWNE.

H

Hail, horrors, hail!

John Milton: *Paradise Lost*

Hadley, Ruth. *See* Edward LAWRENCE.

Hagger, Harold, lorry-driver, was hanged by a yellow string bag—just as surely as by the actual noose which was put around his neck in Wandsworth Prison on 18th March 1947. It was on 31st October 1946 that the body of a middle-aged woman was found strangled on Labour-in-Vain Hill, outside Wrotham, Kent. The body was lying in a clump of bushes at the side of the A20 highway between Maidstone and London. There were no signs of a struggle, which led the police to conclude that the woman had been killed elsewhere. Within a few hours, the dead woman had been identified as Dagmar Petrzywalski—known locally as Dagmar Peters—an eccentric spinster of forty-eight, who had lived by herself in a wooden hut on the Hever Estate at Kingsdown. Her eighty-years-old mother lived close by. She told the police that her daughter had been in the habit of making a weekly visit to London to see her brother, and that she had usually made the thirty-mile trip by 'thumbing a lift' in a passing lorry; she had been engaged upon such an expedition on the morning she had been killed. Miss Peters had set out soon after 5 a.m., intending to hail the first lorry that should happen to come by. Her mother was sure that she must have been carrying, as she always did, an attaché case (with a packet of sandwiches in it) and, just as certainly, a yellow string bag, which one of her sisters-in-law had crocheted for her. But when the body had been found, there had been no trace of either the case or the bag. Chief-Inspector (later Superintendent) Fabian, one of the most brilliant Scotland Yard officers of his time, was put in charge of the investigation. Convinced that the missing string bag was the 'lead' he was looking for, he visited Miss Peters's sister-in-law at Woking. 'Could you crochet another yellow handbag exactly like the first one?' he asked her. She replied, 'If it will help you to get the murderer, I will sit up all night and make it.' In the morning, Chief-Inspector Fabian had in his hands a replica of the bag Miss Peters had been carrying when she had 'thumbed' her last fatal ride. A photograph of it appeared in the evening papers, and was seen by a fifteen-years-old boy named Peter Nash, the son of a farmer at West Malling. He recognized the bag as being identical with one he had fished out of Clare Park Lake three days after the discovery of Miss Peters's body. He had given the bag away, but it was soon traced, and, although it had since been washed, three hairs were clinging to it, one of which was shown to have come from the head of the dead woman. The missing string bag had been found. How had it come to be floating among the weeds on Clare Park Lake, which was separated from A20 by a large field and an eight-foot fence? A local Girl Guide mistress supplied the answer. She described to Fabian how girls in her troop used to amuse themselves by putting messages into bottles and throwing them into the old mill stream at East Malling. A few hours later, the same bottles would be found entangled in the weeds on Clare Park Lake; they had been carried there by an underground stream. The Chief-Inspector visited the mill at East Malling, which had been converted into a cider works. Watched by the village children—'too awed to giggle', as he puts it in his book, *Fabian of the Yard*—he tossed two marked bottles into the stream and watched them vanish under a culvert running beneath the factory. He returned to Clare Park Lake—an hour later he saw the first of the bottles glinting among the weeds. Back went the Chief-Inspector to the mill. This time, he threw into the stream the actual string bag which Miss Peters had been carrying at the time of her death. Three hours later it was found floating at the edge of the lake. In the meantime, torn pieces of what had once been an attaché case had been found scattered by the side of the A20 over a distance of more than a mile. Inquiries now centred upon the cider works. Fabian noticed a pile of bricks. He was told that they had been delivered—on 31st October—by a lorry used by a firm of haulage contractors in Cambridge. The firm supplied the name of the driver—Sydney Sinclair; after a vain attempt at bluff, Sinclair admitted that his real name was Harold Hagger, an 'old lag' with sixteen convictions behind him, including one for an assault upon a woman. This admission was followed by others more damaging. He admitted that Miss Peters had asked him for a lift in his lorry. On the road, she had tried to steal his wallet from his jacket pocket, and this had led to a struggle. 'I didn't mean to kill her,' he said. 'I must have pulled the scarf too tight.' (The 'scarf' was, in actual fact, a woollen vest which Miss Peters was wearing round her neck as a protection against the cold.) Fabian probed the fatal flaw in this artfully contrived story. 'Where was your jacket?' he asked, and Hagger incautiously replied, 'Hung up on a peg inside the cab of the lorry.' Thus, one of the many things he was subsequently required to explain to a sceptical jury at Maidstone Assizes was why he had been driving in his shirt-sleeves at first light on a bitterly cold morning at the end of October! He failed to convince the jury—and paid the penalty at the hands of the hangman.

[59.

Haigh, John George, was the well-spoken, dapper little man with the nice eyes and friendly smile who usually ate by himself in the hotel dining-room. One found it agreeable to exchange a few words with him after dinner. Being a killer who notched up corpses with terrifying facility, he was liable to melt one down in a bath of sulphuric acid, if one possessed any loose capital, or even a few nice pieces of jewellery. But, of course, one did not know that when, amidst the pleasing tinkle of the after-dinner coffee-cups, one bade him 'Good evening' and remarked how mild it was for the time of year. He seemed so very pleasant. That, needless to say, was a gigantic mistake, but it was one easily made, and Mrs. Durand-Deacon made it. Olive Henrietta Helen Olivia Robarts Durand-Deacon, an active, intelligent woman, was the widow of a colonel, who had left her well provided for. In the early part of 1949, when, presuming upon a casual acquaintanceship, she mentioned a small matter of business to the obliging Mr. Haigh, and in so doing signed her death warrant, she was sixty-nine years of age, and had been living for the past six years at the Onslow Court Hotel, Queen's Gate, South Kensington, London. Five people had already shared the fate that was to befall her at the hands of that smiling little man. (Haigh, himself, claimed to have killed three other persons besides, but this was almost certainly untrue; at the time, he was seeking to support a plea of insanity and wished it to be supposed that he had committed more murders than in fact he had.) What manner of man —or monster—was John George Haigh? He was born at Stamford of sturdy Yorkshire stock on 24th July 1909. Both his parents were Plymouth Brethren. Newspapers were not allowed in the house, nor was the wireless; all forms of sport and entertainment were forbidden. Haigh's father, who worked in the Yorkshire coalfield, built a high wall around his garden to shut out the sinful world; it was the symbol of the 'exclusive' character of the religious beliefs of the 'Peculiar People'. The young Haigh lived a life entirely withdrawn, finding in music his only emotional outlet. When, as a pupil at Wakefield Grammar School, he won a choral scholarship which required him to attend the services at Wakefield Cathedral, he was brought into sudden contact with a ritualistic form of religion in violent contrast with the Puritanical austerities of his home. This dichotomy was bound to be disturbing;

Haigh seems to have collapsed under it and other psychological pressures. He left school a congenital liar and cheat and took to crime as a duck to water. In November 1934 he served his first prison sentence—for fraud. In November 1937 he pleaded guilty to an indictment charging him with attempts to obtain money by false pretences, and was sentenced to four years penal servitude. He was released on licence in August 1940, but in the following year he was sent back to prison for stealing. Haigh completed his third sentence in September 1943. In the following year, he acquired a basement at 79 Gloucester Road, Kensington, for use as a workshop. At about the same time he had a chance meeting in a public house with a young man named William Donald McSwan, who confided to Haigh that he planned to 'go underground' to avoid the 'call-up'; soon afterwards he disappeared. Under the date 9th September 1944, Haigh marked his diary with a red cross in crayon. Years later, Haigh provided an explanation of this mysterious entry. He said that the young man had come to the Gloucester Road workshop with a pin-table that needed repair. Haigh had hit him over the head, and had lifted the dead body into a water-butt filled with sulphuric acid; after decomposition, he had poured the residual fluid down a manhole in the basement. To McSwan's parents he had explained that their son had disappeared to avoid military service. In the following year, some time in the early part of July, Haigh killed both the parents, Donald and Amy McSwan, disposing of the bodies by the same method, and then, having exterminated the entire family, proceeded, by means of a forged power of attorney and other devices, to appropriate to his own use everything of which they had died possessed. Altogether, he seems to have enriched himself to the tune of some four thousand pounds. No suspicions were aroused; the disappearance of the McSwan family was never reported to the police. By August 1947 Haigh had run through all the money, having squandered most of it on a singularly unprofitable greyhound racing system. At this time, he had already been living at the Onslow Court Hotel for some two years; he now began negotiations for the purchase of a house, undeterred by the fact that he had no money. It was in this way that he met Dr. Archibald Henderson, a genial Scotsman of fifty, invalided out of the R.A.M.C., and his wife, Rosalie, who had advertised that their house in Ladbroke Grove was for sale. Although his plan to buy the house fell through, Haigh became extremely friendly with the Hendersons. He was now acting as London representative for a firm called Hurstlea Products, with premises in West Street, Crawley, and a storehouse—of which he had the keys—on the outskirts of that agreeable town. In December 1947 he ordered three carboys of sulphuric acid and two 40-gallon drums for delivery at the storehouse, a two-storey building standing on a vacant lot in Leopold Road. In the following February, on some pretext, Haigh persuaded Dr. Henderson to go with him to Crawley. 'Archie was to be the next victim,' Haigh wrote later. 'I drove him to Crawley, and in the storeroom at Leopold Road I shot him in the head. . . . I then returned to Brighton and told Rose that Archie had been taken ill very suddenly and needed her. I said I would drive her to him. She accompanied me to the storeroom at Crawley, and there I shot her.' Both bodies were melted down in sulphuric acid. Haigh's diary for 12th February 1948 contained the laconic entry: 'A.H.' 'R.H.', followed by a red cross. No time was lost in disposing of the Hendersons' property. Haigh sold the doctor's car, forged deeds by which he acquired his house—which he afterwards sold—and, by these and sundry other transactions, cleared something like seven thousand seven hundred pounds. Haigh went through this larger sum even more quickly than he had the smaller. As before, most of it went to bookmakers. By the beginning of 1949 he was substantially in debt, his bank account was overdrawn, and the Onslow Court Hotel was pressing him to settle his long-overdue account. This was Haigh's parlous situation when Mrs. Durand-Deacon, who occupied the adjoining table to his in the hotel dining-room, was foolish enough to mention to him a little idea she had for manufacturing plastic finger-nails. Haigh was most interested, and offered to take Mrs. Durand-Deacon to his 'workshop' at Crawley. On the afternoon of 18th February he drove her there in his car. At the Leopold Road storehouse he shot her in the back of the head, stripped her of her Persian lamb coat and her jewellery, and tipped her body into a 40-gallon metal drum. Having briefly interrupted his horrid work to eat an egg on toast in Ye Olde Ancient Prior's Restaurant in Crawley, he filled the drum with sulphuric acid and went off to dine at the George Hotel. At breakfast at the Onslow Court Hotel the next morning, he approached a fellow-resident, an elderly lady named Mrs. Constance Lane, a close friend of Mrs. Durand-Deacon. He asked her: 'Do you know anything about Mrs. Durand-Deacon? Is she ill? Do you know where she is?' Mrs. Lane said she did not know, adding, rather disturbingly, 'Do not *you* know where she is? I understood from her that you wanted to take her to your factory at Horsham?' Smoothly, Haigh replied, 'Yes, but I was not ready. I had not had lunch, and she said she wanted to go to the Army and Navy Stores, and would I pick her up there?' He had, he said, waited for an hour at the Army and Navy Stores, but Mrs. Durand-Deacon had not turned up. 'Well,' said the disquieting Mrs. Lane, 'I must do something about it.' Later that day, Haigh sold Mrs. Durand-Deacon's watch for £10 to a firm of jewellers at Putney, and sent the Persian lamb coat to a cleaner at Reigate. The next morning at breakfast he went to Mrs. Lane's table again. Had she yet had any news of her friend? Mrs. Lane had not; she intended to report the matter to the police. Later in the morning, Haigh approached Mrs. Lane once more. 'I think we had better go together to the Chelsea Police Station,' he said, and in her gentle way the old lady replied, 'I think so, too.' That afternoon, Haigh drove Mrs. Lane to the police station, where they jointly reported the disappearance of Mrs. Durand-Deacon. Haigh proceeded methodically with the task of collecting the proceeds of his latest killing. He took Mrs. Durand-Deacon's jewellery to Horsham for an expert valuation. He then went on to Crawley, where he looked in at the storeroom, and, finding that the reaction was still not complete, tipped out some sludge from the drum, and replenished it with a fresh supply of acid. The next day he returned to the shop at Horsham, where he had obtained a valuation of the jewellery. There he sold the lot for £100. A further visit to Crawley satisfied Haigh that disintegration was now complete. In the yard outside the storehouse he poured away the whole of the contents of the drum. Since the main facts were never in question at Haigh's trial, it is unnecessary to trace the patient police work by which the whole story was exposed—the tracing of the watch, the jewellery, the fur coat, the finding of pieces of eroded bone, part of a left foot, false teeth, the handle of a red plastic bag, and other fragments in the sludge tipped out in the yard. It is sufficient to say that on 2nd March Haigh was charged with the murder of Mrs. Durand-Deacon; he replied, 'I have nothing to say.' But in the forty-eight hours preceding the charge he had said a very great deal. Of all the things he had said, perhaps the most significant was contained in an apparently casual question he had put to a police officer at Chelsea Police Station on the evening of 28th February. 'Tell me frankly,' he had said. 'What are the chances of anyone being released from Broadmoor?' Later, upon being cautioned, he had said: 'Mrs. Durand-Deacon no longer exists. She has disappeared completely and no trace of her can ever be found again. I have destroyed her with acid. . . . How can you prove murder if there is no body?' He had then made an immensely long and detailed statement describing the murder and disintegration of Mrs. Durand-Deacon, and before her, the McSwans and the Hendersons, and three other persons besides—sketchily identified, and almost certainly imaginary. Haigh insisted that in each case he had drunk a glass of his victim's blood. This gruesome claim formed an important element in the defence of Haigh at his trial, which took place at Lewes Assizes before Mr. Justice HUMPHREYS in July 1949. Insanity was pleaded. Haigh was presented to the jury as a pure paranoic, so far advanced in mental disorder that he conceived himself to be under the control of a guiding spirit whose authority was infinitely superior to that imposed by the ordinary standards and restraints of human society. This defence—conducted by Sir David Maxwell Fyfe K.C. (afterwards Viscount KILMUIR)—was based upon the conclusions of a highly distinguished psychiatrist, Dr. Henry Yellowlees, who in the witness-box discussed the early formative influences in Haigh's home life, which in his opinion encouraged the development of the paranoic condition.

> *Sir David Maxwell Fyfe:* In the statement he made he has given a history, which we have heard, that in each case, as he put it, he 'tapped' the victim and drank some blood. What do you feel as to the truth or otherwise of that statement?
>
> *Dr. Yellowlees:* I think it pretty certain that he tasted it; I do not know whether he drank it or not. From a medical point of view I do not think it is important, for the reason that this question of blood runs through all his fantasies from childhood like a motif and is the core of the paranoic structure that I believe he has created, and it does not matter very much to a paranoic whether he does things in fancy or in fact.

The Attorney-General, Sir Hartley (afterwards Lord) SHAWCROSS K.C., who appeared for the Crown, put this to the doctor: 'I am asking you to look at the facts and tell the jury whether there is any doubt that he must have known that, according to English law, he was preparing to do, and subsequently had done, something which was wrong?'

> *Dr. Yellowlees:* I will say 'Yes' to that if you say 'punishable by law' instead of 'wrong'.
>
> *Sir Hartley Shawcross:* Punishable by law and, therefore, wrong by the law of this country?
>
> *Dr. Yellowlees:* Yes, I think he knew that.

Bearing in mind what had to be proved to satisfy the criterion of the M'NAGHTEN RULES, that answer was fatal to a defence of insanity. The jury took only a quarter of an hour to decide upon a verdict of 'Guilty'. Haigh was executed at Wandsworth Prison on 6th August.
  [*I.*

Hall, Sir Edward Marshall, K.C. (1858-1927). The late Lord Birkenhead once remarked that no one *could* be as splendid as Marshall Hall looked. It is unlikely that a more handsome man ever practised at the Bar, or one with a more magnificent presence. He was six feet three inches tall, proportionately broad, with the figure and gait of an athlete, a nobly shaped head, silver hair curling at the temples, aquiline features, a pair of fine penetrating eyes, his whole appearance giving the impression of a man of quite remarkable vitality, buoyancy, and power. Right up to the end, after forty-four years in practice at the Bar, he retained, undimmed, his naïve enthusiasm, youthful optimism, and innocent zest; he never quite grew up. In so many ways he was rather more than lifesize. His emotions were bigger, his impulses more generous, his sympathies wider, his knowledge of men and women more profound. His heart, as they say, was as big as a house. All this had its reverse side, which at one stage in his career almost ruined him. His biographer, the late Mr. Edward Marjoribanks, wrote in his *Life of Sir Edward Marshall Hall*: 'The advocate must have a quick mind, an understanding heart, and charm of personality. . . . Moreover, he must have the power of expressing himself clearly and attractively to simple people, so that they will listen to him and understand him. He must, then, be histrionic, crafty, courageous, eloquent, quick-minded, charming, great-hearted. These are the salient qualities which go to make a great advocate, and Marshall Hall possessed them all to such a marked degree that he became the best-known advocate of the day, *despite other characteristics which would have meant certain failure to a lesser man*.' (Italics supplied.) Those 'other characteristics' were a violence of temper which seemed, sometimes, to be quite outside his power to control, and an uncertainty of judgment which inclined him towards the most absurd indiscretions. These are grave defects in an advocate, and such reverses as befell him in the course of his brilliant career were entirely due to them—to his hot temper, in particular. This led him into fiery altercations with the Bench and, more rarely, with opposing counsel. Most of those 'scenes'— which later became much less frequent—had their origin in Marshall Hall's extraordinary facility for identifying himself, heart and soul, with his clients and with his clients' interests; it was truly said that the client who briefed him did not simply hire an advocate—he bought the whole man. What eloquence he had, what an astonishing flow of language! No doubt those great speeches of his to the jury would be thought old-fashioned today. In cold print, they sometimes look bombastic, sentimental, overblown. That was not how they appeared to those who were in court to hear them. To the words were added the charm and magic of that golden voice, above all the passionate earnestness with which they were spoken. His speeches were emotional, of course they were—Marshall Hall was an extremely emotional person. Often, as he addressed the jury, the tears would be coursing down his cheeks. They were genuine tears. That does not mean, of course, that he was entirely unaware of the effect they were likely to have upon a susceptible jury. There was, undeniably, a great deal of the actor in him. 'I have no scenery to help me', he would say, 'and no words are written for me to speak. . . . There is no curtain. But out of the vivid dream of somebody else's life I have to *create an atmosphere*—for that is advocacy.' Frankly, as a lawyer, he did not amount to very much. Indeed, he made no secret of his ignorance of the law, was inclined to leave difficult legal points to his juniors, dreaded the Court of Appeal, and only once appeared in the House of Lords. As Mr. Marjoribanks notes: 'Of all leading counsel, his name was most frequently in the newspapers, and most rarely in the official law reports.' This was inevitable, since for the whole of his professional life Marshall Hall practised almost exclusively in the criminal courts, and appeared in many of the most famous murder trials of the day. Thus, unlike Chancery lawyers, who are seldom in the public eye, Marshall Hall was never out of it; he was always the darling of the Press. Whatever lawyers of superior learning might say of him, there was no doubt about his fame and popularity with the public; these have never been equalled, or even approached. To them he was 'The Great Defender'. So he remained until that February day in 1927, when, worn out by the day-to-day strenuous practice of his profession, and having no strength left to withstand influenza that developed into bronchitis, and finally into pneumonia, his great heart ceased to beat. On the day he died they flew the flag over the Middle Temple at half-mast. It was the last tribute of the lawyers to the 'Rupert of the Bar'. Edward Marshall Hall was born in Brighton on 16th September 1858, the son of Dr. Alfred Hall, a well-known local physician. After leaving Rugby, he was employed as a clerk by a firm of tea merchants in Mincing Lane, but within a few months he had exchanged his office stool for a place at St. John's College, Cambridge, where he took a pass degree in 1882. In the following year, he was called to the Bar by the Inner Temple, and began to practise at the Old Bailey and the Middlesex Sessions; he took silk in 1898. In the General Election of 1900, he was returned as Conservative M.P. for Southport, but, like many another eminent lawyer, he was never much of a success in the House of Commons, and it is somewhat surprising that after his narrow defeat in the General Election of 1906 he should have troubled to stand again. He did so, however, at a by-election in the East Toxteth division of Liverpool in January 1910, and found himself an M.P. once more; in the General Election of the following November he increased his majority. He gave up his seat in 1916, and was knighted in the following year. Marshall Hall died 'in harness'. In January 1927 he was appearing in a case before the Recorder at the Quarter Sessions in Derby when he fell ill. He returned to London at the week-end during the hearing of the case, intending to go back on the Monday. But on the Sunday—16th January—he took to his bed. He never left it again; at about midnight on 23rd February he died. Mr. Marjoribanks, in his fascinating *Life*, wrote his epitaph: 'There was something noble about him. He was the last of his kind; his mantle has fallen on no successor.' Men and women he defended in capital cases included Herbert John BENNETT; Edward LAW-RENCE; Frederick Henry SEDDON; Jeannie BAXTER; George Joseph SMITH; Harold GREENWOOD; Frederick Rothwell (Eric) HOLT; Madame FAHMY; Lock Ah TAM; and Alfonso SMITH. He was also associated with Sir Patrick HASTINGS K.C. in the prosecution of Jean Pierre VAQUIER.

Hall, Julian Bernard. *See* Jeannie BAXTER.

Hallett, Sir Hugh Imbert Perriam (*b.* 1886). Judge of the Queen's Bench Division of the High Court since February 1939. Called by the Inner Temple in 1911, his career at the Bar, where he enjoyed a considerable Common Law practice, was interrupted by five years military service during, and immediately after, the first World War; he was raised to the Bench a few months before the outbreak of the second. Mr. Justice Hallett presided, *inter alia*, over the trials of JENKINS, GERAGHTY and ROLT; and George RUSSELL.

Hamilton, Evelyn Margaret. *See* Gordon Frederick CUMMINS.

Hastings, Sir Patrick, K.C. (1880-1952). For at least thirty of the fifty years covered by this book, Patrick Hastings was a great and glittering figure at the Bar, where he will long be remembered as one of the greatest of jury advocates. His sharply distinctive style reflected the coolness, the poise, the sardonic undertones of a highly sophisticated person. Mr. Edgar Lustgarten, in his book, *Defender's Triumph*, points out:

> More than any other counsel of comparable eminence, Hastings was a sophisticated advocate—in fashionable practice when fashionable people were setting new standards in advanced sophistication. Sophisticated people do not care for strident emphasis; they stand on guard against assaults on the emotions; they like effects to be subtle and power to be concealed. In the language of the theatre, they prefer to have their dramas underplayed. Hastings introduced, or, at any rate, perfected, the art of underplaying in the English jury courts.

It was this which gave his famous cross-examinations their especial flavour; it was this which added an extra touch of distinction to his arguments, always elegantly deployed, and expressed with wonderful clarity. Born in 1880, the son of a solicitor, he was educated at Charterhouse, but his father fell on evil days, and on leaving school at sixteen, young Hastings was thrown on the world to make his way as best he could. For a time he worked as a navvy on an engineering site in North Wales; then he enlisted in the Army and fought as a trooper in the South African war. Being invalided home, he found his way into journalism, and managed out of his slender earnings in Fleet Street to save up the fees he needed to read for the Bar. In 1904 he was called by the Middle Temple. But the newcomer was unnoticed. Briefs were few and far between. Somehow he held on. In 1906 he was given the opportunity to enter the chambers of Mr. Horace AVORY. It was a turning-point. From that time forward things began to go right for him. Soon he possessed one of the biggest junior practices on the Common Law side, thus proving once again that a slow starter is often a good finisher. In 1919 he took silk and in 1922 entered the House of Commons as Labour M.P. for Wallsend. When Mr. Ramsay MacDonald formed his first Government in 1923, Patrick Hastings was the obvious choice for Attorney-General. His political life was brief, and ended in bitterness and disillusionment. In 1924, as Senior Law Officer of the Crown, he authorized the prosecution of Mr. John Ross Campbell, Communist editor of the *Worker's Weekly*, who had written for his paper an article which was alleged to be an incitement to disaffection among the armed forces. The Prime Minister, however, yielding to pressure from the left wing of his party, agreed to withdraw the charges against Campbell, and in so doing repudiated the action of the Attorney-General. Out of this episode came the downfall of the Labour Government. Hastings considered, with some reason, that he had been shabbily treated by MacDonald; he was deeply wounded by the episode, which effectively disabused him of any illusions he might have had about the ways of politicians. It was with a sense of relief that he returned to private practice at the Bar. In 1926 he gave up his seat in Parliament and took no further part in politics for the rest of his life. Thereafter, his interests were divided between the Bar, the theatre, and the fashionable life. He wrote for the stage with great facility and skill, and had at least two considerable successes—*Scotch Mist* and *The Blind Goddess*. Hastings retired in 1948; his health had already begun to deteriorate, and on 26th February 1952 he died, being then in his seventy-second year. As Attorney-General, Patrick Hastings led for the Crown against Jean Pierre VAQUIER. He defended John WILLIAMS; Mrs. Elvira BARNEY; and Ludomir CIENSKI.

Hawke, Sir Edward Anthony (*b.* **1896**). Recorder of the City of London since 1959. Son of Mr. Justice (John Anthony) HAWKE, he was called to the Bar by the Middle Temple in 1920; practised on the Western Circuit and at Devon Sessions. In 1932 he was appointed a junior Treasury counsel at the Old Bailey; promoted Senior Prosecuting Counsel for the Crown, 1945-7. In 1954 he became Common Serjeant of the City of London, and in 1959 Recorder, in the place of Sir Gerald Dodson. He led for the Crown in many notable murder trials, including those of Neville HEATH; Arthur Robert BOYCE; LEY and SMITH; JENKINS, GERAGHTY, and ROLT; and Donald George THOMAS.

Hawke, Sir John Anthony (**1869-1941**). Judge of the King's Bench Division of the High Court (1928-41). This burly Cornishman, being immensely kind, friendly, and companionable, was held in great affection by his colleagues on the Bench and at the Bar. Everything about him was attractive, even his pomposity, for his was such an open, ingenuous nature that what in other men would have been considered a trial and an irritation seemed in him to be an endearing, and even lovable, trait. He was not a profound lawyer, perhaps, but he possessed one shining quality which has sometimes been lacking in others whose claims to be remembered as great judges are otherwise far superior—he had a passionate love of justice, and strove to the limit of his capabilities to see that justice was done. On the Bench, his most conspicuous weakness—and even this charmed rather than exasperated—was a tendency he could seldom resist to hold up the business of his Court while he exchanged amiable reminiscences with counsel about past times and forgotten faces. Those who had business at the Law Courts in the 1930s will recall the characteristic attitude of Mr. Justice Hawke on the Bench, where he was usually to be seen leaning on his right elbow, holding up to his round, florid, amiable face an enormous white handkerchief rolled into a ball; for very many it will be an affectionate memory. John Anthony Hawke was called to the Bar by the Middle Temple in 1892, joined the Western Circuit a year later, and took silk in 1913. In 1923, he succeeded Sir Douglas Hogg (afterwards the first Viscount Hailsham) as Attorney-General to the Prince of Wales. Twice he sat in the House of Commons as Conservative M.P. for St. Ives, first in 1922-3, and again from 1924 until 1928, when he was appointed a judge of the King's Bench Division of the High Court. Mr. Justice Hawke died 'in harness', as no doubt he would have wished. On Wednesday, 29th October 1941, he opened the Essex Assizes at Chelmsford. The following morning he was found dead in his bed at the Judge's Lodgings. Murder trials over which he presided included that of James Thomas COLLINS.

Healy, Maurice, K.C. (1887-1943). This massive, genial Irishman, connoisseur of music, wine, and wit, lover of the good things of life, nephew of 'Tim' Healy, first Governor-General of the Irish Free State, embodied in his own person, which was considerable, all the legendary charm of the Southern Irish. Good talk was his passion, as it is of so many Irishmen, and his own contribution to the wise, witty, discursive conversation in which he delighted was heightened by a rich brogue and by a gift of picturesque expression which called to mind a character in Synge or Sean O'Casey—Joxer Daly would have thought him a 'darlin' man'. An incomparable raconteur, some of his most delightful stories are on permanent record in his book, *The Old Munster Circuit*, just as his love and knowledge of wine are preserved in the pages of *Stay Me With Flagons* and *Claret and the White Wines of Bordeaux*, two notable additions to the literature of the subject. His was a warm, rich personality; the profession of the law has produced many such, but none more civilized or more gratefully remembered than Maurice Healy. He was born on 19th November 1887, was called to the Irish Bar at Dublin in 1910, and to the English Bar by Gray's Inn four years later. He was only fifty-five when he died—on 9th May 1943. Murder trials in which he appeared included those of Frederick NODDER; and Leslie George STONE.

Hearn, Sarah Ann, emerged in 1931 from the total obscurity of a hard, penurious life into the fierce white light of a trial for murder. She was found 'Not Guilty', and bruised and shaken from her savage ordeal she retreated once more into an anonymity never afterwards disturbed. She was born at Market Rasen in Lincolnshire, the daughter of a farmer, but little of her early life came to light at the trial. She was not even sure of her age, although she believed she must be 'over forty'. Her marriage was even more conjectural. The Court had her word for it that she had been married to an electrician named Leonard Wilmot Hearn in 1919; he had left her with indecent haste, since when she had heard nothing of him and regarded herself as a widow. The Court was concerned with Mrs. Hearn only from 1925 onwards, in which year she and her sister, Lydia Mary (Minnie) Everard, came to live at Trenhorne House, Lewannick, Cornwall. Miss Everard was an invalid, having been for most of her life a martyr to gastric troubles; her sister, Sarah Ann, tended her with every appearance of loving solicitude. The two sisters were badly off, and were sometimes hard put to it to make ends meet. Presently they became very friendly with a local farmer, Mr. William Henry Thomas, and his wife, Alice Maud, of Trenhorne Farm, from whom they received much kindness and many favours. In May 1930, Miss Everard's health, always precarious, began to give even graver cause for anxiety. Complaining that the medicine she was taking was 'too strong' for her, and that it was 'going into her hands and legs', she told the doctor she thought she was being poisoned by it. 'Oh, Minnie,' exclaimed Mrs. Hearn, 'how could you say such a thing?' By summer, Miss Everard's condition had declined still further, and on 21st July she died from chronic gastric catarrh and colitis; such was the opinion of her doctor. Three months later—on 18th October 1930—Mrs. Hearn accompanied her friends Mr. and Mrs. Thomas on a drive to Bude, where they had tea at a café. Tea, bread and butter, and cakes were ordered, and, as an additional delicacy, Mrs. Hearn produced some tinned salmon sandwiches she had brought with her. Each of the three ate a sandwich. Afterwards, Mrs. Thomas complained of a 'sweety taste' in her mouth, and on the way back to Lewannick she was extremely sick; reaching home, she had to be helped up to bed. Dr. Saunders, who was called in, found her to be suffering from cramp in the legs and pain in the abdomen; her pulse was rapid. The doctor was told about the sandwiches and formed the opinion that his patient was suffering from food poisoning. Both Mr. Thomas and the patient herself pressed Mrs. Hearn to stay at the farm and help with the nursing. For the next eleven days, Mrs. Hearn was in charge of the sick room, and did the cooking as well. When Mrs. Thomas's mother, Mrs. Parsons, arrived on 29th October, Mrs. Hearn still remained at Trenhorne Farm, sharing the cooking, although no longer in direct attendance upon the patient. Mrs. Thomas was quite helpless. On 31st October her husband carried her downstairs, and again on 2nd November, when, after eating leg of mutton at lunch, she was violently ill. The next day her condition was such that Dr. Saunders advised a consultation. Dr. William Alexander Lister, consultant to the Plymouth City Hospital, was called in, and diagnosed arsenical poisoning. Mrs. Thomas was removed to hospital, and died there the next morning, 4th November. There was an unpleasant scene after Mrs. Thomas's funeral, when a brother of the dead woman asked Mrs. Hearn some pointed questions about the tinned salmon sandwiches, and added the sinister remark, 'This must be looked into.' Mrs. Hearn now returned to her own home. On 10th November Mr. Thomas received the following letter from her:

Dear Mr. Thomas,
    Good-bye. I am going out if I can. I cannot forget that awful man and the things he said. I am *innocent, innocent,* but she is dead and it was my lunch she eat. I cannot bear it. When I'm dead they will be sure I am guilty, and you, at least, will be cleared. May your dear wife's presence guard and comfort you still. Yours, A.H.

Mrs. Hearn disappeared after writing this letter, and nothing more was
seen or heard of her for several weeks, despite a nationwide hue-and-cry.
Then, on 12th January 1931, Mrs. Hearn was accosted by a police
officer in the street at Torquay, where, under a false name, she had
obtained a situation as a general servant. Whilst she had been away, the
body of her sister, Miss Everard, had been exhumed in Lewannick
churchyard—on 9th December. About three-quarters of a grain of
arsenic had been found in the organs of the body. In the case of Mrs.
Thomas, analysis had detected the presence in the body of ·85 grains.
On 15th June 1931 Mrs Hearn was indicted before Mr. Justice (afterwards Lord) ROCHE at Bodmin Assizes. Although the indictment
referred only to the murder of Mrs. Thomas, the judge ruled that
evidence touching upon the death of Miss Everard was admissible. A
terrible ordeal was in front of Mrs. Hearn, but in facing her accusers,
the lonely woman in the dock was sustained by the knowledge that
she had on her side the forensic skill of one of the greatest jury
advocates of the day, Mr. Norman (afterwards Lord) BIRKETT K.C.
The Crown case was that Alice Maud Thomas had been poisoned by
arsenic in the sandwich she had eaten at Bude on 18th October, and
that at some time before 29th October, when her mother took over the
nursing from Mrs. Hearn, she had been given a second dose. It was
shown that Mrs. Hearn had bought a weed killer from a local chemist
in 1926; this had contained seventy per cent. of white arsenic, and a
few grains could easily have been used in the form of a solution. It was
further alleged that over a period of seven months Mrs. Hearn had
administered arsenic to her sister, with intent to kill her. An important
witness for the prosecution was Mr. Thomas, but Mr. Birkett elicited
from him in cross-examination several points which told strongly in
Mrs. Hearn's favour, particularly in regard to the salmon sandwich:

> *Q:* There was no pushing of the plate or juggling with the sand-
> wiches?
> *A:* No, there was no juggling at all.
> *Q:* No particular sandwich was pressed upon anybody?
> *A:* No.

A valuable admission was drawn from the doctor who had conducted
the exhumation of Miss Everard's body. It had come to Mr. Birkett's
knowledge that, because of local tin deposits, *every yard* of soil in
Lewannick churchyard contained more arsenic than had been found
in Miss Everard's body. He dealt with the point in this way:

> *Q:* You know we are dealing with very minute quantities of
> arsenic?

A: Yes.

Q: You know, do you not, that in the soil over the grave there were 125 parts per million of arsenic?

A: Yes.

Q: Am I right in saying that a piece of soil so small that you could hold it between your fingers dropped on to this body would make every single calculation wrong?

A: Yes.

That 'Yes' represented an admission of incalculable help to Mrs. Hearn. Not until the cross-examination of the accused, who made a good and consistent witness in her own behalf, was any mention made of a possible motive for the murder of Mrs. Thomas. In the last question put to her by prosecuting counsel the suggestion plainly appeared, and was emphatically denied:

Q: Did it occur to you that if at any time Mrs. Thomas died, Mr. Thomas might have made a match of it with you?

A: No, never.

Instantly, Mr. Birkett was on his feet to re-examine:

Q: Mrs. Hearn, until this moment has anyone in the world suggested that you wanted to marry Mr. Thomas?

A: No.

In his closing speech to the jury, Mr. Birkett submitted that if there had been weed killer in the salmon sandwiches it would have stained the bread blue. This must have been very much in the judge's mind when, in his summing-up, Mr. Justice Roche said: 'The sandwiches are the very kernel of this case. If you are not satisfied that the arsenic was put in the sandwich by Mrs. Hearn, then you should acquit her.' After a retirement of fifty-four minutes, the jury returned to the court with a verdict of 'Not Guilty'. There remained the indictment of Mrs. Hearn for the murder of her sister. The Crown offered no evidence upon this and, as instructed by the judge, the jury entered a formal verdict of 'Not Guilty'.

[*30, 55, 206.*

Heath, George Edward. *See* Elizabeth Maud JONES.

Heath, Neville George Clevely, was drinking and dancing at the Panama Club, South Kensington, London, on the night of 20th June

1946, with a Mrs. Margery Annie Brownell Gardner, a woman of thirty-two, and of easy virtue. At about midnight they left the club together and went by taxi-cab to the Pembridge Court Hotel in Pembridge Gardens, Notting Hill. At 2 o'clock the following afternoon a chambermaid knocked on the door of Heath's room and, getting no answer, went in. Lying on one of the two beds, under the bedclothes, was the naked body of Margery Gardner. She had been suffocated, apparently with a pillow, and before death had been savagely maltreated. Her body bore the weals of seventeen lashes with a whip; her nipples had been practically bitten off, her private parts brutally lacerated with some implement. Her ankles were bound with a handkerchief, and although her hands were free there were marks on the wrists which suggested that these, too, had been tied together. It was probable that she had also been gagged, since no one in the hotel had heard any noise during the night. At the time this hideous discovery was made, 'Lieutenant-Colonel Heath', as he called himself, was a long way from the Pembridge Court Hotel. He was in Worthing, where he had engaged a room at the Ocean Hotel; that evening he was dining and dancing at the Blue Peter Club in Angmering. Two days later—on Sunday, 23rd June—he wrote this letter to Superintendent William Barratt at Scotland Yard:

Sir,

I feel it my duty to inform you of certain facts in connection with the death of Mrs. Gardner at Notting Hill Gate. I booked in at the hotel last Sunday, but not with Mrs. Gardner, whom I met for the first time during the week. I had drinks with her on Friday evening, and whilst I was with her she met an acquaintance with whom she was obliged to sleep. The reasons, as I understood them, were mainly financial. It was then that Mrs. Gardner asked if she could use my hotel room until 2 o'clock and intimated that if I returned after that, I might spend the remainder of the night with her. I gave her my keys and told her to leave the hotel door open. It must have been almost 3 a.m. when I returned to the hotel and found her in the condition of which you are aware. I realized that I was in an invidious position and rather than notify the police I packed my belongings and left. Since then I have been in several minds whether to come forward or not, but in view of the circumstances I was afraid to. . . . I have the instrument with which Mrs. Gardner was beaten and am forwarding this to you today. You will find my fingerprints on it, but you should also find others as well.

N. G. C. Heath

(Heath did not, in fact, 'forward the instrument' as he had promised.) Leaving Worthing, he travelled on to Bournemouth, where under the guise of 'Group-Captain Rupert Brooke' he had engaged a room at the Tollard Royal Hotel. On Wednesday, 3rd July, after he had been in Bournemouth for ten days, he made the acquaintance of a Miss Doreen Marshall, who had recently been in the W.R.N.S. and was convalescing at the Norfolk Hotel, following an attack of influenza. He took her to tea at the Tollard Royal Hotel, and that same evening she dined there with him. Afterwards, they sat in the lounge until shortly after midnight, at which time Heath appeared to be rather the worse for drink. Miss Marshall looked pale and distressed. She asked someone staying in the hotel to call her a taxi, but this was counter-manded by Heath, who said that Miss Marshall preferred to walk. They then left the hotel together, Heath remarking to the night porter that he would be back in half an hour. 'No, in a quarter of an hour,' Miss Marshall corrected. Some time later, Heath came back to the hotel. The time of his return is not known, since he did not use the front door, but got into his second-floor room by scaling a ladder which was leaning against the wall. He did this, he said afterwards, to play a joke upon the porter. Miss Marshall did not return to the Norfolk Hotel. Her absence, however, was not remarked until Friday, 5th July, when the manager notified the police that she was missing. On that day, Heath telephoned a Bournemouth police station, and the next morning he called there and identified Miss Marshall's photograph as that of the girl who had dined with him on the previous Wednesday. He was recognized as the man whose photograph and description had been circulated to police forces all over the country in connection with the murder and mutilation of Mrs. Gardner, and he was detained, pending further inquiries. On the evening of Monday, 8th July, the body of Doreen Marshall was discovered under some rhododendron bushes in a lonely part of Branksome Chine. She was naked except for her left shoe. Like poor Margery Gardner, she had been mutilated, and in the same hideous fashion, although instead of being wealed with a whip, the body had been slashed four times with a knife. The cause of death was a deep cut in the throat. Heath made a statement to the police in which he said that on the Wednesday night he had walked part of the way with Miss Marshall, but had left her at the pier, where he had watched her cross the road and enter the gardens. When Heath was tried at the Old Bailey before Mr. Justice Morris in the following September, it was on an indictment charging him only with the murder of Mrs. Gardner. No mention was made of Miss Marshall by the prosecution; it was Mr. J. D. CASSWELL K.C., representing Heath, who brought out the facts of that case, since, to support a plea of 'partial insanity', it was necessary, or at least desirable, to make it clear to the jury that the man in the dock had killed two women, not one. The medical evidence called to sustain this defence and, later, to rebut it, is of the greatest interest. Mr. Casswell called Dr. William Henry De Bargue Hubert, a leading specialist in psychiatry, who said that while there was nothing to suggest 'ordinary insanity', Heath was, in his view, 'certifiable as morally insane'. The injuries inflicted upon both women were 'extremely savage and of a nature which could almost certainly only be done by a sadist'. Dr. Hubert thought that in committing these terrible acts Heath had appreciated what he was doing, but not that it was wrong. Dr. Hubert did not stand up with conspicuous success to the skilful cross-examination of prosecuting counsel, Mr. (Edward) Anthony HAWKE, who afterwards became Recorder of the City of London. The following passage indicates the tone and character of the exchanges between counsel and witness:

> *Q:* At the time he was inflicting those injuries he thought it was right?
>
> *A:* Yes, he thought it was right.
>
> *Q:* Did he think it was right, in your opinion, because he is a perverted sadist?
>
> *A:* Yes.
>
> *Q:* Because he could only obtain his sexual satisfaction by inflicting cruelty, you say he thought it was right to inflict it, do you?
>
> *A:* Yes, I do.
>
> *Q:* Is that your answer, Dr. Hubert?
>
> *A:* Well, he was doing what he wished to do.
>
> *Q:* I asked if that was your answer?
>
> *A:* If you like, yes.
>
> *Q:* That inasmuch as he desired to satisfy a perverted lust he thought it was right to satisfy it?
>
> *A:* Yes.
>
> *Q:* Are you saying, with your responsibility, standing there, that a person in that frame of mind is free from criminal responsibility if what he does causes grievous bodily harm?
>
> *A:* At the time, yes.
>
> *Q:* Would it be your view that a person who finds it convenient at the moment to forge a cheque in order to free himself from financial responsibility is entitled to say that he thought it was right, and therefore he is free from the responsibility of what he does?
>
> *A:* He may think so, yes.
>
> *Q:* Do you say that a person who has been proved to commit

forgery for the purpose of improving his financial stability is entitled to claim insanity within the M'NAGHTEN RULES as a defence?

A: I think he does it because he has no strong sense of right and wrong at all.

Q: With great respect, Dr. Hubert, I did not ask you what he thought. I asked you whether you thought he was entitled to claim exemption from responsibility on the ground of insanity?

A: Yes, I do. I think that if a man commits crimes in most fields and then the most peculiar and horrible crime and crimes, he does consider he is entitled to do so.

Dr. Hubert's remark about a man who commits 'crimes in most fields' was a reference to Heath's past record. This was restricted mainly to convictions for fraudulently obtaining credit, housebreaking, theft, obtaining goods by a forged banker's order. He had been three times court-martialled during his service career, which was first with the R.A.F., then with the R.A.S.C., and, towards the end of the war, again with the R.A.F. Three times he had been commissioned, three times dismissed the service. There was also a conviction against him for unlawfully wearing military uniform and bogus decorations. The prosecution sought to rebut Dr. Hubert's evidence by calling Dr. Hugh Arrowsmith Grierson, Senior Medical Officer at Brixton Prison, who said he did not consider Heath insane, although perverted and sadistic. Under cross-examination, Dr. Grierson agreed that Heath was a psychopathic personality and 'a most abnormal individual'.

Mr. Casswell: The man who did that sort of thing must have been a most abnormal sort of man?

Dr. Grierson: Yes, I have never yet said that any murderer is normal.

Dr. Grierson would not agree that a psychopath was a person suffering from a disease of the mind. 'It is a disorder,' he said. 'It is temperamental character—abnormality of character and temperament . . . an abnormal state of character, really.' The jury resolved the conflict of medical evidence for themselves by bringing in a verdict of 'Guilty', and Heath was sentenced to death. That sentence was carried out at Pentonville Prison on 26th October.

[*I.*

Hefeld, Paul, and a man named **Jacob Meyer,** both of them Russians, were engaged in a running fight with the police on the northern outskirts of London, which for reckless desperation and sheer ferocity is eclipsed in the criminal history of this country only by the more famous SIEGE OF SIDNEY STREET three years later. This extraordinary episode began at 9.30 a.m. on 24th January 1909, outside Messrs. Schurmann's rubber factory in Chesnut Road, Tottenham. At that hour, a young clerk, Arthur Keyworth, returned from the bank in a motor car with the week's wages, amounting to £80 in golden sovereigns, silver, and bronze. As he made to enter the factory, Hefeld and Meyer, who had been lying in wait for him, stepped forward and grabbed the money, which was in a large canvas bag. The chauffeur of the car leapt from his seat. At once the two desperadoes, both of whom were armed with revolvers, opened fire; one bullet seared the man's coat, another took off his cap. Under cover of these first reckless shots, the two men made off. Police-Constables William Frederick Tyler and Albert Newman rushed from the police station some forty yards away, jumped into the car and set out in pursuit. A passer-by threw himself in Hefeld's path—and received a bullet wound in the head, fortunately not fatal. But by now the thieves had lost the advantage of their quick start, and the pursuing car was close at their heels. With amazing calmness, Hefeld turned, rested his gun on his left arm, and fired shot after shot at the oncoming car; one of the bullets shattered the windscreen, another pierced the radiator. Both policemen jumped out of the car, to continue the chase on foot, followed by an excited crowd. As they ran the two men continued to shoot. A fifteen-years-old boy named Ralph John Joscelyn, who had come running up to see what all the commotion was about, strayed into the line of fire and fell dead. P.C. Tyler, who was gaining on the thieves, shouted, 'Give it up—the game's over!' Whereupon, Hefeld turned in his tracks, sighted with care, and shot the constable through the head, killing him instantly. P.C. Newman, himself hit in the cheek with a bullet, helped to carry his comrade into a neighbouring house. Meanwhile, a great force of police, many of them armed, summoned by telephone and telegraph from stations all over north London and further afield, began to converge upon Tottenham marshes and along the banks of the River Lea. They were reinforced by following crowds, which by now had grown to immense proportions. Men on horseback, in motor cars, on bicycles, and in horse-traps, joined in the chase; an omnibus was requisitioned and loaded with policemen. The pursuit went on. A policeman was shot in the leg, a boy was wounded, a workman who threw a brick at the fugitives was shot down. (From first to last, no fewer than sixteen persons were injured.) Hefeld was clearly an expert shot, so much the superior of the other man that most of the firing was left to him, Meyer contenting himself for the most part with reloading the revolver and handing it back to his companion. The most dramatic point of the chase was reached in the Chingford Road, where the desperadoes held up an electric tramcar at pistol point. Chased upstairs by a spatter of bullets, the driver took refuge on the upper deck. The men boarded the tram. Hefeld put his revolver at the conductor's head and ordered him to drive. One of the passengers, an elderly man, threw himself at Meyer —and was shot in the neck. (The only other occupants were a woman and her child, who were huddled in terror on the floor.) As the tram, driven by the conductor under threat, gathered speed, clanging and swaying over the track, Meyer opened a fierce fire upon the pursuers from the rear platform. Police officers jumped into a trap which was standing at the kerbside and whipped up the horse. A minute later the animal was shot down and the occupants of the trap were thrown into the road. In the meantime, a tramcar going in the opposite direction was stopped by the police further back along the road, put into reverse, and sent in headlong pursuit after the other tram, from which the bullets sprayed in a continual fusillade. The frenzied ride was brought to an end when a motor car was put broadside-on in front of the tram, forcing it to a halt. Hefeld and Meyer leaped out, shot down a milkman, and drove off in his cart. This they crashed into a wall. They then commandeered a greengrocer's cart, but it was secured by a chain brake, and although the two men lashed the horse to exhaustion they could make little headway against their leading pursuers, who were rapidly closing in upon them. At last, the two men abandoned the cart. They were now in desperate straits. A party of sportsmen with shotguns had joined in the chase, and were firing at them from a motor car. They took to the fields, but they were nearly exhausted, and for Hefeld the end came when he found his escape cut off by a high fence topped with barbed-wire. Meyer managed to get over, but the other had no strength left; failing to find a foothold, he collapsed on the ground. A police sergeant on a bicycle was in the van of the chase, but before he could reach him, Hefeld put his revolver to his own head, and with his last remaining cartridge tried to blow out his brains. He succeeded only in inflicting a head wound; it turned out, however, to be a fatal injury, and he died in hospital nineteen days later. Meyer, in the meantime, had taken refuge in a four-roomed cottage occupied by a coalman— Charles Rolston and his wife and their young family. He got in through the back door, which he locked behind him, whilst Mrs. Rolston, gathering her youngest child in her arms, ran screaming out of the front door. Meyer tried to hide himself in the kitchen chimney, but it was too small, so he ran upstairs and shut himself in the front bedroom. He incautiously showed himself at the window, but retreated hastily when a volley of police bullets knocked all the glass out of the frame. Three policemen—P.C. Eagles, P.C. Cater, and Detective Dixon, all of whom subsequently received the King's Police Medal—entered the house. Dixon's own account of what happened then was extremely vivid, and may be given here (in part):

> I got to the landing and opened the bedroom door—not too quickly and not too widely—and the first thing I knew was that Jacob Meyer was standing on the stairs with his pistol pointed at me. He instantly fired, but I had sprung back before he could get at me. I swiftly closed the door again and called on him to surrender. . . . I saw that he did not mean to surrender, so I suggested . . . that as there was a mongrel dog tied up near the back door it should be released and taken inside and told to go upstairs, to see if it could drive Jacob out of the bedroom, or at least take his attention off us and give us a better chance to take him. . . . So it was agreed that the dog should have a chance. . . . It was not an easy matter to deal with the animal, which appeared to be very ferocious. The dog sprang up the staircase and promptly did what we had not been able to do—it frightened Jacob so much that he bolted away from the door after shutting it. . . . Cater and I had got our revolvers loaded and we set to work. The door was very thin deal, so that our bullets went through with ease, making holes which enabled us to see into the room. . . . Jacob was tearing about the room in a terrible excited state and was literally at bay. . . . Eagles, without the slightest hesitation, hurled himself against the door, burst it open, thrust his arm round until it was well inside the room, and fired two shots. . . . Jacob was leaping about and laughing wildly. He shouted to us, 'Come on now!' Whereupon, the man sprang on to a child's bed which was in the room, and instantly tried to pull the clothes over his head. . . . Eagles rushed into the room and up to the bed, and I went after him. Like a flash, Eagles snatched the pistol from Jacob's hand, and I seized him by the throat and dragged him on to the floor and down the staircase, pulling him backwards. The blood was oozing from his forehead, and it was clear that he was wounded by one or more bullets. I dragged him down the stairs into the yard, where he was lying on his back. A crowd came round him instantly. Jacob was between life and death, and there was a horrible grin on his face. He never stopped grinning, and that awful look was on his face when he died, which was soon, with the crowd round him and his eyes staring.
> [*130*.

Heilbron, Rose, Q.C. (*b.* **1914**.) On 7th January 1957 this brilliant woman, one of Her Majesty's Counsel learned in the law, took her seat upon the Bench as Recorder of Burnley, Lancashire. It was a notable milestone on a long and arduous road littered with the obstacles placed there by male prejudice, obstinacy, and conceit. One by one, those obstacles had been demolished as, slowly and painfully, the professions, exclusively male, guarded as jealously as game preserves, surrendered to the clamorous march of the women, an army with time on its side, as well as courage and pertinacity. There at last, on that January morning, sat 'Madame Recorder' in her bob wig, the first woman ever to hold such an appointment. To many, it seemed a portent of something greater still to come, something that had now advanced appreciably nearer—the appointment of a woman as a judge of the High Court. Was 'Madame Recorder' to become Heilbron J.? From the ghostly ranks of the pioneers of women's emancipation, long since dead, there seemed to come an echo of a cheer. Rose Heilbron was born in Liverpool in the first weeks of the 1914-18 war, the daughter of a Jewish hotel-keeper. At the age of twenty-one, she secured a first-class honours degree at Liverpool University, and four years later, in 1939, was called to the Bar by Gray's Inn. From the first, she made it clear that she asked for no consideration on account of her sex, and would indeed have scorned any favours as an insult, had any been offered. None were. Miss Heilbron achieved her success at the Bar on a basis of absolute equality with her male colleagues on the Northern Circuit. Swiftly the honours accumulated: a practice reputed to be worth something like £5,000 a year; the distinction of being the first woman to plead a case in the House of Lords. Finally, in 1949, she was one of the first two women to take silk. Miss Heilbron is in private life Mrs. Nathaniel Burstein, the wife of a Liverpool surgeon. She defended George KELLY (both trials).

Henderson, Dr. Archibald.⎱ *See* John George HAIGH.
Henderson, Rosalie. ⎰

Hewart of Bury, Viscount (1870-1943). Lord Chief Justice of England (1922-40). It might have been expected that the qualities which brought to this subtle, suave, genial and ingratiating man so great a success at the Bar would have served him equally well in the great position of Lord Chief Justice of England. But somehow they did not. The truth was that Gordon Hewart was incorrigibly partisan; he was unable to stand above the battle. The appearance of judicial impartiality was repeatedly disturbed by his bad habit of making up his mind about the merits of a case before he had heard all the evidence, or even the greater part of it—sometimes none of it. And once he had arrived at an opinion he was inclined to hold to it with stubborn tenacity, even if it meant ignoring inconvenient arguments which might otherwise have disturbed it. It is more agreeable to turn to the unchallenged achievements of Gordon Hewart at the Bar, as a Member of Parliament, and as Law Officer of the Crown. He was born in 1870 in the Lancashire town of Bury, the son of middle-class parents. Educated at Manchester Grammar School and at University College, Oxford, he graduated in 1891, but did not at once enter the profession of the law, being under the necessity to seek a more immediately profitable means of livelihood. He found it in journalism. For a time he was leader writer on an important daily newspaper and a frequenter of the Press Gallery of the House of Commons. But his heart was in the law, and eventually, in 1902, he was called to the Bar by the Inner Temple. He possessed few of the conventional advantages—such as impressive stature, a fine presence, a melodious voice—which are thought to make for success at the Bar, especially in jury cases. He was short, almost squat, a rotund little man with a button-nose and pendulous lower lip; his voice was anything but melodious, and was marked with an unmistakable Lancashire accent which it never entirely lost, although it was none the worse for that. Indeed, in his appearance he flouted every popular or romantic notion of how a great advocate ought to look. He was, nonetheless, an immediate success when he started in practice in Manchester. From the first he eschewed the bold, bullying frontal attack; all was accomplished smoothly and suavely, with tact and courtesy, and by the nicely calculated use of a bland and equable manner which somehow managed to convey that he was *understating* his client's case out of a natural distaste for anything that could be called extravagant; it was a device which was wonderfully effective. By 1912 he had won a commanding position at Manchester and was ready for the wider triumphs which were presently to be his. In that year he became a King's Counsel and also, as the result of winning a by-election, Liberal M.P. for East Leicester. His great local reputation followed him to London. In 1916 he was appointed Solicitor-General; three years later, when Lord Birkenhead became Lord Chancellor, he succeeded to the vacant post of Attorney-General. In 1921, Lord Reading went to India as Viceroy, and the great office of Lord Chief Justice was open to Gordon Hewart. But by that time, as its chief legal adviser, he had become indispensable to the Coalition Government, and Mr. Lloyd George persuaded him to stay where he was for the time being. Mr. Justice Lawrence (Lord Trevethin) became Lord Chief Justice in Lord Reading's place, but this was correctly understood to be a 'holding' appointment, and in the following year Hewart succeeded to the office he was to hold for the next eighteen years. In the meantime he had attained the rare distinction of being both a Law Officer of the Crown and at the same time a member of the Cabinet, in which capacity he set his signature to the treaty setting up the Irish Free State in 1921. Upon taking up his appointment as Lord Chief Justice, he became a baron in the peerage of the United Kingdom; in 1940, when he retired in favour of Lord Caldicote, he was created a viscount. In 1943 he died, being then in his seventy-fifth year. Lord Hewart presided over a number of sensational murder trials, including the trial of Leslie STONE. As Attorney-General, he prosecuted Lieutenant-Colonel RUTHERFORD; and Frederick Rothwell (Eric) HOLT.

Hilbery, Sir Malcolm (*b.* **1883**). Judge of the Queen's Bench Division of the High Court since 1935. Called to the Bar by Gray's Inn in 1907, he took silk in 1928, and was raised to the Bench after twenty-eight years in practice as a highly successful advocate; he now ranks first in seniority among the Queen's Bench judges. His deceptively languid manner is apt to conceal from the unwary the strength of a formidable personality—as many a wrongdoer has discovered. Mr. Justice Hilbery has presided over a number of celebrated murder trials, including those of James CAMB; and Donald George THOMAS.

Hobday, Stanley Eric, a dull-witted man of uncommon callousness, had the dubious distinction of being the first murderer to be traced through a police message broadcast by the B.B.C. On an August night in 1933, he broke into a house in Moor Street, West Bromwich, occupied by a Mr. Charles William Fox, a metal-strip cutter, who supplemented his modest wage by acting as a collector for a clothing company. On the previous afternoon, Mr. Fox had collected about fourteen shillings. It was for this paltry sum that Hobday broke into the house; it was for this that he committed murder. He got into the house by breaking the window of the ground-floor sitting-room. The tinkle of falling glass awakened Mrs. Fox, who was asleep upstairs. She roused her husband, who, clad only in vest and shirt, crept downstairs by candlelight to investigate. He went into the sitting-room, and as he crossed the threshold the draught from the broken window blew out the candle. Mrs. Fox, waiting anxiously on the landing, heard a scuffle and a groan. Terrified, she cried out to her husband to come back to her, and ran back into the bedroom. A few moments later, Mr. Fox staggered up the stairs and into the bedroom, where he fell to the floor without a word. His wife knelt down beside him, and he died in her arms. The handle of a bowie-knife was protruding from his back. Mrs. Fox flung wide the bedroom window to call for help; her frantic screams, echoing across the silent street in the first light of dawn, must have rung in

Hobday's ears as he stumbled away from the little house whose life and happiness he had so wantonly destroyed. It might have been imagined that his only thought would have been to get as far away as possible from the scene of his crime. Instead, he acted as if he had all the time in the world, time enough, certainly, to break into a butcher's shop in Bromford Lane, only a short distance away. There he helped himself to a few pounds in cash, washed his hands in a bowl of water, which he did not trouble to empty, and as a crowning audacity, borrowed the butcher's safety razor and shaved himself. Finally, he took a work-basket out of a cupboard and with needle and cotton darned a tear in the left elbow of his jacket. He then had a drink from a bottle of milk which he found in the shop. Milk is regarded as a blameless drink; in Hobday's case it was a fatal one, for he left his fingerprints on the bottle. He had a criminal record, and his prints were in the files at Scotland Yard. These supplied the police with the name and description of the man they were looking for, since it was evident to them from the first that the two burglaries were the work of the same hand. In the meantime, the leisurely Hobday had at last made good his escape. He stole a car from a garage in Bromford Lane and headed north. He drove it as far as High Legh in Cheshire—nearly seventy miles from West Bromwich—where he met with a 'freak' accident, the car leaving the road and turning a complete somersault. But Hobday was unhurt. He pushed on northwards as best he could on foot, and got as far as Carlisle before he was recognized as the man whose description had by this time been broadcast by the B.B.C. from one end of the country to the other. A farmer saw him walking along a country road and told the police of his suspicions. Soon afterwards, Hobday was overtaken by a police car at a little place called Rockcliffe, not far from Gretna Green. He was picking blackberries. Tried at Birmingham Assizes before Mr. Justice TALBOT in the following November, he was found guilty and sentenced to death; he was hanged at Winson Green Prison, Birmingham.

[*42*.

Hoffman, Karl. *See* SIEGE OF SIDNEY STREET.

Holland, Camille. *See* Samuel Herbert DOUGAL.

Holmes, Leonard, demobilized at the end of October 1944, returned to his home at New Ollerton, Nottinghamshire, to find that his wife, Peggy Agnes, had been unfaithful to him whilst he was away at the war. On 19th November, after an uncomfortable evening at a public-house, where it seemed to the jealous husband that his wife was altogether too familiar with R.A.F. men in the bar, the couple went home to a violent quarrel, which ended in Mrs. Holmes declaring, 'If it will ease your mind, I have been untrue to you.' Whereupon, Holmes grabbed a hammer and hit his wife over the head with it. Then he strangled her with his hands. Holmes was tried for murder before Mr. Justice CHARLES at Nottingham Assizes in February 1945, was found guilty, and sentenced to death. He appealed to the Court of Criminal Appeal, where complaint was made of the ruling of the judge at the trial that it was *not open to the jury to find a verdict of manslaughter*. The Court upheld this ruling and dismissed the appeal. Giving judgment, Mr. Justice Wrottesley (afterwards Lord Justice WROTTESLEY) said this:

> It cannot be too widely known that a person who, after absence for some reason such as service, either suspects already, or discovers on his return, that his wife has been unfaithful during his absence, is not, on that account, a person who may use lethal weapons upon his wife, and, if violence should result in her death, can claim to have suffered such provocation as would reduce the crime from murder to manslaughter.

In view of the important bearing of the case upon the law of PROVO-CATION, the Attorney-General, Sir Hartley Shawcross K.C. (after-wards Lord SHAWCROSS), granted his fiat to allow it to be taken to the House of Lords, where for four days the issue of how far a con-fession of adultery could be sufficient to reduce to manslaughter what would otherwise be murder was argued before Lord Simon, Lord Porter, Lord Simonds, and Lord Du Parcq. For Holmes, it was contended that this was a question which it was open to a jury to decide, and that Mr. Justice Charles had been at fault in saying that it was not. Against this, the Solicitor-General, Sir Frank Soskice K.C., submitted on behalf of the Crown that in law, words could never amount to sufficient justification, where the killing was done with a settled inten-tion. It would, he argued, be in the highest degree unfortunate if there should be a general impression that a confession of adultery provided something like a licence to kill. Their Lordships unanimously upheld the decision of the Court of Criminal Appeal, and confirmed the ruling of the trial judge. In his statement of the reasons for rejecting the appeal, Lord Simon pointed out that the doctrine of provocation seldom applied in cases where there was an intention to kill—such as Holmes had admit-ted. 'Even if Iago's insinuations against Desdemona's virtue had been true', he said, 'Othello's crime was murder and nothing else.' It was the duty of the judge at a trial, in relevant cases, to tell the jury that a confession of adultery was never sufficient in itself to reduce an offence which would otherwise be murder to manslaughter, and that in no case could *words alone*, save in circumstances of some extreme and exceptional character, so reduce the crime. (The discovery of a wife or husband in the act of adultery had long been held to be sufficient provocation to justify a verdict of manslaughter.) The highest court in the land having decided the issue, the death sentence passed on Leonard Holmes was carried out—on 28th May 1945.

See PROVOCATION and HOMICIDE ACT, 1957.

[*198.*

Holt, Frederick (Eric) Rothwell, indicted for the murder of his mistress, Harriet Elsie (Kitty) Breaks, sat expressionless and indifferent in the dock during a recital of his love letters which moved the jury, and even the judge, to tears. At the end of the trial, after he had been sentenced to death, his only remark was, 'Well, that's over. I hope my tea won't be late.' Was this apparent callousness in reality a symptom of insanity? Sir Edward Marshall HALL K.C., who had fought with his accustomed ardour to establish that the man had been under the influence of a sudden uncontrollable passion acting upon a mind enfeebled by shell-shock and disease, remained to the end of his life convinced that in sending Eric Holt to the scaffold the State had done that thing from which humanity revolts—hanged a lunatic. The facts are these. Eric Holt, called up as a Territorial officer in 1914, had been invalided out of the Army, and after a brief interlude in Malaya had returned in 1918 to his native Lancashire, where he met charming Kitty Breaks, an extremely pretty woman, who had made an unhappy marriage and was living apart from her husband. He fell deeply in love with her and she with him, and for more than eighteen months they lived happily together; as the letters they exchanged plainly suggested, theirs was a singularly tender and sweet relationship. In the early morning of Christmas Eve 1919, after a wild night of wind and rain, ·the body of Kitty Breaks was found lying half-buried on the sandhills at St. Anne's, near Blackpool; she had been shot three times with a revolver. Her lover was arrested and charged with murder. At his trial, which took place at Manchester Assizes in February 1920 before Mr. Justice Greer (afterwards Lord FAIRFIELD), Marshall Hall submitted that Holt, whose grandfather and aunt had been in an asylum, had had his mind unhinged by his war experiences—he had been through the Festubert bombardment—and that if he committed the murder it was done in a fit of madness, precipitated by a frenzy of jealousy for the woman he adored. With the tears coursing down his cheeks, the great advocate read one touching passage after another from the love letters which Holt had written to Kitty Breaks and she to him. The Court was stilled; tears were in the judge's eyes; several members of the jury wept unashamedly. It was an impressive example of this counsel's mastery of the emotional appeal, always most effective when most sincere. The reply of the Attorney-General, Sir Gordon Hewart K.C. (afterwards Lord HEWART), acted like a cold douche as, quite without emotion, he rehearsed the prosecution's case, which sought to show the prisoner in quite a different light, that is, as a man who had killed his mistress to rid himself of an embarrassing liaison and, at the same time, to put his hands on the £5,000 for which she had insured her life and bequeathed to him in her will. Indifferent to the end, Holt was cramming an evening paper into his pocket when he was brought back into court to hear the jury find him guilty. The Home Secretary caused a special inquiry to be made into Holt's mental condition, but found nothing in the doctors' report to justify him in interfering with the ordinary course of the law. On 13th April 1920 the enigmatic Eric Holt was executed at Strangeways Prison.

[*30, 131.*

Homicide Act, 1957. This measure, an admitted compromise, was carried into law in the aftermath of the persistent and powerful campaign for the total abolition of capital punishment which, between 1948 and 1956, had repeated successes in the House of Commons and met with repeated disaster in the House of Lords. Under its provisions, the death sentence is retained only in five classes of 'capital murder', and in cases where a person convicted of murder has previously been convicted of another murder done on a different occasion, both murders having been committed in Great Britain. In all other cases of murder the death sentence is replaced by a sentence of imprisonment for life. The five categories of capital murder are:

(1) Murder in the course or furtherance of theft.
(2) Murder by shooting or by causing an explosion.
(3) Murder in the course of resisting arrest or of escaping from legal custody.
(4) Murder of police officers in the execution of their duty, and persons assisting them.
(5) Murder by prisoners of prison officers in the execution of their duty, and persons assisting them.

If two or more persons should be guilty of a murder falling within those categories, only the one who actually brought about the death of, or who inflicted grievous bodily harm upon, the murdered man or woman would be liable to the death penalty. The foregoing provisions apply equally to Scotland as to England and Wales. Those which follow, each a very considerable reform of the law of murder, apply only to England and Wales. The first provides for the abolition of the doctrine of CONSTRUCTIVE MALICE. It holds that where a person kills another in the course or furtherance of some other offence, the killing shall not amount to murder unless done 'with the same malice aforethought (express or implied) as is required for a killing to amount to murder when not done in the course or furtherance of another offence'. The effect of this is to say that in the case of a murder done in the course of a felony, involving violence or the threat of violence, or in resisting arrest, *intent to kill or to cause grievous bodily harm* must be shown, as in the case of every other class of murder. The second reform provides that a person suffering from such abnormality of mind —whether arising from a condition of arrested or retarded development, or any inherent causes, or induced by disease or injury—as substantially impairs his mental responsibility shall be liable to be convicted of manslaughter, not murder. (*See* DIMINISHED RESPONSIBILITY.) One of the gravest defects of the criminal law in England had been its refusal to make any allowance for mental infirmity short of insanity. Now, by the adoption of Scottish practice, the English courts are brought into closer accord with modern psychiatric and medical experience. The Home Secretary, Major Gwilym Lloyd George (afterwards Viscount Tenby), moving the second reading of the Homicide Bill—which became the Homicide Act—said this:

The effect of the Clause is that if a person charged with murder can satisfy the jury that at the time of the killing he was probably suffering from such abnormality of mind from one or other of certain specified causes, that his mental responsibility for the act in question was substantially diminished, he will be entitled to a verdict of manslaughter. At present, a person's mental state affects the verdict only if the defence can show that he was insane within the meaning of the M'NAGHTEN RULES, that is, that he was suffering from such a defect of reason due to disease of mind that he either did not know what he was doing, or did not know that it was wrong. *This will remain the test of insanity leading to a verdict of 'guilty but insane'.* A new defence will be open to those who, although not insane in this legal sense, are regarded in the light of modern knowledge as insane in the medical sense and those who, not insane in either sense, are seriously abnormal, whether through mental deficiency, inherent causes, disease or injury. The defence is intended to cover those grave forms of abnormality of mind which may substantially impair responsibility.

It is not intended, however, to provide a defence to persons who are merely hot-tempered or who, otherwise normal, commit murder in a sudden access of rage or jealousy. Persons found guilty of manslaughter under this Clause will be liable to such punishment as the court sees fit to impose, including imprisonment for life, as are those in Scotland who plead diminished responsibility.

The third reform provides that where there is evidence that the accused was provoked—*whether by words or conduct*—to lose his self-control, it shall be left to the jury to decide whether the provocation was enough to make a reasonable man do as he did; if they so decide, their verdict will be one of manslaughter, not murder. In deciding this issue, the jury are to act according to their own opinion of the effect on a reasonable man of the provocation, *whether or not given by words alone*. (*See* PROVOCATION.) (It had been laid down, by a judgment of the House of Lords, that in no case could *words alone*, save in circumstances of a most extreme and exceptional character, amount to provocation sufficient to reduce murder to manslaughter.) The fourth reform provides that a person who kills another, or is a party to the other killing himself, or being killed by a third person, shall be liable to be convicted of manslaughter, not murder, if he were acting in pursuance of a *genuine* suicide pact. Two or more murders may be charged in the same indictment and—unless separate trials are desirable in the interests of justice—may be tried together. Part III of the Act makes amendments in the law as to the form and execution of sentence of death for murder in England and Wales, and provides (1) a shortened form of sentence, which makes no reference to the manner of execution or place of burial; and (2) that notices of execution shall no longer be required to be posted at the prison, and that the Home Secretary shall publish the time and place fixed for the execution, and, after execution, the fact that it has taken place and also a copy of the coroner's inquisition. During the Committee stage of the Homicide Bill in the House of Commons, attempts were made to widen the categories of capital murder, in particular to add to them murder by poisoning. But the Government of Sir Anthony Eden rested itself firmly upon the principle that capital punishment was to be retained only for those forms of murder which most clearly strike at the maintenance of law and order. This point was forcefully made by Major Lloyd George:

> We propose to confine capital punishment, broadly speaking, to murder by professional criminals; murder of the agents of law and order—policemen and prison officers; murder by shooting and causing an explosion, methods which are particularly dangerous

and indiscriminate and are associated with gang warfare and political terrorism; and murder by a man who makes a practice of murder. In this way, we keep capital punishment where it is most needed and most effective; that is, in the main, as a deterrent against professional criminals carrying and using lethal weapons, and as a protection for public servants who are particularly exposed to attack.

The Government, even at the cost of creating obvious anomalies, resisted all attempts to weaken this principle by adding new classes of capital murder based upon 'moral heinousness' and not upon their relevance to the maintenance of law and order. No alteration was made to the Bill during its passage through Parliament; it received the Royal Assent on 1st March 1957. The first person to be sentenced to death for a capital murder, as defined in the Homicide Act, was a twenty-four-years-old labourer named Ronald Patrick Dunbar, who before Mr. Justice Ashworth at Newcastle Assizes on 16th May 1957, was found guilty of the murder of Mrs. Selina Mewes, aged eighty-two; she had awakened during the night to find a burglar in the house and had been effectively silenced. Dunbar, who had pleaded 'diminished responsibility' under the Act, appealed to the Court of Criminal Appeal, which on the ground that in dealing with this defence the judge's direction to the jury had been faulty, quashed the conviction for murder, substituting a verdict of manslaughter and a sentence of imprisonment for life.

Hopwood, Edward, forty-five years of age, a married man living apart from his wife, fell in love with an actress named Florence Dudley, whom he saw in a play at the Tivoli Theatre, Manchester, in May 1912. Miss Dudley—whose real name was Florence Alice Bernadette Silles—found Hopwood an exacting lover. He was insanely jealous, and their liaison, from the beginning, was punctuated with violent scenes, all of which arose from his tormenting suspicion that Florence was going about with other men; he even went to the length of having her watched. Miss Dudley had imagined that Hopwood was a single man; when she discovered that he had a wife and family—and, incidentally, that he was wanted by the police for passing worthless cheques—she tried to break with him. On the night of 28th September 1912 she met Hopwood in London and told him, finally and flatly, that she was determined to have nothing more to do with him. At fifteen minutes to midnight, after a long, earnest, and no doubt exhausting conversation, the two of them left the Holborn Viaduct Hotel in a taxi-cab to drive to Fenchurch Street Station. At the approach to the station, the cab-driver was startled by the report of a pistol shot. He pulled up, got down, and opened the door—Florence Dudley fell out of the taxi into his arms, and died in a matter of seconds. As the driver was bending over her, there was a second shot inside the cab. Edward Hopwood was sitting huddled up in a corner of the cab. He had tried to commit suicide, but had made a poor shot at it, and, after treatment at Guy's Hospital, soon recovered. Hopwood was tried for murder at the Old Bailey, before Mr. Justice AVORY. Declining the services of counsel, he conducted his own defence, which rested upon the statement he had made to the police that he had taken out his revolver in the taxi-cab with the idea of killing himself, and that, in trying to wrest it from him, Miss Dudley had been accidentally shot. His final speech to the jury had great pathos, and even some nobility. He said that Florence Dudley had been the only woman he had ever loved, and that when everything in life had gone from him—his home, his children, his business—he would still have been happy if only she had remained true to him. At the end of his address he broke down and sat sobbing in the dock, with his head buried in his hands. Neither his eloquence nor his tears availed. The jury took only twelve minutes to decide that he was guilty of murder. Edward Hopwood was sentenced to death, and was hanged.

[*62, 121.*

Horridge, Sir Thomas Gordon (1857-1938). Judge of the King's Bench Division of the High Court (1910-37). He began his career as a solicitor in Manchester, and did not enter the senior branch of the profession until 1884, when he was called to the Bar by the Inner Temple. He quickly established himself in one of the most prosperous junior practices on the Northern Circuit; he took silk in 1901. It was however his astonishing success in the General Election of 1906, when as the Liberal candidate for East Manchester he defeated Mr. Balfour, the former Prime Minister, which paved his way for his appointment to the Bench four years later. The High Court judgeship he received at the hands of the Liberal Lord Chancellor, Lord Loreburn, was a frankly 'political' appointment, and as always in such cases, it attracted criticism. Nonetheless, he proved to be an able, hard-working, and above all, conscientious judge. It was his invariable habit to copy into his notebook in longhand every answer given by a witness; not until he was satisfied that he had a true and correct record of what had been said would he allow a further question to be put, and with each reply this process would be repeated. It cannot be said that he was very popular with counsel who appeared before him. An imposing figure in his judicial robes, he was, perhaps, rather too conscious of his own dignity—a fault exaggerated by the fact that he was totally without a sense of humour—and in the course of years came to adopt a somewhat

Olympian air. Unhappily, this encouraged a tendency to be unnecessarily brusque, and even downright rude, both to witnesses and counsel. He had one peculiar mannerism, a trick of screwing his face into a sort of grin, as if he were finding some secret amusement in what was being said. This sometimes led to unfortunate results, since those who were unprepared for these sudden grimaces received from them a mistaken impression of geniality; counsel or witness who fell into that trap were apt to be sharply disillusioned. Mr. Justice Horridge continued to sit on the Bench until he was within a few months of his eightieth birthday; in spite of increasing deafness, he retained his keenness of intellect to the last. A serious illness compelled him to retire in May 1937, and, fourteen months later—on 25th July 1938—he died. Murder trials over which he presided included those of Ronald LIGHT; and Mrs. PACE.

Houghton, Charles, had been for twenty-two years butler to the Woodhouse family at stately Burghill Court, with its three hundred acres of parkland, not far from the city of Hereford. By 1929 he had come to regard himself as indispensable to the two maiden ladies, Elinor Drinkwater Woodhouse, and her younger sister, Martha Gordon Woodhouse ('Miss May'), who were his employers. As an Old Family Retainer, whose position was as privileged as his duties were light, he felt at liberty to indulge his besetting weakness. Put less elegantly, the butler took to drink. For a time, the Misses Woodhouse did their best not to notice. So matters continued until at dinner-time on 31st August Houghton waited at table in a condition so painfully evident that the two sisters were compelled to recognize that as an Old Family Retainer he was no longer serviceable. With much heart-searching, they decided that Houghton Must Go. On 6th September the elder Miss Woodhouse gave him twenty-four hours notice of dismissal and two months wages. On the following morning, the butler attended family prayers as usual, served the breakfast with a steady hand, gave no sign of any murderous intention. But a little later, when Miss Elinor was in the kitchen discussing with the cook the menu for luncheon, in he came with a sporting gun, and without a word, shot his mistress dead. He saved a second shot for Miss May, who was killed a few moments later. Then he ran upstairs to his bedroom, took out his razor, and tried to cut his throat, but succeeded only in inflicting a superficial wound. When the police came, he observed, 'Oh dear, this is a bad job. It is passion.' Houghton was charged with the murder of both sisters, but at his trial before Mr. Justice SWIFT at Hereford Assizes in the following November, he was indicted for the murder of Miss Elinor alone. It was pleaded in his defence that as a child he had been subject to fits, and a medical witness said that in Houghton's condition he detected symptoms of epilepsy. In spite of this, Houghton was found guilty, and being sentenced to death was duly hanged on 6th December.

Hulten, Karl Gustav. *See* Elizabeth Maud JONES.

Humphreys, Sir Travers (1867-1956). Judge of the King's Bench Division of the High Court (1928-51). When, at the age of eighty-four, Mr. Justice Humphreys stood down from the Bench and went into retirement, a remarkable chapter in the history of the criminal courts of this country came to an end. For more than half a century, the criminous and the unfortunate, guilt rampant and innocence misunderstood, had passed in and out of the dock at the Old Bailey under the close regard of one of the shrewdest pair of eyes that ever looked out from under a bob wig. For twenty-three years he had been a King's Bench judge, presiding over many of the most celebrated murder trials of the day; for thirty-nine years before that he had been in practice at the Bar, twenty of them as counsel to the Crown at the Old Bailey. His had been a lifetime spent in the administration of justice, which he regarded in the light of an abstract ideal, to be served selflessly, without passion, and with as near an approach to absolute impartiality as is possible to a fallible mortal in an imperfect world. Rarely, before or since, had the case for the Crown been presented with such formidable skill as when it rested in the hands of Travers Humphreys. In cross-examination, of which he was a master, he possessed most conspicuously the gift of going directly to the heart of the matter, sometimes with just a few crisp, shattering questions; lucid and concise, he never wasted time in skirting the outside of a case. Always master of the facts and of the law, especially with regard to the admissibility of evidence, he never bullied, seldom raised his voice, strictly refrained from getting into arguments with opposing counsel, still less with the judge, whom he treated with becoming deference. All these qualities served him equally well when he was raised to the Bench. He had the true judicial temperament, being blessed with a dispassionate mind. But there was that tough, formidable streak as well. People sometimes said he was a 'hard' judge—by which they probably meant that he was a hard judge to deceive. No judge, indeed, was ever less likely to be taken in by a plausible witness or a specious argument, or by any of the fashionable tricks of advocacy. He wanted the facts, and the less fancifully adorned they were, the better he liked it. He had a dry sense of humour, but perhaps because any form of time-wasting was abhorrent to him he kept it under restraint; as he mellowed with age and experience he allowed his Court more generous glimpses of it. Travers Humphreys was often compared with his great contemporary, Mr. Justice AVORY. There were certainly marked similarities between them. Both men were made judges with the express purpose of strengthening the Bench in dealing with criminal offences; in each case, the Lord Chancellor of the day took the extremely rare course of offering a High Court judgeship to a barrister practising at the Old Bailey and primarily—in Humphreys' case, exclusively—engaged in criminal work. Temperamentally, both men had much in common, although Travers Humphreys, for all his dry exterior, had a warmth that Avory lacked, a kindliness less dourly disguised. Physically, he was spare and very finely made—like Mr. Justice Avory—much wrinkled in his old age, with the actor's long upper lip, a heavy, even pendulous, lower lip and deep-set, extremely watchful eyes, which conveyed an irresistible impression of shrewdness and wisdom. In a crowd he would have stood out for what he was—a judge of men. Travers Humphreys was bred to the law. He was born in 1867, the fourth son of Charles Octavius Humphreys, senior partner of a well-known London firm of solicitors. Called to the Bar by the Inner Temple in 1889, he was appointed Counsel to the Crown at the Middlesex Sessions and North London Sessions in 1905. Thereafter, his advance was steady and sure; 1908, Junior Counsel to the Crown at the Old Bailey; 1916, Senior Treasury Counsel; 1924, Chief Senior Treasury Counsel. In 1925 he was knighted and three years later he was raised to the Bench. Retiring in 1951, he died on 20th February 1956, being then in his eighty-ninth year. The capital trials in which he appeared make up in themselves a formidable 'Companion to Murder': As counsel: Hawley Harvey CRIPPEN; the SEDDONS; George Joseph SMITH; Lieutenant Douglas MALCOLM; Lieutenant-Colonel RUTHERFORD (defence). As judge: Chung Yo MIAO; Wallace BENTON; Mrs. Elvira BARNEY; Ernest BROWN; Theodosios PETROU; Edward Royal CHAPLIN; Ludomir CIENSKI; and John George HAIGH.

Hutchinson, St.John, K.C. (1884-1942). In appearance not unlike an intellectual Mr. Micawber, St.John Hutchinson had a formal stateliness which distinguished him in any company. He was an examplar of the Grand Manner—sartorially and in other ways—and it is difficult to imagine that he could ever have entered a crowded room unnoticed. Like his contemporaries, Sir Henry CURTIS BENNETT and Sir Patrick HASTINGS, he moved a great deal in Society, and was also a well-known and popular figure in artistic, literary, and theatrical circles. In the legal world, he was recognized as a criminal lawyer of the first rank, a lucid and persuasive speaker, deadly in cross-examination. Keenly interested in criminal pathology, he was much in demand in that class of case which lies in the borderland between crime and abnormal psychology, yet, curiously enough, he appeared comparatively rarely in capital trials. Students, however, will remember his conduct of the defence of Alfred Arthur KOPSCH; and Frederick FIELD (second trial). At the trial of Edward Royal CHAPLIN he appeared for Mrs. Casserley, who was charged as an accessory. St. John Hutchinson was born on 8th April 1884, the son of the late Sir Charles Hutchinson, one-time Liberal M.P. for Rye. A pupil of Sir Holman Gregory, a later Recorder of the City of London, he was called to the Bar by the Middle Temple in 1909, and joined the South-Eastern Circuit; he took silk in 1935. At one time he was Progressive member for Poplar on the London County Council. He died at Merton Hall, Cambridge, on 24th October 1942, at the comparatively early age of fifty-eight.

Hutchison, John James, put enough arsenic in the after-supper coffee to poison a whole roomful of people. And poison a whole roomful of people he did—seventeen in all. By good luck rather than design, fifteen of them recovered. Of the two who died, one was Hutchison's father, Charles Hutchison, an employee on the Duke of Buccleuch's estates at Dalkeith, the other a Mr. Alexander Clapperton, who kept a grocer's shop at Musselburgh. The occasion of this wholesale poisoning was a party given on 3rd February 1911 by Mr. and Mrs. Charles Hutchison to celebrate their silver wedding. Twenty-one persons sat down to supper; eighteen of them were guests, the party being completed by the host and hostess and by their son, John James, who worked as a chemist's assistant in his uncle's shop at Musselburgh. John James Hutchison was a versatile young man of twenty-four, with a weakness for skating-rinks, motoring—still something of a novelty in 1911—and Stock Exchange speculation, by which he was understood to have made a fortune. (He had, in fact, made serious losses, as was presently to appear.) After supper, the son of the house handed round coffee. Fortunately for themselves, three of the guests declined. So did John James, who knew the potency of the brew. Within a few minutes, the dining-room resembled a battlefield, with most of the guests writhing in agony upon the carpet. Mr. Hutchison had emptied his cup. So had his friend, the grocer from Musselburgh, and after a few hours, during which they suffered violent internal pains, accompanied by vomiting and the other distressing symptoms of arsenical poisoning, both died. Mrs. Hutchison, too, was in a parlous condition; ultimately she survived, but only after a long and painful illness. John James was indefatigable in his attentions to the sufferers in the stricken dining-room, among whom was the girl he was engaged to marry. No one, it was agreed, could have shown a more touching solicitude during those hours, or have been more ready with the healing word. When on 14th February it was given out that young Hutchison had gone to stay for a few days with some friends of his in Newcastle-upon-Tyne, none suspected evil. Had he not been compelled to stand helplessly aside and watch his father die? None knew that in the bitterness of that hour he had been sustained by the pleasing knowledge that Mr. Hutchison's life was insured for £4,000, a comforting sum, and one which was more than sufficient to extricate him from the consequences of unwise investment in copper, oil, and South African mining shares. It was thus a severe shock to the neighbourhood to learn that nothing had been seen of John James Hutchison in Newcastle upon Tyne, and that a warrant had actually been issued for his arrest on a charge of murder. On Monday, 20th February, a Scotland Yard officer, by name Sergeant Burley, landed upon the island of Guernsey and began a round of visits to boarding-houses on the sea-front at St. Peter Port. At the second house he visited, the sergeant found the landlord scanning a London newspaper in which Hutchison's photograph and description were prominently displayed. The landlord said he was convinced that the missing man was at that very moment seated in the front parlour. Sergeant Burley went in. There, reclining in an armchair, was John James Hutchison. Although protesting that the sergeant was 'making a great mistake', he agreed to accompany him to the local police station. The scene that followed is best told in Sergeant Burley's own words:

He stood up, still keeping his right hand in his pocket. When we were near to the door he made a rush up the stairs, taking two steps at a time. I followed right at his heels. . . . His bedroom was situated at the top of the second flight, at the right-hand side. The door was open. Just as he entered, he drew his hand from his pocket and raised it to his mouth. As he raised it, I saw that it contained a phial filled with liquid. I struck out at his hand and sent the bottle flying across the room. We then closed together and struggled for an instant or two. Then I felt the man collapse. I thought he was done and I laid him on the floor.

A doctor was summoned and arrived within a few minutes. But he could do nothing for the young man, who, in the instant before the phial had been struck from his hand, had swallowed a fatal dose of prussic acid. An inquest was held at St. Peter Port by the *Procureur du Roi*, and a verdict of suicide was returned. So ended this most astonishing and melancholy case.

[*180, 206.*

I

I am in blood
Stepp'd in so far, that, should I wade no more,
Returning were as tedious as go o'er.

Shakespeare: *Macbeth*

Insanity as a bar to Execution. By a provision of the Criminal
Lunatics Act, 1884, if it should appear to the Home Secretary that a
person under sentence of death may be insane it is an absolute obligation
upon him to appoint two or more qualified medical practitioners to
examine the prisoner and report upon his or her mental condition.
(There is in Scotland no such statutory obligation upon the Secretary
of State, but where there is any doubt about a prisoner's mental condition, two Medical Commissioners with special psychiatric qualifications and experience are appointed to hold an inquiry.) The practice in
England has been to hold an inquiry whenever there is anything to
suggest that the prisoner may have been insane or mentally abnormal
at the time of the crime or have become insane since his or her conviction, and in particular where a plea of insanity has been raised at the
trial and rejected by the jury. Normally, these inquiries have been
conducted by three mental specialists, usually including the Medical
Superintendent of Broadmoor. They have had access to full reports of
the case, including police reports, medical reports, and a verbatim
record of the trial. The Royal Commission on Capital Punishment,
1949-53, pointed out in its report that for the purposes of their inquiries
the specialists

> are not bound by the criterion of legal responsibility laid down by
> the M'NAGHTEN RULES, but are free to consider without
> restrictions the medical aspects of insanity or other mental abnor-
> mality, including psychoneurosis, psychopathic personality,
> mental defectiveness, or borderline states.

If the doctors have, as a result, certified insanity, the death sentence
has been respited and the Home Secretary has directed the immediate

removal of the prisoner to Broadmoor or to a local mental hospital. In the past, such inquiries repeatedly demonstrated the incompatibility of the legal and the medical view of what constituted insanity: the doctors, it will be observed, have had the last word.

Insanity as a bar to Trial. Under the Criminal Lunatics Act, 1884, a person who has been committed for trial may be certified as insane and removed from prison to Broadmoor or to a local mental hospital *before trial*. In practice, the Home Secretary authorizes this procedure only in exceptional cases; he acts on the basis that the issue of insanity ought, whenever possible, to be determined by a jury. During the fifty years, 1900-49, there were only forty-nine cases in which a person charged with murder was certified insane and removed to Broadmoor or to a mental hospital before trial; since 1930 there have been only nine such cases. (These figures are quoted in the report of the Royal Commission on Capital Punishment, 1949-53.) Secondly, under a statute over a century and a half old—the Criminal Lunatics Act, 1800— if, when an accused person is brought up for trial, he appears to the jury to be insane and unfit to plead, they may find him (or her) 'insane on arraignment'. The Court may then order the accused person to be detained during Her Majesty's pleasure. The issue of unfitness to plead may be raised by the prosecution, the defence, or the judge. The test which the jury are instructed to apply is whether the prisoner is able to understand the charge, to distinguish between a plea of guilty or not guilty, to challenge jurors, to examine witnesses, to instruct counsel, to follow evidence, or to make a proper defence. Between 1900 and 1949, of 3,130 persons committed for trial on a charge of murder, 428 were found insane on arraignment.

Insanity as a Defence. *See* M'NAGHTEN RULES.

Insanity on Arraignment. *See* INSANITY AS A BAR TO TRIAL.

Irresistible Impulse. *See* M'NAGHTEN RULES.

J

Justice, while she winks at crimes,
Stumbles on innocence sometimes.

Samuel Butler: *Hudibras*

Jelf, Sir Arthur Richard (1837-1917). Judge of the King's Bench Division of the High Court (1901-10). Born in Prussia, the son of the Rev. Richard William Jelf, Principal of King's College, London, and Emmy, Countess Schlippenbach, Maid of Honour to the Queen of Hanover, he was called to the Bar by the Inner Temple in 1863, practised on the Oxford Circuit, and in 1880 took silk. Irascible by nature, he frequently enlivened the cases in which he appeared by quarrelling with opposing counsel, a fact which may possibly have delayed his promotion to the Bench, for which he possessed most, if not all, the necessary qualifications. It was not until November 1901, when he was sixty-four, that he was appointed a judge of the King's Bench Division, in the place left vacant by the retirement of Mr. Justice Day. The choice was, in general, approved by the profession, although, remembering the various 'scenes in court' in which he had figured during his long career at the Bar, there were those who feared that the new judge would turn out to be an irritable and impatient one. They need not have worried. From the beginning, Mr. Justice Jelf had his admittedly quick temper under perfect control, and, rather to the general surprise, treated all who practised in his court with impeccable courtesy and consideration. Failing health compelled him to retire after only nine years service as a judge; he died on 24th July 1917. Mr. Justice Jelf presided over a number of murder trials which attracted public attention, including that of Edward LAWRENCE.

Jenkins, Charles Henry, twenty-three, handsome, self-confident, diamond-hard, with a vicious police record behind him that had begun before he was out of his teens, was the leader of a gang of thieves and hold-up men responsible for various robberies in London in the years immediately after the second World War: they called him the 'King of Borstal'. On 29th April 1947, at about 2 p.m., Jenkins, accompanied by his friend, **Christopher James Geraghty,** aged twenty-one, and a seventeen-years-old youth named **Terence Peter Rolt,** raided the premises of Jay's, the jewellers, in Charlotte Street, London. Carrying loaded revolvers, they entered the shop with masks over their faces. One of them jumped over the counter. With great presence of mind, Alfred Ernest Stock, director of the firm, slammed the safe door shut, whereupon one of the raiders threw one pistol at his head and, leaping upon him, hammered him with the barrel of another. Mr. Stock fell bleeding to the floor. Meanwhile, another of the trio was demanding the keys of the safe from the seventy-years-old manager, Bertram Thomas Keates—who replied by throwing a heavy wooden stool. The youth fired, but fortunately the bullet lodged in the wall without doing harm. The thieves turned and ran, but when they got outside it was to find that the stolen Vauxhall 14 saloon which they had left by the kerb was now hemmed in behind a lorry. As people on the pavement scattered, they ran down Charlotte Street, still wearing their masks and brandishing their revolvers—stolen from a gunsmith's shop in the Borough. Alec de Antiquis, a garage owner, who happened to be passing on his motor-cycle, made a quick decision. In an extremely courageous effort to stop the raiders, he switched off his engine and skidded the machine into their path. Their answer was to shoot him through the head, with as little compunction as if he had been a dangerous dog. Escaping into the busy traffic of Tottenham Court Road, they left the gallant man, the father of six children, dying in the gutter, with the motor-cycle lying across his limp body. An ambulance was sent for. As Mr. de Antiquis was lifted into it he gasped out, 'I'm all right . . . stop them . . . I did my best.' They were the last words he ever spoke: shortly afterwards he died. Before the trail petered out, two of the youths were traced as far as an office building in Tottenham Court Road, where a raincoat was afterwards found in a disused room on the top floor; in one of the pockets was a scarf folded into a triangle for use as a mask. This raincoat provided the first profitable clue. Through the cloth stock ticket of a firm of multiple-branch tailors the coat was traced to a shop in High Street, Deptford, where the manager had a record of the sale—to Jenkins's brother-in-law, who lived in Bermondsey. This man admitted that a few weeks before the murder he had lent the coat to Jenkins. It was but one step further to Jenkins's known associates, Geraghty and Rolt. Geraghty refused to say a word that might implicate his friend Jenkins, but was not so scrupulous about Rolt. As for Rolt, the newest and least regarded member of the gang, he talked enough to put a rope round the necks of both Jenkins and Geraghty—and of himself, had he not been too young to hang. The three youths were tried for murder before Mr. Justice HALLETT at the Old Bailey in

July, and were found guilty. Jenkins and Geraghty were sentenced to death and were hanged at Pentonville Prison on 19th September; Rolt was ordered to be detained during His Majesty's pleasure. Nearly three years before the murder of Mr. de Antiquis, Jenkins's elder brother, Thomas James Jenkins, had been convicted of the manslaughter of another passer-by who had gallantly lost his life in trying to prevent the escape of a gang of jewel thieves—Captain Ralph Binney, R.N. [59, 65, 193.

Jesse, Frederick William Maximilian, throttled and dismembered his aunt, but lost his nerve before he was able to dispose of the pieces. He waited a week, then confessed to the police. They found the dead woman's legs on the table in the top floor back room at her house in York Road, Lambeth; the trunk was on the bed, parcelled up and tied with rope. Jesse, a man of twenty-six, lived with his aunt, Mabel Jennings Edmunds, a married woman separated from her husband. On Saturday, 21st July 1923—according to the story he told at his trial —Mrs. Edmunds quarrelled with him over a family matter. To get away from her he went to his room. But his aunt followed him upstairs and hit him a violent blow with a police whistle on his left eye. He fell on to the bed, whereupon Mrs. Edmunds threw some liquid over his face from a bottle; this 'more or less stupefied' him. He tried to wrest the bottle away, and his aunt hit him again, this time over the right eye, then threw some more of the liquid at him. The next thing he knew, his aunt was on the bed and he had his hands around her neck; she was dead. He carried the body into the back room on the top floor. The next day when he went into the room and saw the body lying on the bed he was filled with horror. 'I became almost frantic,' said Jesse. 'Something seemed to say "cut off the legs" and I did.' He had intended to dispose of the remains, but lacked the courage—there were so many difficulties in the way. Some days later he confessed to the police: 'It's a terrible thing to say, but I killed my aunt last Saturday week.' Tried at the Old Bailey before Mr. Justice SWIFT in September 1923, Jesse was found guilty and sentenced to death; he was hanged on 1st November. [61.

Johnston, John. *See* Susan NEWELL.

Jones, Alfred Poynter. *See* Jean Pierre VAQUIER.

Jones, Elizabeth Maud, blonde and pretty, a 'good-time girl', was born in Wales in July 1926. In November 1942, when she was sixteen, she married a soldier, but he struck her on the wedding night and that was the end of the marriage. She came to London in the following February and for a short time earned her living as a barmaid. After that, under the name of 'Georgina Grayson', she obtained engagements at various night clubs as a strip-tease dancer. Her last engagement ended in May 1944; after that, she lived on her husband's Army separation allowance. In September she went to live in a furnished room at 311 King Street, Hammersmith. For some of her meals she went to a café in Hammersmith Broadway, and it was there, on the night of Tuesday, 3rd October, that a malignant fate placed her in the path of a young man wearing the uniform of a lieutenant in the U.S. Army, who was introduced to her as 'Ricky' Allen. He was, in fact, entitled neither to the uniform nor to the name. **Karl Gustav Hulten,** to give him his proper style, was a private in the 501st Parachute Infantry Regiment, United States Army, who for several weeks past had been absent without leave. Born in Stockholm in 1922 of Swedish parents, he had been taken to the United States as a baby, and had grown up in Boston, where he was later employed as a clerk and as a mechanic. He was inducted into the U.S. Army in May 1943, and came to England in the early part of 1944. Surprisingly enough, he was short, stocky and dark-haired, and also, apparently, a Roman Catholic—a rare combination in a Scandinavian. So far he had no criminal record—it was a lack he was about to supply. Hulten's association with 'Georgie' Grayson, as he knew her, lasted for only six days. It began with a piece of petty banditry, and it ended with murder. The story of those six hectic days rests mainly upon the rival statements of Hulten and Jones. They diverge at crucial points. According to the girl's account, she was intimidated by Hulten, and followed him out of fear. Not so, said Hulten—the girl urged him on and, indeed, had it not been for her there would have been no murder at all. It was common ground between them that at their first meeting in the café Hulten asked 'Georgie' to meet him at 11.30 that same night. He turned up driving a stolen ten-wheeled U.S. Army truck. They drove towards Reading, and on the way the girl said she would like to do 'something dangerous'. This is Hulten's version of the conversation:

> I told her I was a paratrooper, and she said that was a dangerous profession to be in. I told her it was. 'Well,' she said, 'I would like to do something dangerous, like becoming a gun moll. . . . I thought she was kidding at first and I didn't take her serious, but she did say she was serious about it.

Here is the same conversation as recounted by the girl, Jones:

I told him in the truck that I would like to do something dangerous, meaning to go over Germany in a bomber. I meant that, but he got me wrong. He told me he had been a gunman in Chicago, that he was the leader of a gang operating in London. He showed me a gun and said he would use it on me if I told other people about this.

Whatever may have been said, the pair certainly set out to do 'something dangerous', and brilliantly they succeeded. That first night, at a village outside Reading, they robbed a girl cyclist of her purse. Two nights later—on the Thursday—they went out again in the stolen truck. At Runnymede, Hulten hit a girl over the head with an iron bar and half-strangled her. After 'Georgie' had gone through the girl's pockets, between them they carried her to the river's edge and threw her in. The girl was lucky to escape with her life. So much for the Thursday exploit. The events of Friday were to lead to murder. Here, not unnaturally, the accounts given by Hulten and by Jones are most at variance. Jones said that on the Friday night Hulten 'whistled' for her outside her house and that when she joined him in the street he said, 'Come on, let's go and get a taxi,' by which she understood he was intending to rob a taxi-driver. Hulten's version put the blame on the girl. It was she who talked about going out and robbing a cab. 'I argued against her,' said Hulten at the trial, 'and she just kept on arguing with me, and she told me to give her my gun, and she was going to go out by herself.' Whichever way the truth lies, the upshot was that the pair walked together along Hammersmith Road, where they presently saw a grey Ford V8 saloon coming towards them, very slowly, as if it were plying for hire. Whilst Hulten waited in a doorway the girl hailed the car. The driver was George Edward Heath, thirty-four years of age. He was using the car as a hire-service vehicle; it was not a taxi-cab, and by rights he ought not to have picked up casual passengers in the street. It was a small offence for which he had to pay with his life. Heath agreed to take the couple to King Street. When they got there Hulten told Heath to drive on. They got as far as the beginning of the Great West Road and there Hulten asked the driver to stop. This is the girl's account of what happened next:

Heath leaned over from his seat towards the middle of the car with the obvious intention of opening the near-side back door for me to get out. Ricky was sitting to my right, and as Heath was leaning over I saw a flash and heard a bang. I was surprised that there was not a loud bang because Ricky had told me it would make a big noise when it went off. I was deafened in my right ear by the bang.

Heath moaned slightly and turned a little towards his front. Ricky said to him, 'Move over or I'll give you another dose of the same.' ... Heath seemed to understand what Ricky said, because he moved further over to the left-hand side of the front seat until his shoulder was almost touching the near-side door. I heard him breathing very heavily and his head slumped on his chest. The next I realized was that Ricky was in the driving seat and the car was moving.

Jones went through Heath's pockets—under threat from Hulten, she insisted—and relieved him of his wallet, fountain pen, wristlet watch, silver cigarette case, lighter, silver pencil, and about £1 in silver. All the while Heath was 'breathing very heavily'; after a time he 'stopped breathing altogether'. Outside Staines Hulten stopped, dragged Heath's body out of the car, and rolled it into the ditch. The pair then drove back to London. They had something to eat at a café in Hammersmith Broadway; it was now about 3.45 on Saturday morning. Jones said:

After leaving the car we walked home. When we got indoors, I said, 'He's dead, isn't he?' and he said, 'Yes.' I said, 'That's cold-blooded murder, then. How could you do it?' and he said, 'People in my profession haven't time to think what they do.'

That evening they went to the greyhound racing at the White City Stadium. According to the Hulten version of these events, the shooting of Heath was an accident—also, Jones helped him to dump the body in the ditch. The body was found early on the Saturday morning and was quickly identified. Because Heath had a hollow in his chin, the case was at once christened in the Press the 'Cleft Chin Murder'. Naturally, it became of the first importance to trace the missing Ford V8; a description of it was circulated to all police stations. On the Monday evening a vigilant constable saw the car drawn up outside a house in Fulham Palace Road. Presently, Hulten, wearing the uniform of a U.S. Army officer, came out of the house, climbed into the driving seat, and was promptly arrested. Later that same day, a War Reserve policeman who knew Jones slightly had a chance meeting with her and remarked how ill and tired she was looking. She replied, 'If you had seen someone do what I have seen done *you* wouldn't be able to sleep at night.' This curious remark so impressed the policeman that he reported it to Inspector Tansill at Hammersmith Police Station. To the inspector, the girl said: 'I was in the car when Heath was shot. I didn't do it.' The U.S. Government waived its rights under the United States of America Visiting Forces Act, 1942, which provided that no criminal proceedings might normally be taken in any British court

against a member of the American armed forces. On 16th January 1945, Jones and Hulten were put on trial at the Old Bailey on an indictment charging them jointly with the murder of George Edward Heath. After a six days trial both were found guilty, the jury adding a recommendation to mercy in the case of the girl. Both were sentenced to death by Mr. Justice CHARLES. Hulten was duly hanged—five days after his twenty-third birthday—but, forty-eight hours before the time fixed for her execution, Jones was reprieved. She was released from prison nine years later, in May 1954, being then twenty-seven years old.
[2.

Joscelyn, Ralph John. *See* Paul HEFELD.

Jouannet, Doris. *See* Gordon Frederick CUMMINS.

Justifiable Homicide is of three kinds: (1) Homicide in the execution of the law, as when the hangman carries out an execution; (2) Homicide for the advancement of public justice, that is to say, justifiable by permission rather than command of the law, as when a policeman unintentionally kills a person resisting lawful arrest; and (3) Homicide in just defence of person and property, or for the prevention of some 'atrocious' crime—such as murder, rape, arson, burglary, etc.—which could not otherwise have been avoided (Jervis, *On the Office and Duties of Coroners*). *See* EXCUSABLE HOMICIDE.

K

Kill men i' the dark!

Shakespeare: *Othello*

Kassel, Max, otherwise Émile Allard, known to the French Sûreté as Max le Roquin, and to the international underworld as 'Red Max' or 'Max the Red', had a long and unsavoury record as a trafficker in drugs and women. Ostensibly a dealer in cheap jewellery, operating in Soho, Red Max, a Latvian by birth, specialized in finding husbands for foreign women seeking British nationality so that they could carry on their trade as prostitutes in the West End of London without risk of deportation. For a time he had a partner, a Frenchman who called himself Charles Lacroix, but whose real name was Roger Vernon, an escaped convict from Devil's Island. In 1936 Red Max was down on his luck, so much so that he could not raise the £25 he needed to pay off a debt to Lacroix's mistress, French-born Suzanne Naylor, who was continually pressing him for the money. Lacroix agreed to collect the debt for her. Signing himself 'Suzanne', he sent a note to Kassel proposing a meeting in Naylor's flat in Little Newport Street, Soho. When Kassel turned up—it was the evening of 23rd January 1936— he found to his discomfiture that it was Lacroix, not Suzanne, with whom he had to deal. He pleaded that he had no money. Whereupon Lacroix pumped six bullets into him from an automatic pistol. Amazingly, it took Kassel some time to die: indeed, he made a desperate fight of it, and actually succeeded in smashing a window in a fruitless attempt to summon help before expiring on the bathroom floor. Next morning, in the small hours, Kassel's body, wrapped in a blanket, was stowed in the back seat of an American car owned by a compatriot of Lacroix, a man named Alexandre, and driven out of London along the Great North Road. In Cell Barns Lane, on the southern outskirts of St. Albans, Lacroix and Alexandre tipped the body into the hedge, where it was discovered at about 10 o'clock that same morning by a carpenter cycling into town through the rain. It was not until three days later that the body was identified, by which time Lacroix and Suzanne had fled to Paris. Application was made for their extradition, Lacroix on a murder charge, Suzanne as an accessory, but the French authorities refused to surrender either: Lacroix was an escaped convict from a French penal settlement, and as for Suzanne, it turned out that her *mariage de convenance* to the unknown Naylor was a bigamous one, she having married a Frenchman named Emile Bertron eight years previously: she was, therefore, a French, not a British, subject. Lacroix (under his proper name of Vernon) was tried for murder at the *Assize de la Seine* in Paris in April 1937. Suzanne Bertron was charged with him as an accessory after the fact. Lacroix was found guilty and sentenced to ten years imprisonment with hard labour, to be followed by expulsion from France for a period of twenty years. The woman was acquitted.

[*34, 80.*

Keen, Ruby. *See* Leslie George STONE.

Kelly, George, aged twenty-seven, a small-time gangster on Merseyside, pushed his way into the manager's office at the Cameo Cinema, Liverpool, soon after 9.30 on the evening of 19th March 1949; he was armed with a revolver and was wearing a mask. In the office, the manager, Leonard Thomas, and his assistant, John Bernard Catterall, were checking the night's takings. Within a matter of seconds the box-office cashier, Mrs. Jackman, who had just left Mr. Thomas's office, was horrified to hear the staccato rattle of six shots fired in rapid succession. Courageously, she ran towards the door of the office. In the doorway she and the cinema doorman were thrust aside by Kelly, who, gun in hand, and still wearing his mask, ordered them to 'stand back', and then made his escape down an emergency staircase. Both Mr. Thomas and the assistant manager lay stretched out on the floor of the office; both died later from gunshot wounds. All this time, unaware of the real-life drama going on outside the darkened auditorium an audience of some seven hundred persons was watching the feature film. Energetic police inquiries were continued for six months, without result. Then an anonymous letter was received; it offered information about the Cameo Cinema murders—in return for a guarantee of police protection. As requested, the police inserted in *The Liverpool Echo*: 'Letter received. Promise definitely given.' The sequel to this was the arrest of George Kelly and with him **Charles Connolly,** aged twenty-six, another Liverpool thief; they were charged jointly with the murder of Leonard Thomas. The case against Connolly was that he had aided and abetted Kelly in the murder by keeping watch outside the cinema, where he was ready to give the alarm; when he had heard the shots, however, he had run away in a panic. Miss Rose HEILBRON K.C.

was briefed to defend Kelly at the trial, which opened at Liverpool Assizes in the following January. Miss Heilbron had only lately become a King's Counsel; she was now to make legal history as the first woman to *lead* for the defence in a murder trial. 'I want no Judy defending me,' Kelly is alleged to have said upon hearing that Miss Heilbron had been briefed. The brilliant handling of his defence was to change his opinion very quickly. The thirteen days trial—presided over by Mr. Justice Oliver—ended in disagreement among the jury, who were unable to arrive at a verdict. They were discharged, and Kelly and Connolly were put back for re-trial at the next Assizes in February. This time they were tried separately. At Kelly's second trial—before Mr. Justice Cassels—he was again represented by Miss Heilbron. She fought valiantly for him, but this time the jury were of one mind and brought in a verdict which led to Kelly's execution at Walton Prison on 28th March 1950, a few days after the first anniversary of the Cameo Cinema murders. Connolly was charged for the second time—also before Mr. Justice Cassels—on 13th February. No evidence was offered against him on the murder charge and, upon the judge's direction, the jury returned a verdict of 'Not Guilty'. Instead Connolly pleaded guilty to robbing the manager of £50, the night's takings, and also to conspiring with Kelly and other persons to carry out the robbery. On the first charge he was sentenced to two years imprisonment and on the second to two years, the sentences to run concurrently.

Kennedy, William Henry. *See* Frederick Guy BROWNE.

Kerrigan, Daniel. *See* John M'GUIGAN.

Kilmuir of Creich, Viscount (*b.* **1900**). Lord High Chancellor since October 1954. Called to the Bar by Gray's Inn in 1922, success came early to David Patrick Maxwell Fyfe in the form of a busy and rewarding practice. In 1934 he became a King's Counsel, and in the following year he entered the House of Commons as Conservative M.P. for the West Derby Division of Liverpool, which he continued to represent until he went to the Woolsack nineteen years later. From 1942 until the wartime Coalition Government went out of office in 1945 he was Solicitor-General, and during the brief lifetime of the so-called 'Caretaker' Government, Attorney-General. When Winston Churchill formed his post-war administration in 1951, Maxwell Fyfe became Home Secretary and Minister for Welsh Affairs. In the major reconstruction of the Cabinet which took place in October 1954, he was appointed Lord Chancellor and took his seat on the Woolsack as Viscount Kilmuir of Creich, a post he retained in the two succeeding

Governments. Murder trials with which he was associated include those of Chung Yo MIAO; Dr. Buck RUXTON; and John George HAIGH.

King, William Laurie, a young man of twenty-two, who lived with his parents in Murrayfield Gardens, Edinburgh, had a strong natural bent for things scientific, liked pottering about with 'the wireless'—then in its crystal and cat's whisker days—and was addicted to chemical experiment, for which purpose his father, James Rae King, allowed him the use of an upstairs room as a laboratory. He had hoped to follow a scientific career, but his father was set upon the lad becoming a chartered accountant, like himself. Against his will, young William was apprenticed to a firm of accountants in Edinburgh, his indenture being afterwards transferred to his father's office. In May 1924 he was supposed to take his C.A. intermediate examination. But he did not sit for it. When his mother, Agnes Scott King, broke the news to her husband, he was naturally angry and disappointed, but accepted the obvious fact that the youth would never make an accountant and had better be allowed to go his own way. Before supper on the evening of 30th May, the father discussed with his son plans for sending him to a university to study for his B.Sc. in chemistry. Supper in the King household was a frugal meal. It consisted that evening of bread, butter, cheese, jelly, and coffee. Four people sat down to table—Mr. and Mrs. King and their two sons, William, and his younger brother, Alexis, aged sixteen. William cut the bread, handed a slice to each of his parents. Alexis cut the cheese, of which Mr. King complained that it caused 'a burning sensation' in his throat. His wife, on the other hand, found nothing amiss with it. Soon after the meal was over both Mr. and Mrs. King were violently sick; at intervals, for some hours afterwards, the vomiting recurred. The family doctor was sent for, but he was out. Mr. King went to bed in the spare room; he was sick at 12.30 a.m., and again at 2 a.m. Afterwards he went into his wife's room to see how she was, and found her lying dead. Organs of the body submitted for analysis were found to contain 3·01 grains of arsenious oxide, the residue of what had clearly been a considerable dose—at least ten grains. In the pocket of a jacket belonging to young William King, which was hanging in a wardrobe, the police found a glass bottle containing a white powder. The bottle was labelled *Potass. Ferricyanide*, but inside was three-quarters of an ounce of white arsenic. It now transpired that on 26th May young William had obtained one pound of arsenious oxide from a wholesale chemical dealer in Edinburgh. King was put on trial, before Lord Constable within the High Court of Justiciary at Edinburgh, charged with the murder of his mother and the attempted murder of his father. The Crown case was embarrassed from the start by the fact that there seemed to be too much arsenic and too little motive. The prosecution need not, it is true, establish motive, but it would have been convenient to have been able to show that King had been on bad terms with his father and mother and wished them ill. Instead, all the evidence was to the contrary; the young man had been a devoted son and had never been heard to express himself unkindly about either of his parents. The Solicitor-General for Scotland, Mr. J. C. Fenton K.C., did the best he could with some rather flimsy material. He submitted that King, whilst cutting the bread, had taken a pinch of arsenic between his finger and thumb and had sprinkled it on the slice of bread he had handed to his father; his mother's death had been an accident which he had not intended. Giving evidence in his own behalf, King explained that he had purchased the arsenic for certain chemical experiments, particularly for deriving a magenta dye from coal-tar. He had also wished to produce a crystal for his wireless set, a process which involved the use of arsenious oxide and sulphur. His mother had found a packet containing arsenious oxide and had taken it downstairs. On the Monday after her death, he had found it in the right angle formed by the first shelf and the sliding door of the pantry press— where the stale bread was put when taken out of the crock. Upon finding the packet, which had 'kind of burst', he had taken from it what he had required for his experiments—two ounces—and had put it into a bottle which bore an old label *Potass. Ferricyanide*; the remainder he had poured down the pantry sink. In his closing speech to the jury, defence counsel, Mr. Condie Sandeman K.C., suggested that the cheese had been the medium for transmitting the poison; his theory was that Mrs. King had put the cheese on the shelf, and that, by a fatal accident, it had come into contact with the split packet of arsenious oxide. It undoubtedly told heavily with the jury that King himself had been taken ill after supper, having been very sick on three separate occasions. After a twenty-six minutes retirement, the jury came back into court with a verdict of 'Not Guilty' on both charges. It was received with loud applause, instantly suppressed, and King was discharged.

[72, *180*.

Klosowski, Severin. *See* George CHAPMAN.

Kopsch, Alfred Arthur, living with his parents at Highbury, in north London, was a gentle, sensitive boy, shrinking from any sort of violence. In 1921, when he was fourteen, his mother's brother, Arthur Walter Thornton, brought his young wife back from India. Beryl Lilian Thornton was the daughter of an English mother and an Eurasian father; at seventeen she was passionate and wilful, extremely attractive to men. The impact she made upon the adolescent boy whose home she had come to share was explosive. Calf love can be agonizing and cruel as well as tender; as Kopsch grew older it developed into a passion beyond his control. Beryl Thornton, only a few years older than her nephew, but emotionally far more mature, responded. When they met on the stairs they would exchange notes in which they professed for each other a high romantic passion. The inevitable happened. They became lovers. In September 1925 Beryl Thornton told the boy—he was now eighteen—that she thought she was going to have a baby and that he was the father of it. She begged him to kill her. On the night of 15th September they went to Hampstead Heath, and by scrambling through a hole in the fence found themselves in Ken Wood. The next morning the body of Beryl Thornton was found lying beneath a tree, a necktie fastened with a double knot gripping her tightly about the neck. Later that day Kopsch told the police: 'We lay down by the side of a tree and she asked me to strangle her while she was asleep. At 2 a.m. I thought she was asleep. I put my thumb on her neck and tied my necktie round her neck. I then covered her with my overcoat.' At his trial at the Old Bailey in October before Mr. Justice Branson, Mr. St.John HUTCHIN-SON unsuccessfully endeavoured to establish a defence based on *irresistible impulse* (*see* M'NAGHTEN RULES). The following passage, which occurred during the cross-examination of Dr. Cecil MacFadden, a police surgeon, illustrates the skilful development of this line of defence by a counsel who was throughout his professional life keenly interested in abnormal psychology:

> *Mr. Hutchinson:* If someone had reiterated commands given to him, such as 'Kill me', might not he, in his state of mind, have done things without appreciating what he was doing?
> *Dr. MacFadden:* I suppose so.
> *Mr. Hutchinson:* Suppose a boy—very emotionally moved and in a curious condition altogether—suddenly loses control of himself, his sub-conscious mind might take charge of him and make him do something without his appreciating what he was doing?
> *Dr. MacFadden:* I suppose so.
> *Mr. Justice Branson:* I don't quite understand this. Is the theory that the prisoner's condition of mind was such that his conscious mind ceased to function and he strangled the woman through the action of his sub-conscious mind?
> *Mr. Hutchinson:* Yes, my Lord.
> *Dr. MacFadden:* I do not think the conscious mind was lost in this

case. We know the sub-conscious mind plays an important part, but I cannot say it takes up the work if the conscious mind is absent.

Mr. Hutchinson called evidence to show that Kopsch was 'a particularly gentle character', and also that there was a history of insanity in his family. Counsel submitted that the boy had known what he was doing when he had strangled Beryl Thornton, but that he had been unable to control his feelings—to such a degree that, under the law, he was not responsible for his act. Under the stress of circumstances his mind had given way, and the woman's repeated command, 'Kill me! Kill me!' had taken command of his sub-conscious mind and had urged him to the act. That, said Mr. Hutchinson, constituted a disease of the mind. This plea, although powerfully presented, did not convince the jury, who found Kopsch guilty—with a recommendation to mercy. The boy was sentenced to death, but was reprieved a few weeks later.

L

Let me have
A dram of poison, such soon-speeding geer
As will dispense itself through all the veins.

Shakespeare: *Romeo and Juliet*

Lacroix, Charles (otherwise **Vernon, Roger**). *See* Max KASSEL.

Lalcaca, Dr. Cowas. *See* Madar Lal DHINGRA.

Lawrence, Edward, a wealthy brewer of Wolverhampton, notorious for his drunkenness, violence, and licentious habits, called at the home of a local doctor on the night of 29th December 1908, and although far gone in drink and distraught besides, managed to make the doctor understand that he had 'shot a woman'. It was a bitterly cold night, and snow was falling as the doctor hurried back with Lawrence to the latter's house. There, stretched out on the floor of the dining-room in her outdoor clothes, was a young and pretty woman, bleeding from a bullet wound in her right temple and another in her right arm; shortly after the doctor's arrival she died. The woman was a local barmaid named Ruth Hadley, who had been named in a divorce suit brought against Lawrence by his wife. Lawrence was in an hysterical condition; he seemed heart-broken, yet at the same time brazenly defiant. At one moment he was imploring the doctor to do everything he could to save the woman's life, and at the next he was boasting: 'I am glad I did it. She is best dead. She drove me to it. You don't know what a wicked woman she has been.' When the police came he was charged with murder. To that he replied: 'Murder, you say, do you? That's all right.' Later on he adopted a different tone: 'Well, there's one thing—I didn't do it. She shot herself.' Such was the unpromising situation which faced Mr. (later Sir) Edward Marshall HALL K.C., when he accepted the brief to defend Lawrence at his trial, which took place before Mr. Justice JELF at Stafford Assizes in the following March. It was expected that Marshall Hall would invite a verdict of man-slaughter, that being the best he could hope for; instead, he boldly demanded an acquittal, representing the death of Ruth Hadley to be the accidental result of a drunken brawl between herself and her lover. First, he called witnesses to show that the woman had repeatedly threatened to shoot Lawrence, had stabbed him with a hatpin, and had broken the steel handle of an umbrella over his head. Of the revolver which had killed her she had been heard to say, 'This is the thing I will do him in with—I shall only get eighteen months.' Gradually the picture emerged of a violent, drunken woman who had made Lawrence's life unendurable. (She had said on one occasion, 'It has been my privilege to drive him potty.') On the night of the fateful quarrel, Marshall Hall suggested to the jury, Ruth had been in a particularly vicious mood, because Lawrence had lately taken another woman to his bed and had turned her out of it. It was against this background, adroitly prepared by his counsel, that Lawrence, a well-educated, and in his sober moments, pleasant-spoken man, went into the witness-box to describe the events which had ended in Ruth Hadley's death. That night, he said, both he and Ruth had been drinking heavily. Ruth had thrown crockery and fire-irons at him, and he had ordered her out of the house—for good. Intending only to frighten her, he had rushed upstairs to his bedroom to fetch his revolver—a relic of his earlier years in South America—and had fired it at her. He had tried to make the shot go wide, but he now realized that he had slightly wounded Ruth in her right arm. He had then gone back upstairs and had hidden the revolver under the mattress in his bedroom. Hardly had he returned to the dining-room when Ruth had pushed past him, and, going upstairs herself, had ransacked his bedroom to find the revolver. She had come downstairs and had pointed the weapon at him; he had seen the hammer rising and had flung himself forward to save his life. He had gripped her wrist and in the struggle the revolver had gone off. Marshall Hall invited Lawrence to demonstrate to the jury how the revolver pointed automatically upwards when the wrist of the person holding it was gripped by another hand. This was followed by another demonstration even more dramatic, when, at Mr. Justice Jelf's invitation, Lawrence grappled with the judge's clerk within a few feet of the jury, and showed them how the revolver, whose mechanism was admittedly defective, had been discharged in the struggle. This performance was repeated three times; three times the revolver was forced upwards as Lawrence gripped the clerk's wrist; three times the jury heard the tell-tale click as the hammer fell. 'It shows that it was possible to be done,' said the judge, thoughtfully. The prosecution now invited the jury to return a verdict of manslaughter if they felt unable to convict Lawrence of murder. They preferred acquittal, and it was with a verdict of 'Not Guilty' that they filed back into court after a retirement of only twenty minutes. It is stated in Edward Marjoribanks's well-known *Life of Sir Edward Marshall Hall* that the great advocate always regarded this acquittal as his 'greatest victory in a murder trial'.

[*131.*

Lee, Minnie Freeman, a widow of ninety-four, lived alone in a big, neglected house in Ray Park Avenue, Maidenhead, Berkshire. Once she had been rich, but that had been long years before when her barrister husband and her three sons had been alive; by 1948 all she had besides the house, with its seventeen rooms (and maybe her memories of gay days at the turn of the century when she had lavishly entertained there), was a small monthly stipend from a legal benevolent society. However, since few people were ever admitted to the once grand house, to see the moth-eaten carpets, the rotting furniture thick with dust, and the extraordinary collection of old junk which littered the rooms, there was nothing to disturb the legend, widely believed in the neighbourhood, that Mrs. Lee, besides being eccentric and a recluse, was also a wealthy woman. It was a fiction which brought this poor old lady to an agonizing end. On 1st June 1948, the milkman noticed that the bottles he had been leaving at the house during the past two days had not been taken in. He remarked upon this to a carpenter who was working next door. This man peered through Mrs. Lee's letter-box, and saw in the hall a large black leather trunk and beside it on the floor a woman's court shoe and a bunch of keys. He found this prospect vaguely disquieting and called the police. An entry was forced and the trunk in the hall was opened. Doubled up inside it was the body of Mrs. Lee, her arms tied behind her back with a woollen shawl. She had been struck savagely about the head, but these injuries had not been the cause of death. Mrs. Lee had been put inside the trunk whilst still alive, and had been allowed to suffocate slowly, perhaps over a period of several hours. Scotland Yard was called in, and Chief-Superintendent Cherrill, chief of the Fingerprint Bureau, carried out a methodical search of the house. Ransacking drawers and cupboards, the murderer had left confusion behind—but not a single fingerprint; clearly, he was an experienced operator. Superintendent Cherrill persisted. Eventually he found, among the tumbled folds of the eiderdown quilt on the bed, a cardboard box two inches square, and under the bed the lid to it. On the edge of the lid were two fragmentary prints. They were faint and half effaced, but they were sufficient to identify one **George Russell,** a many times convicted thief, whose prints were on the files, as the man who had been in Mrs. Lee's house. Russell was arrested at St. Albans a few days later. He broke down and wept. Yes, he said, he had been at the house—to see the old lady about a job as a gardener. But his next words contained a most damaging implication: 'I was told she had a lot of money by another man. Did I murder this poor aged woman for *something she was supposed to have, and had not*? No, I did not figure in such a murder. I am not a man of such disposition. I am not prepared to risk my life, bad as my financial position may be. I am not prepared to "take the can back" for someone else.' When he faced his trial at Berkshire Assizes before Mr. Justice HALLETT, those words printed in italics were fatal to Russell, for they made plain to the jury who it was who had searched for hidden treasure—*and had not been able to find it*. Russell was convicted, sentenced to death, and in due course hanged at Oxford.

[*42, 85.*

Le Neve, Ethel. *See* Hawley Harvey CRIPPEN.

Lennox, William. *See* Thomas Mathieson BROWN.

Ley, Thomas John, formerly Minister of Justice in New South Wales, Australia, died from a meningeal hæmorrhage in Broadmoor Criminal Lunatic Asylum (now Broadmoor Institution) on 25th July 1947, four months after he and a man named **Lawrence John Smith** had been jointly convicted of the notorious 'Chalk-pit Murder', that nightmare essay in *Grand Guignol*. The processes by which it was to be revealed in all its strangeness and horror began on the afternoon of Saturday, 30th November 1946, when Walter Tom Coombs, returning to his home at Woldingham, Surrey, came upon the dead body of a man lying across a newly dug trench at the top of an old chalk-pit a little way off the road. Two pieces of rope were twined loosely around the body and there were deep grooves in the neck. It was concluded from a post-mortem examination that the man had been slowly strangled, having first received a severe blow on the head—sufficient to cause unconsciousness—and another in the stomach. This was later somewhat elaborated to suggest that the man had been hanged, but hanged without a 'drop', or, at any rate, that death had been caused by a rope which had been 'pulled upwards'. In the dead man's pocket was a card which quickly led to the identification of the body as that of John McMain Mudie, a barman at the Reigate Hill Hotel, Reigate, Surrey, who had been missing since the previous Thursday, 28th November. Mudie was a decent, unoffending, kindly person, of whom everyone spoke well. Events were to show how cruelly he had been sacrificed to the insane illusions of a man whose portly dignity and consequential air helped to conceal the fact that he was a hopeless paranoic. Thomas John Ley enters the story at a very early stage in the police investigation. It may be convenient now, rather than later, to examine his background. He was born at Bath, Somerset, in 1880, but was taken by his parents to Australia whilst still a boy. After leaving school he went to work as a butcher's boy, but by diligent study so far improved himself that he was eventually able to qualify as a solicitor. In 1917 he was elected to the Legislative Assembly of New South Wales and in due course became Minister of Public Instruction, then Minister of Labour, and finally, from 1922 to 1925, Minister of Justice. In the latter year, he was elected to the Australian House of Representatives, but lost his seat in 1928. He had combined his busy public life with a career as company promoter. Some of his enterprises in this line had been distinctly dubious, and when the police started to make inconvenient inquiries, which they did round about the time he lost his parliamentary seat, Ley thought it prudent to return to the land of his birth. He came to London in 1929, and was followed some months later by a Mrs. Brook, a widow, who afterwards became his mistress. Maggie Evelyn Byron Brook was the unwitting, and unlikely, cause of Mudie's death. At the time of the murder she was sixty-six years of age and of homely appearance, hardly the sort of woman, it might have been thought, to drive a man to desperate deeds. But by 1946, despite the fact that it had been twelve years since he and Maggie Brook had been lovers, Ley was in the grip of a possessive jealousy that had long since passed the limit of what is possible to a sanely constituted mind. He was presently inhabiting a world of pure fantasy in which the unfortunate Mrs. Brook had only to exchange a casual word with a man for Ley to be convinced that his ageing *inamorata* had taken to herself a new lover. Mudie comes upon the scene in June 1945. He was at that time a lodger in the house at Wimbledon where Mrs. Brook had a flat, and one day, in a luckless moment for him, the landlady introduced him to Mrs. Brook as he was passing through the hall. They exchanged a few polite words. Mrs. Brook never saw or spoke to him again. Out of this trivial incident, magnified and distorted by the workings of a diseased mind, grew a monstrous conspiracy which took eighteen months to mature. On 14th December, a fortnight after the discovery of Mudie's body, a curious trio presented themselves at New Scotland Yard—an ex-boxer named John William Buckingham, now engaged in the hire-car business; his son (also John William); and a Mrs. Lilian Florence Bruce, a cook-housekeeper from Putney. They had a remarkable story to tell. Mr. Buckingham, the father, described how in the early autumn of 1946, the hall porter at the Royal Hotel, Woburn Place, Bloomsbury, had advised him to get in touch with Ley, who, it appeared, was looking for a car driver who could keep his mouth shut. Buckingham had telephoned Ley, and had met him at the Royal Hotel next evening, by appointment.

Ley had not been alone. With him had been a certain Lawrence John Smith, the foreman of the workmen engaged upon converting Ley's home at 5 Beaufort Gardens, Kensington, into flats. At this and later meetings Buckingham had been given to understand that, as a solicitor, Ley was interested in protecting two women, mother and daughter, who were being blackmailed by the barman at the Reigate Hill Hotel. What Ley had wanted was to decoy Mudie to the house in Beaufort Gardens, to confront him with the proof of his blackmailing activities, and extract from him a promise to leave the country. Various ways of getting Mudie to the house had been discussed. Finally, it had been agreed that, posing as a woman of means, Mrs. Bruce, the cook-housekeeper, a friend of Buckingham *père*, should visit the Reigate Hill Hotel once or twice, and, having thus scraped an acquaintance with Mudie, invite him to be barman at a cocktail party she was supposed to be giving at Beaufort Gardens on 28th November. All had turned out as planned. Mudie had agreed to act as barman at the party, since, by a not so curious chance, the date chosen for it happened to be his half-day off. Mrs. Bruce, accompanied by the younger Buckingham, had called for Mudie and had driven him up to London, arriving at Ley's house at about 7 p.m. Smith and Buckingham *père* had been lying in wait just inside the basement door. Buckingham had thrown a blanket over Mudie's head, and Smith had tied his ankles and wound a rope round his body. In this helpless condition, he had been 'jumped along' the passage and into a room which Ley used as an office. There Mudie was placed in a swivel-chair in front of a desk and gagged with a piece of rag. Buckingham had then left, first receiving from Ley, who all this while had been standing on the stairs, an envelope containing two hundred one-pound notes, as his and his son's and Mrs. Bruce's share in the kidnapping. Buckingham did not see Smith again until the following Tuesday, 3rd December. Smith had then told him: 'The old man was very pleased with the way things went off. Mudie has signed a confession and was given five hundred pounds and got out of the country.' Ley was interviewed at Scotland Yard. There, in the presence of his solicitor, he made a long statement which amounted to a denial of everything that had been said both by Buckingham and by Smith. He had never mentioned Mudie to Smith; there had been no plot, no kidnapping. The statement ended: 'So far as my knowledge goes, Jack Mudie has never been at 5 Beaufort Gardens, and I have never seen him there.' On 28th December, Ley, Smith, and Buckingham were arrested and jointly charged with murder. But later Buckingham was released, and at the trial of Ley and Smith, which took place at the Old Bailey before the Lord Chief Justice, Lord GODDARD, he was called as a Crown witness. The pair made an odd contrast in the dock; Ley, portly and prosperous-looking, suave, well-dressed; Smith, the working man, thirty years Ley's junior, and in appearance and demeanour the very opposite of his companion. Evidence was given which strongly suggested that on the day before the kidnapping Smith had visited the chalk-pit at Woldingham. From this the jury were invited to draw the conclusion that he had been on a reconnaissance, and had selected the chalk-pit—conveniently remote from Kensington—as a suitable place at which to 'dump' the body of the unfortunate Mudie. A verdict of 'Guilty' was returned against both prisoners, and 8th May was fixed as the date for their execution. But on 5th May, the Home Office announced that following a medical inquiry into Ley's mental condition he had been found to be insane, and had been removed to Broadmoor. That being so, it was inevitable that Smith should be reprieved also; in his case the death sentence was commuted to one of life imprisonment.

[*I, 2.*

Light, Ronald Vivian, the central figure in the celebrated 'Green Bicycle' case, offers an instructive example of how a man innocently involved in a murder inquiry ought *not* to behave. From the account given below it will be seen that there is nothing in his conduct which disturbs the perfect pattern of folly. At about 6.30 p.m. on 5th July 1919, Annie Bella Wright set out on her bicycle to visit her uncle, George William Measures, a roadman who lived at Gaulby, a peaceful hamlet typical of the hunting country around Leicester. Miss Wright lived with her parents at Stoughton, about five miles away. She was a strong, good-looking girl, twenty-one years old, quiet and sensible; formerly a domestic servant, she had been working for the past two years at St. Mary's Rubber Mills in Leicester. At about 7.30 p.m. she arrived at Mr. Measures' cottage. With her was a young man on a green bicycle, who waited outside whilst she went in to see her uncle. It happened that Mr. Measures' son-in-law, a miner named James Evans, was there on a visit. Both he and Mr. Measures were naturally rather curious to know who the mysterious stranger was. Miss Wright said she knew nothing at all about the man; he had overtaken her on the road and she had passed the time of day with him in a casual way. Perhaps if she waited a little while he would go. But when the time came for her to leave, the man was still there. As Miss Wright came out he made a remark to her which somewhat startled Mr. Measures. 'Bella, you were a long time,' he said. 'I thought you were gone the other way.' Both Mr. Measures and his son-in-law were quite certain that the man said 'Bella'—not 'Hello', as was afterwards suggested. The point was to assume some importance, since, on the face of it, the use of her Christian name would seem to contradict Miss Wright's statement that the man was a complete stranger to her. The two of them rode away together. Both Mr. Measures and Mr. Evans put the time as 'about a quarter to nine', but it was probably somewhat later than that. What is indisputable is that at about 9.20 the dead body of Bella Wright was found lying in the middle of the Gartree Road, the old Roman highway—also called the Via Devana—rather more than two miles from Gaulby. It was at first assumed that Miss Wright had met her death as the result of a bicycle accident. But the local constable, P. C. Hall, was not entirely satisfied. Early next morning he returned to the scene of the supposed accident, and after a close search discovered a revolver bullet half-embedded in the roadway. A closer medical examination revealed that Miss Wright had been shot through the head, and from the character and direction of the wound it appeared that she might have been lying on her back in the road when she was killed. There was no scorching of the face, which argued that the bullet had been fired at a range of not less than five feet. This discovery transformed an ordinary routine inquiry into a nation-wide murder hunt—for the man with the green bicycle. Scotland Yard was called in, but despite the most exhausting efforts, more than seven months passed by without bringing a solution any nearer; both man and bicycle had effectively vanished. Then, on 23rd February 1920, a boatman who was taking a load of coal through the canal at Leicester noticed his tow-rope slacken, dip, and then, as it tautened again, drag up from below the surface of the water the frame and front wheel of a green bicycle. It hung suspended from the rope for a moment, then slipped back again. The next day the boatman went back to the spot and fished it out. Subsequent dragging by the police recovered other parts of the machine, and also a revolver holster with live cartridges in it. All the usual marks of identification had been scraped off the bicycle—that is, all except one, the serial number 103,648 on the pillar of the handlebar bracket. By means of this number the purchase of the bicycle was traced to one Ronald Light, who had formerly been living with his mother in Leicester, but was now an assistant master at a school in Cheltenham. To the police officers who went there to question him Light denied (1) that he had ever owned a green bicycle; (2) that he had been in the Gaulby district on the day of the murder; (3) that he had ever seen Bella Wright. Light was taken back to Leicester, where he was identified by Mr. Measures and Mr. Evans as the stranger who had called at the cottage with Miss Wright. He was put on trial at Leicester Assizes before Mr. Justice HORRIDGE in the following June, when he was defended by Sir Edward Marshall HALL K.C. and by Mr. Norman Birkett (afterwards Lord BIRKETT). During a five-hours ordeal in the witness-box, Light told a detailed story of how he had spent the evening of 5th July. He said that after calling upon some friends of his mother in Leicester he had gone for a bicycle ride in the country. Having got as far as Little Stretton, he had made to return home by the Upper Road; this was not the quickest way back, but he had not been in any particular hurry. It was then that he had encountered Bella Wright—a complete stranger to him. He went on:

> As I got up to the young lady she was stooping over her bicycle, and she looked up at my approach and asked me if I could lend her a spanner. I had no spanner with me, and I just looked at her bicycle. As far as I could see, from what she pointed out to me, there was a certain amount of play in the free-wheel. I could not do anything to it as I had no spanner. After that we rode on together. We came to a village. I asked her the name of the village, and she said it was Gaulby. . . . She told me that she was going to see some friends there. She said, 'I shall only be ten minutes or a quarter of an hour,' so we rode into the village together, and I went with her as far as the house where she was going.

When Miss Wright had come out they had ridden away together. At the junction of the Upper Road and the Via Devana, Miss Wright had said, 'I must say good-bye to you here.' Light went on: 'I said, "But isn't this a shorter way to Leicester?" She said, "I don't live there." I said, "Well, I must go this way, because I am late already, and with this puncture I may have to walk part of the way home." '

> *Marshall Hall:* Did you shake hands with her or anything of that kind?
> *Light:* No, we were standing some distance apart.
> *Marshall Hall:* Did you ever see her again after you parted at the Common?
> *Light:* No.

Light was then asked about his conduct after he had read in *The Leicester Mercury* about Miss Wright's death. 'I saw the description of the bicycle and the man in the paper,' he said, 'and came to the conclusion that it must have been the girl I was with.'

> *Marshall Hall:* You made the fatal mistake of not communicating with the police?
> *Light:* Yes.
> *Mr. Justice Horridge:* Did you tell a living soul?
> *Light:* I told no one.

Later, upon being pressed further by the judge, Light said: 'I did not make up my mind deliberately not to come forward. I was astounded and frightened at this unexpected thing. I kept on hesitating and, in the end, I drifted into doing nothing at all.' In fact, what he did do was, first of all, to take his bicycle upstairs to the boxroom, and later, under cover of darkness, to smuggle it out of the house and throw it into the canal, having first, as he thought, obliterated all the identifying marks. He also threw his revolver holster into the canal. (Light swore that he no longer had the revolver which had belonged to it; this he had left behind in France when he was demobilized after the war.) Invited to explain his various denials when, in spite of these precautions, he was traced by the police, Light said, simply: 'They were the result of saying the first thing that came into my head.' If ever a man worked hard to put a rope around his own neck it was Ronald Light. However, in spite of himself and his foolish behaviour, he was found not guilty, the jury's verdict being received with 'salvos of cheers' from the crowds outside the courthouse. The mystery of the death of Bella Wright has not advanced one step nearer a solution since that far-off day.

[*131, 159, 211.*]

Lock Ah Tam was one of the most respected and influential members of the Chinese community in England and certainly one of the best known. He was the European representative of the Jack Ah Tai, an organization of Chinese stevedores, with headquarters in Hong Kong, the superintendent of Chinese sailors for three British steamship companies and, as President of the Koch Mai Tong, a world-wide Chinese republican organization, the agent in England of Sun Yat Sen himself. All this gave him a position of great authority among his fellow countrymen here, and particularly among Chinese seamen on Merseyside, where he lived with his Welsh-born wife, formerly Catherine Morgan, and his two daughters, Doris and Cecilia. It was an authority which drew its strength from the affection in which this gentle, good-hearted man was universally held; his sympathy and kindness were unfailing, his acts of charity innumerable. One unlucky night in 1918 he was wounded in an altercation with some drunken Russian sailors who forced their way into the seamen's club he had founded at Liverpool. This appears to have had a more far-reaching effect upon him than might have been expected from the more or less trivial nature of the injury. At all events, from that time forward he became liable to violent fits of rage, which would come upon him without warning, and apparently without provocation: on such occasions he would foam at the mouth, his face would swell, and his eyes would bulge from his head. This emotional instability reflected a profound deterioration in his character. Heavy drinking aggravated it; crippling losses in a shipping venture and subsequent bankruptcy completed it. But in spite of increasing moroseness there were times when his attractive qualities would reassert themselves, disclosing once again the essential goodness of the man, and the sweetness of his disposition. One such occasion was the party which Lock Ah Tam gave at his flat in Birkenhead on 1st December 1925, to celebrate the coming-of-age of his son, Lock Ling Tam, lately returned from his schooling in China. The host was at his most charming and urbane, warmly affectionate towards his son, solicitious for the comfort and enjoyment of his guests. Nothing occurred to mar the festivities, which were continued into the early hours of the next morning. Yet the last of the guests had not long departed before a terrible change came over the amiable Lock Ah Tam. He began to rage against his wife, stamping and screaming in a manner which showed him to be quite beside himself. Disturbed by the uproar, the son, who had gone up to bed, hurried downstairs to remonstrate with his father. Lock Ah Tam left the room, and was heard shouting to the Chinese maid, Margaret Sing, to bring him his boots. As the terrified servant crept downstairs, she glanced through the open door of her master's room and saw his reflection in the mirror on the wall—he was loading his revolver. A few minutes later he killed his wife at point-blank range with a shotgun, and also his eighteen-years-old daughter, Cecilia. His elder daughter, Doris, aged twenty, hid behind the scullery door, with the maid. 'Oh, Maggie, isn't it awful,' she moaned, as her father, revolver in one hand, shotgun in the other, stormed into the room. Dragging back the door, he shot her with the revolver; she died shortly afterwards. The son had, in the meantime, rushed out of the house to summon help, pausing only to throw a kettle through the window at his father. (He missed him.) By the time he returned with two police officers Lock Ah Tam had already telephoned the police station. 'Send your folks, please,' he said. 'I have killed my wife and children.' Chinese from all over Britain contributed to a defence fund. At his trial, before Mr. Justice (afterwards Lord Justice) MACKINNON at Chester Assizes in February 1926, his counsel, none other than the celebrated Sir Edward Marshall HALL K.C., pleaded that the prisoner had killed his dearly beloved wife and daughters whilst in a state of 'unconscious automatism', brought on by an epileptic fit. A specialist in mental disorders called by the defence said that, like a sleep-walker, a man in such a condition might have every appearance of consciousness, yet have no knowledge of what he was saying or doing. 'I do not suppose,' said Marshall Hall, in a characteristic address to the jury, 'that if you were to search the tragedies of the Greek poets you would find anything more poignant than this tragedy. . . . Some minute happening in the brain caused a change for which none of us can account. It turned a man—a mild, lovable, peaceable man—into a raving madman. . . . Absolutely and entirely motiveless, he killed those whom he loved best. . . . Yes, there is no doubt he did it, but at the time he did it he was insane.' Unhappily for Lock Ah Tam the plea of insanity had to satisfy the test of the M'NAGHTEN RULES before it could succeed, and here his behaviour immediately after the shootings created great difficulty for the defence. The fact that he had telephoned the police station to say that he had killed his wife and daughters showed, on the face of it, not only that he appreciated the nature of his act, but was aware that what he had done was wrong. This must have been very much in the minds of the jury when, after a retirement of only twelve minutes, they came back into court with a verdict of 'Guilty'. Mr. Justice MacKinnon, whose first murder trial this was, was greatly distressed when he came to pass sentence, and was scarcely able to get the words out. By contrast, the prisoner accepted his fate with a stoical indifference which was maintained up to the very moment of his execution.

[*30, 51, 131.*

Lofty, Margaret Elizabeth. *See* George Joseph SMITH.

Lowe, Margaret Florence ('Pearl'). *See* Gordon Frederick CUMMINS.

Luard, Caroline Mary, aged fifty-eight, wife of Major-General Charles Edward Luard, of Ightham Knoll, Ightham, near Sevenoaks, Kent, was, on 24th August 1908, found lying dead on the veranda of a summer house in Fish Pond Woods on the neighbouring estate. She had been shot twice through the head with a small-calibre revolver. Prolonged investigation by the police yielded no clue to the identity of the murderer, but it was not long before the voices of calumny and malice began to suggest whom it might be. General Luard, the distracted widower, received through the post dozens of anonymous letters, some of which, not content with heaping abuse upon him, accused him of having killed his wife. Now, if there were one thing which the abortive police inquiries had established beyond a scintilla of doubt it was that General Luard *could not have been the murderer*. Motive there was none. The Luards were an exceptionally devoted couple who were never seen to treat each other with anything but the most marked and touching affection. General Luard, living in retirement after thirty years' service in the Royal Engineers, a man of means and position, stood to gain nothing, financially, from the death of his wife; he was a man healthy in body and mind and of most equable temper. However, many murders have been committed by persons who appeared to have no motive. Far more important was the fact that ten minutes after Mrs. Luard had been murdered—the time was fixed by two independent witnesses who had heard the shots fired—General Luard was seen on the golf course at Godden Green, at so great a distance from the summer house that even if he had run every step of the way he could not possibly have got there in the time. Hoping that in fresh surroundings he might be able to find some relief from his distress, a friend of his, Colonel C. E. Warde M.P., persuaded General Luard to come to stay with him at his home, Barnham Court, near Maidstone. There the General seemed to be easier in his mind. But early in the morning of 18th September, before most of the household was astir, he walked out of the house, and concealing himself behind a clump of bushes at the side of the railway line, waited until he heard a train approaching, when he threw himself in front of it and was cut to pieces. He had left behind him this pathetic letter, addressed to his host:

My dear Warde,

I am sorry to have to return your kindness and long friendship in this way, but I am satisfied it is best to join her in the second life at once as I can be of no further use to anyone in future in this world, of which I am tired and in which I do not wish to live any longer. I thought that my strength was sufficient to bear up against the horrible imputations and terrible letters which I have received since that awful crime was committed and which robbed me of my happiness. And so it was for long and the goodness, kindness and sympathy of so many friends kept me going. But somehow in the last day or two something seems to have snapped. The strength has left me and I care for nothing except to join her again. So good-bye my dear friends to both of us.

Yours very affectionately,

C. E. Luard.

P.S.—I shall be somewhere on the line of the railway.

Rarely can 'poison pen' letters have led to a more hideous result. On the surface, robbery appeared to have been the motive for the murder of Mrs. Luard. Rings had been stripped from her fingers with such violence as to tear the skin; the pocket of her dress had been cut out and her purse stolen. Yet it seems that the officers who conducted the investigation did not share the popular theory that Mrs. Luard had been killed by some tramp who had surprised her, alone and defenceless, as she was walking through the wood; they were clearly inclined to doubt whether robbery was the motive at all. Let us consult the facts. At about 2.30 on the fatal afternoon, General and Mrs. Luard, accompanied by their Irish terrier, set out together to walk in the woods. Because she was expecting a friend to tea and wanted to be back at the manor house in time to entertain her, Mrs. Luard did not intend to go much further than the summer house. The General, on the other hand, proposed to walk as far as the Godden Green golf course. Therefore, at a point some little way beyond the summer house—La Casa, as it was called—General Luard and his wife parted company. Mrs. Luard started to walk back along the bridle path in the direction of the summer house, and the General continued on his way with the dog. The time was about 3 p.m. General Luard was seen to arrive at the golf course at about 3.25. He got back to Ightham Knoll just over an hour later, having accepted a lift in a friend's car. Mrs. Luard's guest had arrived, but of the hostess there was no sign. General Luard apologized for her as best he could. Tea was served, and immediately afterwards the General said he was feeling so uneasy about his wife's absence that he thought he ought to go to look for her. As he came within sight of the summer house, which was deep in the heart of the wood, he saw his wife stretched face downwards on the veranda. His first thought was that she had fainted, but when he came closer, a pool of blood on the floor and extensive bloodstains on his wife's face and head revealed to him the horrible truth. Two witnesses, each independently of the other, were able to fix the precise hour at which Mrs. Luard had been killed. Both of them had heard the shots fired; both were certain of the time—3.15 p.m. What puzzled Scotland Yard at the time, and what has puzzled most people who have studied the case since, is why, a quarter of an hour after leaving her husband, Mrs. Luard should have got no further on her way home than the summer house. She was hurrying back, it should be remembered, because she was expecting a guest for tea. By 3.15 she ought at least to have reached the edge of the wood; indeed, she should already have been in the meadows leading up to the manor house. Why had she lingered at La Casa? To the officers engaged upon the case the delay carried the strong suggestion that Mrs. Luard may have had an appointment to meet someone at the summer house, and that it was this 'someone' who had killed her. It further appeared to the police that the evidence which suggested robbery as the motive for the crime had a curiously contrived air about it. Why, they asked, should a man who was in so much of a hurry to rob Mrs. Luard of her rings that he had torn the skin of her fingers in wrenching them off bother to cut out her pocket to steal her purse? Why should he not simply have taken the purse out of the pocket? Did not the evidence appear to be a trifle over-done? Nothing of all this ever got beyond the realm of speculation, and in that condition it remains to this day.

[*101, 228.*

Lynch, Gerald Roche (1889-1957), senior Home Office analyst, was probably instrumental in bringing retribution to as many murderers as Sir Bernard SPILSBURY himself. The outward appearance of the man was curiously deceptive. In a crowd he might easily have been mistaken for a mild-mannered country schoolmaster. But once he entered the witness-box at a murder trial there was no longer any possibility of error. There, by his beautifully precise and pellucid answers, he at once revealed the formidable strength of the expert who is supreme in his own field and is perfectly aware of the fact. Yet he rarely dogmatized, refused to follow speculation beyond the point at which it could be checked by demonstration and experiment, preferred understatement to overemphasis, and was at all times scrupulously exact. He was thus able to speak with especial authority, since he was so obviously a dispassionate witness dealing confidently with what he knew—but not with more than he knew. Sometimes the impression this created was strong enough to overlay the tension of a capital trial by the calm atmosphere of the lecture room; it was as if a doctor were discoursing to his students rather than an expert witness giving evidence that might well lead a man to the scaffold. A small, spare man, invariably to be seen with a carnation in his buttonhole, Gerald Roche Lynch, who in the field of toxology and chemical pathology had few equals, belonged to a family which for five generations before him had been engaged in the practice of medicine. He was born in London on 12th January 1889, completed his general education at St. Paul's School, and later entered St. Mary's Hospital, Paddington, where in 1920 he became assistant chemical pathologist, and subsequently director of that department. From 1924 until 1945 he was Lecturer in Forensic Medicine and Toxicology at Westminster Hospital; he held the corresponding appointment at St. Mary's for some twenty years, retiring in 1954. His long connection with the Home Office and, indirectly, with Scotland Yard began in 1920, in which year he was appointed assistant official analyst, succeeding to the senior post eight years later; he occupied it until 1954. Apart from the leading rôle he played in countless murder trials, he will be remembered for the important developments in medico-legal practice associated with his name, particularly with regard to the classification of blood groups. He died suddenly on 3rd July 1957.

M

*Murder, like talent, seems occasionally to
run in families.*

George Henry Lewes
The Physiology of Common Life

McCardie, Sir Henry Alfred (1869-1933), judge of the King's
Bench Division of the High Court (1916-33), ardently believed that the
law must always conform to the spirit of the time and to man's changing
needs, and that it was the duty of a judge to point out at all times those
respects in which it appeared to be lagging behind. He was always
impatient when he had to try a case based upon some principle which
he considered to be obsolete—an action for the enticement of a wife is
a good example. 'The law', he said, 'must be stable, yet it cannot stand
still.' And again: 'It is a profound but sometimes forgotten truth that
the law is made for man, and not man for the law.' Very early on, he
let it be known where his sympathies lay. 'If there be an unconscious
instinct in me as a judge to lean to one side rather than the other,' he
said, 'it is an instinct not in favour of the strong and wealthy, but an
instinct which tends to lean rather towards those who are weak and
those who are poor.' His strong and steady humanitarianism coloured
his whole life. He never forgot that although his career had brought him
great material prosperity it had begun very modestly. McCardie was
of Irish descent, but his father had for many years been a merchant in
Birmingham, and it was in that city that the future judge was born, on
18th July 1869, the fifth child of a family of seven. His father died when
McCardie was only a boy, leaving a widow, a woman of sterling
character, to bring up a family on slender means. McCardie left King
Edward's School, Birmingham, when he was sixteen, and set out to earn
his living. After a few half-hearted attempts at a business career, he
found his true *métier*, and in 1894 he was called to the Bar by the Middle
Temple. His success was immediate. He was soon the busiest junior
practising in Birmingham; when he moved to London his success
followed him and multiplied. Raised to the Bench in 1916, he went
there directly from the junior Bar, in itself a rare occurrence, but in

the particular circumstances of McCardie's background, unique. His latter years on the Bench bore traces of mental and emotional stress. This was tragically resolved on the morning of 26th April 1933, when Mr. Justice McCardie, a lonely and weary man, shot himself at his flat in Westminster. In his time he presided over many murder trials, including those of Lieutenant Douglas MALCOLM; and George Arthur BAILEY.

McClure, George Buchanan (1887-1955). For fourteen years—that is, from 1928 until 1942—McClure appeared for the prosecution at many of the most important murder trials to take place at the Old Bailey, where he was renowned for his 'commonsense approach', which was extremely effective, rather than for his forensic style, which was blunt to the point of awkwardness, or for his eloquence, which was nil. McClure was called to the Bar by the Inner Temple in 1917, and was in chambers with Sir Archibald BODKIN, sometime Director of Public Prosecutions. It was whilst Sir Archibald still occupied that post that McClure, who enjoyed a considerable practice at the Criminal Bar, was appointed Junior Counsel to the Department at the Old Bailey. That was in 1928; thereafter, he advanced by successive steps to become, in 1937, Senior Counsel. In 1942, McClure was appointed Judge of the Mayor's and City of London Court. Ill-health dogged him during much of his judicial career, and in 1953, at the age of sixty-six, he was compelled to retire; he died on 22nd February 1955. Prominent murder trials with which he was associated included those of BROWNE and KENNEDY; Frederick FIELD (first trial); Theodosios PETROU; Edward Royal CHAPLIN; William TEASDALE; Lionel WATSON; and Gordon Frederick CUMMINS.

M'Guigan, John, otherwise known as John Milligan, a young Irish tinker, was put on trial within the High Court of Justiciary at Edinburgh, before the Lord Justice Clerk, Lord Aitchison, in 1935. Three charges were preferred against him—murder, rape, and housebreaking. It was a hideous story the prosecution had to tell. On a fine summer evening of mid-August, nineteen-years-old Daniel Kerrigan, glazier's apprentice, a decent, good-looking lad, was walking home with his sweetheart, Marjory Watson Fenwick, an attractive, slightly built girl, who looked rather younger than her seventeen years. His arm was around her waist as they walked slowly along the shady pathway winding between the trees and bushes of Cuddies Strip, on summer evenings a popular resort for courting couples from the neighbouring city of Perth. Suddenly, from the surrounding woods, there was the sound of a shot, and the girl felt something whizz through her hair. The boy dropped his arm, and for a second he and his sweetheart stood facing each other. 'Don't faint,' said Kerrigan, gazing anxiously at Marjory Fenwick's ashen face. An instant later there was a second shot, and he was lying dead at her feet. The girl bent over him crying, 'Danny, Danny!' Then she realized that a man, wearing a cap and with a day's growth of beard, was standing beside her. Begging him to stay with Danny while she went for help, the girl started to run towards the stile at the end of the footpath; without a word the man came after her and she found him running by her side. As she made to get over the stile he pulled her off, held her down with his knee, gagged her, and tied her hands behind her with a handkerchief. Then he dragged her into the bushes and, having stripped her naked, raped her. To get her clothes off he had had to unfasten her wrists, but when the deed was done he used the same handkerchief to tie them again. Dislodging the gag, the girl screamed for help, whereupon the man gripped her by the throat, as if to choke her. Then he tied her suspender belt over her mouth, bound her feet, and left her lying in the bushes. After a time, she managed to free her hands and feet and, picking up her coat to hide her nakedness, she stumbled off as best she could to find help. On the other side of the field beyond the stile she fell in with a young couple who were on their way home after an evening at Buckie Braes, the public park. They saw her coming towards them, barefoot, sobbing, obviously in deep distress. 'Can you help me, mister?' she gasped. The couple took the girl into Cherrybank, a suburb of Perth, where they telephoned the police. After a pair of shoes had been found for her, Marjory led P.C. Ptolmey and sundry other persons back to Cuddies Strip. Kerrigan was lying where she had left him, dead, but with a green handkerchief decently covering his face. At this time, M'Guigan, otherwise homeless, was living in a tent in a wood near Kirton of Mailer, not far away from the scene of the crime, being employed as a temporary labourer at an adjacent farm. He possessed a rifle and also a double-barrelled shotgun. But the most damning evidence against M'Guigan was the handkerchief which had been used to bind the girl's wrists. This was identified as being among the articles which had been stolen some time before from the neighbouring manor house of Abergeldie, the home of Lady Laura Mary Douglas. It was the property of Mr. David Douglas, who had cause to remember it, as it had been presented to him in South Africa by an Indian trader with whom he had done business; it was also readily identifiable by the laundry mark. Now, in M'Guigan's tent were found at least two of the other articles stolen in the Abergeldie House robbery, a telescope and a purse. And if that were not sufficient to fasten the robbery upon young M'Guigan, he had not only left one of his own handkerchiefs behind, but also a good set of fingerprints.

The next step was to try to prove to the jury that the man who had assaulted Miss Fenwick was also the man who had killed her sweetheart. This proved more difficult. The jury were reminded that the shot had been fired from a distance of some eight yards. Where had M'Guigan come from if not from the bushes whence the gun was fired? But the argument was not sufficient to satisfy the jury, who took a course only open to a Scottish jury and brought in a verdict of 'Not Proven' on the murder charge. Found guilty on the other charges, M'Guigan was sent to penal servitude for ten years.

[*177.*

McKerrow, Grace. *See* Thomas Mathieson BROWN.

MacKinnon, Sir Frank Douglas (1871-1946) was called to the Bar by the Inner Temple in 1897, took silk in 1914, and in 1924 became a judge of the King's Bench Division of the High Court, where his clear mind, scholarly habits of thought, and dry sense of humour were alike advantageously displayed. In 1937 he was promoted Lord Justice of Appeal. On 22nd January 1946 he collapsed on the way to the Law Courts, and died in hospital on the following day, being then in his seventy-fifth year. MacKinnon had had little or no experience of the criminal courts before his appointment to the Bench—he said himself that he had not addressed a jury more than half a dozen times during his twenty-seven years at the Bar—yet presided with unfailing distinction over some of the leading murder trials of his day, notably those of LOCK AH TAM; and Charlotte BRYANT.

McLindon, Elizabeth, aged forty-one, was, in the early summer of 1946, engaged by King George of Greece to take charge of a house he had rented in Chester Square, Belgravia. Whilst the house was still in the hands of the decorators the new housekeeper moved in. So did a man named **Arthur Robert Boyce,** whom Miss McLindon had met at Brighton, and whom she regarded as her fiancé, being unaware that he was already married and had, moreover, served a prison sentence for bigamy. On the evening of 9th June 1946, the King of Greece arrived at 45 Chester Square to inspect the decorations, and was surprised and annoyed to find that Miss McLindon was not there to receive him. The King and his private secretary, M. Papanikolaou, went into several of the rooms, but there was one on the ground floor that they could not enter; it was locked. On 12th June, M. Papanikolaou visited the house again; there was still no sign of the housekeeper. On 14th June the police were called in, and they broke open the door of the locked room. Elizabeth McLindon was seated at a small table, her back to the door.

She was dead, having been shot through the back of the head with a pistol. The indications were that the body had been in the locked room for five days. A spent cartridge case was lying on the floor behind the chair. Letters signed 'Your loving and true hubby, Arthur' put the police upon the track of Arthur Robert Boyce. At Boyce's lodgings at Brighton they found a luggage label bearing the name John Rowland, with an address in Caernarvon. Rowland was traced—on the off-chance that he might have something useful to say. He had. It appeared that he had at one time shared lodgings with Boyce. One day he had shown Boyce his gun—a ·32 Browning automatic pistol. Later he had missed the gun and suspected Boyce of having stolen it. Rowland produced a spent cartridge case belonging to it. The marks on it were identical with those on the cartridge case found beside the body—both had been fired from the same gun. At his trial at the Old Bailey in September, Boyce said that he had given Rowland's pistol to Miss McLindon as protection against certain mysterious strangers who, having come to the house to inquire after the whereabouts of the king, had threatened and abused her when she refused to tell them. The jury were not impressed with this story. Boyce was convicted of murder, sentenced to death by Mr. Justice Morris, and executed on 1st November.

McMillan, Margaret, appeared before the Lord Justice Clerk, Lord Aitchison, within the High Court of Justiciary, Edinburgh, in June 1940, on an indictment charging her with murdering her husband, Robert Drennan McMillan, of Oxgang Farm, Kirkintilloch, Dunbartonshire, by administering arsenic to him over a period of six months, between 1st July 1939 and 6th January 1940. A second count in the indictment charged Mrs. McMillan with earlier but unsuccessful attempts to poison her husband between March and May 1937. Mr. McMillan died on 6th January 1940 after an illness. Analysis of the contents of stomach and intestines yielded no less than 11·06 grains of arsenic, clearly indicating that 'a massive dose' had been administered within twenty-four hours of the man's death. The prosecution was able to show that a large quantity of arsenic had been delivered at Oxgang Farm in March 1937 for use as a rat poison. There was also evidence of a second delivery in December 1939. In both cases the poison had been supplied by one of McMillan's friends, a glass-maker employed by a firm which used something like a hundredweight of arsenic a day in various manufacturing processes. Having established this much, the prosecution set out with equal confidence to show that the poison had not been self-administered, either by accident or design. As to accident, there was some evidence to suggest that McMillan's illness in June 1937 might have been due to the fact that he had not been over-particular about washing his hands after putting down rat poison, and had, in that way, absorbed a certain amount of arsenic. But only upon the assumption that there had been a whole series of such accidents could this be made to apply to McMillan's last illness, since the medical witnesses were all agreed that he had been absorbing arsenic in repeated doses over a considerable period of time, certainly from four to six months before he died. It was equally difficult to believe that any man in his senses would choose to commit suicide by administering arsenic to himself in small doses, thus deliberately prolonging month after month the agony of his death. Having excluded both accident and suicide, the Crown left it to the jury that only one other alternative remained—murder. Lord Aitchison's summing-up contained a remarkable passage dealing with the 'process of exclusion':

If you look at it in abstract logic, it seems very simple and convincing to say, 'Well, there are your alternatives—suicide, accident, murder. We rule suicide out, and you are left with two. And you rule accident out, and you are left with one, and that is murder.' I suppose, logically, there is no answer to that. Then I wonder if it is really sound. Is there not another alternative? Is there not this alternative, that the thing is unexplained? Now, I must emphasize that to you. When you are dealing with a grave criminal case of this kind, you must never leave out of account what I will call the fourth alternative, that the thing is unexplained. . . . I have got this feeling about it, that if you don't apply the method of exclusion with very great care when you are dealing with a serious charge, you may run a grave risk of putting upon the accused the burden of explaining things. Now, the burden of proof is never on the accused in a criminal case, and if you simply proceed by a process of exclusion and say 'We rule suicide out and accident out, and therefore the only thing left is murder,' that is coming very near to saying it is for the accused to explain something that may be inexplicable.

In accordance with the procedure open to them in Scottish law, the jury returned a unanimous finding of 'Not Proven'. Mrs. McMillan was thereupon discharged.

[72.

M'Naghten Rules. For more than a century the English Courts relied upon the M'Naghten Rules as the sole test of criminal responsibility. In the year 1843, a man named Daniel M'Naghten, a Glasgow wood-turner who fancied himself to be aggrieved by the Prime Minister of the day, Sir Robert Peel, shot and killed Sir Robert's secretary, Edward Drummond, in Downing Street. He was charged with the murder before a judge and jury at the Old Bailey and was found to be insane. The verdict created indignation and disquiet in some quarters and was challenged in the House of Lords. Their lordships summoned Her Majesty's judges and put to them five questions for their opinion. The answers to these questions constituted the M'Naghten Rules, which, until the HOMICIDE ACT, 1957 extended to the English courts the Scottish doctrine of DIMINISHED RESPONSIBILITY, dictated the degree of madness which must be proved to show that, because of the condition of his mind, the accused ought not to be held responsible for his act. The crucial answer was expressed as follows:

We submit our opinion to be that the jury ought to be told in all cases that every man is to be presumed to be sane and to possess a sufficient degree of reason to be responsible for his crimes, until the contrary be proved to their satisfaction; and that *to establish a defence on the ground of insanity it must be clearly proved that, at the time of committing the act, the accused was labouring under such defect of reason, from disease of the mind, as not to know the nature and quality of the act he was doing, or, if he did know it, that he did not know he was doing what was wrong.*

At the time the M'Naghten Rules were formulated doctors and lawyers were broadly in agreement upon what constituted madness, but as the years went by and the mystery of the human mind was increasingly revealed by scientific methods undreamed of in 1843, the gulf between the *legal* and the *medical* definition of insanity widened to a point at which the lawyer and the doctor were no longer speaking the same language. Medical knowledge expanded freely, whereas the law found itself, in effect, saddled with an immovable definition of criminal lunacy which became steadily more out of date and impractical as time went on. Fortunately, the wording of the answer did permit a certain latitude of interpretation, and did allow some ground for manœuvre. Thus, Lord Chancellor Haldane was able to say that when justice required an acquittal he had never known the M'Naghten Rules to embarrass any judge. This was because the Rules were sometimes stretched to the utmost limit possible to the English language. Had they always been rigidly construed on the basis that *not knowing an act is wrong means not knowing it is against the law,* then, in the words of Lord Bramwell, nobody would be 'mad enough to come within the definition of madness laid down by the judges' answers'. But even allowing for the most liberal interpretation possible, short of actual distortion of the language, most people would be willing to agree that the M'Naghten Rules had been left hopelessly behind by modern psychiatry, which showed them to be anachronistic and, in the end, obsolete. The trouble has been that imprecision is detestable to the legal mind, which hankers after clear definition. But nothing is more imprecise than the point at which 'sanity' may be said to end and 'insanity' to begin. To a doctor, madness cannot be reduced to a formula. Here lies the irreconcilable point of difference between the medical and what was for over a century the legal view of insanity in this country. Whilst the M'Naghten Rules remained the sole criterion by which criminal responsibility was judged by the courts, there were several attempts to adapt them so as to bring them into closer harmony with the advances of medical science, notably by the Committee on Insanity and Crime, which was set up by the Lord Chancellor in 1922. This Committee included in its report the important recommendation that:

It should be recognized that a person charged criminally with an offence is irresponsible for his act when the act is committed under an impulse which the prisoner may be, by mental disease, deprived of any power to resist.

The Committee (known as the Atkin Committee, it being presided over by Lord ATKIN) was satisfied from the evidence given before it that there are mental disorders in which the impulse to do a criminal act recurs with such increasing force that it eventually becomes irresistible and uncontrollable. The Committee agreed that to embody this principle of *Irresistible Impulse* in English Law would probably require legislation. But the Government of the day took no action, and when, in 1924, Lord DARLING introduced his Criminal Responsibility (Trials) Bill in the House of Lords it failed to secure a second reading. The M'Naghten Rules remained in full force. The Royal Commission on Capital Punishment, 1949-53, heard a great deal of evidence bearing upon the Rules. The British Medical Association proposed that they should be enlarged by adding to the existing tests the test whether the accused was labouring, as a result of disease of the mind, under 'a disorder of emotion such that, while appreciating the nature and quality of the act, and that it was wrong, he did not possess sufficient power to prevent himself from committing it'. The Committee (with one dissentient) reported (1) that the test of responsibility laid down by the M'Naghten Rules was so defective that the law on the subject ought to be changed; (2) that an addition to the Rules on the lines suggested by the B.M.A. was the best that could be devised; and (again with one dissentient) that it would be better to amend them in that way than to leave them as they were; and (3) that a preferable amendment of the law would be to abrogate the Rules and to leave it to the jury to determine whether at the time of the act the accused was suffering from disease of the mind (or mental deficiency) to such a degree that he ought not to be held responsible. (To this three members of the Commission dissented.) In 1957, Parliament at last took legislative action to deal with this extremely troublesome matter of responsibility. It did so, as has been said, by incorporating into the English system the Scottish doctrine of *Diminished Responsibility*. Thus, Clause 2 of the Homicide Act, 1957, reads as follows:

(1) Where a person kills or is a party to the killing of another, he shall not be convicted of murder if he was suffering from such abnormality of mind (whether arising from a condition of arrested or retarded development of mind or any inherent causes or induced by disease or injury) as substantially impaired his mental responsibility for his acts and omissions in doing or being a party to the killing.

(2) On a charge of murder, it shall be for the defence to prove that the person charged is by virtue of this section not liable to be convicted of murder.

(3) A person who but for this section would be liable as principal or accessory, to be convicted of murder shall be liable instead to be convicted of manslaughter.

(4) The fact that one party to a killing is by virtue of this section not liable to be convicted of murder shall not affect the question whether the killing amounted to murder in the case of the other party to it.

McSwan, Amy.
McSwan, Donald.   } *See* John George HAIGH.
McSwan, William Donald.

Major, Arthur, a forty-four-years-old lorry driver of Kirkby-on-Bain, Lincolnshire, died on 24th May 1934, apparently in an epileptic fit, having been taken ill with violent spasms and muscular contortions two days before. On 27th May, the mourners having already assembled, a Coroner's order arrived to stop the funeral. This dramatic move followed upon the receipt of an anonymous letter by Inspector Dodson of the Horncastle police force. This had been delivered the previous day. It read:

Sir—Have you ever heard of a wife poisoning her husband? Look further into the death (by heart failure) of Mr. Major, of Kirkby-on-Bain. Why did he complain of his food tasting nasty and throw it to a neighbour's dog, which has since died? Ask the undertaker if he looked natural after death? Why did he stiffen so quickly? Why was he so jerky when dying? I myself have heard her threaten to poison him years ago. In the name of the law, I beg you to analyse the contents of his stomach.

The letter, which bore no address, was signed 'Fairplay'; the identity of the writer was never discovered. Inspector Dodson made an immediate investigation. He found that a wire-haired terrier belonging to the Majors' next-door neighbour had died during the night of 23rd May, having been seized with muscular contortions. The dog was exhumed from its grave at the end of the garden. The Coroner made an order halting the funeral of Mr. Major, and a post-mortem examination of both man and dog was carried out. Dr. Roche LYNCH, the Home Office analyst, reported the presence of a fatal dosage of strychnine in the organs of Arthur Major and of the terrier. It was his opinion that the man had died from strychnine poisoning administered in two doses, the second having been given shortly before death. After some weeks Scotland Yard was called in, and on 2nd July Chief-Inspector (afterwards Commander) Hugh Young arrived to take charge of the police inquiries. He soon discovered that Arthur Major had not been able to get on with his wife, Ethel, a vain, cantankerous, boastful woman, highly unpopular in the district. In the very week that he died, Mr. Major had arranged to insert in the *Horncastle News* a notice repudiating responsibility for his wife's debts, which were mostly to local tradespeople: one of the first things Mrs. Major had done after her husband's death had been to telephone the newspaper to cancel the notice. In his book, *My Forty Years at the Yard*, Commander Young describes his visit to the Majors' cottage on 3rd July and his impressions of the widow, which were unfavourable.

She impressed me as a cool and resourceful woman suffering no pangs of sorrow at the loss of her husband. In fact, she seemed quite callous about the whole affair, and even informed me that she felt 'much better in health since he was gone'. She began, however, by telling me that she was sure her husband had died through eating corned beef. She appeared over-eager to impress me with the fact that she had nothing to do with providing his meals, explaining that for a fortnight before her husband's death she and her young son had not slept at home, but had stayed with her father. . . . 'My husband bought his tinned beef himself,' she went on, adding with great insistence: 'I know that I never bought any. I hate corned beef and think it is a waste of money to buy such rubbish.' This obvious desire to dissociate herself from any provision or purchase of corned beef seemed to me rather important, because corned beef was the last meal eaten by Arthur Major before he was seized with his fatal illness on the night of 22nd May.

(It was to emerge later that a day or two before her husband's illness Mrs. Major had sent their young son out to buy a tin of corned beef.) It remained for the police to show that Mrs. Major had had access to a supply of strychnine. They had no need to look further than her seventy-years-old father, formerly a gamekeeper, who possessed a phial of strychnine crystals, which he kept locked in a box. He admitted that his daughter knew of this box and where he kept it, but since he always carried the key about with him—'It has never left me, day or night'—it was difficult to see how she could have got hold of the poison. Young solved the riddle when he discovered in Mrs. Major's bedroom a purse containing another key, which unlocked the box. 'I am an old man, mister,' said Mrs. Major's father. 'I will tell you nothing but the truth. I *did* have another key, but I lost it years ago. . . . I never knew the going of it.' The police now considered the case against Mrs. Major complete. She was charged with the murder of her husband, and, in the following November, she was tried at Lincoln Assizes before Mr. Justice CHARLES. Mrs. Major was defended by Mr. Norman (afterwards Lord) BIRKETT K.C., but for once that famous advocate was not upon the winning side. Although Mrs. Major pleaded 'Not Guilty', in effect the defence was less concerned to demonstrate that she had not killed her husband than to show that there had been circumstances in their life together which had amounted to extreme provocation. The married life of the Majors was depicted as one of squalid violence and the husband as a congenital drunkard who, in his cups, thought nothing of turning his wife and son out of the house to sleep in a shed in the garden. In addition, it was said that Mrs. Major had been driven into a state bordering upon hysteria by an anonymous letter which told her that her husband had 'got a nice bit of fluff now'. But Mrs. Major did not go into the witness-box, and in the absence of any direct testimony from her these considerations lost something of their impact, although they were undoubtedly behind the strong recommendation to mercy with which the jury accompanied their verdict of 'Guilty'. As she stood sobbing in the dock, Mr. Justice Charles passed sentence of death upon Ethel Major. No action was taken upon the jury's recommendation, and on 19th December she was

hanged (the first woman to be executed since Louie CALVERT, on 26th June 1926).
[*81, 230*.

Malcolm, Douglas, Army lieutenant, whose life was directed by the loftiest conceptions of honour and chivalrous conduct, attracted nation-wide sympathy when he stood in the dock at the Old Bailey charged with the murder of the man who had sought to seduce his wife. To understand the intensity of feeling with which the course of this sensational trial was followed in millions of homes, it must be remembered that it took place in September 1917, in the fourth year of a war which had seen wearily repeated, over and over again, the tragedy of the lonely wife too lightly engaged, the husband in the trenches too far away, and the lover, the 'Man Who Stayed At Home', much too near at hand. When Lieutenant Malcolm put a bullet through the bogus 'Count de Borch' there were many who felt, in some obscure fashion, that the honour of thousands of soldier husbands, betrayed as much by the inescapable separations of war as by the frailty of their wives, had at last been vindicated. There was undoubtedly something of this feeling behind the hysterical scenes in court when the jury brought in a verdict of 'Not Guilty'. It was an acquittal which could be, and was, justified on the respectable ground that Lieutenant Malcolm had killed in self-defence. It is, however, in keeping with the feverish spirit of the time that many people who should have known better openly applauded the verdict as if by it the jury had meant to condone the so-called 'unwritten law'. Douglas Malcolm, a partner in a prosperous City firm, married the daughter of a solicitor in June 1914. When war came he enlisted at once, leaving behind him in London his bride of a few weeks. An unlucky introduction—in July 1917—put her in the way of Russian-born Anton Baumberg, a professional seducer of women, whose suave address and elegant manners, no less than the coronet on his stationery, sustained the spurious title of 'Count Anthony de Borch'. (Was the dreadful pun intentional?) He lived in a top-floor back room in Bays-water, which he rented for 12s. 6d. a week, but, at the same time, contrived to give the impression that he was a man of position and affluence. On Sunday, 15th July 1917, Lieutenant Malcolm, unexpectedly on leave, found upon returning to his home in Cadogan Square that his wife was spending the week-end at a friend's cottage at New Milton, Hampshire. Following her there that same afternoon, he discovered his wife with the bogus Count in circumstances which made it sufficiently clear to him that he had arrived only just in time to save his wife's honour. Having thrashed the would-be seducer, Lieutenant Malcolm took his wife back to town with him, pausing on the way home to dispatch to 'Count de Borch' a challenge to a duel. (This was primly ignored by the recipient on the ground that duelling was 'illegal'.) Lieutenant Malcolm discovered, however, that he could not, simply by a thrashing or by a challenge to a duel, repair his broken marriage. Mrs. Malcolm was still infatuated with the 'Count', and when upon the expiration of his leave her husband returned to Flanders, she wrote to him to say that she could not give up her lover, and to ask for a divorce. Lieutenant Malcolm promptly wrote to 'Count de Borch':

If I ever hear of you trying to see or talk to my wife again, wherever you are, I will get leave and hunt you out and give you such a thrashing that even your own mother will not know you again. I will thrash you until you are maimed for life. This I swear before God in Whom I believe and Who is my witness.

This so greatly alarmed the 'Count' that he bought a revolver; to a friend he said that if Malcolm were to lay a finger upon him he would use it. On 11th August, having obtained compassionate leave, Lieutenant Malcolm returned home once again. His wife was not there. But in her room was a brand-new travelling trunk—with no initials upon it. All the servants were under notice. It was tragically obvious what was about to happen. Lieutenant Malcolm spent the next three days in trying to discover where 'Count de Borch' lived. At last he succeeded. Then he made his will. On the morning of 14th August he presented himself at the 'Count's' lodging in Porchester Terrace. To the landlady, who opened the door, he introduced himself as 'Inspector Quinn of Scotland Yard'. (He was carrying his right arm very stiffly, as he had a horsewhip up his sleeve. He also had a pistol in his jacket pocket.) The landlady took 'Inspector Quinn' upstairs to her lodger's room on the top floor. 'Count de Borch', wearing only a pyjama jacket, unlocked his door, and the visitor slipped past him. Sounds of a struggle ended in the discharge of four or five pistol shots. Then Malcolm came downstairs to fetch a policeman. 'I have shot a man,' he told the constable. 'Count de Borch' was discovered lying dead on the bed—close by his hand was a half-open drawer containing the revolver he had bought for his protection. Being charged, Lieutenant Malcolm said: 'Very well, I did it for my honour.' At his trial at the Old Bailey before Mr. Justice McCARDIE, Malcolm was brilliantly defended by Sir John (afterwards Viscount) Simon K.C., whose famous speech to the jury in this case is still prized by connoisseurs of forensic eloquence. Sir John relied upon that speech for an acquittal, and upon that speech alone, since he neither put Lieutenant Malcolm into the witness-box nor called any other evidence. He expressly repudiated any attempt to justify the killing by reference to the 'unwritten law'. Neither did he plead PROVOCATION, although by taking that line he might have had a chance of persuading the jury to find manslaughter. Instead, he staked all on the proposition that Lieutenant Malcolm had shot the 'Count' in a struggle to prevent him getting hold of the revolver which was lying in the drawer beside the bed—'the only thing in the room that would save his skin'. Mr. Justice McCardie was particularly careful in his summing-up to warn the jury that the case must not be decided on 'bias, on natural sympathy, or on the appeal and eloquence of distinguished counsel'. He went on:

> I desire to say in clear and unmistakable terms that this so-called 'unwritten law' does not exist in England. It is the negation of law; it is opposed to the most elementary principles of British justice—namely open trial and unbiased adjudication. A husband has no property in the body of his wife. He cannot imprison her; he cannot chastise her. If she refuses to live with him he cannot, nor can the Courts, compel her to do so. She is mistress of her own physical destiny. If she sins, and the husband can prove it, he may obtain a divorce, but if she decides to give her body to another, then the husband is not entitled to murder the lover, either to punish the sin or to secure its correction. (*See* Mr. Justice AVORY's charge in the case of Alfonso SMITH.)

The judge instructed the jury that they were entitled to acquit if they were satisfied that Lieutenant Malcolm, honestly believing that the 'Count' was about to seize a pistol, shot him in self-defence. The jury took only twenty-five minutes to arrive at a verdict of 'Not Guilty', and to spark off one of the most remarkable demonstrations of popular feeling ever staged at the Old Bailey. There was a wild burst of cheering —presently taken up by the crowds in the street outside—and women, with tears streaming down their faces, jumped on to the seats waving and blowing kisses to the man in the dock. In vain the ushers struggled to restore order, whilst against the surrounding tumult the judge, white with anger, was heard to say, 'I am sorry that the deliberation of the Court should be stained . . .' The rest of the sentence was drowned in the hubbub, but perhaps its purport may be guessed.

[*99, 164.*

Malinowski, Henryk. *See* Marian GRONDKOWSKI.

Maltby, Cecil, a forty-seven-years-old tailor, lived alone for five months over his shop in Park Road, Regent's Park, London, with the body of his mistress, Alice Hilda Middleton, decomposing in an empty bath in the kitchen. Mrs. Middleton was the wife of a chief officer in the merchant service. In the early summer of 1922, her husband being in the Far East, she left home and went to live with Maltby, who, mainly because of an over-fondness for the bottle, had so far neglected his tailoring business as to lose nearly all his customers, and thus had plenty of time to take her about, to race meetings in particular, and on motor-cycle jaunts. But after 15th August of that year nothing more was seen of Alice Hilda Middleton. When Mr. Middleton came home from sea in the following December he reported to the police that his wife was missing. A police officer called at the shop, but Maltby refused to let him in. He called out of the window that Mrs. Middleton had left him on 15th August and that he had no idea where she had gone. For over a week the police kept watch night and day upon the house. During that time, the story got into the newspapers and crowds collected in the street; they were rewarded by an occasional glimpse of Maltby at one of the upper windows. On 10th January 1923, the St. Marylebone Borough Council applied to a magistrate for an order authorizing the Medical Officer of Health to enter the premises on the ground of their supposed insanitary condition. The order was issued, and at 1 p.m. the same day the Medical Officer of Health of the borough went to the shop, accompanied by armed police officers. The police split into two parties. Watched by an expectant crowd from the pavement opposite, the first party broke open the shop door with a crowbar. Meanwhile, the second party had forced an entry at the rear by smashing a window. The two police parties met on the first-floor landing, and at that precise moment there was a muffled report from the floor above. Breaking down the locked door of the front bedroom, the police found Maltby lying on the bed; he had shot himself in the mouth and he died a few minutes later. In a bath in the kitchen, under a board which covered it, they found the decomposed body of Mrs. Middleton, wrapped in a sheet. On it was a piece of paper with the message: 'In memory of darling Pat, who committed suicide on 24th August 1922, 8.30 a.m.' Nailed to the bedroom door was another note:

In memory of Alice H. Middleton, who committed suicide on Thursday, August 24th, 1922, 8.30 a.m. Pat darling, why did you do it? Everybody loved you. I cannot live without you. When I can brace up my courage shall soon be with you—Cecil Maltby.

In all, no fewer than seven letters, all written by Maltby, were found in different parts of the house. One of them attempted some explanation of what had happened. It would appear that on 24th August Maltby had taken in an early-morning cup of tea to Mrs. Middleton—'the dear little lady who has been living with me'—and she had told him that she was going to shoot herself. He had struggled with her for possession of the gun, but she had been too strong for him. The note ended: 'I put Mrs. Middleton in the bath, and have not liked to part with the dear soul.' Mrs. Middleton had, indeed, been shot—three times—but from behind, whilst she was either sitting or lying down. The Coroner's jury returned a verdict of murder and *felo de se* against Maltby, adding, rather surprisingly: 'He was in a perfectly sound state of health and mind when he took his own life in order to avoid the consequences of his own act.'

Manslaughter (*Culpable Homicide* in Scotland) is the unlawful and felonious killing of a person *without malice*, either express or implied. Manslaughter is either *voluntary*, from sudden transport of passion, as where persons fight upon a quarrel and one is killed, or *involuntary*, ensuing from the commission of some unlawful act, or from the pursuit of some lawful act criminally or improperly performed, or from the negligent commission of some duty. *The absence of malice is the main distinction between this species of homicide and murder.* Manslaughter has been called 'the most elastic of crimes', as it almost overlaps with *innocent misadventure* at one extreme and *deliberate murder* at the other. In the gravest cases it may be, and is, punished by imprisonment for life.

Marsh, Maud Eliza. *See* George CHAPMAN.

Marshall, Doreen. *See* Neville George Clevely HEATH.

Marshall, Lindsay Howitt, farmed six hundred acres at Blunham in Bedfordshire; he was a popular and respected figure in the district, a man in good financial standing and blessed in his domestic life, which appeared unusually happy and contented. On the evening of 9th September 1926, the weather being fine, Mr. Marshall took his wife, Constance Myra, out for a ride in their car. They called on a friend in Bedford, who found them in their usual good spirits. Later that night, at about 11 p.m., the car was seen to stop at the side of the road not far from South Mills Farm, Blunham, where they lived. A few minutes afterwards the car suddenly burst into flames. A Grenadier Guardsman on leave, who was returning home from a concert, raced to the spot. He saw two people in the car. Sitting erect in the driver's seat was Mr. Marshall, with one hand on the steering wheel. Beside him was his wife, who was leaning against him. By this time the fire had taken such a hold that the soldier was unable to get near the car because of the intense heat. Others came running up, but they could do nothing. The car was almost entirely destroyed, and when the bodies of Mr. Marshall and his wife were recovered from the debris they were so badly charred that it was impossible for the doctor who examined them to say whether either or both had been alive when the fire broke out; he had, he said, never known a case of burning in which cremation was so complete. A petrol tin was found beneath the driver's seat and, in a mound of ashes near by, the brass cap which seemed to belong to it. The next day, a small boy fishing in the river at Great Barford—not far from the scene of the blaze—recovered a revolver from the shallow water near the road bridge. This turned out to be the revolver which, together with fifty rounds of ball ammunition, Mr. Marshall had purchased from a gunsmith in Bedford on 6th September. He had previously obtained a licence for it, on the ground that South Mills Farm was 'a very lonely spot' and he had need of a weapon in case of an emergency. It also transpired that on the morning of the tragedy he had bought an ounce of prussic acid from a Bedford chemist, saying that he wanted it to poison his old spaniel. This was the background against which Mr. Gregory Whyley, Deputy Coroner for Bedfordshire, sitting with a jury in a barn at South Mills Farm, conducted the inquest on Mr. and Mrs. Marshall. One of the men who had reached the car soon after it had burst into flames said in his evidence that neither Mr. Marshall nor his wife had made any attempt to get out, although it seemed to him that they had had 'plenty of opportunity' to do so. He was asked: 'If the car had been completely saturated with petrol inside could the fire have been more extensive than the fire you saw?' and he replied, 'No.' In these circumstances, the question whether anything had been the matter with the car doors became important. Mr. Marshall's chauffeur was called to say that on the very day of the fire there had been difficulty in opening the doors from the inside—and was chided for his omission to mention this fact to the police before the inquest opened. 'I wasn't asked,' he explained. The point was confirmed by a woman friend of the Marshalls, who said that a week before the tragedy she had been in the car and had been unable to get out; to release her, Mrs. Marshall had had to open the door from the outside. This lady was also asked about Mr. Marshall's relations with his wife. She replied: 'Mr. and Mrs. Marshall were extremely happy in their domestic life—noticeably so.' The possibility that Mr. Marshall might have had money troubles was also examined. This seemed to be disposed of by the evidence given by his bank manager, who showed that Mr. Marshall had been a man with substantial resources. But what of that chance discovery of the revolver in the river, by the bridge? If, as the Coroner frankly put it to the jury, Mr. Marshall did not shoot his wife, what reason could he have had for throwing the revolver into the river? The suggestion was that he did shoot her, that he poured petrol over the car and over his wife's body, that he set the car alight, and that he swallowed poison immediately afterwards. All this, said the Coroner, was strongly supported by the weight of the evidence, which seemed to him to be 'almost overwhelmingly' in favour of a verdict of 'murder and suicide'. After debating among themselves for some twenty minutes, the jury found that they agreed with him. The effect of their verdict was that Mr. Marshall had murdered his wife and had then killed himself. They did not attempt to say why.

Martirosoff, Reuben. *See* Marian GRONDKOWSKI.

Mason, Alexander Campbell, called 'Scottie' Mason, otherwise 'Scottie' Munro, was on 14th July 1923 convicted at the Old Bailey of the murder of a taxi-driver named Jacob Dickey in Bay-Tree Road, Brixton, in the previous May, and was sentenced to death by Mr. Justice SWIFT. On 10th August the Home Secretary, Mr. W. C. Bridgeman (afterwards Lord Bridgeman), announced that the death sentence had been commuted to one of penal servitude for life. Why was Mason reprieved? It can only have been because of the doubtful value of some of the evidence upon which he was convicted. That doubt has persisted, and there must be many who, on turning over the files of this half-forgotten case, find themselves assailed by the uncomfortable suspicion that justice may have miscarried. Here, first, is an account of the murder of Jacob Dickey, as told in court by Miss Jessie Maud Findlay, milliner:

> I was returning home along Acre Lane at about twenty minutes to ten on May 9th. . . . I heard some moaning and, as I got to the top of Bay-Tree Road, I could see two people struggling, but I could not detect whether they were men or women or boys until one cried out: 'Save me! He is killing me!' He repeated that twice, and then I saw the other one throw him to the ground and shoot him twice. The man who was shot was lying on the ground, apparently on his side; the other man was crouching close to him. There were no lights in Bay-Tree Road except one just by the bend, and it was nearly dark. I did not see anyone else near the two who were struggling. The last I saw of the man who fired the shots he was running round the bend of Bay-Tree Road towards Brixton Hill. The man who had been shot began to stagger up and come towards Acre Lane. I ran for a policeman.

The wounded man, afterwards identified as Jacob Dickey, collapsed at the corner of Bay-Tree Road and Acre Lane, having first cried, 'Go back, go back!' as if in warning that his assailant was armed; he died a few moments later from bullet wounds in his head. His taxi-cab, both its doors open, was standing in Bay-Tree Road, close to the scene of the struggle; there was five shillings and threepence on the clock. It turned out that it had been hired off the rank outside the Trocadero Restaurant in Shaftesbury Avenue. In the roadway were found a revolver, a jemmy wrapped in paper, a right-hand suede glove, stained with blood, and a gold-mounted walking-stick of peculiar design. Footprints and other tell-tale marks plotted the route of the murderer's escape through the gardens at the back of Bay-Tree Road and Acre Lane. It ended at 15 Acre Lane. There the occupiers, two maiden ladies, had seen a man on their garden wall a few minutes after Dickey had been shot. He had asked their permission to go through the house, and had been allowed to do so; neither of the two ladies seems to have seen anything particularly odd in such behaviour. Publication in the newspapers of a photograph of the walking-stick yielded immediate results. It was recognized as a stick which a convicted thief named James Vivian —known to everybody as 'Eddie' Vivian—had lately been flashing around in Soho cafés and night-spots. Police officers picked up Vivian at a house in Charlwood Street, Pimlico, where he was living with a prostitute named Hettie Colquohon; he made a statement which led to the arrest of 'Scottie' Mason the same evening. In due course Mason was indicted for murder at the Old Bailey, where the Crown case was presented by the formidable Sir Richard MUIR, the defence being in the hands of Mr. A. C. FOX-DAVIES. The trial saw a bitter conflict between Mason and Vivian, the principal witness against him, who was himself accused of the murder by the man in the dock. Both men were convicted criminals; neither was a man who could expect to be trusted on his word alone; every statement each made about the other had to be checked and re-checked and weighed against the probabilities. Mason was only twenty-two at the time of his trial, but he already had a number of convictions behind him for theft, shop-breaking, and burglary. Vivian, who was about the same age, had a similar record, and indeed openly admitted in court that his only regular occupation was housebreaking. Both the men had been jointly convicted of burglary in January 1922. Vivian had been released from prison twelve months later. Mason was not discharged until 5th May 1923. The next day, which was a Sunday, Mason turned up at Vivian's flat; he slept there that night and the next three nights, being supplied by Vivian with various small sums of money. On the Monday—so Vivian's story went— they had gone to see a man named Daniel Nunn, who had, some time later in the day, supplied Mason with a revolver. (At the trial, Nunn denied this.) That same evening they had been in a restaurant in Westminster Bridge Road when Mason had produced the gun and had loaded it from a box containing some twenty-five cartridges. He had then remarked that he felt inclined to use it to 'stick-up' a taxi-driver. By the Wednesday Vivian had no more money, either to spend on himself or to support the penniless Mason; clearly what was needed was another burglary. Unfortunately, at this critical juncture Vivian had fallen ill and had been forced to take to his bed—he suspected food-poisoning. Mason had thus been compelled to set out on his own. He took with him a pair of suede gloves and Vivian's gold-handled stick so that he could 'look a bit posh'. (Mason himself said later: 'Policemen do not follow you up if you have a walking-stick'—an interesting piece of criminal lore, if true.) Hettie Colquohon being out on her nightly business, Vivian had spent the evening alone at the Pimlico flat. At 11 p.m. he had been awakened by a rattling at the window and a whistle from the street below:

I got up and saw the prisoner standing in the middle of the road, and went down and let him in. He comes in and he says: 'I have made a terrible mess of things. I have shot a taxi-driver.' So I says, 'Where?' He says, 'Brixton.'. . . He was covered with dust, dirt, and the middle finger of the left hand was all cut and bleeding and his hat had bloodstains on it . . . and the left knee of his trousers was torn. So he said that when he fired the shot at the taxi-driver he seemed to take no notice and closed with him, so he fired again and yet he took no notice, and commenced to struggle and he fired again—and then he had the taxi-driver's head down between his legs, you see, and fired at his head and shoulders as the taxi-driver's head was down here; and then the taxi-driver commenced running round in half-circles; he could not see; his face was covered with blood, or something, and he said that he shot him seven times, but it did not kill him. . . . He said that the revolver was no damned good because it did not kill him; he says, 'If it had been a ·45 I could have done him. I could have done another half a dozen if I had killed him outright.' . . . I says, 'Where is my stick and the other things?' He said, 'I have lost everything.' So I made the remark, 'That is all right for me now.' So he says, 'Don't think I am going to let you into it'—of course I had my own ideas about that.

When it came to Mason's turn to give evidence he denied every syllable of this. Vivian, he said, had feigned illness that night to divert Hettie Colquohon's suspicions that he was about to risk further trouble with the police. As soon as Hettie had gone out he had joined Mason at a rendezvous near Victoria Station. Vivian had told his confederate that he knew of a 'straight up' taxi, that is, one whose driver might be willing to share in a criminal enterprise. This cab was usually on the rank outside the Trocadero. Vivian had said that he proposed to go to Shaftesbury Avenue, and that if he could find the cab he would ask the driver to take him to Bay-Tree Road, Brixton. Mason was to go to Bay-Tree Road on his own and wait there for the cab to arrive; he would know it was coming when he heard the driver's signal—two long blasts on the horn followed by a shorter blast. Mason had accordingly gone to Bay-Tree Road, and a little later a taxi had appeared, coming from the direction of Brixton Hill. The driver had given the signal, and Mason had stepped into the roadway expecting the cab to stop to pick him up. But it had not stopped:

> When it got near me, I heard the sounds of a dispute. Vivian was leaning out of the right-hand side of the cab; he had his head close to the driver's and they were both shouting. I could not distinguish what they said because of the noise. It passed the turning where I was standing and went towards Acre Lane. I started walking towards it. I saw the taxi stop and as soon as it stopped I saw the right-door open and Vivian jump out of it quickly. . . . I saw the driver catch him either by the shoulder or the collar of the left side . . . and the driver was pulled half out of the taxi. Then there was two flashes and two reports, sir, and both men fell down. The driver fell completely out of the cab then and they both fell just beside the wheels. I would be about fifteen paces from the taxi, when they both got up, locked together. There was another report and I saw the flash. It was kind of dusk, and it illuminated both their faces.

Mason said that after the third flash he had been 'frightened to death', and had run away through the back gardens of Bay-Tree Road and Acre Lane. Vivian had come running behind him, stumbling and falling, and crying out, 'My God, Scottie, help me, I cannot walk.' He had helped him over the wall of one of the gardens, but in the end he had had to leave him. While police whistles shrilled, Vivian had lain on the ground moaning, 'My legs are gone, I can't move.' Mason had got away by asking permission to go through one of the houses, and so back to Victoria by tram. There were obvious errors, falsities, and discrepancies in the stories told by *both* the men. (It should be said that Mason's counsel expressly withdrew any imputation against Dickey suggesting that he had been ready to take part in a burglary or any other criminal enterprise.) But having said this, it is difficult to resist the impression that there was a failure by the police to collect and present to the Court evidence which *might* have helped Mason very materially in his defence. In 1927, ex-Superintendent Francis Carlin, who had been prominently connected with the case, published his memoirs, *Reminiscences of an Ex-Detective*. The author referred to statements which he said had been made to the police by 'Eddie' Vivian before the trial. They were of such a nature that had they been repeated in court—which they were not—they must have gone far to discredit Vivian's story. Mr. Carlin died before the appearance, in 1930, of the Mason case in the *Notable British Trials* series. This publication re-directed attention to *Reminiscences of an Ex-Detective*, and the Home Secretary, Mr. J. R. Clynes, was asked to set up a 'searching inquiry' into the reliability of the evidence tendered at the trial. Mr. Clynes replied, 'I am not aware of any ground for inquiry at the present time.' From this the House of Commons was left to infer that Mr. Carlin's statements were inaccurate, due no doubt to a faulty memory. It would have been better if this had been said quite bluntly. Failure to do so, unequivocally, has left unexplained the discrepancies between Vivian's supposed statements to the police and his later testimony in court. Mason was released in October 1937, after serving fourteen years and three months in prison.

[*I.*

Mathews, Sir Charles (1850-1920), was the stepson of the comedian, Charles Mathews, whose name he assumed by deed poll. (He was born Charles West.) Called to the Bar by the Middle Temple in 1872, he became Junior Treasury Counsel at the Old Bailey in 1886, succeeding Mr. Harry Poland as Senior Counsel in 1888. He was knighted by King Edward VII at the opening of the new Central Criminal Court (the present Old Bailey) in 1907, and in the following year became Director of Public Prosecutions; he died on 6th January 1920, in his seventieth year. 'Willie' Mathews, as he was always called, a small, spare man with an alert face, pallid and even careworn, exerted an extraordinary influence upon juries. Although always in deadly earnest, he employed an unashamedly theatrical technique to display his remarkable oratorical gifts, and often had the satisfaction of moving susceptible jurymen to tears, and on one occasion even a High Court judge. He laboured under the disadvantage of a weak, piping voice—a newspaper critic once said that compared with it the still, small voice of conscience was a mighty roar—and to overcome it he relied upon tricks of varying emphasis, often registering his most deadly points in something not much louder than a whisper. He would frighten an unwilling witness with a stabbing, accusatory forefinger, or by drawing his gown tightly round his hunched shoulders and hissing out a question like a snake; conversely, he would woo a helpful witness with caressing, insinuating tones which were all sweetness and light. Many thought him a vindictive prosecutor; if he gave that impression, it was, perhaps, because he believed so passionately in his mission to root out villainy and expose its evil ways. In private life he was the most genial and companionable of men, who all his life possessed the affection of a host of friends, particularly in theatrical circles, where he had many close personal and family ties. Famous murder trials in which he appeared for the prosecution included those of George CHAPMAN; and Arthur DEVEREUX.

Menzies, 'Lady'. *See* John Donald MERRETT.

Merrett, John Donald, afterwards known as **Ronald John Chesney,** made a promising beginning to what was to be a remarkable career when, as a youth of eighteen, he faced a Scottish jury on a charge of having murdered his mother, and secured from them a majority verdict of 'Not Proven'. It ended almost exactly twenty-seven years later when he shot himself in a wood outside Cologne to avoid being arrested for the murder of his wife and his mother-in-law. The years between he devoted to a variety of criminal enterprises, both great and small—they included blackmail, fraud, false pretences, theft, drug-trafficking, gun-running, smuggling and black market and illicit currency deals—interrupted (or, at least, partially interrupted) by war-service with the R.N.V.R. in the Mediterranean, during which he was promoted Lieutenant-Commander, and played a part of some distinction in taking supplies into beleaguered Tobruk. In later years, Chesney (*né* Merrett) sported a black beard, wore a gold earring in his left ear, and conducted himself in the swashbuckling manner of a sixteenth-century pirate, for which rôle he possessed the build and stature and the appropriate habits, being tirelessly addicted to drinking and gormandizing, gambling and the pursuit of women. There was little hint of this later flowering when, in 1927, a quiet, studious-looking boy, he stood in the dock at Edinburgh, charged with shooting his mother, Bertha Merrett, and with a long series of cheque forgeries by which he had depleted her banking accounts to the tune of £457. 13s. 6d. John Donald Merrett was born in New Zealand, the only child of John Alfred Merrett and Bertha Merrett, daughter of a Manchester wine merchant, and a clever, cultured woman of much charm and many social gifts. In 1924, Mrs. Merrett, who had been deserted by her husband, brought the boy to England to complete his education. He was then sixteen, a promising youth intended for a career in the diplomatic service. After a year at Malvern College, he was entered at Edinburgh University, and began his studies there in 1926. He did not pursue them for very long; indeed, for only a few weeks. However, with his books under his arm, he continued to set out each morning from the furnished flat in Palmerston Place where he lived with his mother, and she, poor lady, did not suspect that the son whose welfare was her constant preoccupation was spending his days in places more amusing than classes and lecture rooms; her only anxiety was lest he should overtax his strength by too much intellectual exercise. She was similarly deceived over the way in which the likely lad spent his evenings. Night after night, whilst Mrs. Merrett fondly imagined him to be asleep behind the locked door of his bedroom, 'Donnie', more often than not, was enjoying himself at the Dunedin Palais de Danse in Picardy Place, where he was prized for his agreeable company. He supported his free-spending habits by forging the signature 'Bertha Merrett' on sundry cheques drawn upon his mother's accounts at an Edinburgh branch of the Clydesdale Bank and at the Midland Bank at Boscombe, Hampshire. Such was his ingenuity and skill, alike remarkable at so tender an age, that he managed over a period of something less than six weeks to drain the Midland Bank account of £196. 19s. 6d., and the Clydesdale Bank account, in a rather shorter time, of £87. 4s. 6d., without giving his mother cause to suspect that anything was amiss with her finances. On the morning of 17th March 1926, Mrs. Merrett was seated at a table in her sitting-room writing a letter; her son, on the opposite side of the room, was reading a book. At about 9.40, Mrs. Sutherland, the daily maid, who was in the kitchen, having cleared the breakfast things, heard the sound of a shot. 'On going into the lobby', Mrs. Sutherland told the police that same morning, 'I saw Mrs. Merrett fall off the chair and on to the floor, and a revolver or pistol falling out of her hand.' The story she told later was quite different. According to this, she was making up the fire in the kitchen when she heard a shot, followed immediately by a scream and the thud of a falling body. A few seconds later 'Donnie' came into the kitchen on the verge of tears and said, 'Rita, my mother has shot herself.' He added that he had been wasting his mother's money and that this had worried her. Together, they returned to the sitting-room, where Mrs. Merrett lay unconscious on the floor, bleeding from a bullet wound in the right ear. A revolver was lying on the top of the writing-bureau, which had been behind and a little to the right of Mrs. Merrett as she had sat at the table. It was this revised version to which Mrs. Sutherland adhered at the trial. The discrepancies between the two accounts, which Mrs. Sutherland attributed to her confused state of mind, did not affect the official view. From the first, the case was accepted as one of attempted suicide, and right up to the last Mrs. Merrett, lying at Edinburgh Royal Infirmary, was treated as a person in custody who, if she recovered, would have to face a criminal charge. (A letter from the Clydesdale Bank informing Mrs. Merrett that her account was overdrawn conveniently suggested a motive.) Mrs. Merrett herself did not appear to have any idea of what had happened to her. She told the ward sister: 'I was sitting writing at the time, when suddenly a bang went off in my head like a pistol.' To a doctor to whom this was reported, Mrs. Merrett said this in elaboration: 'I was sitting down writing letters, and my son, Donald, was standing beside me. I said, "Go away, Donald, and don't annoy me," and the next I heard was a kind of explosion, and I do not remember anything more.' On 27th March Mrs. Merrett passed into unconsciousness, and in the early hours of 1st April she died. During the fifteen days his mother lay dying, 'Donnie', who saw no reason to alter his habits—he saw as much as ever of the Palais de Danse—boldly continued his raids upon her resources. Between 18th March and 27th March he drew out of the Midland Bank Account, by means of six forged cheques, a further sum of £173. 9s. 6d., reducing Mrs. Merrett's credit balance to £4. 3s. 4d. Necessary though they may have been to the maintenance of the good life, as represented by the Palais de Danse in Picardy Place (and the purchase of a motor-cycle), these further drawings proved disastrous. On 30th March Detective-Inspector Fleming of the Edinburgh C.I.D. discovered in Donald's bedroom a Midland Bank cheque book, from which five cheques and the corresponding counterfoils had been removed. It was a discovery which led to the disclosure of the entire series of forgeries, and eventually to the murder charge which was preferred against John Donald Merrett in the following November. On 1st February 1927 he was arraigned before the Lord Justice Clerk, Lord Alness, within the High Court of Justiciary at Edinburgh. Merrett had good cause to be grateful to the eminent pathologist, Sir Bernard SPILSBURY, who, making one of his rare appearances for the defence, said that he saw nothing in the position of the wound, the track of the bullet, or the distance at which it had been fired which was inconsistent with suicide or with an accident. He demonstrated in the witness-box how he imagined an accident might have happened, suggesting that Mrs. Merrett, with the pistol in her hand, might have tilted her chair, lost her balance, and jerked her elbow on the projecting ledge of the bureau behind her. By a majority verdict, the jury found the charge of murder 'Not Proven'. But Merrett was convicted of the cheque forgeries, and for these he was sentenced to twelve months imprisonment, justice being tempered with mercy on account of his youth. He served eight months of this sentence, after which, being discharged, he took easily and agreeably to a life of crime, for which he adopted the name of John Ronald Chesney. The immediate events which led to his violent end are, properly speaking, outside the purview of this book. However, they are detailed here for the sake of completeness. Soon after his release from prison Chesney married a Miss Vera Bonnar. (Vera's mother was later to marry again; after parting from her husband she chose to call herself 'Lady' Menzies, although she had no discernible right to the title.) At the end of 1929, having come into a fortune of £50,000, which had been left in trust for him by his grandfather, Chesney settled the sum of £8,400 upon his wife. Vera was to enjoy the interest for her lifetime; if she should die before him the capital sum was to revert to her husband. By the summer of 1953, having run through his grandfather's fortune and several more besides, these being the proceeds of various remarkably successful enterprises, all of them illicit, Chesney had reached a condition in which it would be a great convenience to him if his wife were to die and so allow him to put his hands upon the money he had so rashly settled upon her in happier times. Husband and wife had by this time gone their separate ways. Chesney, in the intervals between prison sentences, was living in Germany; Vera with her mother, who helped her to maintain a house in Montpelier Road, Ealing, as a home for old people. On 11th February 1954 Mrs. Chesney, wearing a black diaphanous nightdress, was found lying dead in the bath, which was still wet, although the water had drained away. A few minutes later, the body of 'Lady' Menzies was discovered in an unused back room on the ground floor, almost covered by a pile of cushions. She had been bludgeoned over the head, and one of her stockings was tied tightly around her neck. A postmortem examination showed that Mrs. Chesney must have been very drunk at the time of her death. Two recently emptied bottles of gin were found in her bedroom. The police were quickly on the track of Ronald Chesney. He was known to have been in England ('on business') on 3rd February, when he had visited his wife and had taken her to a cinema. Equally certainly he had returned to Cologne the next day, travelling by way of Harwich and the Hook of Holland. For the purposes of their inquiries the police assumed that he had made a second and secret visit to London. This they were presently able to confirm, it being shown that in fact Chesney, travelling with a false passport in the name of 'Leslie Chown', and wearing some sort of disguise, had flown over from Amsterdam on 10th February. According to the police reconstruction of the crime, Chesney reached the house in Montpelier Road at about 10.30 p.m., after everyone had gone to bed, and contrived to get in unobserved. He went to his wife's bedroom and there he made her drunk on the two bottles of gin he had thoughtfully brought with him. Then he carried her into the bathroom, and, half filling the bath, held her under the water until she was dead, carefully stage-managing the scene so as to suggest that Vera had fallen into the bath in a drunken stupor and had been drowned. So far all had gone well. But as he was making his way out of the silent house he encountered 'Lady' Menzies in the hall. After a struggle, during which the old lady fought desperately for her life, Chesney battered her over the head with a brass coffee-pot, and then, dragging her into the back room, strangled her with her stocking. Then he flew back to Germany. The police net was rapidly closing in upon Ronald Chesney when he shot himself in a wood outside Cologne on 16th February. He could hardly have dared to hope that his luck would carry him safely through a second murder trial. It was left to a Coroner's jury to fix upon the dead man the responsibility for the murder of his wife and mother-in-law. This time there was no room for a verdict of 'Not Proven'.

[*1, 101, 209.*

Mersey, Viscount (1840-1929). Born John Charles Bigham, the son of a Liverpool merchant, he was called to the Bar by the Middle Temple in 1870, joined the Northern Circuit, and in 1883 took silk. He was Liberal Unionist M.P. for the Exchange Division of Liverpool from 1895 to 1897, when he became a judge of the Queen's Bench Division of the High Court. In 1909 he was appointed President of the Probate, Divorce and Admiralty Division, but held the office only for a few months, retiring with a barony; in 1916 he was created first Viscount Mersey. He died on 3rd September 1929. On the Bench, Mr. Justice Bigham enjoyed the reputation—enjoyed is the correct word—of being the speediest judge, and was apt to get through the business of his court with such celerity that he often sent to other courts for cases to fill up his list and so give himself an occupation for the rest of the day. His secret was a remarkable ability to disentangle the main question to be decided; once this had been done, he resolutely declined to allow counsel to waste his time (or theirs) upon side issues, however appetising, and sometimes went to extreme lengths to head them off. In his court, direct answers to plain questions were required; otherwise, there were irritable rumblings from the Bench. In spite of these austerities, which were naturally unpopular with discursive counsel, he was a man who was very well liked, being entirely unaffected and unselfconscious, and in his latter days his perambulations through the Temple, leaning on the arm of his clerk, were rather like royal progresses, in the course of which he would exchange amiable pleasantries with everybody he met, down to the humblest junior barrister or law student. As Mr. Justice Bigham, he presided over the trial of Richard BRINKLEY.

Meyer, Jacob. *See* Paul HEFELD.

Miao, Chung Yo, a young Chinese doctor of law, was indicted at Carlisle Assizes in November 1928 for the murder of his wife whilst on their honeymoon in the English Lake District. He was found guilty, sentenced to death by Mr. Justice HUMPHREYS, and executed at Strangeways Prison, Manchester, on 6th December. The tragic bride, Wai Sheung, twenty-nine years old at the time of her death, was the daughter of Mr. Ying Chan Siu, a wealthy merchant prince of the Mandarin class from the island of Macao, Hong Kong. In 1917 she went to the United States to complete her education, and five years later graduated from Boston University. Upon her father's death in 1924 Miss Siu inherited his considerable fortune. Three years later she returned to the United States with a collection of Chinese *objets d'art* for sale in the American market. It was in October of that year, 1927, that she met her future husband in New York, and fell deeply in love with him. The origins of Chung Yo Miao, aged twenty-eight, were somewhat obscure, but there seems no reason to doubt his claim to belong to the Mandarin class. He also claimed to be a wealthy man, but this rested solely upon some dubious statements of his own; it is more than likely that Miss Siu's money represented for him a considerable part of her attraction. However that may be, the couple were married—according to the rites of the Protestant Episcopal Church of the United States—on 12th May 1928. A month later, they sailed for Glasgow on what was to be a two-months holiday trip to Europe, before returning to China. After visiting Edinburgh, the couple set out on a leisurely journey to London, taking in on their way the beauties of the English Lake District. On Monday, 18th June, they arrived at the Borrowdale Gates Hotel, outside the Cumberland village of Grange-in-Borrowdale, at the southern end of Derwentwater. It was an idyllic setting for young lovers, but one in which this particular pair were uncommonly conspicuous, partly because the Lake District has few Oriental visitors and partly because of the bride's partiality for wearing elaborate and costly jewellery. At 2 p.m. in the afternoon of 19th June, the day after their arrival, the honeymoon couple, an incongruous pair, the husband very tall for a Chinese, the wife tiny, went out for a walk. At 4 p.m. Dr. Miao returned to the hotel alone. He said that his wife had gone into Keswick —about four miles away—to do some shopping, and would not be back until six o'clock. Dinner-time came, without any sign of Mrs. Miao. At 10.30 p.m. she had still not returned, and Dr. Miao asked one of the maids: 'What do you think we ought to do? Should we inform the police?' Shortly afterwards he went to bed. At that time, although he did not know it, Mrs. Miao had already been found. At about 7.30 that evening, a farmer had noticed a woman in a fur coat lying, apparently asleep, under an open umbrella, at the edge of a wood by the river, about a mile from the village. It did not occur to him at the time that anything was wrong, but later that evening he mentioned what he had seen to several people he knew, one of whom happened to be a plain-clothes detective of the Southport Borough Police, who was on holiday in the neighbourhood. It chanced that at about 4 p.m. that afternoon this man, Detective Constable Pendlebury, had seen Dr. Miao walking by himself, not far from the spot where the woman had been seen lying under the umbrella. He asked the farmer to take him to the spot. The woman was still lying there—one glance showed that she was dead. Mrs. Miao had been strangled with a piece of string. It appeared that she must have been sitting on the ground when someone, with the string held in both hands, had suddenly drawn it tightly round her throat and knotted it behind. An attempt had been made to give the appearance that she had been sexually assaulted. There were also marks which suggested that rings had been wrenched off the third finger of the left hand. The time was now 8.45 p.m. At 11 p.m., Inspector Graham called at the Borrowdale Gates Hotel and saw Dr. Miao in his bedroom. The officer told him that he would be detained on suspicion of having caused the death of his wife. The bedroom was searched. In one of Dr. Miao's suitcases were found two rolls of used film in their original cardboard cartons. A local photographer was asked to develop them. As he was removing the second roll of film from its wrapping of silver paper a diamond wedding ring and a diamond solitaire ring fell out on to the table. They were the rings Mrs. Miao had been wearing on the day she was murdered. Dr. Miao's explanation was that his wife had hidden them in the spool shortly before they had set out on their walk. This had not surprised him, as his wife had had a habit of conceal-ing her belongings in odd places, such as the top of the wardrobe. It was curious that he should have mentioned the top of the wardrobe, since it was in that unlikely place that an odd discovery had been made by a hotel chambermaid in Edinburgh only a few days before. She had been cleaning the room which Dr. Miao and his wife had occupied during their brief visit when she had noticed on the top of the wardrobe three pieces of paper bearing a series of Chinese characters. These were translated to read:

Be sure to do it on the ship
Don't do it on ship
Again consider on arrival in Europe.

Dr. Miao admitted that the writing was his, but said he could not remember to what the words had referred or how he had come to write them. The matter gave a great deal of difficulty at the trial, and, in the circumstances, Mr. Justice Humphreys thought it best to instruct the jury to disregard the whole episode, since it had not been proved to have any relevance to the charge. But could the jury really be expected to ignore the sinister implications that might be read into the words? It is doubtful. The prisoner's own evidence amounted to this: Mrs. Miao had had an almost childish pride in her beautiful jewellery and had made a great display of it. Because of this she had naturally attracted a great deal of attention to herself on board ship. At Glasgow, at Edinburgh, and again in the Lake District, Dr. Miao had noticed 'two Orientals', who had seemed to be following them. On the day of the murder, he and his wife had returned from their walk at about 3 p.m. because it was raining, but at the entrance to the hotel Mrs. Miao had suggested that she should go in to Keswick by herself to buy some warmer underclothing. He had offered to go with her, but she had said that he had better go in and lie down, as he had a cold. They had kissed and parted, and that was the last he had seen of his wife. After lying down for a while, he had gone out again to take some more photographs of lakeland scenery, and had returned to the hotel at about 4 p.m. A number of witnesses supported Dr. Miao's statement that 'two Orientals', whose business there was unexplained, had been in the neighbourhood immediately before the crime had been committed. However, nothing of this carried conviction to the jury. They returned a verdict of 'Guilty', and Dr. Miao was sentenced to death. He appealed to the Court of Criminal Appeal, where, refusing any further assistance from Counsel, he argued his case in a remarkable speech which occupied something like five hours. The Court could see no reason to interfere with the verdict. The appeal was dismissed, and Dr. Miao went to the gallows.

[95, 97.

Middleton, Alice Hilda. *See* Cecil MALTBY.

Milstein, Luba. *See* SIEGE OF SIDNEY STREET.

Mitchell, Winifred Mary. *See* Walter William BURTON.

Morton, Frederick Ellison. *See* Ernest BROWN.

Mudie, John McMain. *See* Thomas John LEY.

Muir, Sir Richard David (1857-1924), the most feared and most formidable prosecutor of his day, appeared in practically all the great murder trials to take place at the Old Bailey during the first quarter of the century. Slow and ponderous in manner, without any gift of rhetoric or any pretentions to oratory, he was deadly in cross-examination and, above all, immensely skilled in the preparation of his cases, and in the lucid presentation of them. Rarely has a member of the criminal Bar possessed such a phenomenal memory or such power of connected thought; everything emerged from his powerful mind in logical and chronological order. The notes of his cases, which were voluminous, were always carefully arranged. Written in pencil in four or five different colours, they were reproduced on a series of small numbered cards, and were famous at the Old Bailey as 'Muir's playing cards'. (In cases involving two or more persons, each one was allotted his own colour, and in Muir's notes every reference to this prisoner or to that was entered with the appropriate coloured pencil.) All this industry argues complete absorption in the work in hand, and Richard Muir was so absorbed, a man engrossed. Lord Justice Bankes once said that Muir was the 'most thorough man in England'; he may well have been also the most industrious. His friends often told him that he was 'killing himself with work', but the concentrated life he lived was the only one he knew and the only one he wanted; there is no doubt that his famous imperturbability, his astonishing calmness of mind—he was never rattled—helped to save him from the effects of overwork. (He also enjoyed the blessing of great domestic happiness, although he never fully recovered from the loss of his only son, a promising young barrister who was killed in the 1914-18 war.) To those who did not know him very well, he may have appeared unsympathetic, and even cold-hearted, but this was a superficial view of him, induced, no doubt, by the increasing austerity of his later years, when it cannot be denied that he was a man often much feared by the juniors who assisted him in the conduct of his cases. Richard David Muir, one of sixteen brothers and sisters, was born at Greenock in 1857, the son of a shipbroker, by whom he was designed for a commercial career. But after some tentative training in a Glasgow bank, the young Muir came to London to seek his fortune in journalism. For a time, he worked in the Press Gallery of the House of Commons as a member of *The Times* reporting corps. Meanwhile, he was reading for the Bar. He was called by the Middle Temple in 1884 and, abandoning journalism for the law, entered the chambers of Mr. (afterwards Sir) Forrest Fulton, a leading criminal lawyer who later became Recorder of London. His advancement was rapid. He became Counsel to the Treasury at the North London Sessions and later at the Old Bailey. In 1901 he was appointed a Senior Treasury Counsel at the Old Bailey, and in 1908 the Senior Treasury Counsel, which office he held until his sudden death in January 1924, when an attack of influenza developed into double pneumonia and killed him within the space of three days. He had been knighted in 1918. The long list of famous murder trials at which he appeared for the Crown included those of Herbert John BENNETT; Horace George RAYNER; Richard BRINKLEY; Hawley Harvey CRIPPEN; Edward HOP-WOOD; Lieutenant Douglas MALCOLM; Alexander Campbell MASON; and Frederick JESSE.

Mundy, Bessie Constance Annie. *See* George Joseph SMITH.

N

Now does he feel
His secret murders sticking on his hands.

Shakespeare: *Macbeth*

Newell, Susan, aged thirty, took her eight-years-old daughter, Janet, on a terrible and perilous journey from Coatbridge to Glasgow one June morning in 1923. A lorry gave them a lift, setting them down at the corner of Duke Street, Glasgow. Alighting, Mrs. Newell slipped. The go-cart she was carrying was upset, and a bundle which was on it was tipped into the roadway. A woman watching from an upstairs window was horrified to notice that when Mrs. Newell picked it up and put it back on the go-cart, a foot was protruding from one end of the bundle and a head from the other. The woman rushed downstairs to tell her sister. Together, the two women followed Mrs. Newell. She was pushing the go-cart and her little girl was sitting on top of the bundle, which was now covered with a brown coat; presently Mrs. Newell picked the bundle up and carried it on her back. One of the women buttonholed a man who happened to be passing. He sent her to fetch a policeman whilst he himself followed Mrs. Newell into a courtyard, where he was just in time to see her deposit the bundle at the foot of a staircase. She then climbed a six-foot wall and dropped to the ground—and into the arms of a policeman. The bundle was examined and the body of a strangled boy, crudely trussed like a chicken, was uncovered. At the police station Mrs. Newell accused her husband of having killed the child, and described her frenzied but unavailing attempts to stop him. The dead boy was John Johnston, at thirteen the eldest of a family of five living at Coatbridge. It was shown that between 6.30 p.m. and 7 p.m. on the previous day he had gone to Mrs. Newell's room with newspapers he sold to earn himself some pocket-money; that was the last that had been seen of him. Mrs. Newell's husband, John Newell, a tube worker, was arrested, and both husband and wife were indicted for murder before Lord Alness, the Lord Justice Clerk, within the High Court of Justiciary, Glasgow. The case against John Newell collapsed; he was able to prove that he had had nothing whatever to do with the murder, and was formally acquitted upon the direction of the judge. Mrs. Newell was left alone in the dock. A pitiful and distressing feature of the Crown case against her was the evidence given by the eight-years-old Janet, who said that she had been playing in the street when 'the wee laddie' had arrived with his newspapers. The following day her 'mammy' had taken her for a walk into Glasgow. The child was asked:

Q: What did you do with the wee laddie?
A: We put him in a bag.
Q: When you put him in the bag, what did you do?
A: We went downstairs and I got toffee. There was a go-cart and I got a seat on it.
Q: When you sat on it, what did you sit on? The bundle?
A: Yes, of the wee boy.
Q: Was the boy in the bundle?
A: Yes.

People in court wept to hear the little girl piping innocently of horrors she was too young to understand. The defence was one of insanity. Having been deserted by her husband, it was said that Mrs. Newell had strangled the boy in a mad frenzy when he called with his papers. But Professor John Glaister, Regius Professor of Forensic Medicine in the University of Glasgow, who was called for the Crown, could find no evidence of insanity. After a retirement of only thirty-seven minutes, the jury brought in a majority verdict of 'Guilty', but with a recommendation to mercy which was unanimous. Very many people were convinced that the death sentence which followed upon this verdict would never be carried out, but the Secretary of State for Scotland, Lord Novar, could find no ground for recommending a reprieve, and on 10th October 1923, Susan Newell was hanged at Duke Street Prison, Glasgow. She was the first woman to be executed in Scotland for fifty years.

[*94*.

Nisbet, John Innes. *See* John Alexander DICKMAN.

Nodder, Frederick, a man in his early forties, describing himself as a motor engineer, stood in the dock at Birmingham Assizes on 10th March 1937, having been convicted of abducting a ten-years-old child named Mona Lilian Tinsley, and heard Mr. Justice SWIFT say: 'What you did with that little girl, what became of her, only you know. It may be that time will reveal the dreadful secret which you carry in your breast.'

Frederick Nodder went to prison with a seven years sentence, there to await what only time could disclose. The jury which had convicted him had listened to a curious and disturbing story. Mona Tinsley, a happy, intelligent child, living with her parents and her six brothers and sisters at 11 Thoresby Avenue, Newark, attended the Wesleyan School in Guildhall Street, some twenty minutes walk away. On the afternoon of Tuesday, 5th January 1937, she went to school as usual. She never returned. That afternoon, shortly before four o'clock, Nodder was seen standing in a doorway at the end of Guildhall Street looking towards the Wesleyan School. At four o'clock Mona Tinsley left the school. She was next seen standing with Nodder at the bus station by the Robin Hood Hotel. Together they boarded the 4.45 p.m. bus for Retford, twenty-two miles away. Although unemployed—because of his intemperate habits he was frequently in that condition—Nodder was living at this time in quite a substantial semi-detached house in the village of Hayton, some three and a half miles outside Retford. It was to this house—ironically enough, it was called Peacehaven—that he took the child. Nodder was known to the Tinsleys—indeed, he had once been their lodger—and was on affectionate terms with their children, who called him 'Uncle Fred'. At first he denied that he had seen Mona lately, but afterwards, in a second statement to the police, he admitted that on 5th January she had come up to him in the street and had asked him to take her to see her 'auntie' and baby cousin, Peter, who lived in Sheffield. He had allowed her to persuade him, but he had soon begun to regret his action, and the next day, having meanwhile taken the child to his house, he had decided to send her to her aunt in Sheffield, with a letter of explanation. On that dark, blustery winter's evening, he had taken Mona from Retford to Worksop by the 6.45 p.m. bus, and from there had let her go on into Sheffield by herself, a distance of nineteen miles. He had then returned home. With dogged patience, but with a total lack of success, the police continued their search for the child—alive or dead. Peacehaven, indescribably filthy, was ransacked; the whole of the garden was dug up; woods, coppices, gravel-pits, derelict houses were searched; cesspools opened and examined; a five-mile stretch of the Chesterfield Canal, which ran within fifty yards of Nodder's house, was drained; the river Idle, transformed by incessant rains from a quiet stream into a raging torrent, was dragged repeatedly. No trace was found of the missing child. Nodder was put on trial at Birmingham Assizes on 9th-10th March, charged with taking Mona Tinsley away by fraud. The prosecution was conducted by Mr. Norman Birkett K.C. (afterwards Lord BIRKETT), the defence by Mr. Maurice HEALY K.C. Mr. Healy made a powerful plea for Nodder, but did not find it prudent to put him into the witness-box, a fact commented upon with great severity by Mr. Justice Swift when he came to sum up. 'Nobody knows', he said, 'what has become of that little girl. . . . Whatever happened to her, how she fared, who looked after her, where she slept, there is one person in this court could tell you, there is one person in this court who knows, and he is silent—he is silent. He says nothing to you at all. . . . He sits there and never tells you a word.' On Sunday, 6th June, three months after Nodder's conviction, a boating party enjoying an afternoon sail on the river Idle below Bawtry noticed an object floating in two or three feet of water some yards from the bank on the Nottinghamshire side. It was the body of Mona Tinsley. She had been strangled, but decomposition made it impossible to determine whether she had also been sexually assaulted. Nodder was tried for murder before Mr. Justice Macnaghten at Nottingham Assizes in the following November, when Mr. Birkett was again in charge of the prosecution and Mr. Healy of the defence. This time Nodder did go into the witness-box. There he described how he had taken Mona by bus from Newark to Retford. He had given her supper at his house. Afterwards they had gone to bed, Mona sleeping in the double bed upstairs, he in a downstairs room. The next day, realizing how foolishly he had acted, he had decided to send the child to her aunt in Sheffield. Mona had spent most of that cold, windy day playing about the house, 'reading books and writing', while he was working in the garden. They had left Peacehaven between six and seven o'clock, and at Retford had boarded a bus for Sheffield. He had left Mona at Worksop, after giving her two shillings for her fare, written and verbal instructions upon how to reach her destination, and a full explanatory letter to her aunt. He had never seen the child again. It was suggested in Nodder's defence that somewhere between Worksop and Sheffield the child had been lured from the bus and murdered. Nodder was found guilty. 'Justice has slowly but surely overtaken you,' commented the judge in passing sentence of death. That sentence was duly carried out at Lincoln Prison on 30th December.

[*I.*

Not Proven. In a Scottish criminal court one of three verdicts may be returned—'Guilty', 'Not Guilty', 'Not Proven'. A verdict of 'Not Proven' has the force of, and the same result as, an acquittal. There is no basis for the popular belief that a case which ends in a verdict of 'Not Proven' may be re-opened if, at some future date, new circumstances should come to light.

O

One to destroy is murder by the law
And gibbets keep the lifted hand in awe.

Edward Young: Love of Fame

Oatley, Evelyn (also known as **Nita Ward**). *See* Gordon Frederick CUMMINS.

O'Connor, Sir Terence James, K.C. (1891-1940). A typical Irishman, with a full share of the more attractive qualities of his race, Terence O'Connor was called to the Bar by the Inner Temple in 1919, and took silk ten years later. In 1924 he entered the House of Commons as Conservative M.P. for Luton, but lost his seat in the General Election of 1929. Victory at a by-election brought him back to the House again in the following year, this time as the member for Central Nottingham. In 1936 he became Solicitor-General. He died suddenly on 8th May 1940, at the age of forty-nine, having strained his heart in the hunting field, where he was a bold and adventurous rider. As Solicitor-General, he prosecuted Charlotte BRYANT.

O'Dwyer, Sir Michael Francis. *See* UDHAM SINGH.

O'Sullivan, Joseph. *See* Reginald DUNN.

P

Put this in any liquid thing you will,
And drink it off; and, if you had the strength
Of twenty men, it would dispatch you straight.

Shakespeare: *Romeo and Juliet*

Pace, Beatrice, accused of poisoning her husband, suffered the ordeal of 'Trial by Inquest', an ordeal which, following upon her dramatic arrest on a Coroner's warrant, continued to drag its way through lengthy police-court proceedings, and came to an end only after a five days hearing at Gloucester Assizes, when the judge stopped the trial and directed the jury to return a formal verdict of 'Not Guilty'. Harry Pace, sheep-raiser and quarryman, of Fetterhill Farm, Coleford, on the fringe of the Forest of Dean, was a rather peculiar and distasteful character, of sadistic impulses, given to violent fits of rage, during which he was capable of acting with extreme brutality towards his long-suffering wife. In the summer of 1927 he was taken ill after dipping some lambs. The chief symptoms were pains in the stomach and 'burning pains' in the throat; eventually his condition became so acute that he was removed to Gloucester Royal Infirmary. He was discharged in October, but two months later he was seized with a similar attack. In the New Year he was prostrated with severe abdominal pains, and on 10th January he died. On 15th January the funeral was stopped by order of the Coroner, Mr. Maurice Carter, acting upon the representations of a brother of the dead man. The inquest on Harry Pace, which was to attract so much criticism, opened on 16th January. It appeared that between Christmas Day 1927 and 10th January 1928 three doses of arsenic must have been administered to Harry Pace, the last, a large dose, between six and forty-eight hours before death. The total amount of arsenic found in the organs was 9·42 grains. Professor Walker Hall was asked about the effect of arsenic if absorbed through the skin. He said that a healthy skin would not absorb white arsenic if applied only for a limited period, but it could be absorbed through a cut or abrasion. Sir William Willcox, medical adviser to the Home Office, who was called to confirm the post-mortem findings, considered that Pace had been suffering from acute arsenical poisoning since the previous July. The inquest proceedings lingered on until the end of May. After a short summing-up by the Coroner who pointed out that there was nothing to support a suggestion that Pace had been poisoned by accident, the jury retired to consider their verdict. They returned after an hour. 'Harry Pace', the foreman announced, 'met his death by arsenical poisoning administered by some person or persons other than himself, and in our view the case calls for further investigation.' But the Coroner would not accept this verdict. He told the jury: 'Only the committal of a person after a Coroner's inquiry can bring about an investigation, which cannot take place unless there is some person named. It is necessary for you to name a person if a person is to be charged.' Armed with this instruction, the validity of which was afterwards sharply challenged, the jury retired for another twenty-five minutes. At the end of that time they came back into court with an amended verdict: 'We find that Harry Pace met his death by arsenical poisoning administered by Beatrice Pace.' A cry was wrenched from the ashen lips of Mrs. Pace —'I didn't do it, I didn't!' She was arrested then and there, and half carried, half dragged from the courtroom sobbing piteously. There was an immediate outcry in the Press over the conduct of the Coroner, of which the most practical result was the raising of a public subscription to provide Mrs. Pace with the funds necessary for her defence; the brief was accepted by the eminent jury advocate, Mr. Norman Birkett K.C. (afterwards Lord BIRKETT). The trial of Beatrice Pace for the murder of her husband opened at Gloucester Assizes before Mr. Justice HORRIDGE on 2nd July, the Crown case being presented by the Solicitor-General, Sir Frank Boyd Merriman K.C. It came out in evidence that Pace had said that he thought his illness was due to getting into the water when dipping the sheep. Against this, a representative of a firm which manufactured sheep-dip said that although sheep were often known to die from arsenical poisoning after dipping, eighty per cent. of these casualties were due to the *swallowing* of the dip. When Sir William Willcox was called he stressed that Harry Pace had died as the result of 'protracted poisoning'. Arsenic could not be absorbed through the skin unless the skin was damaged. He agreed in cross-examination, however, that a man handling dipped sheep might get arsenic on his hands, and in that way it might be possible for the poison to get into his food—but not in the amount that had to be accounted for here. Mrs. Pace's view of the matter was expressed very clearly in her statement to the police: 'I am convinced that my husband poisoned himself, and I don't think anyone else could have done it.' After the case for the Crown had been concluded, Mr. Birkett submitted that there was insufficient evidence for the trial to proceed further. The scientific evidence, he argued, was equally consistent with suicide as with any other theory. Mr. Justice Horridge agreed that it would 'not be safe' to ask the jury to proceed further with the case. He therefore instructed them to return a formal verdict of 'Not Guilty', and this being done, Mrs. Pace was at once discharged. Following upon this sudden and dramatic end to the trial, which was received with jubilation, the *Law Journal* commented severely upon the inquest proceedings: 'The Coroner's jury returned, as we suggest, with no jurisdiction whatever a verdict of murder against Mrs. Pace.' In the House of Commons a few months later Mr. (later Sir) Rhys Hopkin Morris introduced a bill to limit the duty of a Coroner to finding the cause of death, and to debar him from naming guilty persons in his verdict. It was given a second reading, but failed to become law.

[*30, 206.*

Page, Vera, a little girl of ten, was found by a milkman on the morning of Wednesday, 16th December 1931, lying strangled in the shrubbery of the front garden belonging to a house in Addison Road, Kensington. She had been violated, and had been dead for two days. The child was fully dressed, but had no hat. There was coal dust on her face and clothing, and her coat was spotted with candle-grease. Marks—made after death—suggested that a cord had been round her neck, probably when the murderer was carrying the body to the place of concealment. Apparently it had been brought to Addison Road early in the morning on which it was found, perhaps in some conveyance, such as a coster's barrow, possibly in a sack. This was evident from the fact that although it had rained heavily during the night the little girl's clothes were quite dry. Vera Page, the only child of a painter employed by the Great Western Railway Company, had disappeared from her home in Blenheim Crescent, North Kensington, two days before her body was found. She had arrived home from school at about 4 p.m., but had left almost at once to run round to her aunt's house, only a few doors away, to call for some swimming certificates she had won. Having collected the certificates, which she had proudly left for her aunt's inspection earlier in the day, the little girl had then set out on the short walk home. A little later, that is, at 5 p.m., she was seen gazing at a display of soap 'dominoes' in the window of a nearby chemist's shop. (She was hoping to buy some of these 'dominoes' as a Christmas present.) That seems to have been the last that was ever seen of her—alive. The next day Vera's red beret was found lying in a basement area in Stanley Crescent, Montpelier Street, about three hundred yards away from the chemist's shop. Also lying in the area was a candle-end. Both candle and beret smelt strongly of paraffin. There was a disused, unlocked cellar giving on to the area, but the most thorough examination revealed nothing to suggest that this had been the scene of the murder. It seemed most probable, therefore, that the beret and the candle-end had been thrown into the area from the pavement above. A finger-stall consisting of a piece of pus-stained lint and a dirty bandage was found in the bend of the little girl's right elbow. The police concluded that this had been accidentally pulled off a finger—probably from the left hand—of the murderer as he was laying the body down within the shelter of the shrubbery. It was stained with soot or coal dust and smelt of ammonia. Subsequent developments appeared to emphasize the significance of this clue. Those developments are described by the late Mr. Ingleby Oddie, the Westminster Coroner, in his book, *Inquest*. He writes:

On Thursday, December 17th, a man whom I will call X was interrogated by the police. He worked in a laundry, and lived on the top floor of a house only 170 yards away from the Pages' house. He knew Vera quite well. . . . Inquiries showed that X had two cuts on the little finger of his *left* hand which were discharging, and he had been seen wearing a finger-stall bandage to protect the wound. The finger-stall found on the body fitted his little finger exactly. It smelt of ammonia. X used ammonia at his work. . . . The finger bandage was shown to Mrs. X, who said it was the one worn by her husband—but such lint and bandage are in common use, and the evidence was far from being conclusive. . . . X also had a locked coal-cellar in the basement, and a paraffin-soaked rag was found on a chest of drawers which stood on the landing outside his rooms. . . . He worked at a laundry in Kensington situated about twenty-five minutes' bus journey from his home. On December 14th he left off work at 5.55 p.m. He said he did not hurry home as his wife was away visiting her mother, and would not be back until about 8.30 p.m. So he did a little shopping, and arrived home at about half-past eight, to find that his wife had returned. He had his evening meal and did not go out again at all. . . . Dr Roche LYNCH, the Home Office analyst, made experiments with an old pyjama cord found in X's pocket. X said he had picked it up in the yard of the laundry where he worked. This cord fitted the mark on the child's neck, made after death. . . . A woman who saw a man wheeling a coster's barrow early on the Wednesday morning, the day the body was found, from the direction of X's house and in the direction of Addison Road, with a bundle on it covered with a red cloth similar to one found in X's home, failed on two occasions to identify X as this person.

Reluctantly, Mr. Oddie was compelled to record a verdict of murder against 'some person unknown'.

[*145.*

Parker, George Henry, boarded a London-bound train at Eastleigh, Hampshire, on the afternoon of 17th January 1901. He took his seat in a third-class compartment, of which the only other occupant was a Mrs. Rhoda King of Southampton. At Winchester a well-to-do farmer named William Pearson entered the compartment. Parker, a personable young man, over six feet in height and of powerful build, noted Mr. Pearson's prosperous appearance, and decided that for his purpose he would do as well as any other, and distinctly better than some. The train was now running non-stop to Vauxhall. As it reached Surbiton, Parker drew his revolver and shot Mr. Pearson dead. He then turned the gun on Mrs. King and fired again. Mrs. King, who had been looking out of the window when the first shot was fired, felt the bullet graze her cheek. 'My God,' she cried, 'what have you done?' 'I did it for money,' replied Parker calmly, adding, 'I want some money. Have you got any?' Poor Mrs. King, the blood streaming down her cheek on to her dress, fumbled desperately with her purse and drew out a shilling, at the same time imploring Parker to save her life, for the sake of her husband and children. Parker ignored the shilling. He had been rifling the body of the dead man, and now had possession of Mr. Pearson's purse; he was gratified to see that it was well filled. From it he took a golden sovereign and, no doubt intending if he could to implicate her in the crime, offered it to the distraught Mrs. King, who was so beside herself with fear that, although she refused the money, she promised to say nothing about the murder if only she might herself be spared. 'What shall I do with this bloody thing?' inquired Parker, casually twirling the revolver. 'How would it do to put it in the old bloke's hand so that people will think he killed himself?' Mrs. King saw her chance, perhaps the only one she had to save her life. She advised Parker to throw the weapon out of the window; this, rather surprisingly, he did, just as the train was passing Nine Elms. As it slowed down on nearing Vauxhall, Parker opened the door of the compartment, and got his foot on the step. Directly the train reached the platform, and whilst it was still moving, he jumped out, ran along the platform, thrust Mr. Pearson's ticket into the hand of the collector at the barrier, and bounded down the stairs towards the street. Meanwhile Mrs. King had staggered from the train and was filling the station with her cries: 'Stop him! Stop him! He has killed a man!' Within seconds the chase was on. Parker was overtaken and captured. In the following March he was charged with murder, before Mr. Justice Phillimore (afterwards

Lord PHILLIMORE) at the Old Bailey, where it was urged in his defence that he had killed the farmer in a fit of temporary insanity. The defence failed; Parker was found guilty, sentenced to death, and executed on 19th March.

[*33, 112.*

Pearson, William. *See* George Henry PARKER.

Peters, Dagmar (Dagmar Petrzywalski). *See* Harold HAGGER.

Peters, Jacob. *See* SIEGE OF SIDNEY STREET.

Petrou, Theodosios, a Cypriot waiter employed at the Café Monico, Piccadilly Circus, was accused of murdering a fellow-countryman named Dr. Angelos Zemenides in January 1933. He was said to have been enraged because Dr. Zemenides, a teacher turned marriage broker, had accepted a fee of £10 to find him a bride with a £200 dowry, but had failed to produce one. Pressed to return the money, which Petrou had borrowed in the first place, he was supposed to have handed back only £5, having spent the rest. Whereupon, it was alleged that the indignant waiter had stormed into the Hampstead boarding-house where the doctor lived and had shot him dead. But when Petrou was indicted at the Old Bailey for murder he was able to establish an unshakable alibi to satisfy the jury that whoever it was who had killed Dr. Zemenides it was not the man in the dock. Petrou was found not guilty and discharged.

[*18.*

Phillimore, Lord (1845-1929). Walter George Frank Phillimore was the embodiment of austerity and decorum, who viewed with mingled incredulity and disgust the distasteful ways in which men and women were inclined to behave outside the somewhat rarified circles in which he himself moved. A wealthy man—he owned a profitable slice of the Royal Borough of Kensington—he was never required to concern himself with such mundane matters as are involved in the mere process of earning a living, and this lent to him a certain air of remoteness from the ordinary, and no doubt sometimes sordid, commerce of life. When he was first appointed a judge of the Queen's Bench Division of the High Court he had had no experience of criminal cases, and much of the evidence to which he was now compelled to listen plainly shocked him to the core; anything, for instance, which seemed to imply a loose standard of sexual morality was sure to arouse in him feelings little short of horror. He was a purist in all things, not least in language and diction. References to him in the legal memoirs of the period make much of his 'dainty, refined voice'—as of his moustache and side-whiskers—which was said to suggest clerical rather than legal associations. His interest in Church matters was indeed profound; probably no greater authority on ecclesiastical law has sat upon the Bench in recent times. Called to the Bar by the Middle Temple in 1868, he took silk in 1883, succeeded to his father's baronetcy in 1885, and was raised to the Bench in 1897. In 1913 he became a Lord Justice of Appeal, retiring in 1916; two years later, in recognition of his long judicial career, and of his eminence as an ecclesiastical and international lawyer, a peerage was conferred upon him, and he became the first Baron Phillimore. He died in 1929, at the age of eighty-three. Mr. Justice Phillimore presided over the trials of George Henry PARKER; and Stephen TITUS.

Piatkow, Peter ('Peter the Painter'). See SIEGE OF SIDNEY STREET.

'Porthole' Murder. See James CAMB.

Priestly, Helen Wilson Robertson. See Jeannie DONALD.

Provocation. Provocation can never render an unlawful homicide excusable or justifiable, but if the act by which death is caused is done in the heat of passion caused by provocation, this may reduce the crime from murder to manslaughter. The Royal Commission on Capital Punishment, which reported in 1953, pointed out:

> Provocation in its legal sense may take various forms, but is usually physical. The commonest case is an assault, but even an assault will not constitute sufficient provocation unless it inflicts either actual bodily harm or great insult. Another common case is that in which, on a sudden quarrel, two persons fight, on equal terms and in the heat of the moment, and one kills the other. Each party is then deemed to have given provocation to the other and the homicide amounts only to manslaughter. An unlawful arrest or imprisonment may also be a provocation to the person arrested or imprisoned, but rarely, if ever, to other persons present who may seek to assist him. Finally, it has long been held that if a man finds his wife in the act of adultery and instantly kills her or her lover, he has received such provocation as makes the killing only man-slaughter. But the House of Lords has recently ruled that 'a confession of adultery without more is never sufficient to reduce an

offence which would otherwise be murder to manslaughter' and laid down the general proposition that 'in no case could words alone, save in circumstances of a most extreme and exceptional character, so reduce the crime'.

The Royal Commission concluded: 'We think that if the issue is left to the jury and they are allowed to consider each case on its merits, irrespective of whether the alleged provocation was by word or deed, they can be trusted to arrive at a just and reasonable decision and will not hesitate to convict the accused of murder where he has acted on only slight provocation, whether by words or otherwise.' This recommendation was embodied in the HOMICIDE ACT, 1957, a measure which effected many liberalizing reforms in the law of murder. Clause 3 of that Act provides that:

Where on a charge of murder there is evidence on which the jury can find that the person charged was provoked (whether by things done or by things said or by both together) to lose his self-control, the question whether the provocation was enough to make a reasonable man do as he did shall be left to be determined by the jury; and in determining that question the jury shall take into account everything both done and said according to the effect which, in their opinion, it would have on a reasonable man.

Q

Quit, O quit this mortal frame.
Alexander Pope: *The Dying Christian*

Queen, Peter, aged thirty-one, a clerk in his father's business, called at the Partick Police Office in Glasgow at 3 a.m. on Saturday, 21st November 1931, and putting two house keys on the counter said this: 'Go to 539 Dumbarton Road. I think you will find my wife dead.' Two constables went at once to Queen's two-roomed apartment, where they found lying in the bed the dead body of a woman in pyjamas and boudoir cap. Tied tightly round her neck was a piece of cord, which had strangled her; there was no sign of a struggle and the bedclothes had not been disturbed. The woman was identified as Christina Gall, aged twenty-eight, who had been living with Queen at the house in Dumbarton Road since the previous August; she had formerly been employed as a maid by Queen's parents. Some friends of Queen and Christina, a Mr. and Mrs. Johnston, had been at the house that night. Mrs. Johnston spoke of Christina, a confirmed drunkard, as having been in a 'helpless condition'. Mr. Johnston, on the other hand, considered that she had been at least sober enough to have 'walked about' had she chosen to leave her bed. Her precise degree of insobriety at that time was highly important since at Queen's trial for murder, which took place within the High Court of Justiciary at Glasgow in January 1932, it was contended that she had been physically capable of *strangling herself*, and that this was, in fact, what she had done. Obviously, in these circumstances, the medical evidence was vital. The experts called by the Crown were agreed that the appearances of the body were not consistent with self-destruction. Dr. Allison, Professor of Medical Jurisprudence at Glasgow, spoke for them all when, after describing the medical reasons for that opinion, he added: 'I cannot conceive of a woman strangling herself and then placing her right arm under the bedclothes, arranging the bedclothes in an orderly fashion over her body, and leaving the ends of the cord tucked under the top of the bedclothes.' Queen, however, had on his side the prestige attaching to the name of that eminent pathologist, Sir Bernard SPILSBURY, who said that in his opinion the

217

force used in the strangulation was not considerable and was of a degree associated with suicide. Queen's own evidence contained this most vivid and striking passage: 'I drew the curtains to see if Chris was asleep. . . . It was then that I saw the cord round her neck. I got hold of her and shouted: "Chris, Chris, speak to me!" I got a terrible shock when I saw the rope round her neck. Her face was swollen, too. I do not know what happened. I must have collapsed or something. I got a terrible shock; it knocked me out.' After a two hours retirement, the jury returned a majority verdict of 'Guilty', accompanying it with a unanimous recommendation to mercy. Queen was condemned to death by the Lord Justice Clerk, Lord Alness, but was later reprieved.

[*174.*

R

Revenge his foul and most unnatural murder.

Shakespeare: *Hamlet*

Rayner, Horace George, a handsome but shiftless young man, walked out of Lancaster Gate tube station shortly after noon on 24th January 1907 with a sixpenny piece and six pennies in his pocket, leaving behind him in the cloakroom a parcel containing, among other miscellanea, nineteen pawn tickets; he had nothing else to pledge; his prospects extended no further than his next scanty meal, certainly not as far as the one beyond it. But in his breast pocket he had a revolver and a box of 'dum-dum' bullets, and in his mind he had a plan by whose aid he might yet hope to escape from his present penury. A few minutes walk brought him to the fashionable emporium in Westbourne Grove, Bayswater, founded, and at that time still directed, by Mr. William Whiteley, the 'Universal Provider', who had given London its first great department store. It was the last week of the January sales and the store was crowded. Rayner went in and asked to see Mr. Whiteley, pretending that Sir George Lewis, the well-known solicitor, had sent him. There was nothing in the outward appearance of this desperate and penniless man to conflict with his pretensions; his frock coat and shining silk hat seemed to guarantee his respectability. So Rayner was shown into Mr. Whiteley's private room. The 'Universal Provider', now in his seventy-sixth year, whiskered, portly, and affable, with a weakness for quoting the Scriptures, waved him to a seat. The door was closed upon the pair. Half an hour later it was opened by a very different Mr. Whiteley; pale and agitated, his customary geniality quite gone, he emerged from his room into the crowded store and told one of the assistants to fetch a policeman. His visitor appeared behind him in the open doorway.

'Won't you come in again?' asked the young man.

'No, no, go away!' cried Mr. Whiteley.

'Aren't you going to come back?' asked Rayner. 'Is that your final word?'

'Yes.'

'Then you are a dead man, Mr. Whiteley.'

With these words Rayner pulled his revolver from his pocket and fired two shots; the second of these, entering the head behind the right ear, killed Mr. Whiteley instantly. Rayner then turned the gun upon himself and fired again. The bullet entered the left temple, but it did not kill him. At the Old Bailey, in March, he was tried for murder; it was the first capital trial to take place in the new building which had only recently been opened by King Edward VII. The key to the tragic story unfolded there was to be found in a pencilled note—written on two leaves torn from a notebook—which was found in Rayner's breast pocket. This read:

To all whom it may concern: William Whiteley is my father, and he has brought upon himself and me a double fatality by reason of his own refusal of a request perfectly reasonable. R.I.P.

Whatever may have been the truth behind the mystery of Rayner's parentage—and nothing that was said at the trial did anything to clear it up—it seemed sufficiently clear that Rayner, by dint of much brooding on the matter, had genuinely persuaded himself that Mr. Whiteley was his father. His counsel, Mr. George ELLIOTT K.C., declared that it was not for the defence to prove, or even to assert, that the belief was well-founded; it was enough to show that it had preyed upon Rayner's mind ('never of a powerful equilibrium') to such an extent that it had come to govern all his actions. Although he was not to be regarded as 'insane' as the law understood the word, he was nonetheless a degenerate whose mental heritage had been tainted by 'at least two generations of alcohol'. He suffered from 'mental explosions' and at certain moments was capable of acts of 'impulsive insanity'. Rayner himself went into the witness-box to describe the fatal interview with William Whiteley: 'We sat facing each other. He said "What can I do for you?" I said, "I believe I am right in stating that a son is speaking to his father?" He said, "Is that so?" ' The conversation led up to a request for assistance:

Mr. Whiteley said, 'I cannot recall the past,' or words to that effect. . . . Mr. Whiteley then asked me if I would like to go abroad. I said that needed capital. He said, 'Many young fellows go abroad and do well without having started with capital. I should advise you to go to the Salvation Army.' I was very much nettled at this, seeing so little sentiment, and I had a considerable revulsion of feeling in my mind. I said, 'Do you absolutely refuse to help me, either in kind, or in employment?' He said, 'Yes.' 'Then,' I said, 'I must tell you I have made up my mind to blow my brains out if

I am unsuccessful.' Mr. Whiteley said, 'Don't talk so silly!' I produced a revolver and put it to my head. He said, 'Put that thing down!' And I put it behind my back. My head was in a whirl. . . . I thought if he is not amenable to sentiment and sense of duty, he may be amenable to a sense of fear, and I made up my mind to play that last card, with no intention of carrying it into effect. So I put the revolver back in my pocket and tore two leaves out of a pocket-book and started to write. Mr. Whiteley sat opposite me. He got up and went to the door. I said, 'Won't you wait?' But he took no notice. My head was in a state of blankness, and I did not know what to do, having practically condemned myself to death. . . . The last I remember is his statement that he had sent for a policeman.

After a retirement of only ten minutes the jury returned a verdict of 'Guilty', and Rayner was sentenced to death by the Lord Chief Justice, Lord ALVERSTONE. But on 27th March the Home Secretary announced in the House of Commons that he proposed to take into consideration the 'peculiar circumstances' of the case; four days later a reprieve was granted and the death sentence commuted to one of penal servitude for life. Rayner received the news without joy. He would have preferred, he said, to 'get the whole business over and done with, instead of having to endure years of misery behind iron bars'. He was certainly not a tractable prisoner. In October 1907 he tried to commit suicide by opening an artery in his wrist; a few months later he was charged before a visiting magistrate at Parkhurst with having set fire to his prison bedding. He duly paid for these railings against fortune by spells of solitary confinement on bread and water. Rayner was liberated on medical grounds in 1919, after twelve years in gaol; he died not long afterwards.

[*62, 113, 117.*

Rentoul, Sir Gervais, K.C. (1884-1946). This well-known criminal advocate, who, for the last twelve years of his life was a Metropolitan Police Magistrate (West London), had a close family connection with the law, his father being Judge Rentoul of the City of London Court and a Commissioner at the Old Bailey. A barrister of Gray's Inn (called 1907; K.C. 1930), with a large practice in the criminal courts and in licensing cases, he was besides, as Conservative M.P. for Lowestoft (1922-34), extremely active in politics. During his years as a magistrate (1934-46) the atmosphere of the West London Police Court reflected his own buoyant personality. Someone with a talent for wry comment once said of him that he was 'an excellent magistrate for the defence', and perhaps in his manifest anxiety that the man in the dock should have every possible chance to make the most of his case he did sometimes give the impression of 'leaning over backwards'; if this be counted a fault, it was a very genial one. He died on 7th March 1946 at the comparatively early age of sixty-one. The most celebrated of the murder trials in which he was engaged was that of the SEDDONS, when he appeared for Mrs. Seddon, who was acquitted. He also prosecuted James Thomas COLLINS.

Reprieve. *See* ROYAL PREROGATIVE OF MERCY.

Ridley, Sir Edward (1843-1928). Judge of the King's Bench Division of the High Court (1897-1917). Legal memoirs of the period do not, as a rule, deal very generously with Mr. Justice Ridley, who has had many to draw attention to his faults; even so kindly a critic as the late Sir Samuel Ronald Bosanquet found him a 'curiously futile and undignified judge' (in *The Oxford Circuit*). He was a judge perpetually at odds with counsel appearing before him. They seem to have found his inconsequence irritating and distracting, and his tendency to arrive at premature conclusions intolerable; both were fruitful sources of discord, and sometimes of undignified squabbling, between Bench and Bar. Yet this much maligned man had many good qualities. 'With all his faults as a judge,' says Bosanquet, 'Ridley was a gentleman, and he never bore malice.' Edward Ridley, brother of Sir Matthew White (later Viscount) Ridley, sometime Home Secretary, was called to the Bar by the Inner Temple in 1868 (Q.C. 1892), and joined the Northern Circuit, practising chiefly in Durham and in his native county of Northumberland. For a few years (1878-80) he was Conservative M.P. for South Northumberland. In 1886 he became an Official Referee. This is not a post usually regarded as a stepping-stone to a High Court judgeship. However, in this case it was so; in 1897 Lord Halsbury, a Lord Chancellor responsible for some curious appointments, nominated him for a vacancy in the Queen's Bench Division. He retired in 1917, after twenty years on the Bench, and died on 14th October 1928, being then in his eighty-sixth year. Murder trials over which Mr. Justice Ridley presided included those of Arthur DEVEREUX; and William Walter BURTON.

Robinson, John, deposited a large black trunk in the left luggage office at Charing Cross Station on 6th May 1927. Four days later an attendant noticed an unpleasant smell emanating from it and called the police. The trunk was found to contain the dismembered remains of a woman—wrapped in four separate parcels—a pair of black shoes and a handbag. In the first parcel were the arms, severed at the shoulders; these were wrapped in towels and a pair of grey knickers with a tab bearing the name 'Holt'. The legs were in parcels two and three, the head and torso in the fourth. The head was wrapped in a yellow duster, and the torso in a blue jumper and some underclothes. One of these garments carried a laundry mark. This was traced to a Mrs. Holt, who supplied the police with the names of ten maids who had been in her service during the past two years. By a laborious process of elimination each of these girls was accounted for—except one. This was a certain Minnie Bonati, a married woman living apart from her husband. Naturally, the Press made a great deal of the trunk. It figured in every headline; most newspapers carried photographs of it—circulated by Scotland Yard. This publicity had two immediate results: (1) a Brixton dealer reported that on 6th May he had sold a similar trunk to a dark man of medium height, with a slight moustache; and (2) a taxi-driver came forward to say that on or about 6th May he had driven a man with such a trunk from an office building in Rochester Row to Charing Cross Station. The taxi-driver had helped the man to carry the trunk downstairs from the third-floor landing. He had remarked how heavy it was, and his fare had explained that it was full of books. The tenant of the office, on the third-floor front, outside which the trunk had been standing, turned out to be a 'Mr. J. Robinson', carrying on business as an estate agent; he had not been seen there since 9th May, when he had left a note saying that he was 'broke' and would not be returning. Inquiries at his lodgings showed that Mr. Robinson had gone away, without leaving a forwarding address. In his room was a notice from the Post Office to say that a telegram to 'Robinson, Greyhound Hotel, Hammersmith' could not be delivered as no person of that name was known there. This, it transpired, was an error. There *was* a 'Robinson' working at the Greyhound Hotel—a 'Mrs. Robinson'. This lady believed herself to be married to the defaulting estate agent. But in this he had deceived her; it had been a bigamous marriage. She was interviewed by the police and that evening Chief-Inspector (later Superintendent) Cornish, the experienced Scotland Yard officer in charge of the case, accompanied her to the Elephant and Castle public house, Walworth, where she was to meet her 'husband'. John Robinson made no demur when asked to go to Scotland Yard to make a statement. This amounted to nothing more than a simple denial that he had ever seen or heard of Minnie Bonati, or had ever purchased a trunk, at Brixton or anywhere else. Neither did Robinson object to being confronted with the taxi-driver, the porter who had helped with the trunk at Charing Cross Station, and the dealer who had sold it. *None of the three recognized him.* Robinson was allowed to go. Prodigal as he had been with the clues he had left behind him, the significance of the most vital clue of all had so far evaded Chief-Inspector Cornish. But on 21st May during a Scotland Yard conference, he was examining once again the yellow duster in which the head had been wrapped when he fancied that beneath the bloodstains and surrounding grime he could discern some letters which appeared to make up a word. 'I am going to have this washed,' he announced. The duster was accordingly washed, and when it was brought back, still wet, to the Conference room it was possible to make out, faintly written in marking ink, the word 'Greyhound'. Here, by way of the Greyhound Hotel, was the first definite link between John Robinson and the Charing Cross trunk murder. Robinson was invited back to the Yard. He came, but with nothing of his former self-assurance. His second statement was also very different from his first. 'I realize this is serious,' he said. 'I met her at Victoria and took her to my office. I want to tell you all about it. I done it and cut her up.' He went on to describe how he had met Mrs. Bonati at Victoria Station, and how he had taken her to his office in Rochester Row. She had, he said, asked him for money and when he had refused made as if to attack him. He had pushed her away and she had fallen, struck her head, rolled over and lain still. He had gone out, leaving her to recover. But when next morning he had returned to the office he had been horrified to discover that the woman was still lying where she had fallen—she was dead. 'I decided to cut her up in pieces and cart it away in parcels,' said Robinson. He had had to take particular care over it, for his office windows exactly overlooked Rochester Row Police Station, where, no doubt, an inconvenient interest would have been taken in this particular surgical operation. There in that grubby office, under the very eyes of the police, as it were, he had proceeded to dismember the body with a chef's knife, which he had bought for the purpose. Having parcelled the remains, he had left them in the office overnight and the next morning had returned with the trunk. This, with its ghastly contents, he had deposited at Charing Cross Station later that same day; the knife he had buried under a tree on Clapham Common, from which secret place it was, with Robinson's assistance, duly recovered. A further discovery was made during an inch-by-inch search of Robinson's office. Caught in the plaited cane of a wastepaper basket was a matchstick. The stain upon it responded to tests for human blood. It was the last in the long trail of clues left behind by this excessively careless man. At Robinson's trial for murder, which took place at the Old Bailey in July, the accused was questioned by Mr. Justice SWIFT as to his view of the likely reactions of an *innocent man* confronted by such a situation. 'The position I was in was terrible,' said Robinson. 'I did not know what to do.'

Mr. Justice Swift: Why was it terrible? It was unpleasant to find somebody dead in your room, but where was the difficulty, if you had done nothing wrong, in going to the police station across the road and saying, 'I had a few words with a woman in my office, and this morning I found her dead'?
Robinson: I did not look at it in that light.

That, however, was the light in which the jury looked at it, having heard from the Home Office pathologist, Sir Bernard SPILSBURY that Mrs. Bonati had been struck on the head *and afterwards suffocated.* They brought in a verdict of 'Guilty' and Robinson was sentenced to death. He was hanged at Pentonville Prison on 12th August.
[*61, 216, 230.*

Roche, Lord (1871-1956). Alexander Adair Roche, being called to the Bar by the Inner Temple in 1896, discovered in the Commercial Court the *milieu* best suited to his particular talents. His success as a junior was immense, and after he had taken silk in 1912 all that was most attractive (and most lucrative) in commercial practice seemed to gravitate naturally towards him. But he was in silk for only five years; in 1917 he accepted from Lord Chancellor Finlay the offer of a judgeship in the King's Bench Division. In October 1934 he was nominated to succeed the late Lord Justice SCRUTTON in the Court of Appeal, and a year later, when Lord Wright became Master of the Rolls, he took his place as a Lord of Appeal in Ordinary (with a life peerage). He retired in 1938, and eighteen years later, on 22nd December 1956, he died. Perhaps the most famous murder trial over which he presided during his seventeen years as a King's Bench judge was the trial of Mrs. Sarah Ann HEARN.

Rogerson, Mary Jane. *See* Dr. Buck RUXTON.

Rolt, Terence Peter. *See* Charles Henry JENKINS.

Roome, Henry Delacombe (1882-1930) was called to the Bar by the Middle Temple in 1907; seven years later he became Counsel to the Crown at Middlesex Sessions, and in 1920 Junior Treasury Counsel at the Old Bailey; he was promoted Third Senior Prosecuting Counsel in 1928. A motoring accident at Retford on 8th June 1930 prematurely ended a career which to a man much spoken of as one of the soundest criminal lawyers at the Bar had held out the promise of great advancement; he was only forty-eight when he was killed. Murder trials at which he acted for the Crown included those of John STARCHFIELD;

Alexander Campbell MASON; Jean Pierre VAQUIER; Alfred Arthur KOPSCH; and BROWNE and KENNEDY. As a young barrister he acted as junior counsel for Hawley Harvey CRIPPEN.

Rosen, John. *See* SIEGE OF SIDNEY STREET.

Rouse, Alfred Arthur, was hanged, one might say, because he stepped into the cruel light of the moon a little too early. If only this much-harrassed commercial traveller had waited a few moments longer he might have successfully buried his past—and his even more trouble-some present—and the 'Blazing Car Mystery' might never have been recognized as a mystery at all. In the early hours of 6th November 1930, William Bailey and Alfred Thomas Brown—they were cousins—were returning from a Guy Fawkes Night dance at Northampton. To reach their homes in the neighbouring village of Hardingstone they had to walk along the main road until they came to a side-turning known as Hardingstone Lane. They arrived at this junction at about 1.45 a.m., and just as they were turning the corner a man wearing a light mackin-tosh, hatless, and carrying an attaché case, climbed out of the shallow ditch, crossed the grass verge, and stepped into the road—and into the revealing light of the moon—only a few yards ahead of them. He passed the two men without a word. Neither did they say anything to him, their attention being partly diverted by a fire which was casting an angry red glow above the hedge at the bend of the road some little distance ahead of them. Bailey called out to his cousin, 'What is the blaze?' It was the stranger who answered. From behind them the men heard his voice. 'It looks as if someone has had a bonfire,' he said. They looked back. The man had reached the main road. Turning to the right, he made towards Northampton, but after only a few steps he checked himself and began to walk back in the opposite direction, towards London; the last the two men saw of him he was standing irresolutely in the roadway. Wasting no further time upon him, they ran as fast as they could towards the distant blaze, and, some hundred and fifty yards short of the village of Hardingstone, they came upon a motor car on fire at the side of the road; it was burning so fiercely that the flames were leaping fifteen feet and it was impossible for them to get near it. Eventually, with the aid of buckets of water brought from the village, it was extinguished. The car had been almost entirely burned out. In it was the charred, unrecognizable body of a man. Meanwhile, having thumbed a lift from a passing lorry, Alfred Arthur Rouse—for such was the hatless stranger with the attaché case—was making his way back to London, with his plan in ruins. It is a convenient moment to try to piece together the background to this extraordinary case. At a first meeting, Alfred Arthur Rouse would probably have struck you as quite a decent fellow in his own way, and if you were charitably disposed that impression might even have survived a closer acquaintance. But sooner or later, unless you were very long-suffering, he would have exhausted your patience by his boastfulness, his everlasting aggrandizement of himself, his lies and petty deceits, and above all, perhaps, by the smirking complacency with which he retailed his many successes as a seducer of women. When Rouse, the son of a shopkeeper in South London, was invalided out of the Army in 1916—he had been seriously wounded in France—he applied himself to the laudable task of improving his position and prospects in life, and by 1930, being the possessor of a ready tongue and a persuasive manner, he had established himself as a commercial traveller with a good connection, a modest income, and a house which he was buying on mortgage at Friern Barnet, where he lived with his wife, Lily. The regular rounds of his customers, which took him not only to various parts of London, but also to the South Coast and into the Midlands, provided him with unending opportunities to satisfy his voracious appetite for women. Most of his innumerable amours faded, as it were, with the morning light and gave him little trouble; others landed him in plenty. As early as 1921, a fifteen-years-old girl, having been seduced by Rouse, bore him a child, who died after a few weeks. Rouse renewed his association with the girl, who became pregnant by him a second time. He went through a form of marriage with her in 1924—it was bigamous, since Rouse already had a wife—and the pair set up house together in Islington, where their second child was born in the following July. The so-called marriage broke up after a year or two, and in October 1929 the girl obtained a magistrate's order obliging Rouse to contribute ten shillings a week towards the maintenance of the child; his payments were spasmodic. Troubles over women continued to press. There was, for instance, the tiresome case of Nellie Tucker, who in May 1928 had presented him with a child for whose maintenance he was responsible under another court order; here again his payments were irregular. It must therefore have been a blow to him when, on 29th October 1930, Nellie Tucker added to his various embarrassments by bearing him a second child. He was in even graver difficulty over Ivy Muriel Jenkins of Gellygaer, Monmouthshire, who believed herself to be married to him, and was about to give birth to his child. To satisfy the inquiries of the Jenkins family he had been at pains to concoct an elaborate story of how he had purchased and furnished a £1,250 house at Kingston as a home for Ivy and himself; since they were supposed to take possession of this entirely imaginary property during the first week in November, Rouse had not much time left in which to extricate himself from this, the most embarrassing of his many commitments. Taking one thing with another, it must have seemed to him that death alone could release him from his troubles. We have here the genesis of the Plan. Outside the Swan and Pyramid public house in Whetstone High Road he had made the casual acquaintance of a man with no home, no family, no friends, no job, no settled background, a man, it seemed to Rouse, who could remove himself, or be removed, from life without leaving a ripple behind him. Rouse was right. To this day no one has ever been able to suggest who the man was whose charred body was found in the burned-out car. Rouse sought out this nomad and told him that in a few days' time he would be driving to Leicester; as he had hoped, the man, being anxious to find work in the Midlands, asked him for a lift. At about eight o'clock on the evening of 5th November, Rouse picked up the man outside the Swan and Pyramid and they set out together for Leicester. As they neared Northampton in the early hours of the following morning, Rouse turned his car into Hardingstone Lane and drew up at the side of the road. There he strangled the unknown man, who was half-fuddled with whisky, poured petrol over him, loosened the petrol union joint and removed the top of the carburettor. From about ten yards away he laid a trail of petrol to the car and set a match to it. The car was a mass of flames in a few seconds. (The above account of the murder is based upon Rouse's own confession, which appeared in the *Daily Sketch* on 11th March 1931, after his conviction.) Rouse trusted that the body in the car would be so badly burned that, in the absence of any positive means of identification, it would be mistaken for his own. Whatever chance of success this plan may have had was ruined by Rouse's hapless encounter with Bailey and Brown. This threw him completely off his balance. He could think of nothing better to do than to go back to London as quickly as he could. From there he immediately departed by motor coach for Gellygaer and the Jenkins family. This gave him no respite. In their accounts of the 'Blazing Çar Mystery', the newspapers of 7th November carried a description of the hatless man which tallied only too obviously with his own; he left at once by motor coach for London. An unpleasant surprise awaited him at the end of the journey. A Cardiff journalist had communicated with the police, and when the coach reached Hammersmith Bridge Road two plain-clothes police officers boarded it and invited Rouse to accompany them to the nearby police station; there he made a statement which was the basis of his defence at the subsequent trial. In it he said that on the Great North Road, near St. Albans, a man had asked him for a lift. In Hardingstone Lane he had left the car to relieve himself, at the same time asking his passenger to empty some petrol into the tank from a can. The man had asked, 'What about a smoke?' and he had replied, 'I have given you all my cigarettes as it is.' He had been relieving himself some distance along the road when he had noticed 'a big flame from behind'. The statement went on:

> I pulled my trousers up quickly and ran towards the car, which was in flames. I saw the man was inside and I tried to open the door, but I could not, as the car was then a mass of flames. I then began to tremble violently. I was all of a shake. I did not know what to do, and I ran as hard as I could along the road, where I saw two men. I felt I was responsible for what had happened. I lost my head, and I didn't know what to do, and really I don't know what I have done since.

That was well enough, but it was not in Rouse's character to leave matters there. The urge to brag about his successes with women was so strong in him that on the following day he could not resist having a little chat with a police officer. 'My wife is really too good for me,' said Rouse. 'I like a woman who will make a fuss of me. I don't ever remember my wife sitting on my knee, but otherwise she is a good wife. I am very friendly with several women, but it is a very expensive game. . . . My harem takes me to several places and I am not at home a great deal, but my wife doesn't ask questions now.' These tasteless remarks did Rouse immeasurable harm. They provided the prosecution with the first clue to what might lie behind the 'Blazing Car Mystery', and during the committal proceedings before the magistrates full use was made of the evidence given by various women in Rouse's life to show that he had had a motive for committing murder. But when Rouse was brought to trial at Northampton Assizes before Mr. Justice TALBOT in the following January, nothing more was heard of this evidence. Much of the criticism attaching to the conduct of the prosecution, which was in the hands of Mr. Norman Birkett K.C. (afterwards Lord BIRKETT), was founded upon the proposition that Rouse's chances of a fair hearing before a jury had been gravely prejudiced by the police-court proceedings, which, with all the attendant press publicity—how snugly that word 'harem' fitted into the headlines—had included evidence attacking his character which was, and could not be, repeated at the trial, since it was plainly inadmissible, and must have been so ruled by the judge. A great point was made of this in the Court of Criminal Appeal after Rouse's conviction. But the Court held that the evidence which *was* given at the trial, largely directed, as it was, to the technical examination of the possibility of the car having been destroyed by accident rather than by design, was sufficient to allow the jury to come to a proper conclusion upon the guilt or innocence of the accused.

The appeal was dismissed. Rouse was hanged at Bedford on 10th March 1931.
[*I*.

Rowlatt, Sir Sidney Arthur Taylor (1862-1945). Judge of the King's Bench Division of the High Court (1912-32). Before reading for the Bar, to which he was called by the Inner Temple in 1886, he was for a short time a master at Eton College. His advancement in his new profession was rapid; in 1900 he was appointed Junior Counsel to the Inland Revenue, and five years later Junior Counsel to the Treasury, that well-trodden avenue to judicial honours. These came to him in October 1912, when, at the invitation of Lord Chancellor Haldane, he succeeded Mr. Justice Hamilton in the King's Bench Division. He brought to his work on the Bench a scholarly precision, particularly valuable in taxation cases, with which his name will be most readily associated. He possessed, at the same time, a warm humanity of outlook and a delightful sense of humour. He was less fortunate in a curious mannerism, a sort of nervous chuckle which became habitual with him. This trick was quite outside his control, and at solemn moments, as, for instance, when he was pronouncing sentence of death, the effect of its sudden intrusion was distressing, even macabre. He retired from the Bench in 1932, and died on 1st March 1945, in his eighty-third year. Mr. Justice Rowlatt presided over many notable murder trials, including those of Jeannie BAXTER; Edward Ernest BLACK; and, most celebrated of all, Sidney Harry FOX. At the Bar, he was junior counsel for the prosecution of Madar Lal DHINGRA and of the SEDDONS.

Royal Prerogative of Mercy. The Royal Prerogative of Mercy is exercised by the Sovereign upon the advice of the Home Secretary (in Scotland, the Secretary of State). It is the practice of the Home Secretary (and of the Secretary of State for Scotland) to review every capital case in which there has been a conviction and to consider whether there are grounds for advising the Crown to exercise clemency by commuting the death sentence to one of imprisonment for life. The grounds upon which he makes his final decision in any particular case are not disclosed. The Royal Commission on Capital Punishment pointed out in its report (published in 1953): 'The importance of the part played by the Prerogative in the administration of the law of murder is shown by the fact that during the past fifty years no fewer than 45 per cent. of the persons sentenced to death for that crime have been reprieved.'

Russell, George. *See* Minnie Freeman LEE.

'Russian Robert'. *See* Marian GRONDKOWSKI.

Rutherford, Norman Cecil, lecturer in anatomy and embryology at London Hospital, joined the Royal Army Medical Corps on the out-break of war in 1914, served with distinction in France in the rank of Lieutenant-Colonel, and was awarded the D.S.O. for 'conspicuous gallantry and devotion to duty'. He was married to a woman of some means, by whom he had six children. Godfather to his youngest child was an old friend, Major Miles Charles Cariston Seton, a doctor like himself, who, having qualified at Edinburgh, had established himself in private practice in Melbourne. After wartime service with the Australian Army Medical Corps, he had been appointed to a medical post at Australian headquarters in the London district. Such were the leading figures in the tragedy which is now to follow. Major Seton was spending the evening of 13th January 1919 at the home of his cousin, Sir Malcolm Seton, in Clarendon Road, Holland Park. At about ten o'clock Colonel Rutherford called and asked to see the major. The two men were alone in the dining-room for a quarter of an hour. So far as anyone could tell, they seemed to be peaceably engaged; certainly no sound reached Sir Malcolm and Lady Seton, or any of the servants, to suggest that there was a quarrel. But suddenly the quiet of the house was shattered by the sound of half a dozen revolver shots. Sir Malcolm rushed downstairs, to find his cousin lying mortally injured on the floor close by the dining-room door. Colonel Rutherford, a tall, hand-some man of thirty-six, was standing by the window; beside him was a revolver, still smoking. Lady Seton followed her husband into the room a few seconds later. Bending over the dying man, she cried, 'Oh, you've killed Miles!' 'Yes,' said Rutherford, calmly. 'I only wish I had another bullet for myself.' Sir Malcolm hastened to call a doctor and the police. Rutherford made no effort to leave. Lady Seton heard a click and saw him with the revolver in his hand. With remarkable courage, she ordered him to put it down; he obeyed without demur, surrender-ing the gun. When Sir Malcolm arrived with a policeman, who told Rutherford that he would have to go with him to the station, that most imperturbable man asked the officer to be kind enough to bring him his hat and gloves, and on that lordly note took his leave. The inquest proceedings elicited from one of the maids employed at the Rutherfords' large house at Carshalton, Surrey, that there had lately been fierce quarrels between the colonel and his wife. Earlier in the evening of the murder Rutherford had locked her in her bedroom and had told the maid to pack his bag, as he was leaving home. The Coroner read a letter which Mrs. Rutherford had written to her husband some little time before, telling him that she could no longer endure to live with him and asking for a divorce. At the committal proceedings at West London Police Court the prosecution used this domestic background to the crime to suggest a motive for it—jealousy. Evidence was called to show that Major Seton had been on terms of close friendship with Mrs. Rutherford, and had frequently stayed in the house at Carshalton while its master was away. The prosecution did not suggest that Rutherford had any cause for jealousy, for there had been none—this was made abundantly plain; its purpose, rather, was to establish that the accused *believed* that his friend had been false to him and, in a fit of jealous rage, had killed him. Rutherford was committed for trial at the Old Bailey in the following April. At this period, the country having but lately emerged from a long and exhausting war, there was much talk of the 'unwritten law', which, although much frowned upon by the courts (*see* Lieutenant Douglas MALCOLM), was held by some unthinking persons to justify murderous acts by returning soldiers who found or thought themselves betrayed by their wives. Thus, when Colonel Rutherford came to trial before Mr. Justice Salter (afterwards Lord Justice Salter), there were many who expected that the defence would make the best use it could of the emotional atmosphere which, in the peculiar circumstances of the time, almost always surrounded this class of case. They were wrong. The case for Colonel Rutherford made no appeal to false sentiment. It was simpler than that, and more terrible. Colonel Rutherford was held to be insane. All the cross-examination of the Crown witnesses was directed to supporting the evidence which the parlour-maid had given during the committal proceedings, when she had spoken of Rutherford as being 'like a man who has been dozing and is waking up'. Soldiers who had served with Rutherford in France were called. They testified to his abnormal behaviour, which had become particularly noticeable after an incident in which he had been buried under shell debris; to his sudden fits of fury, occurring regularly two or three times a month. A well-known mental specialist said of him: 'The opinion I formed was that he was incapable of appreciating the difference between right and wrong.' The jury were convinced. After a retirement of only five minutes, they returned a verdict of 'Guilty but insane', and the judge took the opportunity to say that he agreed with them. Colonel Rutherford was removed to Broadmoor; he was discharged as cured some years later.

[*18, 61, 62.*

Ruxton, Buck (formerly known as Bukhtyar Rustomji Ratanji Hakim), a Parsee doctor practising in Lancaster, was delighted to read in the *Daily Express* that unidentified human remains found in September 1935 in the ravine below the bridge of Gardenholme Linn on the main road from Moffat to Edinburgh were those of *a man and a woman*. 'You see, Mrs. Oxley,' he remarked to the charwoman, 'it is a man and a woman; it is not our two.' He burst out laughing. By 'our two' the excitable Dr. Ruxton meant his wife, Isabella, and the nursemaid for his children, twenty-years-old Mary Jane Rogerson; nothing had been seen of either for several weeks past. Dr. Ruxton had, at various times, sought to explain their absence by saying: (*a*) that they had gone to Scotland for a holiday; (*b*) that they had gone to Blackpool; (*c*) that Mrs. Ruxton had gone to London; (*d*) that she had gone off with another man; (*e*) that Mary Rogerson was pregnant and that Mrs. Ruxton might have taken her away with the idea of procuring an illegal operation. But already rumour was suggesting that the ravine where the Gardenholme Linn ran into the river Annan had been their more likely destination. Dr. Ruxton's satisfaction with the newspaper report which appeared to scotch this rumour was short-lived. It is true that preliminary examination had suggested that one of the mutilated bodies was that of a man. But this error was soon corrected. Both the bodies were female. They were, indeed, 'our two'. These pitiable remains, the severed heads, mutilated so as to be entirely unrecognizable, the sundered limbs, the torn bodies, skilfully dismembered, disjointed, parcelled up, thrown into a ravine a hundred miles away, provided mute and ghastly witness to what may happen when jealousy rages in a man's blood like fire, consuming him utterly. Buck Ruxton—he had taken the name by deed poll—was a Bachelor of Medicine of the Universities of Bombay and London, and a Bachelor of Surgery of the University of Bombay. In 1927 he met Isabella Van Ess (*née* Kerr), who worked in an Edinburgh restaurant. At the beginning of 1928 she left her husband, a Dutchman, and went to live with Dr. Ruxton as his wife. In 1930 the doctor set up in practice at 2 Dalton Square, Lancaster. There is no doubt he was deeply attached to Isabella—'My Belle', as he called her—and she to him. This did not prevent them from quarrelling bitterly and continually. 'We were the kind of people who could not live with each other and could not live without each other,' Dr. Ruxton was to say at his trial, quoting the French phrase, 'Who loves most chastises most.' Buck Ruxton was a man with little control over his wayward tongue, and none at all over his emotions, a man given to passionate outbursts of rage, during which he would look and act like a lunatic. He suffered agonies over what he supposed to be his wife's infidelities—these were entirely imaginary—and she had only to look at another man to bring upon herself torrents of frantic abuse, wild threats, and sometimes physical violence. In September 1935 he was obsessed with the suspicion—again baseless—that Mrs. Ruxton was having an affair with a young man in the Town Clerk's Department of the Lancaster Corporation. This provided the disturbed background for all his actions at this time; he has to be regarded as a man made frantic by jealousy, whose emotional balance, always precarious, was now even more finely poised than ever. On Saturday, 14th September, Mrs. Ruxton drove her husband's car to Blackpool to meet her two sisters and to see the illuminations. At 11.30 p.m. that same night she left Blackpool to drive back to Lancaster. Undoubtedly, she returned home, for the car was there the next morning. But no one ever saw Mrs. Ruxton alive again. At Ruxton's trial, leading counsel for the Crown, Mr. J. C. Jackson K.C., attempted a reconstruction of what had happened inside the doctor's house after Mrs. Ruxton's return:

> You will hear that Mrs. Ruxton had received before her death violent blows in the face and that she was strangled. The suggestion of the prosecution is that her death and that of the girl, Mary, took place . . . on the landing at the top of the staircase, outside the maid's bedroom. . . . I suggest that when she went up to bed a violent quarrel took place; that he strangled his wife, and that Mary Rogerson caught him in the act and so had to die also. Mary's skull was fractured; she had some blows on the top of her head which would render her unconscious, and then was killed by some other means, probably a knife, because of all the blood that was found down those stairs.

All this was presumed to have happened in the early hours of Sunday, 16th September. Dr. Ruxton was occupied for some time thereafter cutting up and dismembering the two bodies and draining the blood vessels. He also had to find time to remove the numerous traces of his crime. At 4.30 p.m. on the Sunday he called at the house of Mrs. Mary Hampshire, a patient of his, and asked her if she would help him to prepare for the decorators, who were coming in the morning, by scrubbing down the stairs. Mrs. Hampshire went back with him to the house. She found that the carpets had been removed from the stairs and landings right up to the top floor. Straw was scattered about on the staircase; more straw was sticking out from under the doors of the two bedrooms occupied, respectively, by Dr. Ruxton and his wife. Both these doors were locked. Dr. Ruxton asked Mrs. Hampshire to clean the bath, which was a dirty yellow up to about six inches from the top. Carpets—two from the landings and the rest stair carpets—one in particular badly stained with blood, were lying in the backyard, as well as a bloodstained shirt and some badly stained—and partly burned— towels. Dr. Ruxton told Mrs. Hampshire that she could have the carpets in the yard, and other stair carpets in the waiting-room, also a blue suit, copiously stained with blood, which he said he had been wearing when he had cut his hand with a tin-opener whilst opening a can of peaches for the children's breakfast. (Undoubtedly, Dr. Ruxton had a badly cut hand. But at his trial the prosecution held that it was not the sort of injury that could have been made by a tin-opener. Mr. Jackson suggested either that the knife had slipped whilst the doctor was dismembering the bodies, or that he had deliberately cut his own hand to be able to account for the blood on the carpets and in other parts of the house.) Later, Mrs. Hampshire tried to clean the most badly stained of the carpets by throwing twenty to thirty buckets of water over it; at the end of this operation the water running off the carpet still had the colour of blood. Late that Sunday night, or so it was charged against him, the doctor set out for Moffat with the parcelled remains of Mrs. Ruxton and the nursemaid in the back of his car. Having arrived at Gardenholme Linn, he threw the parcels over the bridge, and drove back to Lancaster. Some parts of the remains had still to be disposed of, either at Moffat or elsewhere, and it was not until the following Thursday that Dr. Ruxton was able to rid himself of the last of his unpleasant parcels. Mrs. Oxley, the charwoman, at work in the kitchen, heard him go up and down the stairs and backwards and forwards to his car. When he drove off Mrs. Oxley discovered that the doors which had been locked were open again. It was on 29th September that a Miss Susan Haines Johnson, on holiday at Moffat, looked over the parapet of the bridge at Gardenholme Linn and saw in the gully below a human arm. A little further downstream four bundles containing human remains were retrieved, together with two severed heads, a thigh bone, and two arms. The first bundle was wrapped in a blouse, the second in a pillow-slip, and the other two in pieces of a bed sheet. One of the two heads was wrapped in a pair of children's rompers. Further search in the Linn and along the river Annan resulted in the discovery within the next day or two of other remains. On 28th October a left foot, wrapped in a page torn from the *Daily Herald,* was discovered about nine miles south of Moffat on the main Edinburgh-Carlisle road. Finally, on 4th November, a right forearm and hand were found on the Edinburgh road, south of the bridge over the Linn. The field of inquiry was from the start drastically narrowed by the fact that among the various bundles, together with straw that had been used for packing, was part of the issue of the *Sunday Graphic* for 15th September. This turned out to be the special 'slip' edition containing pictures of Morecambe Carnival which was sold only in Morecambe and Lancaster and surrounding districts; a copy of this edition had been delivered to Dr. Ruxton's house. The blouse was identified as one which had belonged to Mary Rogerson; her mother was able to recognize it by the patch under one arm. Similarly, the rompers were identified—through a peculiar knot in the elastic—as a pair belonging to one of Dr. Ruxton's children. The strips of sheeting also proved to be highly important. They were compared with a sheet taken from Mrs. Ruxton's bed, and were found to be identical with it; a fault in the selvedge (revealed under a microscope) was common to both, showing them to be the product not only of the same loom, but of the same warp whilst in the loom. The piecing together of the various remains, so as to make up (although not completely) two female bodies, was undertaken by Professor James Couper Brash, Professor of Anatomy in the University of Edinburgh. He was one of a brilliant team of professors in the Universities of Edinburgh and Glasgow whose work on this case—the reconstruction and examination of the bodies, and the systematic establishment of their identity, in spite of the care that had been taken to efface every recognizable peculiarity—has long been regarded as a classic achievement of forensic medicine. The trial of Dr. Buck Ruxton for the murder of his wife was opened at Manchester Assizes before Mr. Justice (afterwards Lord Justice) SINGLETON on 2nd March 1936. It lasted eleven days. Two of those eleven days—or the greater part of them—were occupied with the examination and cross-examination of Dr. Ruxton. An early exchange between himself and Mr. Norman (afterwards Lord) BIRKETT K.C., the distinguished counsel who appeared in his defence, set the tone for much that was to follow:

> *Mr. Birkett:* It is suggested here by the Crown that on the morning of the Sunday after your wife had come back you killed her?
>
> *Dr. Ruxton:* That is an absolute and deliberate and fantastic story; you might as well say the sun was rising in the west and setting in the east.
>
> *Mr. Birkett:* It is suggested by the Crown that upon that morning you killed Mary Rogerson?
>
> *Dr. Ruxton:* That is absolutely bunkum, with a capital B, if I may say it. Why should I kill my poor Mary?

The high-pitched note is characteristic. Dr. Ruxton made the worst possible witness. He was voluble, discursive, and often hysterical, his evidence being repeatedly interspersed with paroxysms of weeping. One had the impression of a man at the edge of total moral collapse who was fighting for his life with increasing desperation—and mounting despair. The jury found Dr. Ruxton guilty; he was hanged at Strangeways Prison, Manchester, on 12th May.

S

She drank prussic acid without any water.
Richard Harris Barham: *The Tragedy*

Sach, Amelia, and her accomplice, **Annie Walters,** made a living at the turn of the century out of the prompt and efficient dispatch of unwanted infants. Mrs. Sach kept a so-called 'nursing home' at East Finchley. Unmarried women who were 'expecting' found her advertisement attractive: 'ACCOUCHEMENT: Before and during, skilled nursing. Home comforts. Baby can remain'. The allurement, of course, was in those last three words—'Baby can remain.' Women giving birth at Mrs. Sach's establishment had the comfort of her assurance that for a reasonable fee she would arrange for their babies to be received into good homes. Taken from their mothers immediately after birth, the babies were handed over by Mrs. Sach to her crony, Mrs. Walters, who removed them to her own lodging for disposal; from long experience she knew how pitifully easy it is to end a frail life that has barely begun. The precious pair might have continued their profitable career for many years to come if a fellow-lodger of Mrs. Walters—he happened to be a policeman—had not become suspicious of what was going on. In November 1902 Mrs. Walters was arrested at South Kensington Station whilst carrying a brown-paper parcel containing the dead body of a new-born infant whom she had lately dispatched with a few drops of chlorodyne. Mrs. Walters and Mrs. Sach were put on trial at the Old Bailey before Mr. Justice DARLING in January 1903, and being found guilty, they were sentenced to death; they were the first women to be executed at Holloway Prison, following the closing of Newgate Gaol. Of the two, Mrs. Sach was the more interesting and the less repulsive. Brutal Mrs. Walters was in the business for what she could get out of it. But Amelia Sach, young and attractive, a good mother to her own children, seems to have been able to persuade herself that she was being cruel to these unwanted babies only that she might be kind. Was she not—admittedly for a fee—saving them from a life of poverty and wretchedness, which was all that most of them could expect?
[*106, 202.*

237

Scrutton, Sir Thomas Edward (1856-1934) was called to the Bar by the Middle Temple in 1882, and, upon the basis of his massive knowledge of commercial law, built up a practice in the Commercial Court which few could equal. He took silk in 1901, and nine years later was appointed a judge of the King's Bench Division of the High Court. As a judge he was respected for his erudition, industry and conscientiousness, but it could hardly be said that he was entirely popular with those who practised in his Court, certainly not in the early days. This was because of his brusque manner, irritability, occasional petulance, and, no doubt, also because of his inability to suffer gladly those whose minds worked less nimbly than his own; he mellowed considerably after his translation to the Court of Appeal in 1916. Lord Justice Scrutton had a fine presence, being tall and strongly built, a short, snowy-white pointed beard lending an additional touch of distinction to his appearance. A regular concert-goer and patron of the opera, music provided his principal interest off the Bench. He died in a Norwich nursing home in August 1934, after a short illness; he was seventy-seven. The most celebrated murder trial over which he presided was that of George Joseph SMITH.

Seddon, Frederick Henry, was so much in love with money that he would tot up a column of figures as if it had been an amatory exercise. He not only loved money, but he was entirely absorbed in the mechanics by which money is made, being in this sense a dedicated man, to whom the art of buying cheap and selling dear was a vocation, like healing the sick. In the year 1910 this rapacious man, his wife, Margaret Ann Seddon, his five children, his old father, and a servant girl whose mental condition exhibited alarming signs of disorder, occupied a large house at Tollington Park, Islington. Seddon, who owned the house, had a good and improving position with the London and Manchester Industrial Insurance Company, being the District Superintendent for Islington. Every penny he earned over and above the amounts required for the meagre household budget was put to work to earn more. He spent little on pleasure, for he needed none, but in a sense his life was all pleasure, pleasure in watching the pennies turn into shillings, the shillings into pounds, and the pounds into a chain of small house and shop properties in different parts of London. He was now to acquire the most valuable property of all, in the bulky and unattractive shape of Miss Eliza Mary Barrow, a vulgar, blousy woman of forty-nine, and of singularly unpleasing habits, very irritable and very deaf, whose obstinate insistence upon having her own way was combined with an entire ignorance of the way she ought to go. She had been living near by with her cousins, a Mr. and Mrs. Vonderahe, but having fallen out with them she was on the look-out for a more congenial lodging. On an evil day for her she learned through an agent that the three rooms on the top floor of 63 Tollington Park were to be had unfurnished for twelve and sixpence a week. She moved in on 25th July 1910, bringing with her eight-years-old Ernie Grant, whose mother had been her friend, and upon whom she lavished all her affection. The rather touching relationship between this orphan boy and the coarse-grained, quarrelsome woman he called 'Chickie' provides the only element of relief in this story of squalid greed. Miss Barrow also brought with her a Mr. and Mrs. Hook—Mr. Hook was Ernie's uncle—who were to have one of the rooms rent-free. This arrangement did not last longer than a week or two. Miss Barrow having quarrelled with them over some trifle, the Hooks were given peremptory notice to leave by Seddon. They departed the next day, after a stormy scene with the landlord, who was accused by Mr. Hook of trying to get hold of Miss Barrow's money. He added as a parting shot, 'I will defy you and a regiment like you to get it!' Mr. Hook under-rated Seddon's talent. In a little over a year that most persuasive man had contrived to get into his own hands Miss Barrow's entire property. It was well worth having. Miss Barrow owned £1,600 worth of 3½ per cent. India Stock and the leasehold interest in a public-house called The Buck's Head and in a barber's shop next door, the whole bringing her in an income of £120 a year. She also had £216 on deposit at the Finsbury and City of London Savings Bank, as well as a considerable sum in gold and notes, which she kept by her in a cash box. Suspicious though she was of everybody else, Miss Barrow seems to have placed complete trust in Seddon. The Hooks had not been gone more than two months before she transferred to him her holding in India Stock. In return he promised to pay her a life annuity of £103. 4s. a year. Three months later she handed over her leasehold interest in The Buck's Head and the adjoining shop, in consideration of Seddon's further promise to pay her an additional annuity of £1 a week. On 19th June 1911 she closed her account with the Finsbury and City of London Savings Bank, drawing out £216 in gold. This having gone the same way as the money in her cash box, there was nothing more to be made out of Miss Eliza Mary Barrow, who had, indeed, become a continuing liability to Seddon. On 1st September 1911 she complained of stomach pains, diarrhoea, and sickness. Dr. Henry George Sworn was called in. He prescribed various remedies and palliatives, and for the next two weeks was in regular attendance. At about 7 a.m. on 14th September Seddon called at the doctor's house to tell him that Miss Barrow was dead. He said that he and his wife had been up with her all night; she had been in considerable pain, and had then 'gone off sort of insensible', dying at about 6 a.m. Dr. Sworn issued a burial certificate, ascribing the cause of death to 'epidemic diarrhoea'. That same morning Seddon arranged with an undertaker for Miss Barrow to be buried in a common grave for the sum of £4, and squeezed out of him a commission of twelve shillings and sixpence for introducing the business! Since none of Miss Barrow's relatives and friends had any inkling of her death, Seddon, his wife and his father were the only mourners at the funeral, which took place at Islington Cemetery, East Finchley, on 16th September. A few days later, Mr. Frank Ernest Vonderahe called at the house, to be informed by the servant that his cousin was 'dead and buried'. The next day Mr. Vonderahe's wife, accompanied by her sister-in-law Mrs. Albert Edward Vonderahe, paid a call upon Seddon, who opened a somewhat peculiar interview by demanding to know why he had not received any answer to his letter. 'What letter?' asked Mrs. Vonderahe. 'We have not received any letter.' Whereupon Seddon produced a carbon copy of a letter—dated 14th September—which he claimed to have sent to Mr. Vonderahe; it informed him of his cousin's death, and asked whether he or any other relative of Miss Barrow would be attending the funeral. Seddon also handed Mrs. Vonderahe a letter, dated 21st September, signed by himself, and addressed 'To the Relatives'. This contained the information that Miss Barrow had 'disposed of her properties and investments' to purchase a life annuity, which had died with her. Finally, he produced a black-edged memorial card:

In ever Loving memory
of
Eliza Mary Barrow
who departed this life Sept. 14th, 1911
Aged 49 years
Interred in Islington Cemetery, East Finchley
Grave No. 19453, sec. 2.
A dear one is missing and with us no more
That voice so much loved we hear not again
Yet we think of you now the same as of yore
And know you are free from trouble and pain.

An indignant and suspicious Mr. Vonderahe met Seddon by appointment on 9th October. 'Who is the owner of The Buck's Head now?' he asked. 'I am,' replied Seddon, 'likewise the shop next door. I am always open to buy property at a price.' He had, he explained, bought the public-house in the open market. 'Who bought the India Stock?' Mr. Vonderahe persisted. 'You will have to write to the Governor of the Bank of England and ask him,' replied the evasive Seddon, 'but everything has been done in a perfectly legal manner, through solicitors and stockbrokers. I have nothing to do with it.' The cavalier treatment of Miss Barrow's relations was highly impolitic, to say the least; they were justly indignant over Seddon's arrogant behaviour, and the more they thought of it, and the more they discussed it among themselves, the more it seemed to them that something sinister must lie behind it. Mr. Vonderahe decided to communicate with the Director of Public Prosecutions. As a result, on 20th November, Miss Barrow's body was exhumed, and certain of the organs were removed for examination and analysis. They were found to contain arsenic. Seddon was arrested on 4th December. To the murder charge he replied: 'Absurd. What a terrible charge—wilful murder. It is the first of our family that has ever been charged with such a crime. Are you going to arrest my wife as well? If not, I would like you to give her a message for me. Have they found arsenic in her body? She has not done this herself. It was not carbolic acid, was it, as there was some in her room? And Sanitas is not poison, is it?' (In fairness to Seddon, it should be said that he passion-ately denied having said anything about his wife, whom he certainly did all he could to protect.) Mrs. Seddon was arrested six months later on a joint charge of murder. The eight-day trial of the Seddons opened at the Old Bailey before Mr. Justice BUCKNILL on 4th March 1912. The Attorney-General, Sir Rufus Isaacs K.C. (afterwards first Mar-quess of Reading) led for the Crown. Seddon was defended by Mr. (afterwards Sir) Edward Marshall HALL K.C., and Mrs. Seddon by Mr. (afterwards Sir) Gervais RENTOUL. Some commentators who have studied the trial have confessed to an uneasy feeling that Seddon was convicted not because his guilt was firmly established, but because he was unable to prove his innocence, and that the jury allowed them-selves to be too much influenced by the undeniable fact that the whole course of his conduct showed him to be a cold-blooded, vain, greedy, calculating, and altogether odious person, who *would not have thought twice about committing murder if that were what his interests required*. (It was also undeniable that Seddon had had a direct and substantial interest in procuring Miss Barrow's death.) The prosecution set out to show (*a*) that Seddon was in possession of arsenic, and (*b*) that, in conspiracy with his wife, he had administered a fatal dose of the poison to Miss Barrow within forty-eight hours of her death. As to possession, it was the Crown case that Seddon had produced a distillation of arsenic by boiling the contents of a packet of arsenical fly-papers in a little water, and, as to administration, that he had added the poisonous brew to a cup of Valentine's Meat Juice, an invalid preparation which had been prescribed by Dr. Sworn. It could not be shown that Seddon had pur-chased the fly-papers himself. What he *had* done, said the Crown, was to send his fifteen-years-old daughter, Maggie, to the shop of a local chemist to buy a packet for him. The supposed date of this transaction was 26th August, six days before Miss Barrow was taken ill. Since Maggie herself denied that she had been to the shop on such an errand, on that or on any other day, the prosecution relied, for this vital part of the case, upon the evidence of the chemist, Mr. Walter Thorley. The conditions in which this man came to identify Maggie Seddon as the 'fair-haired girl' who had purchased the packet of Mather's Chemical Fly-Papers were sharply criticized by Marshall Hall, who described them as 'deplorable'. It was pointed out—forcefully—that Mr. Thorley already knew Maggie, at least by sight; that he was aware at the time that her father was in custody on a charge of murder; and that the girl's photograph had already been widely published in the newspapers. With his accustomed skill, Marshall Hall seized upon this, as upon other weak points in the prosecution's case. But whatever chance of acquittal Seddon might have had before he went into the witness-box was totally destroyed by his shocking performance when he got there. The Attorney-General's relentless cross-examination failed to disturb his cool self-possession. Yet its total effect was to expose him unmistakeably as a man so obsessed with money and the means of making it that he had become completely insensitive to the promptings and restraints of ordinary, decent, human feeling. The most dramatic moment of a sensational trial was reserved to the very last. After the jury had found him guilty, and had acquitted the woman who stood beside him in the dock, Seddon turned to his wife and gave her a resounding kiss. Weeping bitterly, Mrs. Seddon was half led, half carried from the dock. She had often enough complained that her husband kept her in ignorance of his affairs. For that, as it turned out, she had good cause to be thankful. It had been quite clear to the jury that Seddon's plan to dispose of Miss Barrow had been among the many things which he had—mercifully—concealed from his wife. The Clerk of the Court addressed himself to Seddon. Had he anything to say why judgment of death should not be passed upon him? Without any sign of agitation, Seddon launched himself upon an elaborate analysis of the evidence. He spoke for a good twenty minutes, without reference to a single note, taking up one after another the various points that had told most heavily against him, and showing that for each there was an entirely innocent explanation. Then he played his final card. Raising his hand as if to take the Mason's oath, he declared, in words familiar to every member of the Craft, that 'before the Great Architect of the Universe' he was innocent of the death of Eliza Mary Barrow. Mr. Justice Bucknill, an ardent Freemason, was so much affected by this last desperate appeal from his Brother that he could scarcely find words to exhort Seddon to repent of the 'great crime' for which he had 'forfeited' his life. 'Try to make peace with your Maker,' he faltered. 'I am at peace,' Seddon replied. The judge went on, as best he could: 'From what you have said, you and I belong to one Brotherhood. . . . But our Brotherhood does not encourage crime; on the contrary, it condemns it. I pray you again to make your peace with the Great Architect of the Universe. Mercy—pray for it, ask for it.' With the tears streaming down his cheeks, Mr. Justice Bucknill proceeded to pass sentence of death. It was carried out at Pentonville Prison on 18th April. It would have flattered Seddon's very considerable vanity to know that a record crowd of 7,000 people was waiting in the street outside.

[*1*.

Seton, Miles Charles Cariston. *See* Norman Cecil RUTHERFORD.

Shawcross, Lord, Q.C. (*b.* **1902**). Hartley William Shawcross, a former Attorney-General of conspicuous brilliance, caused some surprise in March 1957 by abandoning his practice at the Bar. 'Maintenance of health and other personal considerations', he wrote at the time, 'have forced me reluctantly to the conclusion that I could not continue the strain of practice at the Bar and at the same time have any chance of pursuing my other interests in public life and elsewhere.' His resignation twelve months later from the House of Commons, where he had sat as Labour M.P. for St. Helens since 1945, came as something less of a surprise, since it had been apparent for some time past that he had fallen out of sympathy with some of the more important tenets of party policy, particularly on the issue of nationalization. Upon ceasing to be a Member of Parliament, he also separated himself entirely from the Labour Party. In January 1959 he accepted a life peerage. Lord Shawcross ranks as one of the ablest lawyers of his time— yet it seems that, as a young man, his ambition was to become a doctor; indeed, he was once enrolled as a student at St. Bartholomew's Hospital, London. However, he soon gravitated to the law, and in 1925 became a barrister of Gray's Inn. He quickly established his position on the Northern Circuit where, as his reputation mounted, he was sometimes compared to the young F. E. Smith (afterwards Lord Birkenhead), whose early successes had been gained in these same courts. He took silk in 1939. The best was yet to come. In the General Election of 1945 he entered the House as the member for St. Helens, and was appointed Attorney-General in the Government which resulted from Labour's 'landslide' victory. It was a very good choice for, in addition to his known qualities as a lawyer, it turned out that Sir Hartley—he had received the customary knighthood upon becoming a Law Officer of the Crown—possessed considerable parliamentary skill; he proved to be a formidable Front Bench debater. His appearance at the Nürnberg trials of Nazi war criminals as Chief United Kingdom Prosecutor set the seal upon his international reputation. Sir Hartley retained the office of Attorney-General until April 1951, when, for the few months which remained to the Labour Government, he agreed to become President of the Board of Trade. He led for the Crown against John George HAIGH.

Siege of Sidney Street. In his book, *Detective Days*, the late Chief-Constable Wensley C.I.D., had this to say of Whitechapel as it appeared to a young police officer at the turn of the century:

> Most of the inhabitants . . . considered that they had a natural right to get fighting drunk and knock a policeman about whenever the spirit moved them. Bruises were our routine lot. Gangs of hooligans infested the streets and levied blackmail on timorous shopkeepers. There was an enormous amount of personal robbery with violence. The maze of narrow, ill-lighted alleys offered easy ways of escape after a man had been knocked down and his watch and money stolen. It was no picnic for a young police officer, but at least it was never dull. *You never knew what might happen.* (Italics supplied.)

Anything was likely to happen in this unpredictable quarter—and frequently did. The remarkable episode known as the Siege of Sidney Street was typical of Whitechapel as it used to be in that it was violent, murderous, bloody, desperate—and completely fantastic. It was the sensational culmination to a series of events which began more than a fortnight earlier, when, some time before midnight on Friday, 16th December 1910, a man named Max Weil of 120 Houndsditch, off Aldgate High Street, heard mysterious noises, as of sawing and drilling, coming from the back of the jeweller's shop next door, at No. 118A. He gave the alarm and a party of five police officers presently arrived on the scene—Sergeants Robert Bentley, Charles Tucker, William Bryant, and Constables Walter Charles Choat, and Ernest Richard Woodhams. The houses and shops in this section of Houndsditch backed on to a short *cul-de-sac* known as Exchange Buildings. Only one of the houses in this little street showed a light—No. 11. Sergeant Bentley knocked at the door of this house. A man answered. 'Is anybody working here?' the sergeant asked. The man did not appear to have much English, and the officer demanded to know if there were anyone in the house who was better acquainted with the language. At this, the man retreated upstairs, after attempting to close the door. Sergeant Bentley went into the house and entered a dimly lit room, the door of which swung to behind him and partly closed. A few seconds later it was thrown open and a man aimed a revolver at the sergeant and fired two shots. At the same moment the man who had answered the door reappeared and began firing from the staircase. Sergeant Bentley fell mortally wounded. There was a sudden stampede, and a number of men dashed out of the front door into the street. Unarmed as they were, the officers waiting outside closed in upon the men—to be met with a fusillade of bullets. Sergeant Tucker was killed and both Sergeant Bryant and Constable Woodhams seriously wounded. Constable Choat was also hit, but in spite of his injuries he grappled with one of the men, who was in fact the leader of the gang, a Polish *emigré* named George Gardstein. One of the gang fired another shot. His aim was faulty and it was Gardstein, not the constable, who received a bullet in his back. P.C. Choat made another gallant attempt to close with the gang. He was dispatched with another shot in the back and left to die in the street. The gang made off, supporting between them the inert figure of Gardstein. The five police officers lay where they had fallen. Sergeant Bentley, Sergeant Tucker and P.C. Choat were dead, Sergeant Bryant and Constable Woodhams so gravely injured that they never wholly recovered. The dying Gardstein was borne through the silent streets. A refuge was found for him more than a mile away, at 59 Grove Street, Commercial Road, where one of the gang, a Russian-Pole named Fritz Svaars, who had carried Gardstein in his arms for part of the way, shared a squalid lodging with the notorious Peter Piatkow, known as 'Peter the Painter'. This was a name bestowed upon him because he painted the scenery for the plays which were staged from time to time at the so-called 'Anarchists' Club' in Jubilee Street, Whitechapel. This club was supposed to be the breeding-ground for all manner of revolutionary and terrorist activity, and was a favourite meeting-place for the gang. Not that there was anything 'revolutionary' about the Houndsditch raid. When Sergeant Bentley knocked at the door of 11 Exchange Buildings he did not intrude upon a political conspiracy; he disturbed a determined, ingenious, but curiously clumsy gang of thieves, who, having forced an entry to the jeweller's shop by knocking a hole through the rear wall, were about to break open the safe, for which purpose they were provided with elaborate equipment, including a large cylinder of acetylene gas. The gang were using two houses in Exchange Buildings —No. 9 as well as No. 11—as bases for the raid; both houses had been rented by members of the gang a few weeks earlier. At Grove Street, Gardstein was left in charge of two women, Sara Rosa Trassjonsky, and

Luba Milstein, Svaars's mistress. At 3.30 a.m. they fetched a doctor from his surgery in Commercial Road. He found Gardstein lying fully clothed on the bed. He advised immediate removal to the London Hospital, but this was desperately resisted by the two distraught women and, so far as he was able to speak, by Gardstein himself. The doctor did what little he could, but when, later in the morning, he called again it was to find the house deserted and his patient lying dead. Both the women were arrested shortly afterwards. By 22nd December three men believed to be members of the gang—Yourka Duboff, Jacob Peters and Osip Federoff—were in custody. 'Peter the Painter', one jump ahead of the police, escaped arrest by a few minutes, and, it is said, escaped to France. On 2nd January 1911 it came to the ears of the police that two more of the men they were looking for had found a lodging at 100 Sidney Street, off the Mile End Road. One was Fritz Svaars; the other went by the name of 'Josef', and was known as 'the man with the limp'. That same night, after a personal reconnaissance by Chief Detective-Inspector Wensley, a cordon of police, some of whom were armed, was thrown around the house. Rain and sleet lashed the empty streets as the police took up their stations. The next step was to rouse from their beds the seven occupants of the house and get them to safety. This was managed, so far as could be seen, without alarming Svaars and 'Josef', who were occupying a room on the second floor of the three-storey building. It was now well after 3 a.m. The police settled down to wait for a bleak dawn. At 7.30 the operation known as the Siege of Sidney Street began. Loud knocking at the front door having failed to draw any response, handfuls of small stones were thrown at the upper windows. This mild opening skirmish—the idea was to let the two men know that the house was surrounded—was answered by a spatter of bullets fired from powerful Mauser automatics. A police officer, Detective-Sergeant Leeson, was hit; he was dragged through an archway leading to a coach yard on the opposite side of the street. A doctor was summoned, but found that the only way to get to the wounded man was by climbing over walls and scrambling along rooftops, since any attempt to reach the coach yard by way of Sidney Street would have been certain to attract a hail of bullets. He did not shirk the disagreeable journey. The problem then was how to get the patient to hospital. The only way it could be done was by lifting him on to the roof of a shed which over-topped the rear wall of the yard and lowering him down the other side. It was a risky proceeding, but there was nothing else for it. The moment Leeson had been lifted on to the roof the bullets began to fly. The wounded man rolled off the stretcher and with amazing courage, and what little help his comrades could give him, crawled inch by inch across the roof. Good luck stayed with him.

Having reached the edge of the roof he was lowered to safety on the other side of the wall. It was a little miracle, but somehow it was accomplished. Wensley, who had been helping in the hazardous operation, was trapped on the roof, and for half an hour was forced to lie flat on his face and quite still, for even the slightest movement attracted a fresh round of fire from the house opposite. In *Detective Days* he wrote: 'At last I took advantage of a moment when the attention of the assassins had been diverted, for by this time they were firing at anything that moved—even killing a cat that slipped out of a doorway—and dropped back the way I had come.' Now military aid was summoned. At 9 a.m. a detachment of Scots Guards was dispatched from the Tower of London. They directed rifle fire at the upper windows of the house, from front and back, and from each end of the street. Exchanges of fire briskly continued throughout the morning, while heavy police reinforcements kept at a safe distance a crowd of thousands of people overflowing into all the adjacent streets. At noon the Home Secretary, Mr. Winston Churchill, arrived, and shortly afterwards a detachment of Horse Artillery, which, if all else failed, apparently intended to blow the house to pieces. But shortly before 1 p.m. smoke was seen to be coming from one of the top windows. The house was on fire. Quickly the blaze took hold, yet—incredibly—at least one of the two men trapped in the burning building was still raking the street with revolver fire. When the fire brigade arrived the firemen were, for their own safety, and in spite of their protests, forbidden to pass the police cordon. So the fire raged unchecked and 100 Sidney Street was burnt to the ground. In the still-smoking debris two charred bodies were found. 'Josef' had been shot through the head; Svaars appeared to have died from suffocation. At the subsequent inquest a verdict of JUSTIFIABLE HOMICIDE was returned. The casualties on the other side were: One police officer (Leeson) seriously wounded; four policemen, one guardsman, and four spectators slightly wounded; one police sergeant and four firemen injured by falling debris after the fire had burned itself out. The police carried on with the search for the Houndsditch murderers. At the beginning of February a man named John Rosen was arrested, and a few days later another suspected member of the gang, a certain Karl Hoffman; also Gardstein's mistress, Nina Vassileva. Eight persons, all of them Poles or Letts, were now in custody. But only Nina Vassileva was convicted—and even she escaped punishment. Her conviction at the Old Bailey on a charge of conspiracy, for which she was sentenced to two years hard labour, was quashed on appeal, on the grounds of misdirection by the judge. Hoffman and Federoff, Milstein and Trassjonsky were discharged by the magistrates for want of sufficient evidence. Jacob Peters, Yourka Duboff, and John

Rosen were committed for trial at the Old Bailey, but all three were acquitted. Shortly afterwards Sara Rosa Trassjonsky went mad and was removed to Colney Hatch Asylum, where she died. [*57, 130, 143, 205, 216.*

Silles, Florence Alice Bernadette. *See* Edward HOPWOOD.

Singh, Udham. *See* UDHAM SINGH.

Singleton, Sir John Edward (1885-1957), a Lancashire man, was called to the Bar by the Inner Temple in 1906, took silk in 1922, was elected to the House of Commons that same year as Conservative M.P. for Lancaster—he did not re-contest the seat at the General Election of 1924—and in 1934, after six years as Judge of Appeal in the Isle of Man, was appointed to a vacant judgeship in the King's Bench Division of the High Court. Mr. Justice Singleton required counsel who practised before him to have particular regard for the niceties of professional decorum, the standards he set being based upon his own book, *Conduct at the Bar.* Anything careless, slovenly, or merely inefficient earned his sharp disapproval; conversely, he was always ready with his praise when he considered a case to have been well prepared and skilfully presented. He did not allow that to influence his judgment upon the merits of the case; it was just that, as a lawyer, he delighted in competent professional work well done. This fair-minded, dispassionate man had a great belief in the jury system, which he thought to be the best for distributing justice as between man and man. Partly because of this, no doubt, his handling of jury cases was always particularly successful. In 1948 Mr. Justice Singleton was appointed a Lord Justice of Appeal. He died in office on 6th January 1957, within a few weeks of his seventy-second birthday. The trial of Dr. Buck RUXTON was the most notable of the murder trials over which he presided.

Smith, Alfonso Francis Austin, former officer in the Dragoon Guards, had a young and attractive wife, Kathleen. He also had a friend, John Derham, who in the course of six months had so far interfered with the domestic happiness of the Smiths as almost to wreck their marriage. Hoping to bring the unhappy situation to some sort of conclusion, Smith, using his wife's name, sent a telegram to Derham, inviting him to the villa called Stella Maris at Whitstable, where they were living. Derham came. That evening—it was 12th August 1926—husband, wife and lover dined at an hotel, returning afterwards to the villa. At 11 p.m. a shot was fired, and Mrs. Smith's younger sister ran into the drawing-room in time to see Derham holding Smith down on the floor and hitting him with a revolver. Mrs. Smith was trying to pull Derham away. Eventually Derham staggered out of the house and fell mortally wounded: he had been shot in the side. Smith was charged with murder. 'I intended to shoot myself,' he said, 'but in the struggle for the revolver it went off and shot Derham.' This was the basis of Smith's defence at his subsequent trial before Mr. Justice AVORY at Maidstone Assizes. It was brilliantly conducted by Sir Edward Marshall HALL K.C., whose last appearance in a capital case this was. He sought to persuade the jury by practical demonstration that the fatal injury might easily have been inflicted by an accidental discharge of the revolver as Derham leapt upon Smith to prevent his killing himself. It was one of the most entirely convincing demonstrations which even this master of experiment ever brought off. But what probably tipped the scale in Smith's favour was his own evidence—and his manner of giving it. He said that the tragedy had occurred in a flash. Derham and Mrs. Smith had been shuffling a pack of playing cards before beginning a game. He had chosen that moment to tell them that he was going to shoot himself. 'It did not appear to distress them,' he added. 'They did not believe it.' He had felt for the revolver in his hip-pocket. He went on: 'The next thing that happened—all I know is—there was a terrific struggle. I was struck on the head, the revolver went off, and the next thing I was absolutely conscious of was speaking to Inspector Rivers.' He swore that he had never touched the trigger. Although the defence had made no other plea than that the revolver had gone off accidentally, the atmosphere surrounding the case was such that Mr. Justice Avory felt it necessary in his summing-up to give this warning to the jury:

> The law you have got to administer is the law of this country and not of any other, and, above all, not that which is erroneously called the 'unwritten law'. That is merely a name for no law at all. It is the name given to the proposition that every man and woman is a law unto himself or herself, and that reverts us to a state of barbarism. I have told you the law of this country as it must be applied. If you apply any other law or notions of your own you are violating the oaths you have taken.

The jury took nearly two hours and a quarter to reach a decision. Then they returned to court with a verdict of 'Not Guilty', both of murder and manslaughter. But the expected discharge of the prisoner did not follow. The judge called attention to another charge on the calendar— 'possessing fire-arms and ammunition with intent to endanger life'; he held that the statute applied to a man who, on his own admission, had intended to shoot *himself*. Smith having pleaded 'Guilty' to this

subsidiary charge, he was sentenced to twelve months imprisonment with hard labour. (*See also* Lieutenant Douglas MALCOLM.)
[*121, 147.*

Smith, George Joseph, murderer, bigamist, swindler, performer on the harmonium, and one of the most consummate scoundrels who ever lived, was born at Bethnal Green, London, on 11th January 1872, the son of an insurance agent. Little is known of his early years, save that as a boy he was sent to a reformatory and later served several terms of imprisonment for larceny and receiving stolen goods, by which time he was ready for his two major discoveries—Women and the Seaside. The first provided him with his livelihood, the second with a suitably romantic background for profitable seduction. In January 1898 he married nineteen-years-old Caroline Beatrice Thornhill—of his many marriages this was the only one which was valid—and, with the aid of 'references' which he himself supplied, obtained various situations for her in London, Brighton and Hastings, maintaining himself upon the proceeds of what she was able to steal. This ended in disaster. Smith was sent to prison for two years for receiving stolen goods. It taught him a useful lesson—that it is better to steal than to receive. Henceforward, Woman was to be the victim, not the agent; the enemy, not the partner. By dint of much practice Smith's methods over the years came to acquire an enviable fluency and ease. In his hands women were, for the most part, malleable creatures who could, with proper contrivance, be made to do exactly what he wished. He picked them up in the street, in the park, on the seaside promenade, married them in front of a registrar—using a variety of false names—separated them from their life savings, and then disappeared, leaving the poor things only with the clothes they stood up in. Of the dreary procession of women he 'married' there was only one to whom he wished no harm. This was Edith Pegler, who represented the solitary element of stability in a life of constant movement. He 'married' Miss Pegler at Bristol in July 1908, intending the union to be a permanent one. And so, indeed, it proved. Between his various matrimonial adventures Smith always returned to Miss Pegler, as to a haven of domesticity. He was—like his French counterpart, Landru—a dealer in second-hand furniture, or, as he preferred to put it, 'antiques', an occupation which provided him with a colourable excuse to be away from home as and when he chose. Having no suspicion of what her husband was up to, Edith Pegler took a philosophic view of Smith's continual absences. She could be sure that however long he might be away he would, at some time or other, be back. (Sometimes he told her he had been in Canada, at other times in Spain.) Although some of his most striking successes had been with deluded servant girls, Smith saw no reason why he should not move a few rungs higher up the social ladder. He forsaw, correctly, that his swaggering virility would prove equally attractive to refined, but frustrated and secretly resentful, maiden ladies. On the prowl among the elegant terraces of Clifton one August evening in 1910, he encountered just what he was looking for. Miss Bessie Constance Annie Mundy, aged thirty-three, well-educated, extremely reserved and ladylike, lived in genteel loneliness upon a modest income derived from £2,500 in gilt-edged securities bequeathed to her by her late father, a bank manager. Smith's bold wooing swept her off her feet. In less than a week they were 'married' at Weymouth by special licence, the bride-groom describing himself as 'Henry Williams', aged thirty-five, a picture restorer. On the very day of the wedding he instructed a solicitor to obtain a copy of the late Mr. Mundy's will. From this he made the unpleasing discovery that he could not touch the capital sum which provided Bessie with her income. But he did discover that Bessie was entitled to a sum of money amounting to £135 which her uncle, who was also her trustee, had in his hands for safe keeping. It was a fortnight or more before he was able to get hold of this, for Bessie's uncle was a shrewd man quite capable of recognizing a fortune hunter when he saw one. In the end, upon legal advice, the uncle reluctantly surrendered the money. The moment it arrived—on 13th September—Smith absconded. In a savage access of cruelty he wrote to the ill-used Bessie:

I have caught from you a disease which is called the bad disorder. For you to be in such a state proves you could not have kept your-self morally clean. . . .

A strong sadistic impulse is in control here. It is not typical. Usually Smith was content to despoil his women; he did not also require to lash them across the face. Wounded and contrite, submissive to the scoldings of her family, Bessie returned to the *longueurs* of her former existence, from which she had believed herself miraculously delivered; she was a sadder but not, as it turned out, a wiser woman. It was just eighteen months later—on 14th March 1912—that Miss Mundy, then living at a boarding house at Weston-super-Mare, went out to execute a small commission for her landlady and encountered on the Promenade her errant husband. The meeting was the result of one evil chance in a million. Smith, on the look-out as usual for some easy pickings by the sea, had had no thought of Bessie in his mind when he had selected Weston-super-Mare for a fresh exploit—indeed, he had not known that she was living there. Bessie saw him 'looking out to sea', went up to him and touched his elbow. He turned round—and coolly took possession of Bessie again; she left the town with her husband that same evening. To Bessie's uncle Smith wrote:

> I . . . vow to take advantage of every hour and day for the future that Bessie and I are spared to outlive the past and to prove myself in the eyes of my wife and her relations a true and worthy husband.

A letter in the same vein to Bessie's brother provides an even finer example of Smith's epistolary style—the opening sentence is particularly to be admired:

> I know not how I shall offend in dedicating my unpolished lines to you, nor how you will censure me for using so strong a prop for supporting so grave a burden; only if you will accept my humble apology for pain and trouble which you share with your sister my wife, and let the past sink into oblivion, I account myself highly honoured, and vow to take advantage of every future day that the great powers have ordained; until the miserable past is absolutely outlived and a character established which will be worthy of your appreciation.

Bessie, poor, deluded creature, added a postscript:

> I trust you will try and forget the past as I have done. I know my husband better now than ever before. You will be pleased to know I am perfectly happy.

In the intervals of writing his affecting letters, Smith was preparing a plan whereby Bessie was to make a will bequeathing to him her £2,500 and he, for his part, was to make a will leaving to her everything he possessed—which was practically nothing. Counsel's opinion confirmed that this arrangement was acceptable within the terms of Mr. Mundy's will; on 8th July the mutual wills were executed. Since the previous May, Smith had been living with Bessie at 80 High Street, Herne Bay, a house he had taken on a yearly tenancy. On 9th July he purchased from an ironmonger in the town a bath, without taps or any other fixtures, which had to be filled by hand. The price was £2, but after some chaffering Smith obtained it for £1. 17s. 6d. (The overheads must be kept down.) On the following day he accompanied the meekly acquiescent 'Mrs. Williams' to a doctor's surgery close by. To Dr. French he said, 'My wife has had a sort of fit.' The doctor prescribed bromide of potassium. On Friday, 12th July, Dr. French was twice summoned to No. 80 High Street; the patient complained of feeling listless—the effect, no doubt, of the exceptionally hot weather—but otherwise there seemed little amiss. That night Bessie, who had surrendered herself entirely to the masterful 'Mr. Williams', wrote to her uncle:

> Last Tuesday night I had a bad fit, and one again on Thursday night. . . . My husband has been extremely kind and done all he could for me. . . . I do not like to worry you with this, but my husband has strictly advised me to let all my relatives know and tell them of my breakdown. I have made my will and have left all I have to my husband. That is only natural, as I love my husband.

At eight o'clock next morning Dr. French was summoned by a note which ran: 'Can you come at once? I am afraid my wife is dead.' The doctor hurried round. Smith took him upstairs to a room at the top of the house. In the bath, which was too small for her, Bessie 'Williams' lay naked and dead, her head submerged beneath the water, and in her hand a tablet of Castile soap. Smith told the police that he had gone out to buy some herrings for breakfast; returning, he had found his wife lying dead in the bath. He wired to the Mundy family: 'Bessie died in a fit this morning', and followed this up with a letter written on black-edged paper:

> Words cannot describe the great shock I suffered in the loss of my wife. The doctor said she had a fit in the bath.

The inquest was held on the Monday, and resulted in a verdict of death from misadventure. Smith having arranged the cheapest possible funeral, Bessie was buried in a common grave on Tuesday, 16th July. Smith then proceeded to the winding-up of his wife's estate. The Mundy family lodged a caveat against the will, but later, realizing the helplessness of their position, they withdrew it, and by the end of the year Bessie's securities were in the sorrowing hands of 'Mr. Williams'. By October 1913 he was ready for another seaside adventure. At Southsea Smith scraped acquaintance with a Miss Alice Burnham, who, within a few days of the first meeting, gratefully accepted his offer of marriage. Miss Burnham, aged twenty-five, a stout, rather jolly woman, was a nurse, very anxious to get married and impatient of the fate which had so far denied her the opportunity. On 4th November Smith 'married' her under his own name ('bachelor, independent means') at Portsmouth Register Office, disregarding the hostility of the Burnham family and, in particular, of Alice's father, a retired coal merchant, of

Aston Clinton in Buckinghamshire, who had met his future son-in-law and had found him odious. Scarcely was the ceremony over before Mr. Burnham found himself involved in an acrimonious correspondence. He had in his keeping £100 belonging to his daughter. It may be imagined with what determination Smith set himself to obtain this money. Mr. Burnham was equally determined not to hand it over, certainly not until he knew a little more about the man his daughter had chosen to marry. He instructed his solicitor to ask Smith to provide some information about himself. In reply Mr. Burnham received from his son-in-law the following postcard:

> Sir—In answer to your application concerning my parentage, etc. My mother was a Buss horse, my father a Cab-driver, my sister a roughrider over the arctic regions—my brothers were all gallant sailors on a steam-roller.

Smith's applications for the £100 became ever more aggressive and threatening, and eventually Mr. Burnham surrendered the money. By now Alice had been insured for £500. The road to the seaside was open. On 10th December Mr. and Mrs. Smith arrived in out-of-season Blackpool. They applied first to a lodging house in Adelaide Street, but Smith rejected the accommodation available there, as it did not include a bath. At a second attempt he engaged a bed-sitting room at 16 Regent's Road; this did possess a bathroom. The very same evening the familiar routine begins. First, the visit to the doctor—Dr. Billing—who finds Mrs. Smith in good health, but rather tired; he gives her a mild purgative and some tablets to ease her headache. Afterwards the submissive Alice writes to her parents:

> My husband does all he can for me, in fact, I have the best husband in the world.

Two days later—on Friday, 12th December—the Smiths went out for a walk in the evening, leaving instructions for a bath to be prepared. They came back shortly after eight o'clock. Mrs. Smith went to the bathroom. The landlady, Mrs. Crossley, and her daughter were sitting in the kitchen, which was immediately below the bathroom, when they saw water seeping through the ceiling and streaming down the walls. At that moment Smith entered the kitchen carrying two eggs. 'I have brought these for our breakfast in the morning,' he said. After he had left the kitchen he was heard calling up the stairs, 'Alice, when you have done put the light out.' Mrs. Crossley's daughter went out into the hall. 'My wife does not answer me,' said Smith. A few moments later he called out from the bathroom landing: 'Fetch the doctor! My wife cannot speak to me. Fetch Dr. Billing; she knows him.' Mrs. Crossley ran for the doctor. She waited on the stairs whilst Dr. Billing went into the bathroom. When he came out she asked him what was wrong, and the doctor told her, 'Oh, she is drowned, she is dead.' After Dr. Billing had gone, Smith came into the kitchen, and Mrs. Crossley said to him, 'How dreadful; what an awful thing this is.' Smith replied that he would not be surprised at anything that might happen thereafter. Mrs. Crossley looked steadily at her lodger; she saw something in his face that she did not like. When she spoke to him again it was in an entirely different tone. 'Now, Smith, you cannot stop here tonight.' 'Why?' he asked. 'Because I won't have a callous man like you in the house.' Smith mumbled, 'When they are dead they are dead.' Smith slept that night in the house next door. The following day he telegraphed to Mr. Burnham: 'Alice died last night in her bath. Letter following.' In this letter, written the same day, he said he had suffered 'the greatest and most cruel shock that ever a man could have suffered'—words could not describe his feelings. The inquest resulted, as before, in a verdict of accidental death, the deceased having been found drowned in a hot bath, 'probably through being seized with a fit or a faint'. Smith left Blackpool immediately after the funeral, which took place on the Monday, leaving with the landlady a postcard with a forwarding address. On the back of that postcard the percipient Mrs. Crossley wrote: 'Wife died in bath. We shall see him again.' Smith collected the insurance without difficulty. In December 1914 he prepared himself for his third killing. He chose as his victim a certain Miss Margaret Elizabeth Lofty, a clergyman's daughter, who earned a modest livelihood in that most genteel of all occupations—lady's companion. Accosted in the street at Clifton—not far from the spot which had seen the first meeting with Bessie Mundy—Miss Lofty, although a woman of great sensitivity and refinement, was no more able to resist the allure of Smith's emphatic masculinity than any of her predecessors in the melancholy sequence of discarded brides; she was still smarting from the hurt of an unhappy love affair, which no doubt made her surrender the more rapid and complete. All Miss Lofty possessed was about £19 in a savings bank, so, to increase her value, Smith dispatched her to the offices of an insurance company in Bristol, where she filled in a proposal form for a £700 endowment policy; the transaction was completed on 4th December, and the first premium paid out of money supplied by Smith—meanness and greed were among his leading characteristics, but this, of course, was a necessary outlay. The couple were 'married' at a register office at Bath on 15th December, the bridegroom giving his name as 'John Lloyd' and his occupation as 'land agent'. Precedent required them to make their way to the sea.

Instead, they set out for London, where they found lodgings at 14 Bismarck Road, Highgate, Smith having first ascertained that the house had a bathroom. Margaret wrote to her sister:

> No doubt you will be surprised to know that I was married today to a gentleman named John Lloyd. He is such a nice man . . . I am perfectly happy.

There follows the usual visit to the doctor—Dr. Bates—who prescribes a bromide for 'Mrs. Lloyd's' headache. At seven o'clock the next evening a bath is prepared for 'Mrs. Lloyd'. The rest is predictable. Mrs. Louisa Blatch, the landlady, described it at the trial:

> I was ironing in the kitchen when I heard someone going upstairs. A few minutes after it I heard a sound from the bathroom. It was a sound of splashing. Then there was a noise as of someone putting wet hands or arms on the side of the bath, and then a sigh. . . . The next sound I heard was someone playing the harmonium in the sitting-room . . . . I should say the harmonium playing went on for about ten minutes. The next sound I heard was the front door slam. About ten minutes after that I heard the front door bell. I went to the door and I found Mr. Lloyd at the door. . . . He said, 'I have been for some tomatoes for Mrs. Lloyd's supper. Is she down yet?'

The reader will not require to be told what happened after that—he is by now sufficiently familiar with the canon. He will not even be surprised to hear that at the inquest, conducted by the Coroner for Central London, Mr. Walter Schroder, a verdict of 'suffocation by accidental drowning' was returned. (The only variant is that macabre performance on the harmonium immediately after the killing.) Nonetheless, Smith had overreached himself at last. The *News of the World* published a report of the inquest on 'Mrs. Lloyd' under the headlines:

FOUND DEAD IN BATH
BRIDE'S TRAGIC FATE ON DAY AFTER WEDDING

Those staring capitals happened to catch the eye of Mr. Charles Burnham of Aston Clinton in Buckinghamshire, who found the report so interesting that he cut it out, pinned to it a newspaper account of his own daughter's death, and forwarded both cuttings to the Aylesbury police. Being entirely absorbed in the business of winding up his wife's estate, Smith heard no pursuing footfall. It was an unpleasant shock to him, therefore, when upon leaving his solicitor's office in Shepherd's Bush on 1st February 1915, he was approached by Detective-Inspector Neil and two other Scotland Yard officers, who arrested him on a charge of having caused a false entry to be made in the marriage register at Bath. Not for another seven weeks were the police ready to charge him with the wilful murder of the three 'Brides in the Bath'. When in June he was put on trial at the Old Bailey before Mr. Justice Scrutton (afterwards Lord Justice SCRUTTON), he was indicted only for the murder of Bessie Mundy, and his counsel, Edward Marshall HALL K.C., challenged the right of the Crown to introduce evidence touching upon the deaths of Alice Burnham and Margaret Lofty. But the judge—whose decision was later upheld by the Court of Criminal Appeal—ruled that such evidence *was* admissible as tending to show that Smith had a 'system'. He told the jury: 'You may use the evidence as to the other deaths for this purpose—to see whether it helps you as to whether the death of Miss Mundy was accidental or designed.' After that, although it dragged on for nine whole days, the trial could have only one result. No jury in the world could be expected to believe that it was no more than a coincidence that the three 'wives' of George Joseph Smith should all have come to a watery end, and in precisely similar circumstances. This particular jury needed only twenty-two minutes to agree upon a verdict of 'Guilty'. When Mr. Justice Scrutton came to pronounce sentence of death upon the prisoner he prefaced the solemn words with, 'I think that exhortation to repentance would be wasted on you.' He was probably right. George Joseph Smith was hanged at Maidstone Prison on 15th August 1915.

[*1, 27.*

Smith, Lawrence John. *See* Thomas John LEY.

Spatchett, Walter. *See* Samuel James FURNACE.

Spilsbury, Sir Bernard Henry (1877-1947), Home Office patho-logist, has been called the 'greatest medical detective of the century'. In his book, *Verdict in Dispute*, Mr. Edgar Lustgarten writes: 'To the man in the street he stood for pathology as Hobbs stood for cricket or Dempsey for boxing or Capablanca for chess.' This, no doubt, had its dangers, for as time went on the immense authority attaching to his opinions, and, indeed, the prestige of his name alone, came to have a mesmeric effect upon juries. Counsel were dismally aware of this, and repeatedly sought to counter it with reminders that no man is infallible and that this applied as much to Sir Bernard Spilsbury as to anybody else. His contribution to the practice of forensic medicine was immeasurable, but the respect, or, as counsel wearily complained, the reverence, with which his theories were received was founded on something more than his professional reputation, high though that was. Sir Bernard Spilsbury possessed remarkable powers of popular exposition. No matter how complex the problem, or how subtle and elaborate his conclusions, he always explained himself simply, clearly, and directly, in language that the intelligent layman could perfectly well understand. Indeed, he never seemed to be arguing, but only to be explaining, and what is more—such was the persuasive clarity of his style—to be explaining something which was really self-evident. He was, without cavil, *the* Perfect Witness, and, as such, regularly collected the compliments of judges who, out of their painful experience of what often passes for 'expert evidence', were in the best position to appreciate his quality. Typical of such compliments was the tribute paid to him by Mr. Justice DARLING in his summing-up at the trial of Major ARMSTRONG:

Do you remember Dr. Spilsbury? Do you remember how he stood and the way he gave his evidence? Do you remember how if there were any qualifications to be made in favour of the defence he always gave it without being asked for it? *Did you ever see a witness who more thoroughly satisfied you that he was absolutely impartial, absolutely fair, absolutely indifferent as to whether his evidence told for one side or the other, when he was giving evidence-in-chief, or when he was being cross-examined?*

No man ever spared himself less than did Sir Bernard Spilsbury in the painstaking examination and assessment of every circumstance, every fact which could help him to make up his mind upon the basic problems of forensic medicine: Is it murder? Or suicide? Or misadventure? Or even, in spite of appearances, death from natural causes? Having made up his mind, he usually stuck to it, with grave, courteous, unshakable persistence. His appearance was impressive, but at the same time misleading. He was tall and spruce and neatly tailored, but with his ruddy complexion and the air he wore of a man who spent much of his life out of doors—instead of in mortuaries and dissecting-rooms—he looked more like a gentleman farmer than a distinguished scientist. Between 1910, when his professional association with the Home Office began, and 1947, when he died, Sir Bernard performed some 25,000 post-mortems. Only about 250 of them had to do with murder, but, inevitably, it was this one per cent. which focused the limelight upon him, and made him the national figure that he became. Bernard Spilsbury (knighted 1923) was born at Leamington Spa, Warwickshire, in 1877, the son of an analytical and manufacturing chemist. He entered St. Mary's Hospital Medical School, Paddington, as a student, qualified in 1905, and in that same year was appointed Resident Assistant Pathologist at St. Mary's, under Dr. A. J. Pepper; when Dr. Pepper retired in 1908, Spilsbury succeeded him. The turning-point in his career came in 1910, when he was called in to examine the mutilated remains of Cora Crippen, and thus to assist in the most sensational murder trial of the century. It was the first of the long series of cases in which he was retained by the Home Office over a period of thirty-seven years. The latter part of Spilsbury's life was clouded with domestic tragedy. He was profoundly affected by the deaths of his two sons and indeed never recovered from the shock of this double bereavement, which coincided with a general decline in his health and mental alertness, largely brought about by overwork. On 19th December 1947 he took his own life by coal-gas poisoning at his laboratory in University College, Gower Street, London. (The work which was formerly carried out by Sir Bernard Spilsbury is done today by a small team of pathologists, whose services are called upon as occasion demands. Its foremost member is Dr. Keith Simpson; others are Dr. Donald Teare and Dr. F. E. Camps.)

Spink, Mary Isabella. *See* George CHAPMAN.

Starchfield, John, sold newspapers outside the Horseshoe Hotel in London's Tottenham Court Road. He was a man of great courage, as was sufficiently demonstrated one September day in 1912, when a mad Armenian tailor named **Stephen Titus**, having shot dead the assistant manageress of the Horseshoe, one Esther May Towers, rushed into the street, revolver in hand. Starchfield left his newspaper pitch to chase the maniac along Tottenham Court Road, closed with him, and although wounded in the desperate struggle which followed, held him long enough to hand him over to the police. At his trial at the Old Bailey Titus was found 'Guilty but insane' and removed to Broadmoor Criminal Lunatic Asylum. The trial judge, Mr. Justice (afterwards Lord) PHILLIMORE, warmly praised Starchfield's bravery and awarded him £50 as some compensation for his injuries. (The Carnegie Heroes Fund afterwards made him an allowance of £1 a week.) Remembrance of his act of heroism had scarcely begun to fade when only fifteen months later—on 8th January 1914—the dead body of his eight-years-old son, Willie Starchfield, was found beneath one of the seats of the 4.4 p.m. train from Chalk Farm to Broad Street; the boy had been strangled with a thin cord, which was still tightly drawn about his neck.

Public sympathy was intense—but it dried up overnight when the Coroner's jury returned a verdict of 'wilful murder' against the bereaved father. Starchfield was tried at the Old Bailey, before Mr. Justice Atkin (afterwards Lord ATKIN), at the end of March, but the case against him—based upon the doubtful evidence of four persons who claimed to have seen the boy in his father's company on the afternoon of the murder—proved to be so flimsy that on the second day it collapsed altogether. Upon the judge's direction, the prisoner was discharged, without being called upon to say one word in his defence. (Mr. Justice Atkin had some extremely scathing things to say about the Coroner's inquisition.) Two years later, almost to the day, Starchfield died in St. Pancras Infirmary from a cause directly attributable to the injuries he had received in his struggle with the madman, Titus. The mystery of Willie Starchfield's murder has resisted solution. The only thing reasonably certain about it is that the boy was not killed on the train, from which it would appear that the murderer, a homicidal maniac, must have boarded it at one of the five intermediary stations between Chalk Farm and Mildmay Park where the gruesome discovery was made—carrying his victim's body in a suitcase, or perhaps a parcel.

[*8, 34.*

Steele, Louisa Maud, domestic servant, left her mistress's house in Lee Road, Lewisham, at about eight o'clock on the evening of Thursday, 23rd January 1931, intending to return a book to a neighbour and to call at a local chemist for some syrup of senna. She usually went for a walk on Thursday evenings, but as it was wet and windy, her mistress, Miss Kathleen Andrews, a music teacher, expected that she would be back at least by 9 p.m. When she had not returned by eleven o'clock, Miss Andrews, much alarmed, informed the police. Shortly before eight o'clock the next morning the dead body of Louisa Maud Steele was discovered by a lamplighter on Blackheath, within walking distance of home. The girl was lying on her back, covered by her coat; she had been strangled and there were extensive injuries to the face, neck, and body, probably caused by heavy kicks as she lay on the ground. There were also what appeared to be bite marks. The girl's clothes had been ripped off her, but there was no sign of any attempt at sexual interference. At the inquest, the Home Office pathologist, Sir Bernard SPILSBURY, said that the girl had been strangled by the length of tape threaded into the neckline of her own dress. 'In my opinion, he said, 'the girl was attacked from behind and the neck of the dress was drawn forcibly backwards, while counter-pressure was made on the back of the head and neck. . . . She would probably lose consciousness in a few seconds, so that she could offer no effectual resistance. Probably the pressure was released before death took place. Most of the other injuries were inflicted during life.' Death would ensue within five or ten minutes, he thought. Detective-Inspector Cory, the Scotland Yard officer in charge of the case, told the Coroner, Dr. H. S. Knight, that there could not be the slightest doubt that the murder was the work of a maniac. The jury returned the only possible verdict—wilful murder by a person or persons unknown. And that is the last that has ever been heard of the matter.

[9.

Stemp, Janie Tremayne.
Stemp, Peggy. } *See* James Thomas COLLINS.

Stephen, William Thomas Scott (Michael). *See* Elvira Dolores BARNEY.

Stewart, Frederick, aged twenty-eight, professional thief, having broken into a luxury flat in Pembridge Square, Bayswater, London, in the late afternoon of 9th February 1928, and having been disturbed by the unlooked-for return of the occupier, Mr. Alfred Charles Bertram Webb, shot his way out with a Spanish revolver he had bought for five shillings. Peering through the shattered glass panel of the front door, Mr. Webb received a bullet in his forehead, and died in hospital. Stewart had spent most of the afternoon knocking at the doors of houses and flats in the neighbourhood. He was, in the vernacular of thievery, 'sounding the drum'. The technique of this operation is simple. The would-be thief knocks at the door—any door. If his knock is answered he asks for an imaginary 'Mrs. Smith' or a fictitious 'Mr. Brown', and goes away—with apologies. The aim is to find a house where there is no answer, because nobody is at home. At one of the houses Stewart 'sounded' he told the woman who came to the door that he was from the 'Warwick Garage'—non-existent—and that he 'wished to see the chauffeur'. For one of the Scotland Yard officers engaged upon the case this faintly rang a bell. He remembered a housebreaker named Frederick Stewart, short, dark, stockily built, who answered well enough to the description of the man who had been 'sounding the drum' in Bayswater that afternoon. He also remembered —and it was this that rang the bell—that Stewart was usually to be found in and around Warwick Mews, Kensington. Being in need of a colourable excuse to knock at the door, might not the word 'Warwick' slip naturally on to Stewart's tongue? Had not Warwick Mews been transmuted into 'Warwick Garage'? This long shot hit the mark. Stewart was questioned. He admitted breaking into the flat, and that the bullet which had killed Mr. Webb had been fired from his revolver. But, he said, the gun had gone off accidentally. At his trial at the Old Bailey in the following April Stewart was convicted of murder, and was sentenced to death by Mr. Justice AVORY; he was hanged at Pentonville Prison on 6th June—Derby Day.

[*91, 92.*

Stillwell, Philip George. *See* Joan WOODHOUSE.

Stone, Leslie George, aged twenty-four, a sand-pit labourer of Heath and Reach, near Leighton Buzzard, put on a new suit he had never worn before when, on 11th April 1937, he went out for the evening with factory girl Ruby Keen. It was a circumstance that helped to hang him. Ruby Keen's nearly naked body was found early next morning lying on a footpath known as The Firs at Leighton Buzzard; she had been strangled with her own scarf. The sandy soil where the body lay had been badly scuffled and trampled down, suggesting to Chief-Inspector Barker of Scotland Yard that the girl had been killed after a desperate struggle to protect herself from being raped. The churned up earth showed the marks of the strangler's knees as he knelt over his victim. Stone made a statement to the police in which he admitted that he had been in various public houses with Ruby Keen on the night she had been killed, but swore that he had left her outside the Stag Hotel at 10.15 p.m. He was betrayed by his new blue serge suit. The knees of the trousers had been vigorously brushed, so hard that the nap had been rubbed away. However, when examined under a microscope, granules of sandy earth, identical with the soil of the footpath, were visible among the dark blue fibres; there were traces of the same soil in the turn-ups. If the soil really had come from that path, then Stone must have been there on the night of the murder, for that was the first and only time he had worn his new suit. Even more incriminating was the fact that in the brushing of the suit a tiny thread of artificial yellow silk had, as it were, been 'embedded' in the fibres of the jacket. The thread exactly matched the dead girl's dress. In the following June, Stone was put on trial at the Old Bailey, where the evidence supplied by the suit, the yellow thread, the tell-tale granules of sandy soil, forced him to change his story. He now admitted that he had quarrelled with Ruby Keen, who had struck him. 'I caught hold of her scarf, I think, and pulled it,' he said. 'I think I knotted it again after that. I was in a kind of a rage.' Whilst the jury were out considering their verdict they sent in a written question for answer by the judge, Lord HEWART, Lord Chief Justice. It was: 'If as the result of an intention to commit rape a girl is killed—although there was no intention to kill her—is a man guilty of murder?' To this Lord Hewart replied: 'Yes, undoubtedly.' Complaint was made of this answer when, following upon his conviction, Stone applied to the Court of Criminal Appeal to have the murder verdict set aside on the ground that the jury had been misdirected. The Court held that Lord Hewart's reply was perfectly adequate, and dismissed the appeal. Stone was hanged at Pentonville Prison on 13th August.

[34.

Sullivan, Ronald Joseph. *See* Dorothea Nancy WADDINGHAM.

Sutton, Beatrice Vilna. *See* Frederick Herbert Charles FIELD.

Svaars, Fritz. *See* SIEGE OF SIDNEY STREET.

Swift, Janie Tremayne. *See* James Thomas COLLINS.

Swift, Sir Rigby Philip Watson (1874-1937). Judge of the King's Bench Division of the High Court (1920-37). Rarely has an occupant of the Bench impressed his personality more incisively upon a delighted and receptive public than did the rare, the one and only, the sadly irreplaceable Mr. Justice Swift. Everything about this extraordinary man was large and warm and generous and rich; even his weaknesses and occasional defects of temper were free from anything petty or mean or spiteful. His wit, which was inexhaustible, had the true rapier glint. In cold print, no doubt, it loses something of its appeal. To savour it fully, perhaps, one needs to be able to remember the man as he was, in his uniqueness. One needs to hear again in one's fancy the drawling voice, with its flattened vowel sounds, the short 'a', the tones which suggested, rather than reproduced, the speech of his native Lancashire, above all the peculiar habit he had of elongating the final syllable of certain words and then snapping it off, explosively. (The very word 'remember' recalls this trick. On the lips of Mr. Justice Swift it would be certain to come out as 'remem-*bah*'. This mannerism was so well-known in the Temple that lawyers used to refer to him—and still do— as 'Rig-*bah*'.) One needs to remember, also, how he looked as he sat on the Bench; the round, rubicund face under the bob wig, the glowing cheeks, the nose like a button, the amiable lift of the mouth, the bright, observant eyes, the endearing air of *bonhomie*. And all the various tricks and mannerisms which were so much a part of the man need to be remembered, too—such as the habit of slowly tapping his pencil three times upon the desk before him as a warning that he was about to say something apt and shrewd, and frequently devastating. (At those premonitory taps, much to his delight, an awful silence would descend upon the court.) This is to say that to enjoy the true flavour of the aphorisms of Mr. Justice Swift it is necessary to have the whole man. He claimed to be plain and blunt, and liked to pretend that his knowledge of the law was something less than it was. But even if it had been no more than was strictly necessary—the infrequency with which his decisions were upset on appeal showed that it was, in fact, very much more than that—his success as a judge, and particularly as a criminal judge, would not have been any the less, since it was based not upon learned books but upon an extraordinary intuitive insight into human nature, perfected by a lifetime's experience in the courts. He was certainly no ordinary man, but he understood ordinary men, sympathized with them in their temptations, and admitted to some of their failings and weaknesses—no judge was ever less inclined to take a 'holier than thou' attitude towards poor sinners who stood before him in the dock. 'I have been an associate of criminals all my life,' he said once. 'I have defended them, prosecuted them, and for years have tried them. I know there is a very great deal of good in the very worst of them. I spend the greater part of my time on the Bench not deciding for how long I should send a man to prison, but whether I can possibly avoid sending him to prison at all, particularly for the first time.' Rigby Swift was born at St. Helens in 1874, the eighth son of Thomas Swift, a prosperous solicitor in the town, who later gave up his practice to become a barrister. The son followed the father as a student of Lincoln's Inn, and received his call in 1895. He first practised at Liverpool, but migrated to London in 1910; two years later he took silk, and by the end of the 1914-18 war ranked as one of the leading King's Counsel in the country. He combined his practice at the Bar with a modest career in politics, securing election to the House of Commons in 1910 as Conservative M.P. for his native St. Helens; he remained there until he was unseated at the 'coupon' election of 1918. Appointed a judge in 1920, Mr. Justice Swift was seventeen years on the Bench. He died on 19th October 1937, six months after the death of Lady Swift, the wife to whom he was so deeply devoted. He presided over many notable murder trials, chief among them being those of Alexander Campbell MASON; Madame FAHMY; Frederick JESSE; Charles HOUGHTON; John ROBINSON; Frederick FIELD (first trial); and Reginald WOOLMINGTON (second trial). As counsel, he appeared for Lieutenant-Colonel RUTHERFORD.

T

Thou canst not say I did it, never shake
Thy gory locks at me.

Shakespeare: *Macbeth*

Talbot, Sir George John (1861-1938). Judge of the King's Bench Division of the High Court (1923-37). Two Lord Chancellors and a fifteenth-century Judge of the Common Pleas were among the forbears of this scholarly High Churchman, a Fellow of All Souls, who was called to the Bar by the Inner Temple in 1887 and became a King's Counsel in 1906. His ample practice was divided between the Parliamentary Bar and rating, local government, licensing and, more particularly, ecclesiastical cases, of whose intricacies he possessed a remarkable store of out-of-the-way knowledge. Yet, curiously enough, when he succeeded Lord DARLING as a High Court judge in 1923, at the age of sixty-two, he was more than ordinarily successful in his handling of criminal cases, in spite of the fact that this class of work had lain entirely outside the scope of his former practice. Sensational cases did not often come his way, but there were exceptions—as, for example, the trials for murder of Alfred Arthur ROUSE and Stanley Eric HOBDAY. Mr. Justice Talbot retired in 1937, and died in the following year, aged seventy-seven.

Taylor, Elizabeth (Bessie). *See* George CHAPMAN.

Teasdale, William, a Metropolitan Police constable, proposed marriage to a woman who accepted him in happy ignorance of the fact that he already had a wife, and that he was living with her at Voltaire Road, Clapham; the wedding was fixed for 28th May 1938. On the evening of 3rd March, P.C. Teasdale took his fiancée to the Victoria Palace theatre to see *Me and My Girl*. In the vestibule as they arrived they were confronted by the indignant Mrs. Teasdale. 'Do you know he is a married man?' she demanded of the other woman. 'I am his wife and he has a baby.' As may be imagined, this sour incident destroyed the evening's enjoyment. Teasdale and the woman he had deceived left the theatre during the interval, and for the next few hours—indeed, the 'explanations' went on far into the night—the harassed constable was busy trying to talk his way out of a highly difficult situation. He, of course, denied that the woman who had made such an embarrassing scene in the vestibule was his wife; she was, he weakly insisted—over and over again—'only a woman he knew'. When eventually he left his fiancée's flat to go home to Clapham, it was to exchange the reproaches of one angry woman for the recriminations of another woman even angrier. 'She told me that she had evidence for a separation,' Teasdale was to say when facing his trial. 'I said she could do as she pleased. She became excited and struck me in the face. I pressed her against the head of the bed and held her there for a short time. I noticed she was unconscious and went away.' That was more than Ruby Jeannie May Teasdale was able to do, for she was dead. The next day Teasdale was arrested in Sunderland—where his parents lived—and was charged with murdering his wife by strangulation. Tried at the Old Bailey before Mr. Justice Goddard (afterwards Lord GODDARD) on 28th April, the accused was found guilty and sentenced to death. He was reprieved on 13th May.

Thomas, Alice Maud. *See* Sarah Ann HEARN.

Thomas, Donald George, exemplary boy at school, captain of the cricket eleven, a member of the Boys' Brigade, was in trouble with the police before he was sixteen. Called up for military service in January 1945, when he was twenty, he deserted a few weeks later. After two years on the run, he surrendered to the police, served a period of detention, then deserted again. He fell in with a man named Winkless, who took him home and introduced him to his wife. Noreen Winkless became infatuated with him. Leaving home, husband and three children, she went off to live with Thomas in a rented room in South London. On the evening of 13th February 1948, Thomas was stopped at the garage entrance to a house in Wade's Hill, Southgate, by P.C. Nathaniel Edgar, who was engaged on plainclothes duty following a series of housebreaking incidents in the neighbourhood. While he was being questioned he drew a revolver and shot the officer three times in the right groin and right thigh. Before he died in hospital ninety minutes later, Edgar stammered out: 'I got his identity card and name. . . . The pocket book is in my inside pocket.' In the constable's book was this entry: 'Thomas Donald, 247 Cambridge Road, Enfield. BEAH 257/2.' Using for the first time (says Sir Harold Scott, former Metropolitan Police Commissioner) a formula which has since become familiar, the police made it known to the Press that they were anxious to interview Donald George Thomas, who 'might be able to help them in their inquiries'. This notice, reproduced in a popular newspaper, was seen by Mr. Winkless, who told the police that his wife, missing for three weeks, had gone off with Thomas; he supplied them with a photograph of Noreen Winkless. This appeared in the morning papers of 17th February, and was seen by Mrs. Smeed, landlady of the house in Clapham where Thomas and the woman were living. She recognized the photograph and called the police. Four officers arrived at the house within a few minutes. It was arranged that Mrs. Smeed should take breakfast up to her lodgers in the top-front bedroom as usual. The officers followed her up the stairs. Mrs. Smeed knocked at the door and put the tray down outside. A few moments later the policemen waiting by the door heard the key turn in the lock. The door opened an inch or two. Thomas, dressed in his underclothes, peered out, saw the officers, and tried to slam the door—but was not quite quick enough. He made a leap for the bed and put his hand under the pillow for his revolver. There was a short, sharp struggle, and Thomas was disarmed before he could fire. 'You were lucky,' he said, on the way to the police station. 'I might just as well be hung for a sheep as a lamb.' In the bedroom the police found seventeen rounds of ammunition, a rubber truncheon, a jemmy, and an instruction manual—written by two wartime Commandos—entitled, *Shooting To Live With The One-Hand Gun*. At the Old Bailey in the following April, Thomas was convicted of the murder of P.C. Edgar, and was sentenced to death by Mr. Justice HILBERY. But, like James CAMB, he did not hang, because at the time of the trial a clause suspending the death penalty for an experimental period of five years had been added to the Criminal Justice Bill, then before Parliament. The clause was later deleted by the House of Lords, but whilst the matter was still at issue between the two Houses death sentences were commuted. So Donald George Thomas, the lucky one, went to prison instead of to the gallows. Sir Harold Scott, in his book, *Scotland Yard*, calls this case 'the classic example of co-operation between the three Ps—police, press and public'.

[*148, 193, 226.*

Thomas, Leonard. *See* George KELLY.

Thornton, Beryl Lilian. *See* Alfred Arthur KOPSCH.

Tinsley, Mona Lilian. *See* Frederick NODDER.

Titus, Stephen. *See* John STARCHFIELD.

Tobin, Sir Alfred Aspinall, K.C. (1855-1939), is remembered, first and foremost, for his lively defence of Dr. Hawley Harvey CRIPPEN. A barrister of the Middle Temple (called 1880), he was for many years one of the busiest juniors in practice on the Northern Circuit. He took silk in 1903, and twelve years later was appointed to a county court judgeship, with jurisdiction in Herefordshire and Shropshire. Upon accepting that post he gave up his seat in the Commons, to which he had been elected in 1910 as Conservative Member for Preston. In 1919 the Lord Chancellor, Lord Birkenhead, a colleague of his early days in Liverpool, transferred him to Westminster County Court; he was knighted in the same year. White-haired and benign, His Honour Judge Tobin, a man of singular charm, presided over his court at Westminster for sixteen years, retiring in 1935 when he was eighty. He died in Switzerland on 30th November 1939.

Towers, Esther May. *See* John STARCHFIELD.

Trapnell, John Graham, K.C. (1876-1949), was called to the Bar by the Inner Temple in 1903, joined the Western Circuit, where he came to have an extensive miscellaneous practice, and took silk in 1931. In the following year he succeeded the future Lord GODDARD as Recorder of Plymouth. He was Judge-Advocate of the Fleet from 1933 to 1943, in which year he was appointed an Official Referee to the Supreme Court. He died in office on 3rd November 1949, at the age of seventy-three. Notable murder trials in which he was engaged included those of William Walter BURTON; and Reginald WOOL-MINGTON (both trials).

Trassjonsky, Sara Rosa. *See* SIEGE OF SIDNEY STREET.

True, Nellie Grace. *See* David GREENWOOD.

Tucker, Sergeant Charles. *See* SIEGE OF SIDNEY STREET.

Tyler, William Frederick, Police-Constable. *See* Paul HEFELD.

U

Unkindness may do much
And his unkindness may defeat my life.

Shakespeare: *Othello*

Udham Singh, a fanatical Sikh, living at Mornington Crescent, in London, where he cherished a consuming hatred of the British, attended a joint meeting of the Royal Central Asian Society and the East India Association at Caxton Hall, Westminster, on 13th March 1940. As the meeting was breaking up he edged his way to the platform and fired six shots from a ·45 revolver at the distinguished group of persons who had lately addressed the audience of some three hundred people. One of the bullets grazed the Marquess of Zetland, Secretary of State for India, who had presided; another pierced the hand of seventy-nine-years-old Lord Lamington, a former Governor of the Punjab; a third broke the arm of Sir Louis Dane, one-time Under-Secretary to the Government of the Punjab. Considering that the shots had been fired at point-blank range it was remarkable that these three should have escaped with so little damage. A fourth victim of the lightning assault was not so fortunate. Sir Michael Francis O'Dwyer, another ex-Governor of the Punjab—he had been in office at the time of the Amritsar riots of 1919, when Udham Singh's brother had been killed—received two bullets in the back, one of which passed through the heart and right lung and killed him instantly. It was all over so quickly that few realized what had happened; at the back of the hall there seems to have been the idea that some high-spirited person, hoping to relieve the almost excessive respectability of the occasion, had let off a firework. A sudden flurry in the aisle dispelled this notion. Recovering from the momentary shock, Sir Percy Sykes, the distinguished Orientalist, whose lecture on Afghanistan had been the main business of the meeting, leapt from the platform in pursuit as the assassin raced for the door, the still-smoking pistol in his hand. At the same time a member of the audience named Claud Riches, a man of sixty, took a flying leap at the escaping Indian and landed on his back. Udham Singh was overpowered and firmly secured, to await the arrival of the police in the person of the Commissioner, Sir Philip Game, who himself took charge of the case. Twenty-five rounds of ammunition were found in the assassin's pockets, as well as a razor-sharp knife; he certainly had the means, if not the will, to commit a massacre. 'Only one dead?' he demanded upon being arrested. 'I thought I could get more. I must have been slow.' In Brixton Prison, whilst awaiting his trial at the Old Bailey, Udham Singh went on a forty-two days hunger strike and had to be forcibly fed. He was tried and convicted on 4th June—which happened to be the day the new Prime Minister, Winston Churchill, announced to the House of Commons the 'miracle of deliverance' at Dunkirk. Mr. Justice ATKINSON had difficulty in pronouncing sentence of death, being constantly interrupted by the prisoner, who, to show his contempt for the hated British rule, spat upon the floor of the court and, gripping the dock rail, shouted, 'I am dying for a purpose.' He was hanged at Pentonville Prison on 25th June. (*See also* Madar Lal DHINGRA.)

Upchurch, Annie Luisa (Norah). *See* Frederick Herbert Charles FIELD.

V

Vengeance is in my heart, death in my hand,
Blood and revenge are hammering in my head.

Shakespeare: *Titus Andronicus*

Vachell, Charles Francis, K.C. (1854-1935), barrister of the Middle Temple (called 1886; silk 1905), was a legal wit in the high tradition of Lord DARLING and Rigby SWIFT, but since, unlike them, he hardly ever appeared in cases commanding general interest his stylish aphorisms, although much relished by judges and counsel, were only rarely reported. His appearance was deceptive; he looked excessively earnest-minded and solemn—an effect produced, no doubt, by his thick owl-like spectacles—and his thin, dry voice was precise to the point of pedantry. Yet he abounded in wit which, at its best, was delicious, always beautifully turned and finished, and only occasionally malicious, although he could, when he chose, be as annihilating as the young F. E. Smith. He enjoyed a fairly substantial practice on the Oxford Circuit and later in London, but somehow his success was never equal to his talents; one reason for that may have been that when he was not particularly interested in his brief he sometimes allowed that fact to be seen—with unfortunate results. He died on 5th November 1935, in his eighty-second year. Mr Vachell helped to present the Crown case against Herbert Rowse ARMSTRONG.

Vaquier, Jean Pierre, looked and behaved like a character in an improbable French farce. Square, squat, endlessly gesticulating, his hair *en brosse*, his bristling black beard smelling of violets (he used a perfumed brilliantine), he displayed precisely those forms of Gallic extravagance which are most outrageous and distasteful to the Anglo-Saxon mind. He was an outsize caricature of a Frenchman, of the sort often seen on the stage—and seldom anywhere else. But the engaging absurdities of 'Monsieur Froggy', the stage Frenchman, masked a tigerish cruelty and ferocity. The famous Blue Anchor murder is a story of passion, jealousy, and hatred, no less appalling because the principal character in it was a vain, ridiculous, posturing exhibitionist. In January

1924, Vaquier, a native of Niort in the Department of Aude, having been a telephonist in the French Army during the 1914-18 war, was engaged in demonstrating to the patrons of the Hotel Victoria at Biarritz the potentialities of the radio as a medium of popular entertainment. That is to say he had obtained the permission of the management to give a regular series of wireless concerts—using his own receiver—in the *salon*. It was thus that he became acquainted with a Mrs. Mabel Theresa Jones, who was recuperating at Biarritz after a nervous breakdown, brought on largely by her financial worries. She spoke no French; Vaquier had no English. This did not prevent the acquaintance-ship ripening into friendship, and friendship into something much more intimate, all at top speed; with the aid of a dictionary—purchased by Mrs. Jones at Vaquier's suggestion—they found that rudimentary conversation was not beyond them. In little more than a week they were sharing a double room at the more modestly priced Hotel Bayonne, also at Biarritz. The idyll was rudely interrupted by a telegram from the lady's husband, Mr. Alfred George Poynter Jones, licensee of the Blue Anchor, Byfleet, Surrey, inviting her to come home. Vaquier, in tears, begged her not to go, but could not prevail upon her. To soften the shock of parting he accompanied Mrs. Jones as far as Paris; from there she went on alone. Vaquier waited for twenty-four hours, then followed her to London, ostensibly to secure the patent rights of a sausage machine which he had invented. From the Russell Hotel in Bloomsbury he telegraphed to Mrs. Jones at the Blue Anchor: 'Arrived from Paris on business. Shall be very pleased to see you and to meet Mr. Jones. Perhaps you will inform me which evening.' (The English was supplied by a helpful receptionist at the hotel.) Five days later—on 14th February—Vaquier arrived unexpectedly and without luggage at the Blue Anchor, borrowed £14 from Mrs. Jones to pay his bill at the Russell Hotel, and proceeded to make himself at home and, as he hoped, indispensable. Mr. Jones was very ill at this time with congestion of the lungs, which made it easier for Vaquier and 'Mabs' (as he called her) to resume their former relationship. For a while it continued with something resembling the ardour of those first romantic days at the Hotel Bayonne. But presently, so far as Mrs. Jones's feelings were concerned, it began to wane. Unhappily, what was a fading infatuation to Mabel Jones was to her lover a raging passion by which he was entirely absorbed. Time and again Vaquier besought her to come away with him. She always refused—no doubt his absurdities were becoming a bit of a bore—and Vaquier perceived that before he could hope to obtain the absolute possession of the wife he must first get rid of the husband. The idea was not displeasing to him, for he was passionately jealous of Mr. Jones and of the rights he enjoyed; the pitilessly cruel means he selected to destroy this inoffensive man shows the measure of his hatred of him. On 1st March Vaquier went up to London. He called at a chemist's shop in Southampton Row, where, during his stay at the Russell Hotel, he had made sundry purchases, and had made himself known to the manager, who spoke excellent French. He explained that for the purposes of 'wireless experiments' he required various chemicals, including ·12 of a gramme (nearly two grains) of strychnine, a quantity sufficient to kill three or four people. After some hesitation the manager agreed to supply him. Vaquier signed the poison register—using the somewhat curious name of 'J. Wanker'— and returned with his purchases to Byfleet. He had observed that Mr. Jones, a heavy drinker, was in the habit of taking bromo salts in the morning to palliate the effects of overnight excesses; he further perceived that this provided him, ready made, with the opportunity he was looking for. There was a party at the Blue Anchor on the evening of 28th March. Mr. Jones retired to bed at one o'clock the next morning in a condition which suggested that he was likely to wake with a 'hangover'. He slept late, which was not surprising, and it was not until after half-past ten that morning that he went into the bar parlour for his bromo salts, which he always kept on the mantelpiece. The blue bottle was in its accustomed place. Mr. Jones poured a teaspoonful of the salts into half a glass of water, stirred the mixture, and drank it in one gulp. 'Oh, God! They're bitter,' he exclaimed. An interested spectator of this proceeding had been Monsieur Vaquier, who had been sitting in the bar parlour ever since he had come down for his breakfast coffee at seven o'clock. From his armchair by the mantelpiece he watched gravely whilst Mrs. Jones picked up the blue bottle and poured out some of the contents into her hand. She was startled to see that mixed with the salts were some crystals. She tasted them, tentatively, and found them excessively bitter. 'Daddy, they have been tampered with!' she cried. 'Quick—some salt and water!' Mrs. Jones poured the crystals back into the bottle and hurried into the kitchen to prepare an emetic. She took the bottle with her, and put it into one of the drawers of the kitchen dresser. Mr. Jones followed his wife into the kitchen; she gave him an emetic, and he was violently sick. Afterwards he complained of being 'numb and cold'. Vaquier helped to carry him upstairs, and a doctor was called. A few minutes later Vaquier came hurrying into the kitchen and stammered out to the cook, Mrs. Fisher, a few of the English words he had culled from the dictionary. Mrs. Fisher understood him to say: 'Medicine—doctor—quick.' At the same time he picked up from the dresser a bottle of Kruschen Salts and held it up for Mrs. Fisher to see. She gathered that he was asking for Mr. Jones's 'medicine', his bromo salts, and she pointed to the drawer where Mrs. Jones had put the bottle. Vaquier went to the drawer, took out the bottle, and left the kitchen with it. Dr. Frederick Carle arrived at 11.50 a.m. Mr. Jones, in an extremity of terror, was calling out for help, but he was already beyond medical aid. He died shortly afterwards in the extremely violent—and agonizing—convulsions which are typical of strychnine poisoning. Dr. Carle asked for the bromo salts bottle. Mrs. Jones went to the kitchen dresser for it. The bottle was there, but in a different place—in the front, not at the back, where she had left it. There was nothing in it but a little water; it looked as if it had lately been washed. (It had. After washing the bottle out, Vaquier had been able to smuggle it back into the drawer whilst the cook was busy in the scullery.) On the floor of the bar parlour Dr. Carle found some of the crystals which Mrs. Jones had spilt when pouring them back into the bottle; he scooped them into an envelope and sent them away for analysis. (They duly revealed traces of strychnine, as did the water which had been used to wash out the bottle.) Rather over half a grain of strychnine was found in the organs of the body. That is a minimum fatal dose; allowing for the vomiting, it is probable that Mr. Jones had swallowed something not far short of two grains. Vaquier stayed on at the Blue Anchor for a few days longer, maintaining the most affable relations with the crime reporters of Fleet Street who, as it may be imagined, descended upon Byfleet in force. Mrs. Jones showed him very clearly that she suspected him of being her husband's murderer, but it was not until he was about to leave the Blue Anchor for his new quarters at the Railway Hotel, Woking, that she taxed him with it to his face. She then said to him: 'You have assassinated Mr. Jones.' Vaquier had made sufficient progress with his English to understand her and to reply, 'Yes, Mabs— for you,' he said. 'I would have killed you', remarked Mrs. Jones, 'if I knew you would have done a thing like that.' After his move to Woking—on 4th April—Vaquier continued to hobnob with the newspaper reporters. His vanity was enormous. He liked to see his name in the Press and, better still, his photograph. This turned out to be his undoing. On 16th April the manager of the chemist's shop in Southampton Row happened to see a newspaper photograph of Vaquier; he recognized him as the garrulous Frenchman who had signed himself 'J. Wanker' in the poison register, and he at once got into touch with Scotland Yard. Thus were the police provided with the 'missing link'. It was the proof they were waiting for that Vaquier had had strychnine in his possession. Now they pounced. Vaquier was arrested at the Railway Hotel, Woking, on 19th April. In reply to the charge of murder he said (through an interpreter): 'I assure you on the tomb of my mother that I am innocent, and that I will make known tomorrow he who administered the poison. . . . I beg of you—do not put me in prison if you can help it. I prefer to die. You will see—I am not guilty.' Vaquier's trial before Mr. Justice AVORY took place at Guildford Assizes in July. As is usual at a poison trial, the prosecution was handled by a Law Officer of the Crown—in this case the Attorney-General, Sir Patrick HASTINGS K.C.; with him was Sir Edward Marshall HALL K.C. The accused was defended by Sir Henry CURTIS BENNETT K.C. The four-day trial was a disappointment to Vaquier, or, rather, he was disappointed that his own part in it was not more spectacular. He was disgusted that he was not 'confronted with his accusers' according to the French system, for he had had agreeable visions of himself hurling defiance at false and perjured witnesses, demanding justice from a bullying judge—whom he would quell with his superior eloquence—and, in the end, emerging from his heroic ordeal triumphant and unscathed, to the astonishment and admiration of the Court, and indeed of the entire British nation. The reality was dismayingly drab. The sphinx-like Mr. Justice Avory was not the ranting *Monsieur le Président* of his imagination. There were no opportunities to defy or to quell. Everything was flat, colourless, and conversational. The outraged Vaquier found that he was required to sit still and allow other people to do the talking. He fell back upon various devices to divert the attention of the Court to himself. He kept the warders continuously busy sharpening pencils for him while he took copious notes of all the evidence, which was interpreted to him one sentence at a time. When a point appealed to him he was sure to offer some comment upon it—usually a frivolous one. For instance, when one of the Crown witnesses described himself as 'a builder and undertaker', Vaquier, highly delighted, remarked to the interpreter, 'Ah, he houses them above and below ground.' His own evidence was a tissue of absurdities. He insisted that he had bought the strychnine to oblige Mrs. Jones's solicitor, a complete stranger to him, who had wanted it to destroy a dog. Under cross-examination by the Attorney-General he said that he had signed the poison register 'J. Wanker' because he had been told that 'When you buy poison you never sign your own name'.

> *Q:* Who told you that?
> *A:* The solicitor.
> *Q:* Did the gentleman who asked you to buy the poison tell you to sign a false name?
> *A:* Yes.
> *Q:* Did it strike you as odd that a complete stranger, who wanted to poison a dog, was telling you to sign a false name?

A: No.

Q: Do I understand you to say that you signed a false name merely because a complete stranger asked you to?

A: Yes; if he had told me to sign my name I should have signed it.

This passage sufficiently indicates the style and tone of Vaquier's performance in the witness-box. It was not until the very end that the Court had a glimpse of the real man, as opposed to the mountebank. It was not a pretty sight. Vaquier listened with obvious incredulity as the interpreter translated for him the jury's inevitable verdict of 'Guilty'. Then, while the death sentence was being pronounced, he screamed abuse at the judge and jury, pounding the dock with his fist. 'I swear on my mother's and my father's graves, still fresh, that I am quite innocent of the crime of which I have been accused. . . . You have given an iniquitous verdict!' (So much was translated by the interpreter; he did not make any further attempt to keep up with the torrent of words that continued to pour from Vaquier's lips.) 'I can listen to nothing more,' said Mr Justice Avory, in his ice-cold voice. 'Let him be removed.' Vaquier, still shouting and struggling, was dragged from the dock. There was a similar violent scene at the end of his unsuccessful application to the Court of Criminal Appeal to have the verdict put aside. '*Je demande la justice, Monsieur le Président!*' he screamed, as harassed warders struggled to break his grip on the dock rail. Fifteen days later—on 12th August—Vaquier was hanged at Wandsworth Prison.

[*I.*

Vassileva, Nina. *See* SIEGE OF SIDNEY STREET.

W-Z

Wither'd murder
Alarum'd by his sentinel, the wolf.

Shakespeare: *Macbeth*

Waddingham, Dorothea Nancy, liked to call herself 'Nurse' Waddingham, which, since she presided over a so-called 'Nursing Home for Aged and Chronic Cases', was quite understandable. She had, in fact, no professional qualifications and no training, other than the knowledge she had picked up whilst working as a ward maid at Burton-on-Trent Workhouse Infirmary. It should be said, however, that those ailing and aged folk who were from time to time accommodated at Nurse Waddingham's 'Home' at 32 Devon Drive, Nottingham, appear to have been well looked after, and rarely had cause for complaint. Certainly, Mrs. Baguley and her invalid daughter, Ada Louisa Baguley, who moved in in January 1935, were content with the arrangements made for their maintenance and care. Nurse Waddingham, however, was considerably less content, and as time went by became increasingly impatient with her own folly in having accepted two patients who required far more attention than they probably had the right to expect in return for the meagre weekly sum they paid for their keep—thirty shillings each. (Mrs. Baguley was eighty-nine, too old and frail to do much for herself; her daughter, aged fifty, was a cripple who for twenty years past had suffered from creeping paralysis, and was now almost entirely helpless.) Nurse Waddingham complained to a cousin of Miss Baguley about the inadequacy of the fees she was collecting from these exacting patients, but no offer was made to increase them. However, some weeks later Ada Baguley sent for her solicitor, Mr. Lane, and told him she wished to settle the whole of her small property upon Nurse Waddingham, who, she said, had promised to look after her and Mrs. Baguley for the rest of their lives. Mr. Lane managed to dissuade her from this imprudent course, but she nonetheless insisted upon some arrangement being made whereby, sooner or later, Nurse Waddingham would get the money. Perceiving that Miss Baguley was set upon this, the solicitor proposed that she should make a new will in Nurse Waddingham's favour. This was done on 6th May 1935, a man named **Ronald Joseph Sullivan** being introduced as an equal beneficiary with Nurse Waddingham; to them, jointly, Ada Baguley bequeathed all her property (which amounted to nearly £2,000 gross value), 'in consideration that they have undertaken to look after me and my mother for and during our joint lives'. Sullivan's position requires some explanation. He was Dorothea Waddingham's lover, at thirty-nine a man five years older than herself, who lived with her at the nursing home and helped her to run it, performing most of the domestic chores, some of the nursing, and all the heavy work. His hand is seen in some of the episodes which, taken together, were to bring Nurse Waddingham to grief. On 12th May 1935 Mrs. Baguley died. Greatly distressed, her daughter Ada attended the funeral in her wheel-chair; she, herself, had only four more months to live. Miss Baguley's death occurred on 11th September, and Dr. G. H. H. Manfield certified the cause of it as cerebral hæmorrhage, due to cardio-vascular degeneration, or weakness of the arteries of the heart. Arrangements were made for the body to be cremated. So far everything had gone smoothly for Nurse Waddingham. She was now to overreach herself. A letter addressed to Dr. Manfield, dated 29th August, written in Sullivan's hand, but bearing Ada Baguley's undoubted signature, was handed to Dr. Cyril Banks, Medical Officer of Health for the City of Nottingham, whose consent was required before there could be a cremation there. The letter read:

To Dr. Manfield,
    I desire to be cremated at my death, for health's sake. And it is my wish to remain with Nurse and my last wish is my relatives shall not know of my death.
Signed,
Ada Baguley
Witness, R. J. Sullivan

Dr. Banks, it is hardly necessary to say, regarded this peculiar missive with some suspicion. He communicated with the Chief Constable, who intervened to stop the cremation and to remove the body for a post-mortem examination. Analysis of the contents of the stomach, spleen, kidneys, and part of the liver revealed the presence of 3·192 grains of morphine. The discovery that Ada Baguley had died from acute morphine poisoning made it necessary and desirable that Mrs. Baguley's body should be exhumed from its grave in Caunton Churchyard. Dr. Roche LYNCH, the Home Office analyst, found in it traces of pseudo-morphine, indicating to him that 'the deceased had taken a considerable quantity of morphine or heroin, or both, prior to death; at all events, a quantity in excess of a medicinal dose'. He was 'driven to the view' that Mrs. Baguley, like her daughter, had died by morphine poisoning. Both Nurse Waddingham and Sullivan were placed on trial before Mr. Justice Goddard (afterwards Lord GODDARD) at Nottingham Assizes in February 1936, charged jointly with the murder of Ada Baguley. But after hearing the Crown witnesses the judge ruled that the evidence against Sullivan was not sufficient, and directed the jury to return a formal verdict of 'Not Guilty'. Sullivan was thereupon discharged, leaving Dorothea Waddingham, short, plump, and homely, to face the capital charge alone. She did not deny that she had given morphine to Miss Baguley—but she had done so only upon the instructions of Dr. Manfield, who had left with her ten tablets, to be used at her discretion for the relief of the patient. Dr. Manfield, however, denied that there had been any occasion to prescribe morphia tablets for Miss Baguley, and he had certainly not done so. He had, on the other hand, prescribed morphia for another of Nurse Waddingham's patients, a Mrs. Kemp, who had died at the nursing home in February 1935. It was the contention of the prosecution, which was in the hands of Mr. Norman Birkett K.C. (afterwards Lord BIRKETT), that Nurse Waddingham had poisoned Miss Baguley with some of the left-over tablets prescribed for Mrs. Kemp. Nurse Waddingham was found guilty, but the jury added to their verdict a strong recommendation to mercy. This did not avail her. On 16th April 1936, Dorothea Nancy Waddingham—'Nurse' Waddingham to the last—was hanged at Winson Green Prison, Birmingham.

[*30, 72, 94, 103.*]

Walls, Inspector Arthur. *See* John WILLIAMS.

Walters, Annie. *See* Amelia SACH.

Waterhouse, Lily. *See* Louie CALVERT.

Watson, Lionel Rupert Nathan, aged thirty-one, a bakelite moulder, poisoned Phyllis Elizabeth Crocker, whom he had bigamously married, and her eighteen-months-old daughter, Eileen Alice, and buried the bodies in the back garden of his house in Goring Way, Greenford, Middlesex. On 26th May 1941 he was seen digging in the garden; on 30th June the bodies were recovered from a two-foot deep grave covered over with flagstones. Watson was tried at the Old Bailey before Mr. Justice Cassels in September. He swore that upon returning home on 19th May he had found Phyllis Crocker and the baby lying dead. 'I was in a bit of a fix', he explained, 'because I had bigamously married her. I could not call in a doctor owing to that. I thought of my children, my job, and my people. . . . I dug a pit in the garden and when it was dark I put the bodies in.' The jury found Watson guilty of murder and he was sentenced to death. He was hanged at Pentonville Prison on 12th November.

[*34.*

Webb, Alfred Charles Bertram. *See* Frederick STEWART.

Webster, Richard Everard. *See* Viscount ALVERSTONE.

Whiteley, William. *See* Horace George RAYNER.

Williams, John, murdered a police inspector at Eastbourne in October 1912. Behind the façade of this commonplace crime was a strange story of love and hate, jealousy and betrayal. Williams was a Raffles in real life, a well-educated young man of good family who had drifted into a life of crime. He lived with a girl named Florence Seymour, who was about to bear his child. The most intimate of his companions, who were mostly criminals like himself, was a certain Edgar Power; out of jealousy of the girl, this unpleasant individual, while professing undying friendship for Williams, watched and waited for an opportunity to destroy him. He was poised and ready when it came. On 9th October 1912 Williams was caught in the act of breaking into a house in Southcliffe Avenue, Eastbourne, the home of Countess Sztaray. A taxi-driver who saw him crouched on the portico above the front door warned the Countess, and she telephoned the police. Inspector Arthur Walls arrived, to find Williams still there. He called out to him to come down. For answer, he received a revolver bullet which killed him on the spot. A few days later, Edgar Power provided the Eastbourne Borough Police with the name of the murderer. Williams, he said, had left his girl, Florence Seymour, sitting on the beach while he had gone away to break into the house. Returning to the beach after the murder, he had confessed to the girl that he had 'shot a policeman'. Then and there they had buried the revolver in the shingle. Without turning a hair, Power described to the police how Williams had come to him for help, and how he had given him money so that he could escape to London. Grateful though the police were for this information, they perceived that a prosecution would require something more substantial to support it than the word of a man like Edgar Power, a known criminal. A trap was ingeniously prepared, the success of which depended upon Power's considerable talent for duplicity and treacherous dealing. In his rôle of devoted friend, Power called upon Florence

Seymour at her lodging in Eastbourne. He told her that the police knew all there was to know about the crime, and that the only chance of saving Williams was to retrieve the gun from its hiding-place on the beach before that, too, was discovered. The unsuspecting girl went with Power to the beach. Almost at once she found the spot where the revolver was hidden and dug it out of the shingle—at which point police officers, who had been watching at a little distance, closed in on the couple and took them both into custody. The arrest of Power was, of course, a pretence, since in the setting and springing of the trap his position had merely been that of a police agent. But poor, terrified Florence Seymour could not know this; to her he was the faithful friend whose efforts to help Williams and herself had landed him in a situation of great peril. But Power made light of his own position; he affected to be much more concerned about hers. The only way to save herself from a charge of murder, he assured her, was to tell the police the whole truth. Torn this way and that, not knowing what to do for the best, the girl accepted this earnest advice, and made a full statement to the police, in which she said that after the murder Williams had confessed his guilt to her. Williams was arrested and brought before the magistrates. Florence Seymour was questioned about her statement —and confirmed it line by line. The prisoner was committed to stand his trial at Lewes Assizes, before Mr. Justice Channell, in December, when he was defended by young Mr. Patrick HASTINGS, whose first murder case this was. Apparently with some kindly, but mistaken intention of shielding him from the eyes of the curious, the police took the accused to and from the court each day with a hood drawn over his head; this, of course, secured the maximum public attention for the 'Hooded Man Murder Trial', as it was gleefully described in the newspapers. The prosecution based its case almost entirely upon the girl's statement, but when Florence Seymour, her quite exceptional beauty hardly at all impaired by her approaching pregnancy, went into the witness-box, her first words were that she knew nothing whatever about the murder. Not a word of her statement was true, she said; she had made it only because Power had told her that otherwise she would be charged with murder. Weeping, she was led from the box, a piteous figure. Edgar Power made an odious impression upon the Court with his story of betrayal, particularly betrayal of the girl, whom he had deceived with protestations of the most tender affection at a time when the police were, so to say, standing at his very elbow. Many years afterwards, when he came to publish his book, *Cases in Court*, Sir Patrick Hastings wrote of Power: 'Never in my life have I met a more utterly contemptible human being.' Mr. Justice Channell's summing-up probably sealed Williams's fate. The jury were directed that if they accepted the truth of Florence Seymour's statement—confirmed before the magistrates and only retracted at the trial—they were entitled to regard it as evidence in the case. They returned a verdict of 'Guilty' and the prisoner was sentenced to death. Soon afterwards Florence Seymour gave birth to his child. Williams was allowed to see the baby in prison. Sir Patrick Hastings movingly describes the scene: 'The warder in attendance, with a not unusual kindness, took the child from its mother and gave it to him. He showed no sign of emotion as he kissed it affectionately, and then pressed a small piece of prison bread into its hand, saying as he did so, "Now nobody can ever say that your father has never given you anything." The next day he was hanged.'

[*89*.

Williamson, Thomas Henry. *See* Wallace BENTON.

Wilson, Field-Marshal Sir Henry. *See* Reginald DUNN.

Wood, Ivy Lydia. *See* Arthur BEARD.

Woodhouse, Elinor Drinkwater. *See* Charles HOUGHTON.

Woodhouse, Joan, aged twenty-seven, a librarian at the National Central Library in Bloomsbury, London, was found strangled in a thicket in Arundel Park, Sussex, on 31st July 1948—Bank Holiday week. Although his inquiries were extended over many months, the experienced Scotland Yard officer in charge of the case was unable to collect sufficient evidence to justify an arrest. Presumably the matter would have rested there had it not been for the pertinacity of two elderly ladies, aunts of the dead girl, who lived in Yorkshire, and who were so dissatisfied with the negative results of the 'official' investigation that they determined to make their own inquiries, independently of the police. To this end they engaged the services of a private detective, who occupied himself with the case for nearly two years. The dramatic sequel came in July 1950, when the father of the murdered girl applied to the magistrates at Arundel for a warrant for the arrest of Thomas Philip George Stillwell, a labourer, the man who on that July day two years before had gone to the police station to report his discovery of the dead body of Joan Woodhouse. The application, made under the Indictable Offences Act, 1848, was granted, and in due course Stillwell appeared at an improvised court held in Arundel's seventeenth-century Town Hall to face a charge of murder—the first instigated by a private individual since 1865. As it is only the Director of Public Prosecutions who can prosecute on the capital charge, he—or, rather, his representative, Mr. J. S. Bass—was required to present the case against Stillwell. It was made clear at the start that the Director thought that case a poor one. Mr. Bass told the magistrates: 'It is right that I should say at once that the evidence against this man is circumstantial. There is not one single piece of evidence which goes directly to show that he was a party to the commission of that crime. If you come to the conclusion that the evidence does no more than to show that he had the opportunity to commit this crime if he so desired, I submit that it would not be proper to commit this man to take his trial.' Thirty-five witnesses were called. Their examination and cross-examination lasted several days. At the end, the Bench of five magistrates—two of them women—stated: 'We are of the unanimous opinion that there is not sufficient evidence to justify putting the accused on trial.' Stillwell was accordingly discharged—amid cheers.

[*149.*

Woodhouse, Martha Gordon. *See* Charles HOUGHTON.

Woolmington, Reginald, a farm labourer aged twenty-one, was convicted in February 1935 of the murder of his seventeen-years-old wife. The far-reaching consequences of that conviction entitle the case to be regarded as one of the most important to be decided in modern times. For, arising out of a passage in the summing-up of the presiding judge, Mr. Justice SWIFT, the House of Lords was presently to overturn an heretical view of the criminal law which had been accepted without demur by successive generations of lawyers for the best part of two hundred years. On the morning of 10th December 1934, Violet, the girl-wife of Reginald Woolmington, was shot dead in the kitchen of her mother's house at Milborne Port, Sherborne, Dorset. 'It was jealousy, I suppose,' said Woolmington when he was charged with murder. He was put up for trial at Taunton Assizes before Mr. Justice Finlay in the following January, but the jury failed to agree. The case was transferred to Bristol Assizes, where in February the prisoner was tried a second time. In the witness-box Woolmington said that after vainly pleading with his wife to come back to him he had pulled out a gun from underneath his coat; as he had done so it had gone off accidentally. When Mr. Justice Swift came to sum up, he quoted a passage from *Archbold's Criminal Pleading*, the criminal lawyer's 'Bible':

All homicide is presumed to be malicious and murder, unless the contrary appears from circumstances of alleviation, excuse, or justification. In every charge of murder, the fact of killing being first proved, all the circumstances of accident, necessity, or infirmity are to be satisfactorily proved by the prisoner unless they arise out of the evidence produced against him, for the law presumeth the fact to have been founded in malice until the contrary appeareth.

These words had been taken over by *Archbold* from *Foster's Crown Law*, published as long ago as 1762. Mr. Justice Swift then paraphrased the quotation in his own words, as follows:

If once you find that a person has been guilty of killing another it is for the person who has been guilty of the killing to satisfy you that the crime is something less than the murder with which he is charged.

The jury found Woolmington guilty of murder, and he was sentenced to death. He appealed to the Court of Criminal Appeal, where his counsel, Mr. J. D. CASSWELL, argued that the words in *Foster's Crown Law*, adopted by *Archbold* and by other authorities, offended against the deep-rooted principle that a man is innocent until the Crown has proved him guilty, and that their citation by Mr. Justice Swift amounted to misdirection. This argument was brushed aside by Mr. Justice AVORY in announcing the court's decision to disallow the appeal. All that he said of the *Archbold* citation was: 'No doubt there is ample authority for that statement of the law.' He did add, however: 'It may be that it would have been better if the learned judge had said to the jury that if they entertained reasonable doubt whether they could accept his [Woolmington's] explanation they should either acquit him altogether or convict him of manslaughter only.' Being convinced that the words cited must be wrong in law, in spite of the summary treatment of the argument by the appeal judges, Mr. Casswell asked the Attorney-General, Sir Thomas Inskip K.C. (afterwards Lord Caldecote), for his fiat, so that the case could be taken to the House of Lords. The Attorney-General's fiat is reserved for cases involving points of law of exceptional importance. Since the establishment of the Court of Criminal Appeal in 1907 it had repeatedly been applied for but rarely granted, and for the past fifteen years not at all. In this instance Sir Thomas Inskip considered the point a proper and necessary one to be decided by the House of Lords, and for that purpose he issued his fiat. On 4th April 1935, the point which appeared to have given so little trouble to the appeal judges was argued afresh before the Lord Chancellor (Lord Sankey); the Lord Chief Justice (Lord HEWART); Lord ATKIN; Lord Tomlin, and Lord Wright. Mr. Casswell was 'led' on this occasion by Mr. (later Sir)

Terence O'CONNOR K.C. For two days the bemused farm labourer, Reginald Woolmington, sat in the gilded chamber of the House of Lords in the custody of a warder whilst counsel in silk gowns and full-bottomed wigs discussed with the Law Lords the fundamental principles of the criminal law. The even-toned arguments circled around and about his bewildered head, and for most of the time soared well above it. For him the examination of a phrase penned by a learned commentator in the reign of George III was not an intellectual exercise or an essay in abstract justice, but rather the means whereby he might hope to save his life—or be made to lose it. In the end his life was saved. At the close of the second day the Lord Chancellor announced that the conviction would be quashed. Their Lordships, he added, would state the reasons for that decision later. Reginald Woolmington was promptly released. It was the first time in the history of this country that a man lying under sentence of death for murder had been freed by the House of Lords. Six weeks later Lord Sankey delivered judgment; the words he chose were memorable.

> Throughout the web of the English criminal law one golden thread is always to be seen—that it is the duty of the prosecution to prove the prisoner's guilt. . . . The principle that the prosecution must prove the guilt of the prisoner is part of the common law of England, and no attempt to whittle it down can be entertained.

Foster was wrong; past decisions based upon Foster's text were wrong; the summing-up of Mr. Justice Swift was wrong. The jury had therefore been misdirected and the conviction could not stand. Thus it was that a long-accepted view of the criminal law, supported by much respectable authority (including Halsbury's Laws of England), became, as it were overnight, the 'Woolmington Misdirection'. Assured of a permanent place in the textbooks of case law, this farm labourer may count, at any rate, upon a sort of immortality.

[61.

Wright, Annie Bella, See Ronald Vivian LIGHT.

Wright, Sir Robert Samuel (1839-1904). Judge of the King's Bench Division of the High Court (1890-1904). Called to the Bar by the Inner Temple in 1865, he practised on the Northern Circuit and was afterwards Junior Counsel to the Treasury; he was raised to the Bench in 1890. Mr. Justice Wright, an erudite lawyer and a classical scholar of some eminence—he edited the Golden Treasury of Ancient

Greek Poetry and the *Golden Treasury of Greek Prose*—was inclined to be impatient of minds inferior to his own, a trait which showed itself on the Bench in a certain sharpness of temper. He was at the same time an extremely solemn and conscientious judge, if occasionally somewhat over-hasty in his judgments. Liberal in politics—he might almost be described as a Radical—and humane in his views, he was sometimes criticized for the supposed leniency of his sentences, at a period when, in the treatment of criminals, severity was admired. Failing health compelled him to offer his resignation to the Lord Chancellor in June 1904. Acceptance of that offer was deferred in the hope that the judge's health might improve, but he died two months later, at the age of sixty-five. He presided over the trial of Samuel Herbert DOUGAL.

Wyllie, Sir William Hutt Curzon. *See* Madar Lal DHINGRA.

Zemenides, Angelos. *See* Theodosios PETROU.

BIBLIOGRAPHY

1. *Notable British Trials* (William Hodge)
2. *Old Bailey Trials* (Jarrold)
3. *Famous Trials* (Geoffrey Bles)
4. ABINGER, EDWARD: *Forty Years At The Bar* (Hutchinson, 1930)
5. ABRAHAMS, GERALD: *According To The Evidence* (Cassell, 1958)
6. ADAM, HARGRAVE LEE: *The Police Encyclopædia* (Blackfriars Publishing Co. *n.d.*)
7.   *do.*   : *C.I.D.* (Sampson Low, 1931)
8.   *do.*   : *Murder By Persons Unknown* (Collins, 1931)
9.   *do.*   : *Murder Most Mysterious* (Sampson Low, 1932)
10. ALEXANDER, GILCHRIST: *After Court Hours* (Butterworth, 1950)
11. ALVERSTONE, VISCOUNT: *Recollections Of Bar And Bench* (Edward Arnold, 1914)
12. *Anatomy Of Murder*, by various hands (John Lane, the Bodley Head, 1936)
13. ANDORSEN, HAROLD F. (ed.): *Memoirs Of Lord Salvesen* (W. & R. Chambers, 1949)
14. ASHLEY, F. W.: *My Sixty Years In The Law* (John Lane, the Bodley Head, 1936)
15. ASHTON-WOLFE, H.: *The Underworld* (Hurst & Blackett, 1926)
16. BANCROFT, GEORGE PLEYDELL: *Stage And Bar* (Faber & Faber, 1939)
17. BECHHOFER ROBERTS, C. E.: *Lord Birkenhead* (Mills & Boon, 1926)
18.   *do.*   : *Sir Travers Humphreys* (John Lane, the Bodley Head, 1936)
19. BELL, EDWARD A.: *These Meddlesome Attorneys* (Martin Secker, 1939)
20. BERRETT, Chief-Inspector JAMES: *When I Was At Scotland Yard* (Sampson Low, Marston, 1932)
21. BEVERIDGE, ex-Chief-Superintendent PETER: *Inside The C.I.D.* (Evans, 1957)
22. BIRKENHEAD, LORD: *Contemporary Personalities* (Cassell, 1924)
23.   *do.*   : *Famous Trials Of History* (Hutchinson, 1926)
24.   *do.*   : *More Famous Trials* (Hutchinson, 1928)
25. BIRMINGHAM, GEORGE A. [Cannon Hannay]: *Murder Most Foul* (Chatto & Windus, 1929)

26. BIXLEY, WILLIAM: *The Guilty And The Innocent* (Souvenir Press, 1957)
27. BOLITHO, WILLIAM: *Murder For Profit* (Jonathan Cape, 1926)
28. BOSANQUET, Sir RONALD: *The Oxford Circuit* (Thames Bank Publishing Co., 1951)
29. BOWEN-ROWLANDS, ERNEST: *In Court And Out Of Court* (Hutchinson, 1925)
30. BOWKER, A. E.: *Behind The Bar* (Staples Press, 1947)
31. BRICE, A. H. M.: *Look Upon The Prisoner* (Hutchinson, 1933)
32. BROAD, LEWIS: *The Innocence Of Edith Thompson* (Hutchinson, 1952)
33. BROOKES, CANON J. R.: *Murder In Fact And Fiction* (Hurst & Blackett, 1926)
34. BROWNE, DOUGLAS G., and TULLETT E. V.: *Bernard Spilsbury: His Life And Cases* (Harrap, 1951)
35. BROWNE, DOUGLAS G., and BROCK, ALAN: *Fingerprints* (Harrap, 1953)
36. BUCKNILL, Sir ALFRED: *The Nature Of Evidence* (Skeffington, 1953)
37. CADOGAN, Hon. EDWARD: *The Roots Of Evil* (John Murray, 1937)
38. CALVERT, E. ROY: *Capital Punishment In The 20th Century* (Putnam, 1927)
39.   *do.*   : *The Death Penalty Inquiry* (Gollancz, 1931)
40. CARR, JOHN DICKSON: *The Life Of Sir Arthur Conan Doyle* (John Murray, 1949)
41. CASTLE, H. G.: *Case For The Prosecution* (Naldrett Press, 1956)
42. CHERRILL, ex-Superintendent FREDERICK R.: *Cherrill Of The Yard* (Harrap, 1954)
43. CHILDS, Major-General Sir WYNDHAM: *Episodes And Reflections* (Cassell, 1930)
44. COLERIDGE, LORD: *This For Remembrance* (T. Fisher Unwin, 1925)
45. CREW, ALBERT: *The Old Bailey* (Ivor Nicholson & Watson, 1933)
46. CURTIN, PHILIP (Mrs. Belloc-Lowndes): *Noted Murder Mysteries* (Simpkin Marshall, Hamilton, Kent, 1914)
47. CUTHBERT, C. R. M.: *Science And The Detection Of Crime* (Hutchinson, 1958)
48. DEANS, R. STORRY: *Notable Trials: Difficult Cases* (Chapman & Hall, 1932)
49. DEARDEN, HAROLD: *The Mind Of The Murderer* (Geoffrey Bles, 1930)
50.   *do.*   : *Some Cases Of Sir Bernard Spilsbury And Others* (Hutchinson, 1934)
51.   *do.*   : *Aspects Of Murder* (Staples Press, 1951)
52. DICKENS, Sir HENRY FIELDING: *Recollections* (Heinemann, 1934)
53. DILNOT, GEORGE: *Triumphs Of Detection* (Geoffrey Bles, 1929)

BIBLIOGRAPHY

54. DOUTHWAITE, L. C.: *Mass Murder* (John Long, 1928)
55. DUKE, WINIFRED: *Six Trials* (Gollancz, 1934)
56. EDDOWES, MICHAEL: *The Man On Your Conscience* (Cassell, 1955)
57. EDDY, J. P.: *Mystery Of Peter The Painter* (Stevens & Sons, 1946)
58. ENSOR, DAVID: *I Was A Public Prosecutor* (Robert Hale, 1958)
59. FABIAN, ex-Superintendent ROBERT: *Fabian Of The Yard* (Naldrett Press, 1950)
60.   *do.*   : *London After Dark* (Naldrett Press, 1954)
61. FAY, E. S.: *The Life Of Mr. Justice Swift* (Methuen, 1939)
62. FELSTEAD, S. T.: *Sir Richard Muir* (John Lane, The Bodley Head, 1927)
63.   *do.*   : *Shades Of Scotland Yard* (John Long, *n.d.*)
64. FIELDING, CECIL: *Justice Triumphant* (John Long, 1958)
65. FIRMIN, STANLEY: *Scotland Yard: The Inside Story* (Hutchinson, 1948)
66.   *do.*   : *Murderers In Our Midst* (Hutchinson, 1955)
67. FORDHAM, EDWARD WILFRED: *Notable Cross-Examinations* (Constable, 1951)
68. FURNEAUX, RUPERT: *The Medical Murderer* (Elek Press, 1957)
69. GARDINER, GERALD: *Capital Punishment As A Deterrent* (Gollancz, 1956)
70. GARSIA, MARSTON: *Criminal Law And Procedure In A Nutshell* (Sweet & Maxwell, 1953)
71. GILES, F. T.: *The Criminal Law* (Penguin Books, 1954)
72. GLAISTER, Professor JOHN: *The Power Of Poison* (Christopher Johnson, 1954)
73. GODWIN, GEORGE: *Crime And Social Action* (Watts & Co., 1956)
74. GOODWIN, JOHN G.: *Insanity And The Criminal* (Hutchinson, 1923)
75. GOWERS, Sir ERNEST: *A Life For A Life?* (Chatto & Windus, 1956)
76. GRAHAM, EVELYN: *Lord Darling And His Famous Trials* (Hutchinson, 1929)
77.   *do.*   : *Fifty Years Of Famous Judges* (John Long, 1930)
78. GRIBBLE, LEONARD: *Famous Manhunts* (John Long, 1953)
79.   *do.*   : *Adventures In Murder* (John Long, 1954)
80.   *do.*   : *Triumphs Of Scotland Yard* (John Long, 1955)
81.   *do.*   : *Famous Judges And Their Trials* (John Long, 1957)
82. GRIMSHAW, ERIC, and JONES, GLYN: *Lord Goddard: His Career And Cases* (Allan Wingate, 1958)
83. HAESTIER, RICHARD: *Dead Men Tell Tales* (John Long, 1934)

84. HARRISON, RICHARD: *Whitehall 1212: The Story Of The Police Of London* (Jarrold, 1947)
85.   *do.*   : *Criminal Calendar* (Jarrold, 1951)
86.   *do.*   : *Criminal Calendar II* (Jarrold, 1952)
87.   *do.*   : *Foul Deeds Will Rise* (John Long, 1958)
88. HASTINGS, Sir PATRICK: *Autobiography* (Heinemann, 1948)
89.   *do.*   : *Cases In Court* (Heinemann, 1949)
90. HOPKINS, R. THURSTON: *Life and Death At The Old Bailey* (Herbert Jenkins, 1935)
91. HORWELL, JOHN E.: *Horwell Of The Yard* (Andrew Melrose, 1947)
92. HOSKINS, PERCY: *They Almost Escaped* (Hutchinson, 1937)
93. HOWGRAVE-GRAHAM, H. M.: *Light And Shade At Scotland Yard* (John Murray, 1947)
94. HUGGET, RENÉE, and BERRY, PAUL: *Daughters Of Cain* (Allen & Unwin, 1956)
95. HUMPHREYS, CHRISTMAS: *Seven Murderers* (Heinemann, 1931)
96. HUMPHREYS, Sir TRAVERS: *Criminal Days* (Hodder & Stoughton, 1946)
97.   *do.*   : *A Book Of Trials* (Heinemann, 1953)
98. HYDE, E. MONTGOMERY: *Cases That Changed The Law* (Heinemann, 1951)
99.   *do.*   : *United In Crime* (Heinemann, 1955)
100. JACKSON, STANLEY: *The Life And Cases Of Mr. Justice Humphreys* (Odhams Press, *n.d.*)
101. JACOBS, T. C. H.: *Cavalcade Of Murder* (Stanley Paul, 1955)
102.   *do.*   : *Aspects Of Murder* (Stanley Paul, 1956)
103.   *do.*   : *Pageant Of Murder* (Stanley Paul, 1956)
104. JERVIS, Rev. EUSTACE: *Twenty-Five Years In Six Prisons* (T. Fisher Unwin, 1925)
105. JERVIS, Sir JOHN, *On The Office And Duties Of Coroners* 7th edition, 1927. Ed. by F. Danford Thomas (Sweet & Maxwell and Stevens & Sons)
106. JESSE, F. TENNYSON: *Murder And Its Motives* (Heinemann, 1924; and in a new edition, Harrap, 1952)
107.   *do.*   : *Comments On Cain* (Heinemann, 1948)
108. JOWITT, EARL: *Some Were Spies* (Hodder & Stoughton, 1954)
109. JOYCE, JAMES AVERY: *Justice At Work* (Chapman and Hall, 1952)
110. *Kenny's Outlines Of Criminal Law*: Ed. J. W. C. Turner (Cambridge University Press, 1952)
111. KINGSTON, CHARLES: *Remarkable Rogues* (John Lane, the Bodley Head, *n.d.*)

112. KINGSTON, CHARLES: *Dramatic Days At The Old Bailey* (Stanley Paul, 1923)
113.   do.   : *Famous Judges And Famous Trials* (Stanley Paul, 1923)
114.   do.   : *A Gallery of Rogues* (Stanley Paul, 1924)
115.   do.   : *The Judges And The Judged* (John Lane, the Bodley Head, 1926)
116. KOESTLER, ARTHUR: *Reflections On Hanging* (Gollancz, 1956)
117. LAMBERT R. S.: *When Justice Faltered* (Methuen, 1935)
118.   do.   : *The Universal Provider* (Harrap, 1938)
119. LAMBTON, ARTHUR: *Echoes of Causes Célèbres* (Hurst & Blackett, n.d.)
120.   do.   : *Thou Shalt Do No Murder* (Hurst & Blackett, n.d.)
121. LANG, Rev. GORDON: *Mr. Justice Avory* (Herbert Jenkins, 1935)
122. LEFEBURE, MOLLY: *Evidence For The Crown* (Heinemann, 1955)
123.   do.   : *Murder With A Difference* (Heinemann, 1958)
124. LUKENS, JOHN: *The Sanger Story* (Hodder & Stoughton, 1956)
125. LUSTGARTEN, EDGAR: *Verdict In Dispute* (Allan Wingate, 1949)
126.   do.   : *Defender's Triumph* (Allan Wingate, 1951)
127.   do.   : *Prisoner At The Bar* (André Deutsch, 1952)
128.   do.   : *The Woman In The Case* (André Deutsch, 1955)
129. MACKINNON, Lord Justice: *On Circuit* (Cambridge University Press, 1940)
130. MACNAGHTEN, Sir MELVILLE: *Days Of My Years* (Edward Arnold, 1914)
131. MARJORIBANKS, EDWARD: *The Life Of Sir Edward Marshall Hall* (Gollancz, 1929)
132. MARTIENSSEN, ANTHONY: *Crime And The Police* (Martin Secker & Warburg, 1951)
133. MATHEW, THEOBALD: *For Lawyers And Others* (William Hodge, 1937)
134. MITCHELL, C. AINSWORTH: *Science And The Criminal* (Pitman, 1911)
135.   do.   : *The Scientific Detective And The Expert Witness* (Heffer, 1931: originally published as *The Expert Witness*, 1923)
136. MORLAND, NIGEL: *An Outline Of Scientific Criminology* (Cassell, 1950)
137.   do.   : *Hangman's Clutch* (Werner Laurie, 1954)
138.   do.   : *Background To Murder* (Werner Laurie, 1955)

139. MORLAND, NIGEL: *Science In Crime Detection* (Robert Hale, 1958)
140. MOYLAN, Sir JOHN: *Scotland Yard* (Putnam, 1934)
141. NEUSTATTER, Dr. W. LINDSAY: *Psychological Disorder And Crime* (Christopher Johnson, 1953)
142.   do.   : *The Mind Of The Murderer* (Christopher Johnson, 1957)
143. NOTT-BOWER, Sir WILLIAM: *Fifty-Two Years A Policeman* (Edward Arnold, 1926)
144. O'BRIEN, BARRY: *Life Of Lord Russell Of Killowen* (Smith, Elder, 1901)
145. ODDIE, S. INGLEBY: *Inquest* (Hutchinson, 1941)
146. O'DONNELL, BERNARD: *Great Thames Mysteries* (Selwyn & Blount, 1929)
147.   do.   : *The Trials Of Mr. Justice Avory* (Rich & Cowan, 1935)
148.   do.   : *The Old Bailey And Its Trials* (Clerke & Cockeran, 1950)
149.   do.   : *Cavalcade Of Justice* (Clerke & Cockeran, 1951)
150.   do.   : *Crimes That Made News* (Burke, 1954)
151.   do.   : *Should Women Hang?* (W. H. Allen, 1956)
152.   do.   : *The World's Strangest Murders* (Frederick Muller, 1957)
153. O'SULLIVAN, A. M.: *The Last Serjeant* (Macdonald, 1952)
154. PAGET, R. T., with SILVERMAN, SYDNEY: *Hanged—And Innocent?* (Gollancz, 1953)
155. PARMINTER, GEOFFREY DE C.: *Reasonable Doubt* (Arthur Barker, 1938)
156. PARRY, Dr. LEONARD: *Some Famous Medical Trials* (Churchill, 1927)
157. PARTRIDGE, RALPH: *Broadmoor* (Chatto & Windus, 1953)
158. PEARCE, CHARLES E.: *Unsolved Murder Mysteries* (Stanley Paul, 1924)
159. PEARSON, EDMUND: *More Studies In Murder* (Arco, 1953)
160. *Penal Reform in England: Introductory Essays On Some Aspects Of English Criminal Policy* (Macmillan, 1946)
161. *Penguin Famous Trials*. Ed. Harry Hodge. Vols. I-V (Penguin Books)
162. PHILLIPS, CONRAD: *Murderer's Moon* (Arthur Barker, 1956)
163. PLAYFAIR, GILES, and SINGTON, DERRICK: *The Offenders* (Secker & Warburg, 1957)
164. POLLOCK, George: *Mr. Justice McCardie* (John Lane, the Bodley Head, 1934)

BIBLIOGRAPHY

165. POSTGATE, RAYMOND: *Murder, Piracy And Treason* (Jonathan Cape, 1925)
166. RENTOUL, Sir GERVAISE: *Sometimes I Think* (Hodder & Stoughton, 1940)
167.   *do.*   : *This Is My Case* (Hutchinson, 1944)
168. RHODES, HENRY T. F.: *Science And The Police Officer* (The Police Chronicle, *n.d.*)
169.   *do*   : *Clues And Crime* (John Murray, 1933)
170.   *do.*   : *In The Tracks Of Crime* (Turnstile Press, 1952)
171. RICHARDSON, ANTHONY: *Nick Of The River* (Harrap, 1955)
172. ROUGHEAD, WILLIAM: *Twelve Scots Trials* (Green, 1913)
173.   *do.*   : *The Fatal Countess* (Green, 1924)
174.   *do.*   : *In Queer Street* (Green, 1924)
175.   *do.*   : *Malice Domestic* (Green, 1928)
176.   *do.*   : *Rogues Walk Here* (Cassell, 1934)
177.   *do.*   : *Mainly Murder* (Cassell, 1937)
178.   *do.*   : *The Seamy Side* (Cassell, 1938)
179.   *do.*   : *Neck Or Nothing* (Cassell, 1939)
180.   *do.*   : *Reprobates Reviewed* (Cassell, 1941)
181.   *do.*   : *Classic Crimes* (Cassell, 1951)
182.   *do.*   : *Tales Of The Criminous* (Cassell, 1956)
183. ROWLAND, JOHN: *Murder By Persons Unknown* (Mellifont Press, 1941)
184.   *do.*   : *The Wallace Case* (Carroll & Nicholson, 1949)
185.   *do.*   : *A Century Of Murder* (Home & Van Thal, 1950)
186.   *do.*   : *Criminal Files* (Arco, 1957)
187. *Royal Commission On Capital Punishment, 1949-1953: Report* (H.M. Stationery Office, 1953)
188. RUSSELL, DONN (edited), *Best Murder Cases* (Faber & Faber, 1958)
189. RUSSELL OF LIVERPOOL, LORD: *Though The Heavens Fall* (Cassell, 1956)
190. SANDBACH, J. B.: *This Old Wig* (Hutchinson, *n.d.*)
191. SAPTE, W.: *A Century's Sensations* (John Barker, *n.d.*)
192. SCOTT, GEORGE RILEY: *The History Of Capital Punishment* (Torchstream Books, 1950)
193. SCOTT, Sir HAROLD: *Scotland Yard* (André Deutsch, 1954)
194. SILLITOE, Sir PERCY: *Cloak Without Dagger* (Cassell, 1955)
195. SINGER, KURT (ed): *My Greatest Crime Story* (W. H. Allen, 1956)
196. SLESSER, Sir HENRY: *Judgment Reserved* (Hutchinson, 1941)
197. SMITH-HUGHES, JACK: *Unfair Comment* (Cassell, 1951)
198.   *do.*   : *Eight Studies In Justice* (Cassell, 1953)
199. SPARROW, Judge GERALD: *Murder Parade* (Robert Hale, 1957)

200. STEPHEN, Sir JAMES FITZJAMES: *Digest Of The Criminal Law* 5th edition (Macmillan, 1899)
201. STEVENS, C. L. McCLUER: *Famous Crimes And Criminals* (Stanley Paul, 1924)
202. *Taylor's Principles And Practice Of Medical Jurisprudence* 8th edition, Ed. Sydney Smith and W. G. H. Cook (Churchill, 1928); 10th edition, 1948
203. TEMPLEWOOD, VISCOUNT: *The Shadow Of The Gallows* (Gollancz, 1951)
204. THOMPSON, Sir BASIL: *The Criminal* (Hodder & Stoughton, 1925)
205.   do.   : *The Story Of Scotland Yard* (Grayson & Grayson, 1925)
206. THOMPSON, C. J. S.: *Poison Mysteries Unsolved* (Hutchinson, 1937)
207. THORP, Chief-Superintendent ARTHUR: *Calling Scotland Yard* (Allan Wingate, 1954)
208. TOTTERDELL, Superintendent G. H.: *Country Copper* (Harrap, 1956)
209. TULLETT, TOM: *Portrait Of A Bad Man* (Evans, 1956)
210. VILLIERS, ELIZABETH: *Riddles Of Crime* (Werner Laurie, 1928)
211. WAKEFIELD, H. R.: *The Green Bicycle Case* (Philip Allan, 1930)
212. WALBROOK, H. M.: *Murders And Murder Trials: 1812-1912* (Constable, 1932)
213. WALKER-SMITH, DEREK: *The Life Of Mr. Justice Darling* (Cassell, 1938)
214. WARD, ARTHUR: *Stuff And Silk* (Gansey Publications, *n.d.*)
215. WEBB, DUNCAN: *Crime Is My Business* (Muller, 1953)
216. WENSLEY, ex-Chief Constable FREDERICK PORTER: *Detective Days* (Cassell, 1931)
217. WEST, REBECCA: *A Train Of Powder* (Macmillan, 1955)
218. WHITELAW, DAVID: *Corpus Delicti* (Geoffrey Bles, 1936)
219. WILD, ROLAND: *Crimes And Cases Of 1933* (Rich & Cowan, 1934)
220.   do.   : *Crimes And Cases Of 1934* (Rich & Cowan, 1935)
221. WILD, ROLAND, with CURTIS BENNETT, DEREK: *'Curtis'* (Cassell, 1937)
222. WILLIAMS, GLANVILLE: *The Proof Of Guilt* (Stevens & Sons, 1955)
223. WILLS, WILLIAM: *An Essay On The Principles Of Circumstantial Evidence* 6th edition, edited by Sir Alfred Wills (Butterworth, 1912)
224. WOOD, WALTER: *Survivors' Tales Of Famous Crimes* (Cassell, 1916)
225. WOODLAND, W. LLOYD: *Assize Pageant* (Harrap, 1925)

226. WYLES, LILIAN: *A Woman At Scotland Yard* (Faber & Faber, 1952)
227. WYNDHAM, HORACE: *Famous Trials Re-Told* (Hutchinson, *n.d.*)
228.   do.   : *Consider Your Verdict* (W. H. Allen, 1946)
229. WYNDHAM-BROWN, W. F.: *The Trial Of Herbert Wallace* (Gollancz, 1933)
230. YOUNG, HUGH: *My Forty Years At The Yard* (W. H. Allen, 1955)

INDEX

of names not given separate entries in the text

INDEX OF NAMES

299

A NOTE ABOUT THE AUTHOR

E. SPENCER SHEW, who was born in 1908, first came to London in 1930 as a news-agency reporter at the Law Courts and the Old Bailey. It was at this time that Mr. Shew was witness to some of the great murder trials and came to know the renowned justices and counsel who now appear, along with many others, with greater or less prominence, in this book. In 1936 he was officially accredited to Buckingham Palace as a Court correspondent and in that capacity covered the abdication of King Edward VIII, now Duke of Windsor. For the past nine years Mr. Shew has been Honorable Secretary of the Parliamentary Lobby Journalists, the elite press corps of political journalists attached to the House of Commons. As representative of the Exchange Telegraph of London, he has covered American visits of the late Ernest Bevin, Lord Attlee, Sir Winston Churchill, and Prime Minister Harold Macmillan. In 1957 he received the Coronation Medal. Mr. Shew is married to Betty Spencer Shew, author of a number of books on the British Royal Family. A novel by Mr. Shew, *Miss Proutie*, was published in 1952.

May 1961

A NOTE ON THE TYPE

The text of this book was set on the Monotype
in *Plantin,* a type face named after
the 16th Century printer, Christophe Plantin of Antwerp.
It was made available in 1914 by
the Monotype Corporation Ltd., London.
Printed by the Murray Printing Company,
Forge Village, Massachusetts.
Paper made by S. D. Warren Company, Boston.
Bound by H. Wolff, New York.